Gender Disparities in Africa's Labor Market

Gender Disparities in Africa's Labor Market

Jorge Saba Arbache, Alexandre Kolev, and Ewa Filipiak

Editors

A copublication of the Agence Française de Développement and the World Bank

ISBN: 978-0-8213-8066-6
eISBN: 978-0-8213-8070-3
DOI: 10.1596/978-0-8213-8066-6

Library of Congress Cataloging-in-Publication Data
Gender disparities in Africa's labor market / Jorge Saba Arbache, Alexandre Kolev, and Ewa Filipiak, editors.
  p. cm.
  ISBN 978-0-8213-8066-6 — ISBN 978-0-8213-8070-3 (ebook)
  1. Sex discrimination in employment—Africa. 2. Sexual division of labor—Africa. 3. Labor market—Africa. I. Arbache, Jorge Saba. II. Kolev, Alexandre. III. Filipiak, Ewa. IV. World Bank.
  HD6060.5.A35G46 2010
  331.4'133096—dc22

                                                                          2010014200

Cover design: Naylor Design, Washington, DC

Africa Development Forum Series

The **Africa Development Forum** series was created in 2009 to focus on issues of significant relevance to Sub-Saharan Africa's social and economic development. Its aim is both to record the state of the art on a specific topic and to contribute to ongoing local, regional, and global policy debates. It is designed specifically to provide practitioners, scholars, and students with the most up-to-date research results while highlighting the promise, challenges, and opportunities that exist on the continent.

The series is sponsored by the Agence Française de Développement and the World Bank. The manuscripts chosen for publication represent the highest quality in each institution's research and activity output and have been selected for their relevance to the development agenda. Working together with a shared sense of mission and interdisciplinary purpose, the two institutions are committed to a common search for new insights and new ways of analyzing the development realities of the Sub-Saharan Africa Region.

Advisory Committee Members

Agence Française de Développement
Pierre Jacquet, Directeur de la Stratégie et Chef Économiste
Robert Peccoud, Directeur de la Recherche

World Bank
Shantayanan Devarajan, Chief Economist, Africa Region
Jorge Arbache, Senior Economist

Contents

5   Addressing Gender Inequality in Ethiopia: Trends, Impacts, and the Way Forward   193

Caterina Ruggeri Laderchi, Hans Lofgren, and Rahimaisa Abdula

PART 3   DISPARITIES IN LABOR INCOME: MACRO–MICRO SIMULATIONS   229

6   Gender, Time Use, and Labor Income in Guinea: Micro and Macro Analyses   231

Juan Carlos Parra Osorio and Quentin Wodon

Figures

Tables

Foreword

In the early 2000s, women's weekly earnings as a fraction of male earnings were 79 percent in Ghana, 51 percent in Nigeria, 45 percent in Mozambique, and 23 percent in Burkina Faso. It is tempting to conclude that this wage gap—which is pervasive throughout Africa—is a sign of discrimination against women in the labor market. This book shows instead that the wage gap is a reflection of a number of factors, ranging from labor market conditions to access to education to cultural values and attitudes in the household.

Specifically, when characteristics that usually explain labor market earnings such as human capital are taken into account, there is still a gap. While this "unexplained component" is often interpreted as discrimination against women in the job market, the authors show that other explanations also play a substantial role. Women suffer from having fewer educational opportunities, limited access to credit, and less time to work in the job market because of their domestic chores. The housework burden on women, which limits their time for market work, often allows them to engage only in productive activities compatible with their household duties. This helps explain why women are more often found in informal activities. Women appear to have lower bargaining power within their households—mostly because they have a smaller share of household income than men, but likely also because of cultural and other social norms—and, therefore, they suffer from a relative lack of control in household investment decisions. Firm-level and sector characteristics are also found to be powerful factors in explaining the gender earnings gaps.

The book documents how gender disparities vary with economic conditions. The wage gap grows substantially whenever there are fewer available jobs in the labor market. More than the effect of discrimination, it seems that job rationing causes those with better human capital and those with more power in the household—usually the men—to take the few jobs available. No wonder that in a region where only a fraction of the labor force finds jobs in the formal sector, gender disparities in earnings are so high.

The finding that gender disparities grow when economies are not functioning well and labor markets are tiny suggest that job creation is central to gender equality. African governments and their development partners must therefore do whatever they can to stimulate economic growth, particularly in sectors that will generate jobs for both men and women. African countries should pursue gender equality in all levels of education and expand education attainment in general.

Finally, the issue of attitudes toward women also deserves attention should Africa want to promote gender equality in the labor markets and promote sustained growth. Faster job-creating growth, better education, and greater bargaining power for women within the household will not only reduce gender disparities, but also improve the lives of *all* Africans.

Ngozi N. Okonjo-Iweala
Managing Director
The World Bank

About the Editors and Authors

Rahimaisa Abdula is a consultant for the World Bank and a doctoral candidate in environmental economics at the University of Gothenburg, Sweden. At the World Bank, Abdula conducts research on countries in Sub-Saharan Africa and Asia, concentrating on the application of Computable General Equilibrium models and other quantitative approaches to environmental policy analysis, including policies related to climate change and bioenergy.

Jorge Saba Arbache is senior economist in the World Bank's Office of the Chief Economist, Africa Region, and director of the Africa Development Indicators. Before joining the Bank, Arbache was a professor of economics at the University of Brasilia and an economist at the International Labour Organization. He served in the Brazilian government, working for the Presidency of the Republic and Ministry of Labor. He has published books and articles on development economics topics, including growth, labor economics, gender, international trade, industrial economics, poverty, and tourism economics. More recently, Arbache has been working on a research agenda on growth acceleration and deceleration and their impacts on poverty, Millenium Development Goals (MDGs), gender, long-term growth, and governance. He has also worked on issues related to labor markets, demographic changes, and youth in Africa.

Prospere Backiny-Yetna is a consultant with the Development Dialogue on Values and Ethics in the Human Development Network at the World Bank. His emphasis in recent years has been on poverty measurement, poverty and social impact analysis, and labor market and informal sector analysis. Previously, he served as head of the Survey and Statistics Department of Afristat and as deputy director general of the Cameroon National Statistical Office.

Ewa Filipiak is a project manager at the Education and Vocational Training Division of the Agence Française de Développement. She holds a master's degree in development studies and a M.Phil. in political sociology from Sciences Po

Paris. From 2003 to 2007, she was a research officer at Agence Française de Développement, working extensively on skills development in Africa.

Alexandre Kolev heads the Employment and Skills Development Programme at the International Training Centre of the International Labour Organization (ITC-ILO). He is also an associate professor at the University of Paris 12. Kolev has a Ph.D in labor economics from the European University Institute, Florence, Italy, and a B.A. in Russian studies from the Institute of Oriental Studies, Paris. He began his professional career as an operations officer for Gaz de France in Russia. He then worked as a research economist for UNICEF Innocenti Research Centre, Florence, Italy, and later joined the Young Professional Program of the World Bank as an economist. At the World Bank, he has held various positions in the Infrastructure Front Office, the Poverty Reduction and Economic Management unit for Europe and Central Asia, and the Social Protection group in the Middle East and North Africa Region. Before joining the ILO, Kolev worked as a task manager for the Education and Vocational Training Division of the Agence Française de Développement (University of Paris 12 and Institut de recherche et documentation en économie de la santé. E-mail: a.kolev@itcilo.org).

Caterina Ruggeri Laderchi is a senior economist at the World Bank with the Poverty Reduction and Economic Management unit for Eastern Europe and Central Asia. She holds a D.Phil. from the University of Oxford. Her current efforts focus on the integration of MDG strategies in government plans and Poverty Reduction Strategy Papers; poverty and distributional analysis, particularly in urban contexts; and impact evaluation and labor markets. Over the past few years, she has worked on Eastern African countries, specifically on Ethiopia.

Hans Lofgren is a senior economist at the World Bank in the Development Economics Prospects Group. His work focuses on model-based analysis of long-run development strategies at the country level and their impact on social and economic objectives, including poverty reduction and other MDG targets. Prior to joining the World Bank in 2004, he was a senior research fellow at the International Food Policy Research Institute. He holds a Ph.D. in Economics from the University of Texas at Austin.

Christophe J. Nordman is research fellow at the French Institute of Research for Development (IRD), assigned to Development, Institutions, and Globalization (DIAL) in Paris, a research center on development economics. He is also an associate research fellow of Skills, Knowledge and Organisational Performance (SKOPE) at the University of Oxford. He received a Ph.D. in economics from University of Paris I Panthéon-Sorbonne. His recent research has focused on the functioning of labor markets in developing countries and gender inequalities using linked employer-employee and household survey data. He has served as a consultant for various multilateral and bilateral organizations, including the World Bank and the Agence Française de Développement. (IRD, DIAL, 4 rue d'Enghien, 75010 Paris, France. E-mail: nordman@dial.prd.fr.)

Juan Carlos Parra Osorio is a consultant with the Development Dialogue on Values and Ethics in the Human Development Network at the World Bank. His emphasis in recent years has been on the economic analysis of household survey data, as well as the design of simulation tools for economic analysis, among others, for social accounting matrices. He is completing a Ph.D. at Georgetown University, with some of his research on social security forthcoming in the *Journal of Political Economy*. (E-mail: jparraosorio@worldbank.org)

Faly Rakotomanana is in charge of employment and earnings statistics at INSTAT, the National Institute of Statistics of Madagascar. He received a master's degree in statistics and economics in 1994 from the Ecole Nationale Supérieure d'Economie et de Statistiques Appliquées (ENSEA) in Abidjan, Côte d'Ivoire. He is currently completing a Ph.D. in development economics on the informal sector, microfinance, and poverty in Madagascar at the University Montesquieu-Bordeaux 4 and DIAL, Paris. He currently serves as United Nations Development Programme consultant for the edition of the fifth Human Development Report on Madagascar, focusing on "Micro-enterprise, Employment, and Human Development." (INSTAT–DSM, Antananarivo. E-mail: rakotomananafaly@yahoo.fr)

Anne-Sophie Robilliard is a research fellow at IRD, where she works in the DIAL research group. She holds a Ph.D. in Development Economics from the University of Paris I Panthéon-Sorbonne. Her research focuses on the use of microsimulation models for the evaluation of development and poverty reduction policy impacts in least-developed countries. She has also worked on poverty and labor market analysis in different Sub-Saharan African countries. She is now carrying out a research project in Senegal on migration, labor markets, and demographic dynamics. (IRD, DIAL, Dakar, Senegal. E-mail: robilliard@dial.prd.fr)

Pablo Suárez Robles is a young expert of the French Government, Ministry of Foreign Affairs, at the International Training Centre of the ILO in Turin. He is also a Ph.D. student in France at the University Paris–Est Créteil Val de Marne, working on a thesis on gender disparities in Africa's labor markets. He graduated from the Paris School of Economics with a Master's degree in international, development, and transition economics and with a *Magistère* in economics.

Nicolas Sirven received a Ph.D. in economics from the University of Bordeaux, France, and conducted postdoctoral work at the Capability and Sustainability Centre (Von Hügel Institute) at St. Edmund's College, University of Cambridge. Sirven's main work in development and health economics deals with social capital, poverty, inequality, and living conditions. He has been a research fellow at the Institute for Research and Information in Health Economics (IRDES) in Paris since 2007. (University of Paris 12 and Institut de recherche et documentation en économie de la santé. E-mail: sirven@irdes.fr)

Diego Angel-Urdinola holds a Ph.D. in economics from Georgetown University. He conducts applied research in the fields of gender, labor markets, international migration, poverty, and human development. Angel-Urdinola has contributed to policy dialogue in World Bank investment projects and operations, as well as to the development of a series of academic and nonacademic publications in Latin America, Sub-Saharan Africa, and Europe and Central Asia. With the World Bank since 2005, he currently works as a senior economist in the Middle East and North Africa Region.

Quentin Wodon is an adviser and program manager for the Development Dialogue on Values and Ethics in the Human Development Network at the World Bank. After engineering and business studies, he worked in business, including as an assistant brand manager with Procter and Gamble. In 1988, Wodon joined the ATD Fourth World, an interdenominational grassroots and advocacy nongovernmental organization concerned with extreme poverty. He later completed a Ph.D. in economics; taught at the University of Namur, Belgium; and joined the World Bank in 1998 as economist and senior economist for the Latin America Region, then as lead poverty specialist for Sub-Saharan Africa. Wodon currently heads the Development Dialogue on Values and Ethics, the unit at the World Bank in charge of work on faith, ethics, and development. (E-mail: qwodon@worldbank.org)

François-Charles Wolff is professor of economics at the Institut d'Economie et de Management of the University of Nantes, France. He is also associate researcher at the Caisse Nationale d'Assurance Vieillesse and the Institut National des Etudes Démographiques, Paris. He received a Ph.D. in economics from the University of Nantes in 1998 and has been Agrégé des Universités since 2004. He is a recipient of the Jacques Tymen Prize and the Novatlante Prize and has written more than 70 peer-reviewed papers. (LEMNA, Université de Nantes, France; CNAV and INED, Paris, France. E-mail: francois.wolff@univ-nantes.fr)

Yvonne Ying is a consultant with the Development Dialogue on Values and Ethics in the Human Development Network at the World Bank. Her emphasis in recent years has been on the econometric analysis of household survey data, among others, on informal safety nets, time use, and household energy use, including electricity tariffs. She holds a D.Phil. in social and cultural anthropology from the University of Oxford.

Acknowledgments

This book is the outcome of a joint project on Gender Disparities in Africa's Labor Markets between the Agence Française de Développement and the World Bank. In particular, we acknowledge a grant from the Gender and Development, Poverty Reduction and Economic Management Network, World Bank, for the production and dissemination of this book.

We are grateful to the authors for their valuable contributions to this volume. We are also grateful to Jean Claude Balmes, Hervé Bougault, Ludovic Cocogne, Laurent Cortese, Paul Coustère, Shanta Devarajan, Blandine Ledoux, Robert Peccoud, and Quentin Wodon for their encouragement, support, and suggestions.

This volume benefited greatly from rich and thoughtful comments on draft chapters provided by Francisco Almendra, Mayra Buvinic, and Sangheon Lee.

Mary C. Fisk and Richard Crabbe, from the EXTOP Team at the World Bank, did a great job in producing this book.

Jorge Saba Arbache, Ewa Filipiak, and Alexandre Kolev

Abbreviations

ALMS	Addis Labor Market Survey
CFAF	Central African CFA franc; Republic of Congo franc
CGE	computable general equilibrium
CIF	cost, insurance, and freight value
CSA	Central Statistical Agency of Ethiopia
CWIQ	Core Welfare Indicator Questionnaire
DHS	Demographic and Health Survey
EIBEP	Enquête Intégrée de Base pour l'Evaluation de la Pauvreté *or* Basic Integrated Poverty Evaluation Survey
FACS	Firm Analysis and Competitiveness Survey (World Bank)
FGM	female genital mutilation
FGT	Foster, Greer, and Thorbecke (1984) class
FHH	female-headed household
GDP	gross domestic product
GEM	Gender Empowerment Measure
GER	gross enrollment rate
GF	Guinean francs
HDI	Human Development Index
HICES	Household Income and Consumption Expenditure Survey
ICA	Investment Climate Assessment
IFPRI	International Food Policy Research Institute
IIA	Independence of Irrelevant Alternatives
ILO	International Labour Organization
I-O	input-output
ISCED97	International Standard Classification of Education 1997
LFS	Ethiopia 2005 Labour Force Survey
LIC	low-income country
MAMS	maquette for MDG Simulations
MDG	Millennium Development Goal (United Nations)
MHH	male-headed household

MVP	marginal value product
NFE	non-farm enterprise
OLS	ordinary least squares
PASDEP	Plan for Accelerated and Sustained Development to End Poverty
PRSP	Poverty Reduction Strategy Paper
RPED	Africa Regional Program on Enterprise Development
SAM	Social Accounting Matrix
SHIP	World Bank Survey-based Harmonized Indicators Program
SPA	structural path analysis
SSA	Sub-Saharan Africa
TFP	total factor productivity
UNDP	United Nations Development Programme
UNFPA	United Nations Population Fund
WMS	Welfare Monitoring Survey

Overview

Why Study Gender Disparities in Africa's Labor Markets?

Jorge Saba Arbache, Ewa Filipiak, and Alexandre Kolev

G ender disparities in terms of opportunities, security, and participation have become important issues for developing economies, and for Africa in particular, not least because of their potential negative effects on both sustainable growth and poverty reduction. This is the reason gender equality is now among the aims of most Poverty Reduction Strategy Papers (PRSPs) and is also one of the United Nations Millennium Development Goals (MDGs).

However, despite receiving increasing attention in Africa, international comparison based on the World Economic Forum's Global Gender Gap Index reveals that most African countries for which data are available rank particularly poorly in terms of economic participation, education, health, and political empowerment (World Economic Forum 2009). Yet, still relatively little is known about gender inequality in many African countries, and even less is known about how to design more effective policies to reduce them.

In the context of gender inequality, gender disparities in labor markets are especially important. Available evidence shows that, in a number of African countries, women are less likely to be in paid jobs, they are disproportionately concentrated in informal and precarious employment, and they are paid less (see, for instance, Appleton, Hoddinott, and Krishnan 1999; Brilleau, Roubaud, and Torelli 2004; Fafchamps, Söderbom, and Benhassine 2006; ILO 2002; Lachaud 1997; Nordman and Roubaud 2005; Nordman and Wolff 2008, 2009).

While there is a consensus on the existence of gender disparities in African labor markets, assessing their nature, extent, and root causes remains, in many cases, a challenge. Often, available data provide incomplete and limited information on the relative situation of men and women, are collected using very diverse methodologies and definitions of employment and earnings, and focus mostly on urban areas. This book sheds light on the multiple dimensions of the gender disadvantage in Africa's labor markets and the way these dimensions tend to interact with and reinforce each other. It relies on a series of datasets that became available recently.

But why the need to know specifically about gender disparities in labor markets when the lack of decent employment for both men and women remains at the heart of the poverty battle in Africa? The focus on gender inequality and the need to understand gender disparities in Africa are important for at least two reasons. First, women's education, employment, and earnings are essential in the fight against poverty, not only because of the direct and interrelated contribution they make to household welfare, but also because of the personal power they provide women in shaping and making family decisions and in redirecting household spending on essential needs, especially in favor of children's health and education (UNICEF 1999). In some developing countries, mother's schooling is also found to have a larger impact on girls' education than that of the father (Hill and King 1995). Second, from a rights-based perspective, gender disparities in labor markets should be narrowed simply from the standpoint that, as recognized internationally, everyone deserves the same opportunities and should receive the same rewards for equivalent work.

There is a consensus that gender disparities generally diminish as nations develop over time. However, a more nuanced examination of gender in Africa will show that, while broad development progress naturally tends to bridge the gap between men and women on many fronts,

> [E]vidence of the heterogeneity of women as a category, the difficulties of reaching those most deprived, and the fact that greater household monetary resources do not necessarily translate into lower gender disparities in various dimensions suggest that there is a place for carefully designed, targeted interventions to support the achievement of the agenda for women's economic empowerment. (chapter 5)

Therefore, a deeper understanding of the determinants of gender disparities in Africa is crucial for implementing effective policies to promote gender equality and to reap its benefits in the shortest time possible.

Objective of This Book

The main aim of this book is to help fill the gap in current knowledge about the nature, the extent, and some of the root causes of gender disparities in Africa, showing what can be revealed about the application of standard and less standard tools and methods to existing survey and national account data. The analysis herein is novel in providing in-depth assessments of some of the sources of gender disparities in different labor market outcomes. A part of the book provides results on the basis that data are as comparable as possible for 18 countries. These results were extracted from multi-topic, integrated household surveys conducted in Africa around 2000 and thus may not represent the latest trends, but they have the merit to be comparable. The cross-national perspective provides a benchmark against which other results for individual countries and more recent data presented here may be compared. Additional goals are to demonstrate the possibilities, as well as the challenges, of analysis of gender inequality in labor market outcomes with existing survey data, to support the improvement of data collection, and to stimulate further research on gender disparities in Africa. We hope to highlight the issues that can be addressed, while at the same time marking out some of the caveats in this area of measurement and analysis. The book touches on policy issues at various points, although it is not principally a book about using policy to reduce gender inequality. Rather, it aims to provide analysis that is relevant to policy design.

This introduction will summarize the content and principal findings of the studies that comprise this volume. After discussing the selection of these country case studies, the main topics to be addressed and the organization of the volume as a whole are provided. Then the data and methodology are reviewed for each chapter, followed by a summary of the main findings discussed around key issues. Although the book addresses some complex topics, the authors have attempted to make the results accessible to as wide an audience as possible without compromising rigor.

Countries Covered in the Studies

The African countries in the country-specific case studies presented in this book differ in a number of dimensions, including the level of economic development, the place of women in society, and the strength of formal labor markets. The countries covered in this book are listed in the table O.1. The extent to which women in Africa are disadvantaged in the labor market and how this compares across countries is analyzed in chapter 1 using standardized survey data for 18 African countries. More detailed country case studies on gender disparities in labor market outcomes are then presented in the following chapters. They cover a subset of seven countries and draw upon recent surveys and national account data. What are the grounds for selection of country case studies for this volume?

Table O.1 Countries Covered in This Volume

General cross-country comparison	Burkina Faso, Burundi, Côte d'Ivoire, Cameroon, Ethiopia, The Gambia, Ghana, Guinea, Kenya, Madagascar, Malawi, Mauritania, Mozambique, Nigeria, São Tomé and Príncipe, Sierra Leone, Uganda, Zambia
Theme-specific studies	
Country-specific	Republic of Congo, Ethiopia, Guinea, Madagascar, Nigeria, Sierra Leone, Tanzania
Cross-country	Benin, Kenya, Madagascar, Mauritius, Morocco, Senegal, Uganda

Ethiopia picks itself: This is the country with one of the largest populations in Sub-Saharan Africa and one of the world's oldest continuous civilizations. Ethiopia is also one of the world's poorest countries. Significant progress has been made since 1991 in key human development indicators, with primary school enrollments tripling, child mortality cut almost in half, and the number of people with access to clean water more than doubled. Notwithstanding the progress in critical aspects of human development, Ethiopia is a long way from achieving some of the MDGs by 2015, given the country's very low starting point and recent economic turbulence. The government's recently completed second Poverty Reduction Strategy (called the Plan for Accelerated and Sustained Development to End Poverty, or PASDEP) includes enhanced plans over the medium-term to accelerate local empowerment and increase transparency and accountability.

Madagascar provides an example of an insular country to contrast with Continental Africa. Located in the Indian Ocean off the southeast African coast, Madagascar is one of the largest islands in the world, with a fairly low population density. Madagascar is also among the world's poorest countries. Since 2002, the country has embarked on an ambitious transformation path by instituting a bold development strategy for 2007–12—the Madagascar Action Plan (MAP), a second-generation Poverty Reduction Strategy that has brought improvements in social, economic, and governance indicators. But it still has a long way to go. However, the macroeconomic situation remains fragile and social indicators are still low and far from achieving the MDGs. Recent political instability also remains an issue.

The Republic of Congo and Nigeria represent countries dominated by the oil sector, but with rather different experiences and states of development. In addition to the availability of data, these countries were important to study for a number of reasons. The Republic of Congo has been marked by a series of conflicts that have imposed a heavy toll on the country. Formerly ranked as a lower-middle-income country, Congo has declined steadily in per capita income since the late 1980s. A political liberalization process has taken place since 1999, and the country is now embarking on a process of strengthening democratic institutions. But poverty remains widespread, growth is dependent on fluctuating commodity prices, and the country has still to secure efforts toward more transparency in managing its natural resources.

In contrast, Nigeria has made important strides in economic reforms and the fight against corruption. Recent elections in Nigeria further consolidated the transition from military to democratic rule that began in 1999. With its large reserves of human and natural resources, Nigeria has the potential to build a prosperous economy, reduce poverty significantly, and provide the health, education, and infrastructure services its population needs. However, if significant progress has been made, at current rates of improvement, Nigeria is still unlikely to achieve any of the MDGs by 2015.

Guinea is illustrative of a country with abundant natural resources and large foreign investors, a fairly peaceful internal situation, but with a rather unstable external environment. The country has been significantly affected by conflicts in neighboring countries, and as a result, poverty is estimated to have increased in recent years. Guinea has attempted several economic reforms but implementation was partly hindered by political and social unrest.

Sierra Leone shares with Congo, Guinea, and Nigeria an abundance of natural resources; however, 10 years of civil war have severely disrupted the country's internal security. Improvements in the security situation since 2001 and the subsequent return of the displaced population to their homes has helped economic recovery. Much of this recovery was concentrated in the informal agricultural, fishing, mining, and services sectors that make up the bulk of the economy.

While Tanzania enjoys political stability and has implemented what are considered sound macro-economic policies, as well as structural changes and governance reforms, it still faces major challenges in terms of socioeconomic development. Having performed well economically throughout the last decade and having achieved significant progress in social services provision including education, health and water access, the country still needs to translate high growth rates into sustainable poverty reduction: roughly a third of the population still lives below the national poverty line. Tanzania also remains strongly dependent on external aid and vulnerable to international conjuncture.

Book Organization and Topics

This volume includes cross-national comparisons and country case studies on the following topics: (1) an overview of gender disparities in labor market outcomes in Africa's labor markets; (2) a microanalysis of disparities in employment, pay, education, and other dimensions; (3) macrosimulations of gender disparities in labor income; (4) disparities in time use; and (5) disparities in bargaining power.

Chapter 1 presents an important contribution to filling a knowledge gap about the extent and nature of gender disparities in African labor markets in general. It is the first study of its kind to use a recently harmonized set of integrated household surveys as its dataset, enabling a cross-country comparison that was hitherto impossible to undertake credibly, as well as bringing more confidence to generalizing results to the whole continent. This collection of 18 comparable surveys—extracted from the World Bank's Survey-based Harmonized Indicators Project (SHIP)—provides a solid base on which the authors describe the severity of gender disparities in the labor market, the nature of such disparities, the relationship between education parity and improvements in women's labor outcomes, and how these issues vary across countries.

The next five chapters comprise a microanalysis of the gender gap in employment, pay, education, and other dimensions. Chapter 2 provides an analysis of the gender pay gap by different age cohorts for Ethiopia in 2005. It sheds light on the Ethiopian gender pay gap using data from a 2005 labor force survey and decomposing the gap by analyzing its properties across different age cohorts, and controlling for human capital and job characteristics. The analysis follows a Cotton-Neumark procedure and focuses on wage employment only.

A similar analysis is conducted in chapter 3 for Madagascar using equivalent national household surveys from 2001 and 2005 and measures the gender pay gap between these two points in time spanned by important external shocks. It also analyzes the determinants of occupational choices across sectors of employment, wages, and earnings. The study brings an interesting perspective to the Malagasy labor market, as it compares data from two national household surveys spaced by four years, bringing a time dimension to the analysis and extracting information about how shifts in human capital attainment and economic shocks influence the choice of sectors and wage gaps between genders over time.

An extension of the gender pay gap analysis to seven African countries (Benin, Kenya, Madagascar, Mauritius, Morocco, Senegal, and Uganda) is provided in chapter 4, using the World Bank's Investment Climate Assessment (ICA) surveys between 2003 and 2005, except for Morocco, which provided similar data from a Firm Analysis and Competitiveness Survey conducted in 2000. Among other variables, this study investigates firms' characteristics as determinants of gender pay disparities in the manufacturing sector in these countries. This chapter goes beyond the usual household survey analysis by using matched employer-employee data in order to control for firm heterogeneity when investigating the determinants of gender disparities. The study—the first of its kind—uses fixed-effect models both for ordinary least squares and quantile regressions to determine to what extent firm characteristics influence wage gaps in different salary brackets in the countries under study.

Chapter 5 examines the case of Ethiopia using two comparable national household surveys conducted in 1995 and 2005 for gender trend comparisons in education, empowerment of women, and monetary poverty. Then, using macroeconomic data, it performs a simulation to show the effects of different policy scenarios on these trends over time. This chapter also breaks new ground in methodological approaches by presenting the first MAMS (maquette for MDG simulation)—a widely used economy-wide simulation model created to analyze different development strategies—broken down by gender. This extension of the MAMS model is welcome, because it yields not only forecasts of a country's overall income level and progress against the MDGs over time as a consequence of different policy scenario simulations, but it also presents these results broken down by gender and by different educational attainment levels.

The third topic, covered in chapters 6 and 7, relies on macrosimulation methods to investigate the role of different scenarios on gender disparities in labor income. These chapters iterate a social accounting matrix (SAM) for Guinea and Tanzania to calculate the multiplicative effects of isolated shocks in specific sectors on the rest of the economy and how these shocks affect overall income levels by gender, sector, employment type, and educational attainment level. These chapters provide a simple general equilibrium framework that is easy to understand, despite strong assumptions and static results that may limit its applicability. A novelty introduced in chapter 7 is the structural path analysis (SPA) added to the SAM procedure—the first time this combination has been performed to study gender issues. The SPA is used to describe the actual transmission routes of these shocks and how they are likely to affect men's and women's incomes differently.

The book's fourth topic focuses in more detail on a subset of two countries, Ethiopia and Sierra Leone, looking at gender disparities in time use. The analysis provided in chapter 8 uses the Ethiopia Labor Force Survey of 2005 to focus on gender disparities in Ethiopian labor markets caused by differences in time allocation between market and household work, time poverty, and labor allocation across employment sectors. The study first constructs estimates of how Ethiopian men and women allocate time differently between different activities—notably market and household work, leisure, and tertiary activities—and then employs Tobit and multinomial logit models to estimate the codeterminants of time allocation decisions by gender within households. This analysis is complemented by similar estimations of codeterminants of employment for men and women across different sectors for different education levels. While the approach is not novel in its own right, it introduces an important topic to readers unfamiliar with this kind of analysis and sheds additional light on the situation in Ethiopia.

A similar analysis is performed in chapter 9 for Sierra Leone, using the 2003 Integrated Household Survey to provide basic descriptive statistics on time allocated to domestic work by different household members (according to the individual characteristics of each member). The chapter also investigates the determinants of domestic time use, including access to infrastructure services. It brings attention to the difficulties researchers face in lack of adequate data and provides insights from simple descriptive statistics and regressions, especially on the potential benefits of better access to infrastructure services toward gender equality (since it tends to reduce the number of hours needed for the same household work, freeing up time for women to spend on other productive activities). The study is valuable because it is the first effort to describe domestic work time in the country, simply because the survey used is the first one in the country for which time use information is available.

The fifth topic of the book deals with the links between labor outcomes and intra-household bargaining. The effect of female earnings on consumption patterns in Congo is covered in chapter 10. The chapter uses a nationally representative household survey conducted in 2005 to test the unitary model of household consumption; it measures the relative inability of women to affect expenditure decisions within households. The estimation uses a noncooperative model of bargaining within the household to formulate a hypothesis that a higher income share held by women leads to more decision power (hence, more money to the above areas), which is then tested through standard econometric estimation procedures.

The impact of gender disparities in employment and income on decision power within households in Nigeria is the subject of chapter 11. This last chapter uses the 2003 Core Welfare Indicator Questionnaire (CWIQ) surveys to document the extent to which income generation by different members affects decision making within the household. It starts by showing descriptive statistics on how household decisions differ by area between gender groups of different ages, and then employs a bivariate probit model to estimate how children reap benefits when women control a larger share of household resources.

The Main Findings on Gender Disparities in Africa

This section provides a brief overview of the principal findings of this book. The findings are structured around key issues rather than on a chapter-by-chapter basis.

Causes of the Gender Gap

What are the main causes of the gender gap at the labor market and household levels? Although most chapters investigate to some extent the causes of gender disparity at the labor market level, chapters 2 through 5 go deeper in their analyses. Generally, most of the gender earnings gaps detected can be explained by differences among individuals, especially in human capital variables, such as educational attainment, vocational training, and years of real or potential experience. In some cases (notably those where adequate data is available for analysis), firm characteristics and gender segmentation in different sectors are also identified as important codeterminants of the observed disparities between men and women.

Controlling for the characteristics that usually explain most individual returns still leaves a part of the observed gap unexplained. While this is often interpreted as "discrimination against women" in the job market, it must be noted that there are several other explanations that must be ruled out before real job market discrimination can be ascertained with any degree of confidence.

What does seem clear, however, is that African women on average do suffer from having fewer educational opportunities (from schooling, training, or otherwise), and less available time to work in the job market because of their domestic chores. Some of the studies in the book also point to women's disadvantage in access to credit, which is probably strongly influenced by their relative inability to control collateral, since men own or otherwise control a larger share of capital than women. These factors then lead the enquiry to disparities at the household level.

Although very difficult to measure objectively, cultural and social norms likely play a large role in allotting to women the largest share of responsibility to take care of children and elders, cooking, cleaning, and other domestic chores. "The housework burden on women limits their time available to market work and allows them to engage only in productive activities compatible with their household duties" (chapter 8). In most of Africa, this is compounded by factors that delay household work, such as lack of access to infrastructure services like water and electricity, which further hampers the ability of women to engage in the job market on equal terms to men.

In addition, it seems clear in recent years that the classic depiction of harmonious households taking decisions together and optimally for all members does not hold in the real world, and this is true for Africa as well. Men and women appear to have different priorities in spending resources under their control, so bargaining power also becomes a factor when attempting to understand gender disparities in general. Women appear to have lower bargaining power within their households—mostly because they have a smaller share of income generation than men, but likely also influenced by culture and other social norms—and therefore they suffer from a relative lack of control in household investment decisions. Echoing other recent micro studies, the evidence from Congo in chapter 10 suggests that the income-pooling hypothesis is not supported by the data:

> This result signals that gender inequalities encompass not just inequalities of opportunities outside the households—such as inequalities in education, employment, labor remuneration, access to credit, and other dimensions—but also inequalities within the household, manifested mainly by inequality of power.

Evidence for Nigeria discussed in chapter 11 shows that "when they are the main contributor of income, women win substantial decision power."

Impact of Education on Labor Market Disparities

By far, the most important and recurring theme in all the chapters is that women lag behind men in educational opportunities. The sad consequences of this relative disadvantage can be seen in every country under study and across many different working environments or activities.

Education plays a large role in the measured gender gaps in employment and earnings. As stated in chapter 1:

> In Africa, education not only has a favorable effect on earnings but also has a positive impact on gender page equity. What is indeed remarkable is that gender disparities in earnings varied with the level of education, and the higher the education level, the lower the extent of inequalities in labor income per hours worked. On average, the male-to-female earnings ratio was as high as 2.8 among individuals with no education, and as low as 0.9 among individuals with tertiary education.

These stylized facts at the beginning of the book are echoed in other chapters, for example, in chapter 2:

> For both men and women, more highly educated workers tend to be disproportionately concentrated in better paid jobs. Public wage employment predominantly comprises workers with general or beyond education, and this is true for both men and women. . . . While formal private wage employment includes workers with all levels of education (from illiteracy to beyond general education), informal private wage employment is predominantly workers with low education levels, especially the case for women.

In chapter 3, the study finds

> . . .a strong positive impact of education on the probability of getting a paid job for both men and women. This effect also increases with education level. For men and women alike, education has the strongest positive impact on the probability of accessing the public sector, followed by private formal wage employment and, finally, informal self-employment.

Taking the example of Ethiopia—a country where enormous gender disparities in education have been narrowed systematically by sound public policy in recent years—chapter 2 asserts that "a non-negligible proportion of the gender wage gap—at least 11 percent but no more than 23 percent on average—was explained by differences in education endowments between men and women," and it varied across age groups. Using a very different approach, but also focused on Ethiopia, chapter 5 asserts that the main results of its simulations imply that "broad-based education expansion reaching (but not limited to) women, combined with selective labor market interventions, may lead to a major reduction in gender disparities in education and the labor market, as well as improved overall macroeconomic performance."

Rural vs. Urban Issues

Many observed gender disparities take on distinct emphasis, depending on whether the study is of rural or urban populations. In general, gender disparities in employment tend to be higher in urban areas, indicating that women's access to employment in urban labor markets may be more difficult. Yet, as stated in chapter 1:

> ... the gender employment gap in favor of men persisted in rural areas in almost all countries in the region. . . . Lower gender inequality in terms of access to employment in rural Africa is indeed not surprising, as it may reflect the large incidence of farm employment and household enterprises.

Education attainment is lacking in most African countries, but differentiated access to schooling seems to be even more of a problem in rural areas, where the majority of Africans live:

> Gender disparities in literacy were much more pronounced in rural areas, but gender differences persisted in urban areas. . . . Gender educational disparities were largely a rural phenomenon and were observed for all education levels. In urban areas, the gender education gap was rather small at the primary and secondary levels, but became an issue at the tertiary level. (chapter 1)

Turning again to the example of Ethiopia, the gender-based division of labor is much more acute in rural than in urban areas. In line with what happens in many other African countries, not only do Ethiopian men engage more often in market work and less often in household work than women, but men also work longer hours on average on market activities, while women spend more time on average on household chores. In addition to this overall gender division of labor, these differences are compounded outside urban centers: "Gender gaps in the incidence, as well as in the average duration, of both market and household work are greater in rural areas" (chapter 8).

However, because Ethiopia also mimics many other countries in that the tradeoff between market and household work tends to be only partial for much of its female population, "the double work burden on women, then, is more pronounced in rural areas, where more men focus only on market work, while more women tend to accumulate both types of work." In that country,

> ... in both urban and rural areas, whatever the share of the population selected, the average work time of women is always higher than that of men. . . . The gender gap in time poverty rates is much larger in rural than in urban areas. Women living in rural areas are more likely to be time-poor than women living in urban areas, and the reverse is true for men. . . . The same picture emerges with measures of time poverty gaps. (chapter 8)

In the same vein as education, access to adequate infrastructure is a problem in most of the continent. However, the magnitude of the issue is much larger in the countryside: lack of access to water and electricity is especially prevalent in rural areas. This exacerbates urban-rural differences in gender gaps by reducing the productivity of household chores on average more in rural areas, thus limiting rural women's available time for productive work and leisure disproportionately over their urban counterparts.

However, despite rural populations being on average more time poor, it seems that time poverty hits households in different income strata relatively evenly:

> In rural areas,. . .the differences in number of hours allocated to domestic work are smaller between the various consumer groups. . . .The fact that differences by consumption group are larger in urban areas than in rural areas could be because of the correlation between consumption and housing infrastructure . . . stronger [in urban] than in rural areas. . . or because hiring domestic workers is easier and more common [in urban] than in rural areas, hence richer households can more easily reduce their domestic work time by employing servants at home. (chapter 9)

Unemployment vs. Underemployment

Is unemployment an issue or is underemployment more relevant, and, if so, why? In the case of Africa, analyzing underemployment may yield deeper insights than purely relying on unemployment numbers. The informal sector is largely dominant in most African countries, and effective formal social protection schemes are the exception. Many experts and development agencies have already recognized that unemployment is often not an affordable option for those facing adverse employment prospects in such conditions. Tracking measures of underemployment—such as the share of the population engaged in subsistence activities or low-paying jobs—may be a better way to determine the real employment situation in African labor markets.

Unemployment may be used together with underemployment when trying to assess the impact of job rationing in different sectors of society. Richer households may be able to afford unemployment, as individuals wait for the next high-paying opportunity to present itself, and may also reflect how intrahousehold gender divisions manifest themselves (for example, richer women may afford to be unemployed, whereas poorer women may be forced to engage in some other kind of economic activity to make a contribution to the household budget) (chapter 1).

As expected from the fact that African women are poorer than men both in monetary and time measures, "women are overrepresented among the underemployed and the incidence of female underemployment was lower among the richest households, confirming that [in Africa] underemployment may be a better measure of economic stress than unemployment" (chapter 1). This is especially true when trying to assess the gender components of employment.

Heterogeneity of Labor Markets

How heterogeneous are labor markets in Africa and how does it help explain gender disparities (heterogeneity regarding variables such as labor market participation by gender, informality, level of development of economies, pay gap, and so on)?

Labor markets in Africa appear to be highly heterogeneous in a number of ways. The studies in the first five chapters found that, on average and in most countries, sex-based segregation was an important issue, and individuals with different levels of education did not seem to compete for the same jobs. The study of 18 African countries in chapter 1 found that, "Workers with a tertiary level of education earned on average more than eight times more than individuals with no education, and more than four times more than individuals with primary education." On the basis of education heterogeneity alone, this characteristic in African labor markets helps explain a large part of observed gender disparities.

Chapter 2 adds that, in Ethiopia, "job characteristics were found to be systematically less favorable for women." When included in the analysis, job characteristics across genders explained an important share of the gender wage gap (25 percent on average). "These differences in job characteristics were largely driven by the differences in education between men and women, but also by an unexplained gender factor that may well reflect a mix of sex-based segregation and gender differences in individual work preferences."

These differences in job preference, together with cultural and social norms, probably contribute to sectoral segmentation between genders, and this is also reflected in earnings gaps between sexes. In Madagascar, as well as in many other countries, the size of the earnings gap differs across wage sectors and is usually much higher in the informal wage sector. There, as shown in chapter 3, the explained share of the gap falls dramatically between 2001 and 2005, probably revealing a greater heterogeneity in earnings and/or greater unobserved heterogeneity among the sample of workers in this sector:

> The gender earnings gap would have been 28.3 percent and 34.3 percent smaller, respectively, for 2001 and 2005, if men and women had been "equally" distributed across the three sectors. These results are driven by the fact that the proportion of women is higher in both years in the informal wage employment sector where earnings are lower. Moreover, the increase in the sectoral location effect between the two years . . . is reflective of the greater proportion of women in the lower paying wage sector in 2005 compared to 2001. . . .

This is a reflection of the economic crisis that Madagascar faced over that period, and which created job rationing conditions that appeared to have affected women more strongly than men.

In the Malagasy non-farm, self-employment sector, "[i]ncluding the branch of activity results in a dramatic decrease in the unexplained share of the gap, from 42.9 percent to 21.3 percent in 2001 and from 41.0 percent to 15.8 percent in 2005" (chapter 3). Firm-level characteristics (such as number of employees and the amount of capital invested in the firm) are also much more powerful than individual characteristics in explaining gender earnings gaps in Madagascar, a sign that heterogeneity at the firm and sector levels may be behind much of what had been previously considered pure discrimination against women.

However, these results are not exclusive to Madagascar: occupation differences are also critical in countries such as Kenya, Morocco, and Uganda,

> ...where they explain about one-half of the total wage differences. ... In addition, including occupations [in the regressions] strongly affects the relative contributions of the other covariates, in particular education. For instance, in Kenya, the weight associated with years of schooling is 65.2 percent without controls for occupations, but it amounts to 17.4 percent once occupations are included in the list of regressors. (chapter 4)

For many countries, heterogeneity is strongly present not only across sectors, but also along different points in wage distributions. "[R]aw gender gaps calculated at the mean of the samples tend to hide significant differences in the magnitude of the gaps along the wage distribution" (chapter 4).

While there is no clear trend across countries as to how these disparities manifest along different wage levels, it is clear that a one-size-fits-all approach to such disparities does not work either across countries or across specific economic sectors—situations must be considered on a case-by-case basis in a context-sensitive manner.

Economic Context

How do economic context and conditions explain gender disparities at the labor market and household levels? In general, the level of gender disparities grows substantially whenever there are fewer available jobs in the labor market. More than an effect of discrimination, it seems that job rationing causes those with better human capital attributes and those with more power in households to take the few available jobs. In both of these cases, the beneficiaries are usually men to the detriment of women, expanding gender gaps.

> In Africa, high male employment is often associated with high female employment and less gender inequity in employment. ... [In] countries with relatively high male employment ratios, the employment prospects of women were relatively favorable and the level of gender inequality in employment was low. By contrast, in countries ... where jobs were especially scarce and few men were employed, gender disparities in employment were particularly pronounced and female employment ratios were remarkably low. ... [O]verall in the region, there was a positive relationship between male and female employment ratios, and countries with the largest male employment ratios tended to also have the lowest gender gap in employment. This suggests that women in Africa tend to be particularly vulnerable to labor market rationing, but that they could also greatly benefit from overall expansion of job opportunities. (chapter 1)

These stylized facts were derived from a static cross-country comparison, but it is very interesting to see that they have held over time in specific places as well. Fortunately, chapter 3 analyzes the Malagasy market at two points in time, before and after important external economic shocks, which serves as a relatively good natural experiment in reducing labor demand in the economy. In Madagascar,

> [d]ecompositions of the gender wage gap show that differences in individual characteristics of men and women account for almost 70 percent of the gap in 2001. However, this share is down to less than 40 percent in 2005. . . . This fall in the explained share is principally explained by the significant decrease in the explanatory power of human capital variables in 2005, in particular, education and professional experience. (chapter 3)

The analysis shows that, when the crisis hit, women were more negatively affected than men, even after controlling for other human capital variables, such as education and work experience. In fact, human capital variables have a lower explanatory power after the crisis, so this may be one of the few instances where it may be less dangerous to consider that women may have suffered more than men from the same kind of negative stimulus for no clear reason.

These findings could support the idea that potential gender segregation may find more fertile ground to manifest itself in adverse economic circumstances than otherwise. On the other hand, it has been widely noted that, "when regular, full-time jobs that provide clear career prospects exist and are accessible to women, they usually contribute to their empowerment and offer alternative interests and achievements to domestic work or motherhood" (chapter 8).

Is Discrimination an Issue?

Is labor market discrimination really a key issue in underdeveloped economies and in labor markets where jobs are scarce? Given the results in these chapters, there seems to be little evidence to support the idea that labor market discrimination is a key explanation for gender gaps in underdeveloped economies, especially those whose job markets are small and can only supply formal employment for a minority of the population. In addition, chapter 4 notes that "in a context where wages usually remain low, it may be that employers tend to limit the use of discrimination against women."

Gender disparities in the African context seem not to be caused predominantly by conscious discriminatory practices in the labor market. Instead, differences in education and other human capital variables, together with women's lack of power within their own households, as well as sociocultural norms, seem to be the most important factors that lead to worsening outcomes for women in Africa's labor markets.

Of course, the crucial factor that creates the initial conditions for the largest gender differences to develop is the widespread lack of economic opportunities on the continent. In places with strong economic growth, disparities shrink, and the inverse is also true for nations in economic doldrums.

Youth Employment

What are the main contributions of the book to understanding youth employment issues?

> On average in the region, and for both men and women, youth employment was substantially lower than that for adults, while the employment of older people was remarkably high.... In almost all countries ... gender disparities in employment were in general much lower for youth. (chapter 1)

By contrast, in chapter 2, which particularly focuses on Ethiopia, a country with some particular challenges and opportunities, especially in relation to its youth and cultural norms, "[t]he ... relative wage disadvantage for women is also more pronounced for younger women. As women get older, the pay differential with men tends to get lower."

While the assertion is valid for Ethiopia in 2005, this claim shows the dangers of trying to extract generalized information from studies performed on individual countries in isolation. In addition, chapter 2 concludes by noting that, while the "raw gender pay differential was found to be more pronounced for younger workers ... the unexplained component was probably much lower for youth." This means that human capital gaps, which the Ethiopian government is actively combating with relative success, are probably more the issue than any form of discrimination in the new generations. The same holds true for many other African countries, since it "is reassuring ... that education parity is progressing among youth" (chapter 1).

Children are burdened with a significant amount of the domestic work in many African countries. In Sierra Leone, for example, children spend long hours fetching wood and water and performing other household duties, reducing their available time for studying or leisure. This work obligation is higher in rural areas and also higher for girls than boys. In contrast to urban areas, in rural areas, "a higher number of children actually reduces the amount of domestic work performed by adults, presumably because the children play a larger role in the domestic work there" (chapter 9).

Policy Recommendations and the Way Forward

The evidence presented in this volume may be used in two ways to inform future policy interventions in African countries. The first is to draw overall conclusions about gender disparities in Africa that seem common or widespread across the continent in general. These overarching facets of gender disparities in Africa may yield general strategic guidance and additional stamina for policy makers to tackle some of the most prevalent and important challenges facing their countries, possibly teaming up with or learning from neighboring nations facing similar problems. The second way to use this book is to draw more context-specific insights, which may be carefully applied on the basis of the conclusions from individual chapters. Some countries may go further and jointly consider different studies that focus on more than one aspect of gender disparities in their population.

Clearly, gender disparities grow when economies are not functioning well and labor markets are tiny. Job creation is central to gender equality: even in the presence of other factors that affect women negatively, robust growth and more opportunities in the labor market greatly diminish the inequalities faced by women in their productive activities. Therefore, national governments must do all they can to stimulate economic growth, particularly in sectors that will generate formal sector jobs for both men and women.

In the same way, policy makers must make efforts to provide adequate infrastructure services to their populations. Efforts to expand water and electricity provision (among other services) will pay off in a variety of ways that will also create positive spillover in other areas of governmental concern. Private investment is likely to grow in the wake of better infrastructure availability, stimulating economic growth and formal jobs; health outcomes are likely to improve, allowing human capital expenditures in households to be shifted toward education and training; women's time may be freed for productive activities, further stimulating income generation. All these facets also help reduce women's disparities while benefiting economies as a whole.

Beyond the common challenge of low growth, African countries must also commit to pursuing gender equity in all levels of education and expanding education attainment in general. In all cases, better education means better outcomes for women, less disparity, and brighter prospects for the country in general. Much has been written about education, but the point here is that, even for countries with the lowest income, widespread provision of and gender equality in education are less of a luxury and more of a necessity for any nation serious about unleashing the economic power of its women and reaping the benefits for everyone in the process.

The last commonality in this book, albeit in a more subdued manner, is the question of attitudes toward women in developing countries in general, and African countries in particular. Starting in the household—sometimes even from birth—women have fewer opportunities than men and are assumed to be responsible for a larger share of household duties. Economic empowerment through access to better jobs and better education will likely have the largest influence in shifting societal attitudes toward women over time. However, it seems that, at least in some countries, there is a case for active public participation in speeding up the process.

Two general policy fronts already implemented with success in some countries include creating public awareness campaigns to gradually shift societal values and economic initiatives to empower women in particular. On this last point, specific strategies will differ according to context, but women-specific access to credit, tax incentives for companies to hire women, conditional transfer programs to families that enroll girls in schools, and other similar programs may prove beneficial. Together with introducing effective and equalitarian legal systems in those countries still lacking them, these interventions may help break the vicious circle perpetuating the women's disadvantaged situation in many African countries, and should allow the other two spheres, growth and education, to take hold more strongly and revert the cycle toward a brighter future for women—and consequently for all—in the continent.

From a more academic point of view, it seems that gender issues are just beginning to be understood within the African context. There is a rampant lack of good quality data, and this is the first place where improvements must be made in order to gain a deeper understanding of gender disparities in the region. Periodic national household surveys, in particular, would benefit from more standardization between countries, and should also include more gender-specific questions, to the extent possible within a country's sociocultural constraints.

There must also be a stronger push to study gender issues specifically in the African context. Many results in the book are highly sensitive to context, stated assumptions, methods, and datasets; deviations in conclusions are possible and even expected when some studies are replicated or applied to different countries by other investigators. In addition, despite the clear value and the pioneering character of the studies herein, some results—one daresay, even some of the prior and unstated assumptions that can be identified in isolated cases in the book—need additional investigation for more robust insights into the subject within the African context. Future investigations of gender issues in Africa would surely benefit from a wider and deeper literature dedicated to the issues particular to the region. This would allow knowledge in this area to mature outside the shadow of results from other, better studied regions—in particular, developed countries— that may not generalize well into the African context.

References

Appleton, S., J. Hoddinott, and P. Krishnan. 1999. "The Gender Wage Gap in Three African Countries." *Economic Development and Cultural Change* 47 (2): 289–312.

Brilleau, A., R. Roubaud, and C. Torelli. 2004. *L'Emploi, le Chômage et les Conditions d'Activité dans les Principales Agglomérations de Sept Etats Membres de l'UEMOA*

Principaux Résultats de la Phase 1 de l'Enquête 1-2-3 de 2001–2002. DIAL working paper 6, L'Union Economique et Monetaire Ouest Africaine (UEMOA).

Fafchamps, M., M. Söderbom, N. Benhassine. 2006. "Job Sorting in African Labor Markets," Working Paper Series 2006-02, University of Oxford, Centre for the Study of African Economies.

Hill, M. A., and E. M. King. 1995. "Women's Education and Economic Well-being." *Feminist Economics, Taylor and Francis Journals* 1 (2): 21–46.

ILO (International Labour Organization). 2002. *Women and Men in the Informal Economy: A Statistical Picture*. ILO, Gender and Employment Sector, Geneva.

Lachaud, J. P. 1997. *Les Femmes et le Marché du Travail Urbain en Afrique Subsaharienne*. Paris: Editions l'Harmattan.

Nordman C. J. and F. Roubaud. 2005. "Reassessing the Gender Wage Gap: Does Labour Force Attachment Really Matter? Evidence from Matched Labour Force and Biographical Surveys in Madagascar," Working Papers DT/2005/06, Développement, Institutions and Analyses de Long Terme, Paris.

Nordman, C. J. and F. C. Wolff. 2008. "Islands through the Glass Ceiling? Evidence of Gender Wage Gaps in Madagascar and Mauritius," Working Papers DT/2008/02, Développement, Institutions and Analyses de Long Terme, Paris.

———. 2009. "Gender Differences in Pay in African Manufacturing Firms," Working Papers LEMNA, University of Nantes, France.

UNICEF (United Nations Childrens' Fund). 1999. *Women in Transition*. Florence, Italy: UNICEF Innocenti Research Centre.

World Economic Forum. 2009. *The Global Gender Gap Report 2009*. WEF, Geneva.

Part 1

Stylized Facts

Chapter 1

Gender Disparities in Africa's Labor Markets: A Cross-Country Comparison Using Standardized Survey Data

Alexandre Kolev and Nicolas Sirven

G ender inequality in the labor market remains a pressing problem in con-
temporary Africa. Although there are large variations across countries in
male and female labor market outcomes, evidence shows that, in several
countries of the region, women are less likely to be in paid jobs, and those that
are employed are disproportionately concentrated in informal and precarious
employment and paid substantially less than men (for example, Appleton, Hoddinott, and Krishnan 1999; Bigsten and Horton 1997; Brilleau, Roubaud, and
Torelli 2004; ECA 2005; Glick and Roubaud 2004; ILO 2002; Lachaud 1997).

While the lack of decent employment for both men and women is at the
heart of the poverty battle in Africa, the fact that women experience greater
difficulties in the labor market is an additional concern and a specific poverty
challenge. Women's employment and earnings are essential in the fight against
poverty, not only because of the direct contribution they make to household
welfare, but also because such employment provides personal power for women
in making family decisions and redirecting household spending on essential
needs, especially in favor of children's health and education (UNICEF 1999).
Supporting employment for women is also instrumental in securing initial
investment in girls' education.

Assessing and comparing women's disadvantages in African labor markets
remains a challenge, however. In-depth comparative analyses are lacking, largely
because reliable and comparable comprehensive data have been scant and have
the following limitations. First, when centralized databases do exist, they typically break down only a few basic labor market indicators by gender, which

This study was prepared as part of a joint research project by the French Development Agency and
the World Bank.

yields incomplete information on the relative situations of men and women and does not allow comparison between indicators. A further problem is that reported labor market indicators by gender are often not comparable across countries because they refer to different survey instruments with different concepts and measures of employment and earnings. Second, while ad hoc comparable survey instruments for several countries in Africa have been developed from time to time, they usually cover only urban areas or capital cities (Brilleau, Roubaud, and Torelli 2004; Lachaud 1997). Third, fairly good poverty and labor market data gathered from multi-topic household surveys that cover urban and rural areas do exist for a number of African countries, but until recently they were not easily comparable because of differences in survey instruments.

The objective of this study is to help correct an important knowledge gap regarding gender disparities in Africa's labor markets. The study is novel in providing a comparative analysis based on standardized, nationally representative survey data for 18 countries. The data were extracted from multi-topic integrated household surveys conducted in the region around 2000 and recently harmonized as part of the World Bank Survey-based Harmonized Indicators Program (SHIP).[1]

The fundamental issue this study addresses is the extent to which women in Africa are disadvantaged in the labor market, and how this disparity might vary across countries. The research questions include: Are gender disparities in the labor market particularly pronounced? What is the nature of women's disadvantages? Is greater gender parity in education likely to result in improved and more equal labor market outcomes?

This chapter is organized as follows. The next section presents the SHIP dataset and the concepts used to compute key labor market indicators. It also discusses comparability and measurement issues. An overview of gender disparities in labor market outcomes is provided in the third section. The fourth section discusses gender inequalities within employment in the sample countries. The role of educational attainment and gender inequalities in education is reviewed in the fifth section, and a summary section follows.

Data and Concepts

This section presents the data used for the comparative analysis of gender disparities in Africa's labor markets. It further defines key relevant labor market indicators and discusses issues related to the measurement of gender disparities in employment outcomes and the comparability and quality of the data.

World Bank SHIP Data
The research used standardized survey data from 18 African countries prepared as part of the World Bank SHIP. The list of household surveys used to derive

gender disaggregated information on a variety of social and economic indicators is shown in table 1.1.

The objective of the World Bank SHIP is to facilitate the monitoring and comparison of social and economic conditions in Africa. Data comparability is achieved through the use of a common set of variable definitions to which individual surveys are harmonized. The procedures designed to ensure good data quality, transparency of data processing, and ease of analysis include verification for internal and external consistencies, extensive documentation of data processing, and harmonization of the standardized files through a common set of variables.

Measures of Key Indicators and Gender Disparities

The analysis of gender disparities draws attention to the gender gap ratio, which is the male-to-female ratio for each variable. For instance, the gender gap in employment (or male-to-female employment ratio) is given by the share of men employed over the share of women employed in the population. Since such

Table 1.1 List of Surveys by Country and Date

Country	Code	Year of survey	N	Title
Burkina Faso	bfa	1994	31,937	Enquête prioritaire auprès des ménages
Burundi	bdi	1998	16,703	Etude nationale sur les conditions de vie
Cameroon	cmr	2001	30,657	Enquête Camerounaise auprès des ménages
Côte d'Ivoire	civ	1998	13,343	Enquête nationale de vie des ménages
Ethiopia	eth	2000	42,672	Welfare monitoring survey
Gambia, The	gmb	1998	8,056	Household poverty survey
Ghana	gha	1998	13,717	Living standards survey 4
Guinea	gin	1994	15,146	Enquête intégrale sur les conditions de vie des ménages
Kenya	ken	1994	27,934	Welfare monitoring survey II
Madagascar	mdg	1999	13,701	Enquête prioritaire
Malawi	mwi	1997	15,364	Second integrated household survey
Mauritania	mrt	2000	20,281	Étude nationale sur les conditions de vie
Nigeria	nga	1996	21,900	Household survey
São Tomé and Príncipe	stp	2000	5,882	Enquête nationale sur les conditions de vie des ménages
Sierra Leone	sle	2003	11,952	Household survey
Uganda	uga	1999	26,246	Household budget survey
Zambia	zmb	1998	49,165	Living conditions monitoring survey

Source: Authors.
Note: N = number of survey participants.

a ratio is based on interpersonal comparison, we use individual data for the population ages 15 to 64, as defined by the International Labour Organization (ILO) as the "active population" age group.

Notice that all variables—and therefore all gender gap ratios—are calculated for each country by area of residence (rural, urban); age group (15–24, 25–39, 40–59, 60–64); and quintile (based on household consumption per capita). When the value of this ratio equals 1, the distribution of men and women for a given variable (for example, employment rate) and for a specific group (for example, rural) is similar. However, when the ratio value is more (or less) than 1, men (or women) are overrepresented. In this study, variables of interest to compute the gender gap ratio refer to education and labor market indicators.

Usual statistics for education have been generated, including literacy status ("can both read and write?"), school attendance ("ever attended school?"), and highest level of education achieved (primary, secondary, and tertiary education) for individuals between 15 and 64 years of age. Net enrollment ratio refers here to individuals between 7 and 12 who were in school at the time of the survey.[2]

Labor market statistics retained for the analysis deal with labor force status[3] (unemployment rate, employment-to-population ratio); sector of activity[4] (agriculture and non-agriculture; sectors I, II, and III); and employment status (wage-employed in the private sector, wage-employed in the public sector, employed in the informal sector, self-employed, employer, homemaker, retired, student, etc.). Special attention was also paid to gender differences in labor income. A value of weekly labor income was calculated as the ratio of annual labor income to the number of hours worked per week, adjusted on the basis of 52 weeks. Gender earnings gap ratios were performed using all these measures.

Comparability and Measurement Issues

The SHIP data provide individual and household data from national surveys for 18 countries in Africa (although because some countries are missing information for particular indicators, the sample will be smaller in some parts of this chapter). Comparability of key indicators across surveys included in the SHIP data is ensured through the construction of a common set of variables. Comparison across countries based on the SHIP data must be treated with great care, however. All surveys were collected between 1994 and 2004, but they do not necessarily coincide with the same dates (table 1.1). Differences in the time period across surveys occur because the cost of such surveys and the lack of human and financial infrastructures in most of these countries do not allow household surveys to be conducted annually. Another weakness of the SHIP data is that only 7 of the 18 countries provide data on labor income and the number of hours worked per week. For this reason, when several datasets were available for a country at different periods of time, this study gave preference to those providing information on labor income and the number of hours worked per week.

Data Quality

Much effort was made to ensure internal and external consistencies of the SHIP data, yet the quality of these data ultimately depends on the quality of the original dataset, which varies from one survey to another. One indicator of data quality (reported in the annex) is the percentage of missing observations for key education and labor market variables. This information is given for all national surveys included in the SHIP data. It shows that missing information for one or more indicators is a problem of moderate to high importance, depending on the survey and the indicator. By and large, the quality of labor market data seems to be lower than the quality of education data. For instance, detailed data on the sector of employment are missing in five countries. In the case of Niger, data on the labor market are simply missing, so the country was dropped from the sample.

The quality problems encountered in the SHIP data are by no means an exception, however. Researchers widely acknowledge that statistical systems are particularly weak in many African countries. As a result, the findings presented here, like those obtained from many surveys conducted in Africa, need to be treated with caution.

Gender Differences in Labor Market Outcomes

Paid work is a key determinant of women's economic autonomy and an important foundation for their empowerment. It is therefore essential to monitor the relative position of women in the region and call attention to places where women may be more at risk of poorer labor market outcomes. This section provides a cross-country comparison of the situation of men and women in terms of labor force participation, employment, unemployment, and underemployment around 2000.

Labor Force Participation

Labor force participation rates in Africa, as elsewhere in the world, are extremely gender-specific. Women are much less likely to be economically active than men in all age groups and in all countries for which data were available, apart from Burundi, The Gambia, and Sierra Leone (figure 1.1). On average in the region, the difference between the labor force participation rate for men (78.3 percent) and women (61.0 percent) stood at 17.3 percentage points, which is higher than in the European Union. There were also large differences across countries, with the female participation rates ranging from below 40 percent in Ethiopia, Kenya, Malawi, and Uganda, to 80 percent and higher in Burkina Faso, Burundi, The Gambia, Ghana, Guinea, and Sierra Leone. High female participation rates in several African countries compared to other regions of the world may be the

Figure 1.1 Labor Force Participation Rate by Gender, around 2000

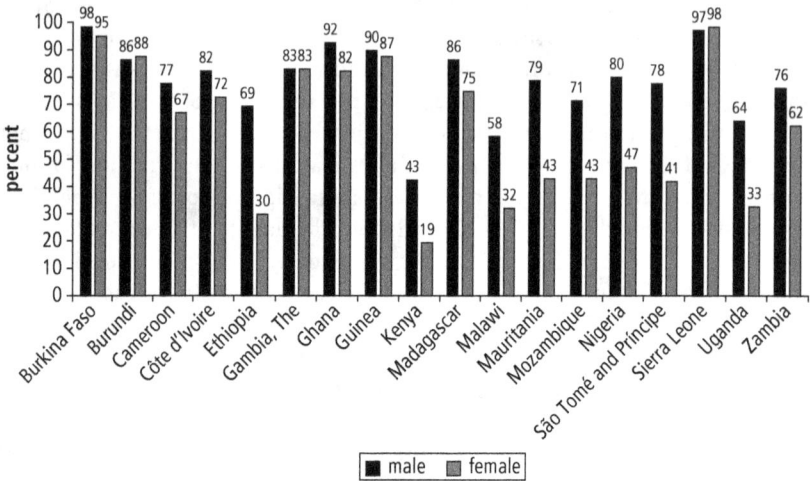

Source: World Bank Survey-based Harmonized Indicators Program (SHIP).
Note: Estimates use ages 15–64.

result of women's traditional participation in subsistence farming and market production in agriculture (World Bank 2007).

Employment

Another key indicator of the economic and welfare situation of men and women in low-income countries is the employment ratio, which is the share of productively employed individuals in the total working-age population. This statistic excludes individuals engaged in unpaid activities, unemployed, or inactive. Table 1.2 presents the share of employed men and women in the working-age population of the region around 2000. It shows that participation in productive employment was significantly lower for women. For the region as a whole, the employment ratio stood at about 53 percent for women, compared to nearly 70 percent for men (1.5 times higher than for women).

These average figures hide large disparities across the region, however. The lowest female employment ratios (below 33 percent) were found in Ethiopia, Kenya, Malawi, Mauritania, Mozambique, and Uganda. In these countries, the gender gap in employment was also very large, ranging from 23 percentage points in Kenya to 42 percentage points in Ethiopia. By contrast, female employment ratios were relatively high (above 70 percent) and closer to male ratios in Burkina Faso, Burundi, The Gambia, Guinea, Madagascar and Sierra Leone.

In Africa, high male employment is often associated with high female employment and less gender inequity in employment. In Burkina Faso and

Table 1.2 Employment Ratio by Gender, around 2000

| Country | Share of the working-age population in employment | | Male-to-female employment ratio |
	Male (%)	Female (%)	
Burkina Faso	89.03	76.77	1.16
Burundi	85.02	86.80	0.98
Cameroon	70.77	62.14	1.14
Côte d'Ivoire	75.52	64.59	1.17
Ethiopia	65.27	23.20	2.81
Gambia, The	78.61	75.12	1.05
Ghana	60.67	54.66	1.11
Guinea	83.59	81.19	1.03
Kenya	42.56	19.29	2.21
Madagascar	84.83	72.22	1.17
Malawi	56.03	31.50	1.78
Mauritania	58.32	28.25	2.06
Mozambique	63.45	30.18	2.10
Nigeria	76.55	45.31	1.69
São Tomé and Príncipe	69.70	35.48	1.96
Sierra Leone	67.09	72.32	0.93
Uganda	62.75	32.40	1.94
Zambia	66.26	55.54	1.19
Africa-18	**69.78**	**52.61**	**1.53**

Source: World Bank SHIP.
Note: Estimates use ages 15–64.

Burundi, countries with relatively high male employment ratios, the employment prospects of women were relatively favorable and the level of gender inequality in employment was low. By contrast, in countries like Ethiopia and Kenya, where jobs were especially scarce and few men were employed, gender disparities in employment were particularly pronounced and female employment ratios were very low.

Figure 1.2, panels a and b, confirm that, overall in the region, there was a positive relationship between male and female employment ratios, and countries with the largest male employment ratios tended to also have the lowest gender gap in employment. This suggests that women in Africa tend to be particularly vulnerable to labor market rationing, but that they could also greatly benefit from overall expansion of job opportunities.

Variations between African countries in gender employment gap are further illustrated in figure 1.3, which shows the share of women among the employed. For the region as a whole, women's share in total employment

Figure 1.2 Relationships Between Male and Female Employment Ratios, around 2000

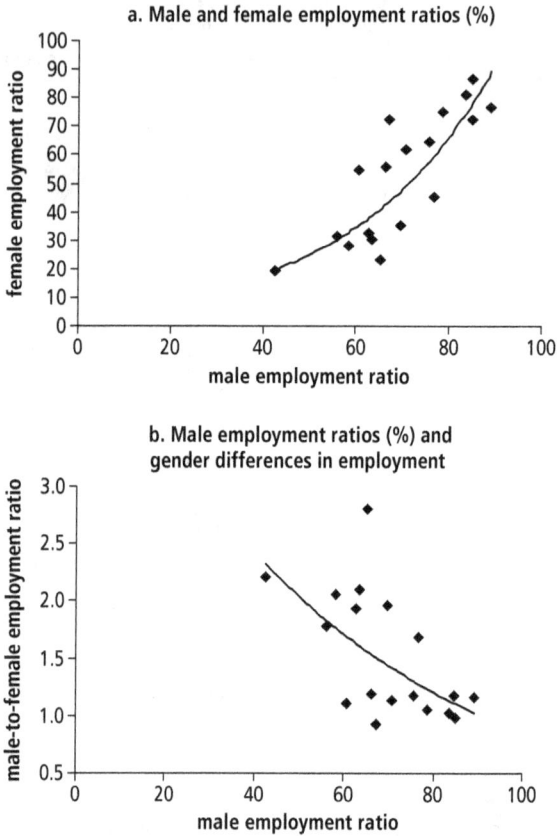

a. Male and female employment ratios (%)

b. Male employment ratios (%) and gender differences in employment

Source: World Bank SHIP.
Note: Estimates use ages 15–64.

stood at around 44 percent, ranging from 35 percent and below in Ethiopia, Kenya, and Mozambique, to as high as 55 percent and above in Burundi, Guinea, and Sierra Leone.

In Africa, noticeable disparities persist in the employment ratio for men and women within different age groups (table 1.3). For the youth age group across the region, employment ratios ranged from 15 to 80 percent for men and from 13 to 73 percent for women. For the older age group, employment ratios were in the range 21–95 percent for men and 4–94 percent for women. On average in the region, and for both men and women, youth employment was substantially lower than that for adults, while the employment of older people was remarkably high. It is also interesting that in almost all countries, with the noticeable

Figure 1.3 Women's Share in Total Employment, around 2000

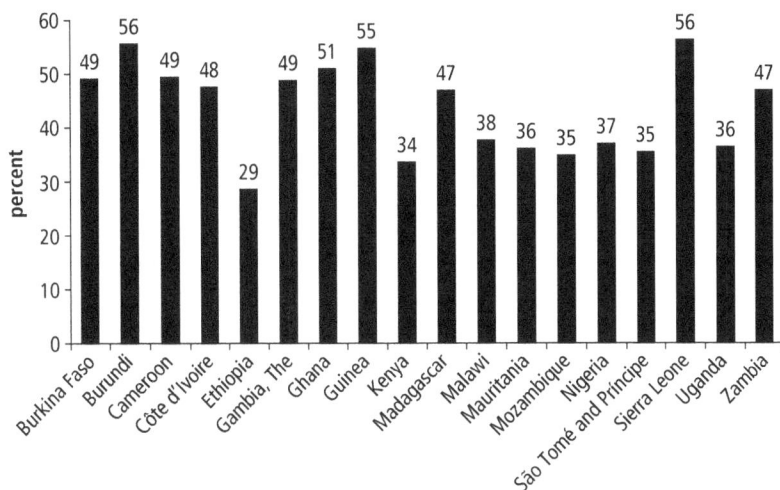

Source: World Bank SHIP.
Note: Estimates use ages 15–64.

exception of São Tomé and Príncipe, gender disparities in employment were in general much lower for youth.

In addition to gender differences between age groups, there seems to be a spatial dimension as well. In 12 of 18 countries for which data were available (Burkina Faso, Burundi, Cameroon, Côte d'Ivoire, The Gambia, Guinea, Madagascar, Malawi, Mauritania, São Tomé and Príncipe, Sierra Leone, and Zambia), gender disparities in employment were somewhat higher in urban areas (figure 1.4). Yet, in five of these countries, the gender employment gap was much higher in rural areas. The gender employment gap in favor of men persisted in rural areas in almost all countries in the region, with the exception of The Gambia and Sierra Leone.

Unemployment and Underemployment

Another commonly used indicator of labor market conditions is the unemployment rate. Table 1.4 shows the ILO unemployment rates separately for men and women by age and location around 2000. It shows that in the region as a whole, gender disparities in aggregate unemployment were limited. Among the 18 countries for which comparable data were available, the average unemployment rate stood at 13.9 percent for women and 10.7 percent for men. Yet, important disparities persist within the region, with a strong female disadvantage in terms of unemployment in Burkina Faso, Ethiopia, Mauritania, and Mozambique.

Table 1.3 Employment Ratio by Gender and Age Class, around 2000

Country	Youth (age 15–24)			Older people (age 60–64)		
	Male (%)	Female (%)	Male to Female	Male (%)	Female (%)	Male to Female
Burkina Faso	80.40	70.70	1.14	89.58	71.28	1.26
Burundi	67.37	72.82	0.93	95.45	91.27	1.05
Cameroon	43.62	41.81	1.04	79.83	68.44	1.17
Côte d'Ivoire	53.45	49.45	1.08	80.72	67.54	1.20
Ethiopia	25.54	14.27	1.79	87.02	34.06	2.55
Gambia, The	47.03	58.64	0.80	95.82	94.65	1.01
Ghana	15.69	19.68	0.80	83.16	72.77	1.14
Guinea	66.26	73.43	0.90	86.22	51.91	1.66
Kenya	16.69	13.61	1.23	21.35	4.54	4.70
Madagascar	70.47	64.89	1.09	82.09	56.08	1.46
Malawi	21.88	18.95	1.15	71.14	52.30	1.36
Mauritania	36.37	21.23	1.71	61.38	25.51	2.41
Mozambique	28.61	16.04	1.78	84.28	50.32	1.67
Niger	27.14	19.62	1.38	92.23	78.92	1.17
Nigeria	31.51	48.46	0.65	91.51	59.29	1.54
São Tomé and Príncipe	22.12	13.88	1.59	91.00	60.10	1.51
Sierra Leone	47.43	18.24	2.60	75.22	18.88	3.98
Uganda	38.14	39.27	0.97	82.18	70.87	1.16
Africa-18	**41.09**	**37.50**	**1.26**	**80.57**	**57.15**	**1.78**

Source: World Bank SHIP.

As in other parts of the world, youth unemployment in Africa was around twice as high as the overall unemployment rate. Recent evidence shows that world regions that have experienced an increase in youth cohorts and new entrants in the work force have also experienced a rise in youth difficulties in entering the labor force and finding living-wage employment (World Bank 2006a). It is interesting that, according to the SHIP data, youth unemployment in Africa was equally balanced overall between men and women: in only half of 18 countries represented in table 1.4 was the youth unemployment rate higher for women.

Unemployment in Africa was also more an urban phenomenon, with unemployment rates on average three times higher in urban than rural areas. Gender differences in unemployment were also much more pronounced in urban areas, where the rate for women was nearly 7 percentage points higher than the rate for men.

Using unemployment as a measure of labor market conditions in Africa is not exempt from problems, however. In most African countries, effective formal

Figure 1.4 Male-to-Female Employment Ratio by Country, around 2000

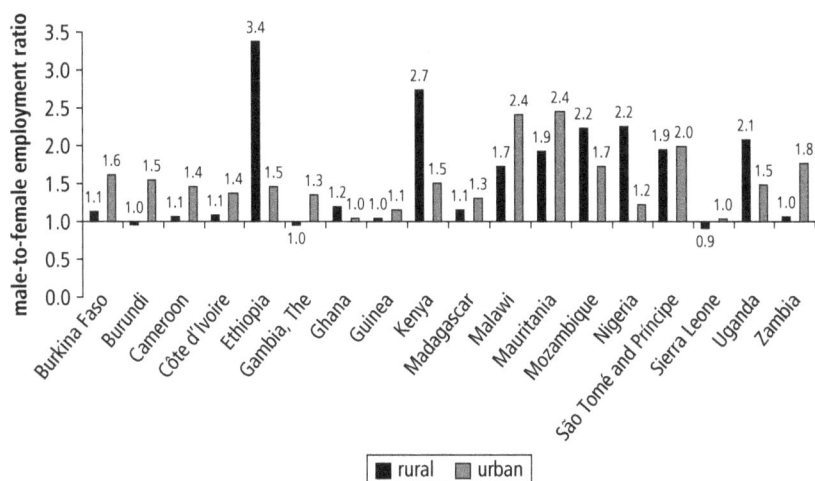

Source: World Bank SHIP.
Note: Estimates use ages 15–64.

social protection systems do not exist and the informal sector is widespread. Under such circumstances, unemployment tends to be a rather poor measure of economic stress and an even worse indicator for capturing gender economic disparities. On one hand, it is well known that, among poor populations, unemployment is not affordable and rationing in the labor market could be better reflected by other indicators, such as the share of the population engaged in subsistence activities or the incidence of underemployment (World Bank 2006b). On the other hand, research shows that for better-off individuals, unemployment reflects more of a queuing process, where people are waiting for well-paid or public jobs to become available (Sender, Cramer, and Oya 2005). Thus, monitoring unemployment in Africa is useful but needs to be interpreted with great care and complemented by other indicators.

Figure 1.5 compares the proportion of unemployed men and women living in the richest households with those in the poorest households. This comparison can help in understanding whether unemployed workers are disadvantaged and whether the welfare position of unemployed workers differs by gender. The numbers reveal, first, that in most countries in the region, the incidence of unemployment in the richest households is not far different from that in the poorest households, confirming that unemployment in the region may not be a very good proxy for economic stress, because many poor individuals can simply not afford to be unemployed in the absence of unemployment insurance systems.

Table 1.4 Gender Differences in Unemployment Rates by Age and Location, around 2000

Country	Youth (15–24)		Rural		Urban		All	
	Male	Female	Male	Female	Male	Female	Male	Female
Burkina Faso	16.4	24.6	4.0	12.1	32.0	56.3	9.5	19.3
Burundi	1.3	0.9	0.6	0.2	16.6	21.7	1.5	0.9
Cameroon	16.4	12.5	2.9	1.8	17.8	20.4	8.7	7.1
Côte d'Ivoire	14.1	18.5	1.8	3.0	15.5	23.3	7.9	10.8
Ethiopia	12.0	23.7	3.5	21.5	16.2	24.4	5.3	22.3
Gambia, The	5.1	2.8	1.5	2.6	10.0	23.9	5.1	9.4
Ghana	81.5	76.0	29.7	28.6	41.1	39.2	34.4	33.5
Guinea	9.1	11.9	2.6	3.3	15.3	17.2	7.1	7.0
Kenya								
Madagascar	1.3	2.5	1.1	2.9	2.7	5.3	1.4	3.3
Malawi	8.2	3.8	3.9	1.3	4.8	5.5	4.0	1.7
Mauritania	40.6	51.9	20.5	25.8	33.3	47.7	26.0	34.1
Mozambique	30.2	51.0	7.9	17.7	22.1	52.5	11.2	29.5
Nigeria	22.5	14.8	3.1	3.0	5.4	4.4	4.0	3.7
São Tomé & Príncipe	21.6	34.2	11.5	16.7	9.5	12.3	10.4	14.4
Sierra Leone	67.7	50.5	22.3	14.9	42.2	43.8	30.9	26.3
Uganda	4.2	3.4	0.9	0.4	4.8	3.3	1.6	1.1
Zambia	25.8	19.4	6.3	5.0	24.2	28.2	12.9	11.1
Africa-18	**22.2**	**23.7**	**7.3**	**9.5**	**18.5**	**25.3**	**10.7**	**13.9**

Source: World Bank SHIP.
Note: Estimates use ages 15–64.

Second, the welfare repercussions of unemployment in Africa seem to be related to gender. While for men a small but positive association exists between unemployment and poverty, the unemployment rates being slightly greater among the richest households in only 2 of 17 countries, the reverse was true for women. For the latter, the proportion of unemployed workers was higher in the richest households in 9 of 17 countries of the region. Extreme examples were Côte d'Ivoire and Malawi, where the female unemployment rate was more than four times higher among the richest households than the poorest households.

Considering that measures of unemployment have limited relevance in the African context, it is useful to complement the reporting of unemployment with other indicators. Table 1.5 provides a measure of underemployment, defined as the share of individuals in the active population (ages 15–64, employed or unemployed) who work for pay less than 30 hours per week. On average, for the nine countries for which data were available, women were overrepresented

Figure 1.5 Ratio of Unemployment Between Richest and Poorest Households, around 2000

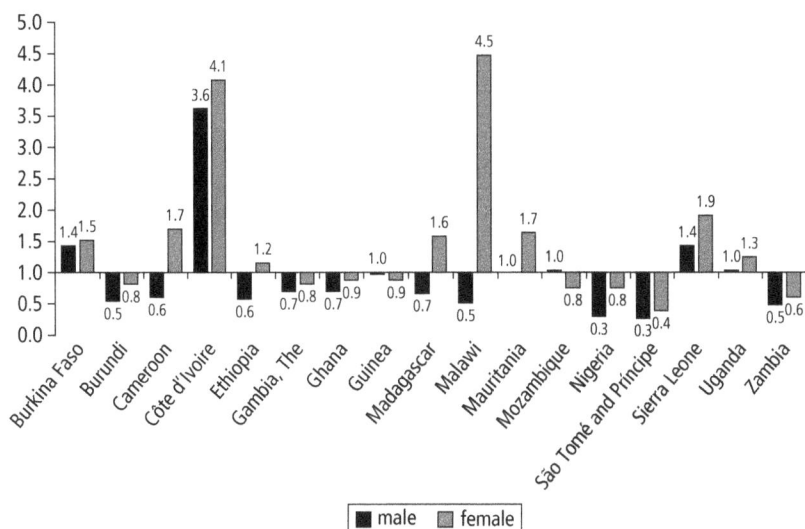

Source: World Bank SHIP.
Note: Estimates use ages 15–64. The ratio refers to the unemployment rate among individuals whose household consumption per capita lies within the top quintile (Q5) over the unemployment rate among individuals whose household consumption per capita lies within the top quintile (Q5).

Table 1.5 Average Incidence of Underemployment (Less Than 30 hours of Work per Week)

	Quintile 1	Quintile 2	Quintile 3	Quintile 4	Quintile 5
All genders (% employed)	41.2	42.3	40.0	40.1	38.9
Men (% employed)	35.9	36.7	35.2	35.0	34.5
Women (% employed)	46.9	48.8	45.7	46.0	33.6
Gender gap ratio	0.7	0.7	0.7	0.7	0.7

Source: World Bank SHIP.
Notes: Average among 9 countries for which data were available (Burkina Faso, Cameroon, Ghana, Guinea, Malawi, Mauritania, Mozambique, Nigeria, and Sierra Leone). Estimates use ages 15–64.

among the underemployed: two out of three underemployed workers were women. For women, the incidence of underemployment was also lower among the richest households. The latter confirms that in Africa, underemployment may be a better measure of economic stress than unemployment.

The fact that women in Africa tend to be overrepresented among the underemployed does not mean that the overall workload may be lower for women, however. Time allocation data show, indeed, that the division of responsibilities between productive (market) and reproductive (household) work is strongly gendered, and that women usually bear the brunt of domestic tasks. Moreover, in the absence of even rudimentary domestic technology, the time and effort required for these tasks is often staggering, and there may be short-term trade-offs between market-oriented and household-oriented activities (Blackden and Wodon 2006).

Gender Disparities at Work

Despite the particular difficulties that women face in access to paid employ-ment, more than half of women in Africa are employed. Thus, it is equally important to examine the nature and conditions of employment in the region and to explore how they may be influenced by gender. This section looks at the following questions: Is gender inequality in low-paid work a concern? How important are gender differences in earnings? Is sex-based segregation in sectors and types of employment an issue?

Low-paid Work and the Working Poor

In many countries, access to jobs does not necessarily allow an individual to escape poverty. This situation is usually a result of a combination of household-level factors, such as a relatively low incidence of employed members in the household, and a relatively large proportion of low-paid workers. In addition to the lack of job opportunities, low-paying work is a concern in Africa, where effec-tive social security systems for workers do not exist and where workers may have no choice but to take whatever job is available. According to International Labour Organization estimates, the working poor may account for almost 45 percent of the employed population in Sub-Saharan Africa (ILO 2004).

To what extent is the distribution of low-paid jobs related to gender in Africa? Figure 1.6 offers insight by presenting the proportion of low-paid workers in total wage employment (1.6, panel a) and total self-employment (1.6, panel b) for seven countries for which comparable data were available (Burkina Faso, Cameroon, Ghana, Malawi, Mozambique, Nigeria, and Sierra Leone). Notice-able disparities in wage employment across countries were observed. Numbers of low-wage workers were disproportionately high among women in Ghana and Mozambique (above 30 percent). By contrast, in Malawi, the incidence of low-wage employment was relatively low for women (13 percent). In Burkina Faso and Cameroon, the gender difference in the incidence of low-paid work was small, but the overall incidence of low-paid wage employment was high for both men and women (above 23 percent).

Among the self-employed, the incidence of low-paid work was higher for women in six out of seven countries. There were also marked differences across countries, with a proportion of low-paid self-employment among women rang-ing from 53 percent in Burkina Faso to 16 percent in Cameroon.

Figure 1.6 Incidence of Low-Paid Work in Total Wage Employment and Self-Employment, around 2000

a. Low-paid work in total wage employment

b. Low-paid work in total self-employment

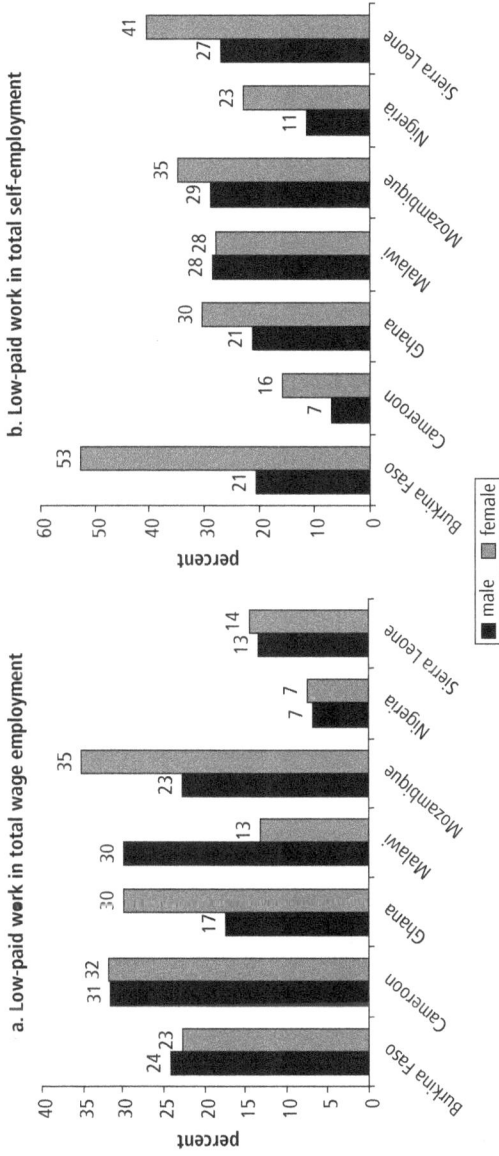

Source: World Bank SHIP.
Note: Estimates use ages 15–64.

37

The Gender Pay Gap

Earnings are important indicators of economic well-being and personal success. The relative level of women's and men's pay is informative about women's progress in the labor market. The first step in exploring the gender gap in earnings is simply to compare the pay for women and men. Studies point to a significant disadvantage for women in earnings. For instance, the ratio of women's to men's earnings was estimated to range from 40 percent in Kenya (Kabubo-Mariara 2003), to 70 percent in Cameroon (Lachaud 1997), 80 percent in Botswana (Siphambe and Thokweng-Bakwena 2001), and 90 percent in Burkina Faso (Lachaud 1997). Similarly, in a study of the size and determinants of gender wage gaps in the urban sector, Appleton, Hoddinott, and Krishnan (1999) found that female earnings represented about 72 percent of male earnings in Uganda, 78 percent in Ethiopia, and 97 percent in Côte d'Ivoire.

Evidence from the SHIP data confirms the presence of large gender pay gaps in several African countries, while pointing to significant differences across countries (figure 1.7). In the seven countries for which comparable data are available, the ratio of average female-to-male weekly labor income ranged from 23 percent in Burkina Faso to 79 percent in Ghana. The clear outlier was Malawi, where weekly labor income appeared to be slightly higher for women than for men.

Gender Differences in Employment Status and Nature

With the implementation of structural adjustment programs in many African countries in the late 1980s and early 1990s, the region has seen a dramatic decline in public-sector employment. At the same time, private employment

Figure 1.7 Weekly Female-to-Male Pay Ratios, around 2000

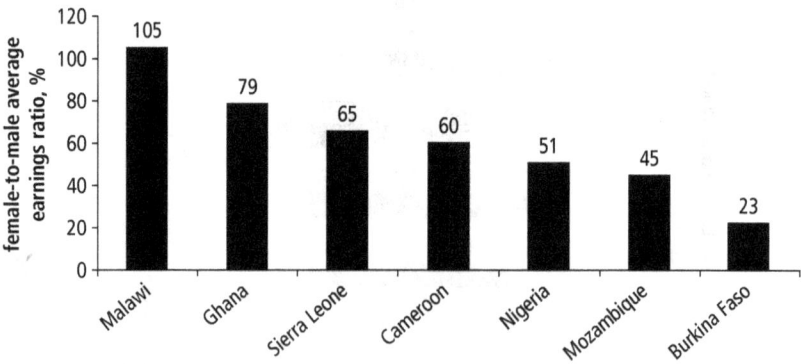

Source: World Bank SHIP.
Note: Female weekly labor income as a percent of male weekly labor income. Estimates use ages 15–64.

has progressed considerably, but most of this expansion has occurred in the low-wage, informal sector (World Bank 2006c). The fundamental question is whether women have had better or worse opportunities, and the related question is how these changes have affected men.

Figure 1.8 offers insight by presenting regionally aggregated information on the share of employed men and women in different employment status around 2000. On average in the region, the nature of employment was characterized by a dominant share of self-employment, a sizeable importance of informal employment, and a fairly minor contribution of public and private formal wage employment. Regionally, the distribution of employed individuals into some of these categories followed clear gender patterns. While there was little gender difference in the share of self-employment and the incidence of the employer category, women were almost twice as likely as men to be in the informal sector and about two times less likely to be in public and private formal wage employment.

Noticeable differences were observed within the region in the extent of the gender differential in employment status (table 1.6). In self-employment, the differential was highest in Burkina Faso, where men were nearly four times more likely to be self-employed than women, and lowest in Kenya, Ghana, and Malawi, where more women were self-employed.

In public wage employment, the gender disparities were remarkably high in Burkina Faso, again, where men were more than four times more likely to be in public wage employment than women, and lowest in São Tomé and Príncipe and Kenya, with a male-to-female ratio close to 1. The extent of the gender differential

Figure 1.8 Share of Employed Men and Women in Different Employment Status, around 2000

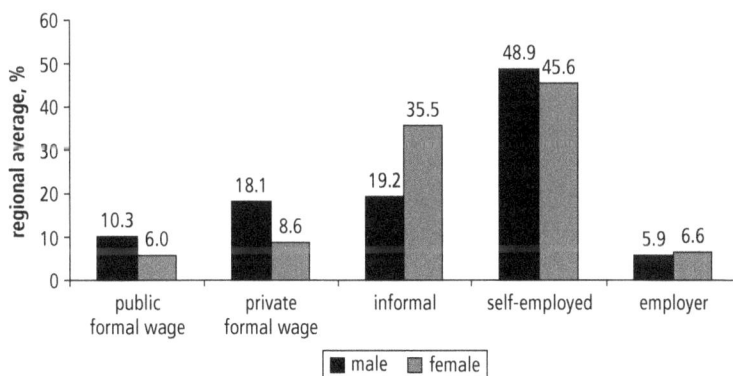

Source: World Bank SHIP.
Notes: Average among 16 countries only for the self-employed, and among 14 countries only for the informally employed and the employer. Estimates use ages 15–64.

Table 1.6 Share of Employed Men and Women in Selected Employment Status, around 2000

	Self-employment			Public wage employment			Informal employment		
	Male (%)	Female (%)	Male to Female	Male (%)	Female (%)	Male to Female	Male (%)	Female (%)	Male to Female
Burkina Faso	44.5	12.1	3.7	3.9	0.9	4.4	46.2	86.0	0.5
Burundi	66.2	25.9	2.6	4.3	1.5	2.9	25.1	71.8	0.3
Cameroon	52.4	59.1	0.9	9.6	3.8	2.5	11.4	3.1	3.7
Gambia, The	58.5	64.9	0.9	8.7	3.0	2.9	15.5	26.3	0.6
Ghana	68.6	88.2	0.8	11.8	4.5	2.6	—	—	—
Guinea	54.5	39.8	1.4	5.0	1.2	4.1	—	—	—
Kenya	20.3	35.7	0.6	27.5	22.3	1.2	—	—	—
Madagascar	59.6	38.6	1.5	3.7	2.1	1.8	21.8	50.6	0.4
Malawi	62.5	78.1	0.8	11.2	5.7	2.0	3.2	8.8	0.4
Mauritania	60.9	44.2	1.4	11.7	4.3	2.7	14.2	38.4	0.4
Mozambique	76.8	89.2	0.9	13.4	6.6	2.0	—	—	0.7
Nigeria	15.8	11.5	1.4	11.7	8.1	1.4	70.0	79.2	0.9
São Tomé and Príncipe	—	—	—	19.1	20.7	0.9	33.7	48.5	0.7
Sierra Leone	78.1	86.8	0.9	8.9	3.0	3.0	—	—	—
Uganda	—	—	1.2	6.6	3.8	1.7	—	—	—
Zambia	57.2	51.3	1.1	13.0	5.4	2.4	15.2	38.5	0.4

Source: World Bank SHIP.
Note: Estimates use ages 15–64. (—) means data not reliable or not available.

in the incidence of informal employment also varied substantially, with a male-to-female ratio ranging from 0.3 to 8.5. Only three countries—Cameroon, Guinea, and Kenya—had more men than women engaged in informal employment.

Within the perspective of SHIP data, it is interesting to note that the findings using the 1-2-3 survey carried out in the economic capitals of seven West African countries (Abidjan, Bamako, Cotonou, Dakar, Lomé, Niamey, and Ouagadougou) showed that discrimination against women, generalization of under-employment, and the importance of the informal sector were the major structural characteristics of the urban labor markets in the region (Brilleau, Roubaud, and Torelli 2004).

Sector of employment on average for the 14 countries for which data were available was characterized by a dominant agriculture sector (accounting for around 70 percent of women and 64 percent of men employed), a small industry sector (6 percent for women and 13 percent for men), and a fairly minor service sector (23 percent of both men and women employed). Overall, women were underrepresented in the industry and service sectors and slightly overrepresented in agriculture. The relative importance of women's employment in the service sector varied substantially across countries, however (figure 1.9). In Burundi and Guinea, men were more than three times more likely to be in the service sector. In contrast, in Ghana and São Tomé and Príncipe, men were slightly underrepresented in service employment.

Figure 1.9 Gender Differences in Sectors of Employment

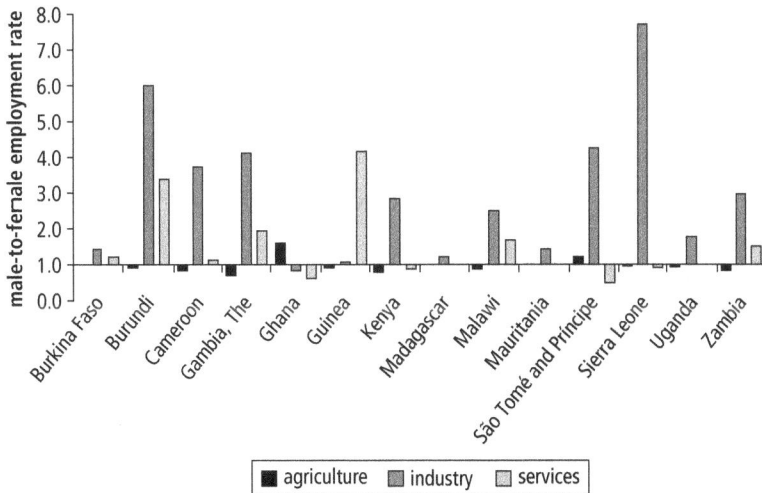

Source: World Bank SHIP.
Note: Estimates use ages 15–64.

The Role of Educational Attainment and Gender Inequalities in Education

Worldwide evidence suggests that higher educational achievement is almost always associated with better employment outcomes. As a result, large gender inequalities in education tend to be represented in women's disadvantage in the labor market. To what extent is this true in Africa? This section reviews the relationship between education and employment outcomes in Africa and investigates the extent of gender inequalities in education.

The Role of Education in Employment Outcomes and Earnings

In Africa, skills and educational achievement have a positive impact on individual labor outcomes for both men and women. Kuepie, Nordman, and Roubaud (2006) studied the effects of education on urban labor market participation and earnings in seven major West African cities. They found that, although education did not always guard against unemployment, it did increase individual earnings in Abidjan, Bamako, Cotonou, Dakar, Lomé, Niamey, and Ouagadougou, and increased the probability that employment would be in the most profitable sectors, that is, the formal private and public sectors.

New evidence from the SHIP data is reported in table 1.7, which provides for the region as a whole, and separately by gender and education level, the share of the active population that is employed, unemployed, low-paid, and underemployed. It shows that, for both men and women, the returns from education in terms of employment and unemployment are ambiguous. The employment

Table 1.7 Employment Status of the Active Population by Gender and Education Level, Regional Average, around 2000

	No education (%)	Primary (%)	Secondary (%)	Tertiary (%)
Employment				
Men	95.4	89.2	81.9	92.7
Women	91.0	83.5	74.7	85.4
Unemployment				
Men	4.5	10.7	18.0	7.2
Women	8.9	16.4	25.2	14.5
Working Poor				
Men	28.8	19.0	6.5	3.2
Women	47.1	29.5	9.9	2.3
Underemployment				
Men	36.8	34.6	29.3	22.0
Women	47.3	43.1	34.9	27.6

Source: World Bank SHIP.

rate was highest for the least educated (no education) and the most educated (tertiary education). At the same time, unemployment was highest for those with primary and secondary education, and it was higher for those with tertiary education than for those with no education.

Looking at the quality of employment provides a somewhat different and more predictable story with regard to the effect of education. For both men and women, the higher the educational level, the lower the incidence of low-paid jobs and underemployment. What is also interesting is that the returns from different educational levels on the quality of employment varied greatly for different indicators. With respect to low-paid jobs, the positive effect of educational attainment was already visible for those with a primary education. As far as the incidence of underemployment, only those with secondary education or more had a substantially lower risk of being underemployed, while this risk was high and almost similar for those with no education and for those with primary education.

In the region, there is also a clear association between level of education and employment status for both men and women (table 1.8). On average for the limited number of countries for which comparable data were available, the proportion of male and female workers in wage employment was much higher among individuals with tertiary and secondary education. By contrast, informal employment and self-employment was disproportionately high among men and women with primary education or less.

The results suggest that labor markets in Africa are highly segmented. Sex-based disparities in employment status are an important issue, and individuals with different levels of education did not seem to compete for the same jobs. Regarding earnings, table 1.9 shows that for the seven countries for which data were available, both the returns from education and the level of gender inequality

Table 1.8 Share of Employed Individuals in Selected Employment Status by Gender and Education, Regional Average, around 2000
(percentage of total employment)

	No education	Primary	Secondary	Tertiary
***Wage employment*[a]**				
Male	17.0	25.6	51.8	78.7
Female	7.1	12.6	42.5	79.2
Self-employment				
Male	60.5	53.6	29.6	12.4
Female	53.5	48.5	31.0	11.9
Informal employment				
Male	18.9[b]	21.5[c]	14.4[c]	4.7[d]
Female	32.7[b]	35.9[c]	22.2[c]	5.5[d]

Source: World Bank SHIP.
a. Average among 14 countries; b. among 11 countries; c. among 14 countries; d. among 12 countries. Estimates use ages 15–64.

Table 1.9 Earnings Gap Ratio by Education Level and Gender

	Men to women					All genders		
	All education	No level	Primary	Secondary	Tertiary	Tertiary to no education	Tertiary to primary	Tertiary to secondary
Burkina Faso	4.43	7.04	2.08	1.52	0.22	2.99	7.68	4.46
Cameroon	1.66	1.90	1.46	1.32	0.93	4.38	5.00	3.01
Ghana	1.27	1.57	1.24	1.16	1.45	3.11	1.91	1.37
Malawi	0.95	1.88	0.88	1.13	1.43	11.50	7.26	2.85
Mozambique	2.21	3.44	1.13	0.86	1.21	33.71	5.54	1.53
Nigeria	1.97	2.41	1.59	2.16	0.83	1.15	1.77	1.19
Sierra Leone	1.53	1.16	5.58	1.01	0.74	4.50	1.83	2.43
Africa-7	**2.00**	**2.77**	**1.99**	**1.31**	**0.97**	**8.76**	**4.43**	**2.40**

Source: World Bank SHIP.
Note: Estimates use ages 15–64.

44

were important. Workers with a tertiary level of education earned on average more than eight times more than individuals with no education, and more than four times more than individuals with primary education. At the same time, on average in the region, men earned twice as much as women.[5] The gender differences in earnings were particularly important in Burkina Faso and Mozambique.

In Africa, education not only has a favorable effect on earnings, but also has a positive impact on gender wage equity. What is indeed remarkable is that gender disparities in earnings varied with the level of education, and the higher the education level, the lower the extent of inequalities in labor income per hours worked. On average, the male-to-female earnings ratio was as high as 2.8 among individuals with no education, and as low as 0.9 among individuals with tertiary education.

Gender Disparities in Education Outcomes

While it has been shown that education had a positive influence on employment outcomes and earnings, the fact that educational attainment is lower for women in the region is a concern. As a whole in the region, the literacy rates stood at 61 percent for men, compared to 41 percent for women. Gender disparities in literacy were much more pronounced in rural areas, but gender differences persisted in urban areas (figure 1.10, panel a). These disparities were highest in Ethiopia, Guinea, and Niger and lowest in Madagascar and São Tomé and Príncipe.

Overall in the region, the primary-educated population in the age group 15–64 stood at 38 percent for men and 32 percent for women, and the secondary-educated population constituted only 27 percent for men and 20 percent for women. Only 5 percent of men and 3 percent of women received tertiary education. In most countries in the region, gender educational disparities were largely a rural phenomenon and were observed for all education levels. In urban areas, the gender education gap was rather small at the primary and secondary levels, but became an issue at the tertiary level (figure 1.10, panels b to d).

If, in fact, gender disparities in Africa's labor markets are to a large extent a result of gender inequality in human capital acquisition among the adult population, what is reassuring is that education parity is progressing among youth. As part of the objective to reach the Millennium Development Goals (MDGs), many governments in Africa have indeed made significant progress toward universal primary education and gender equality in school enrollment (UNESCO 2005).

According to SHIP data, on average in the region, school enrollment ratios among children ages 6–12 were 66 percent for boys and 64 percent for girls. In addition, while the level of gender inequality in school enrollment between rural and urban areas and between rich and poor families varied across countries, these gender differences were limited in most countries. Only Burkina Faso, Guinea, and Mozambique had significant gender inequality in school enrollment that was further amplified in rural areas and poor households. In these countries, girls' disadvantage in terms of school enrollment was in excess

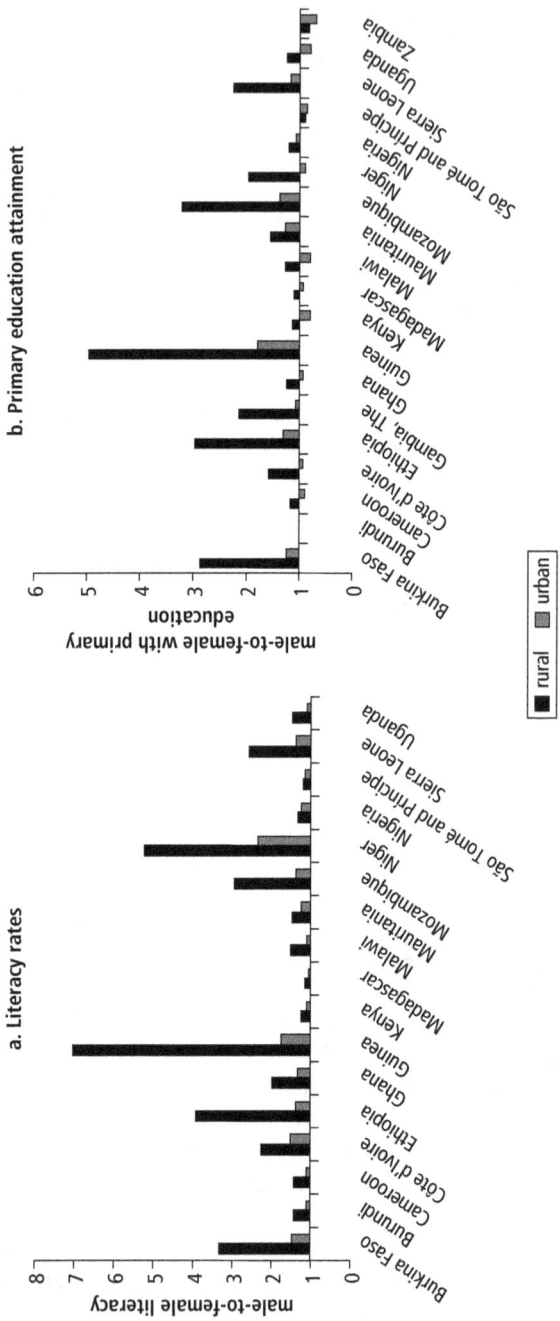

Figure 1.10 Gender Differences in Literacy and Education, around 2000

a. Literacy rates

b. Primary education attainment

rural   urban

c. Secondary education attainment

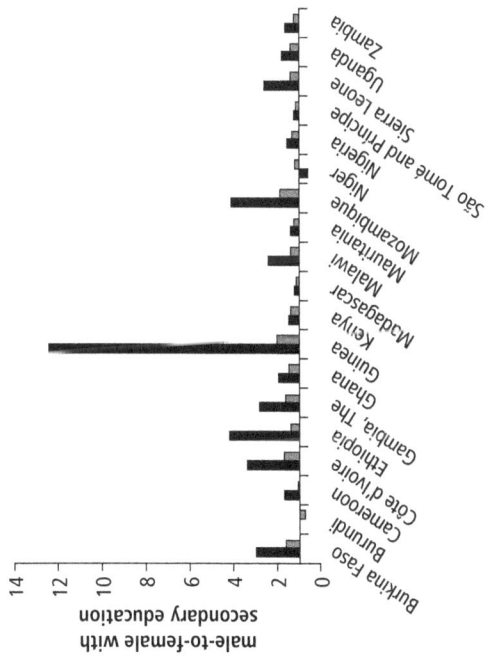

d. Tertiary education attainment

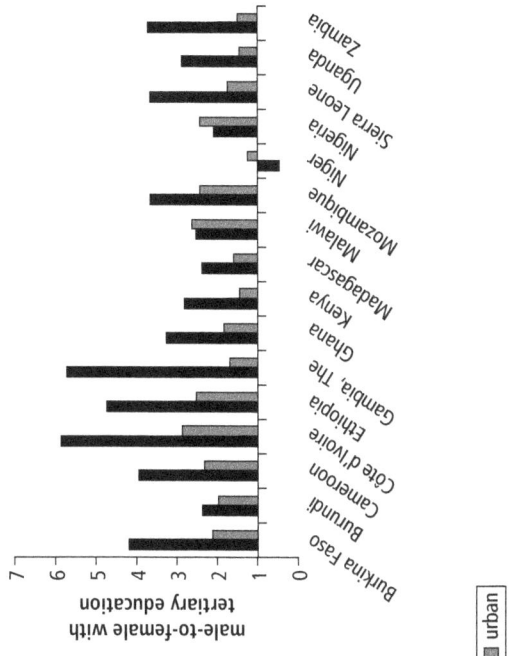

Source: SHIP data.

of 20 percent in rural areas and among poor families (figures 1.11 and 1.12). In the rest of the region, the female-to-male school enrollment ratios were close to 1 in urban areas and among better-off families, and only slightly greater in rural areas and among poor families.

Figure 1.11 Gender Differences in Enrollment Ratios Among Children Ages 7–12 by Location, around 2000

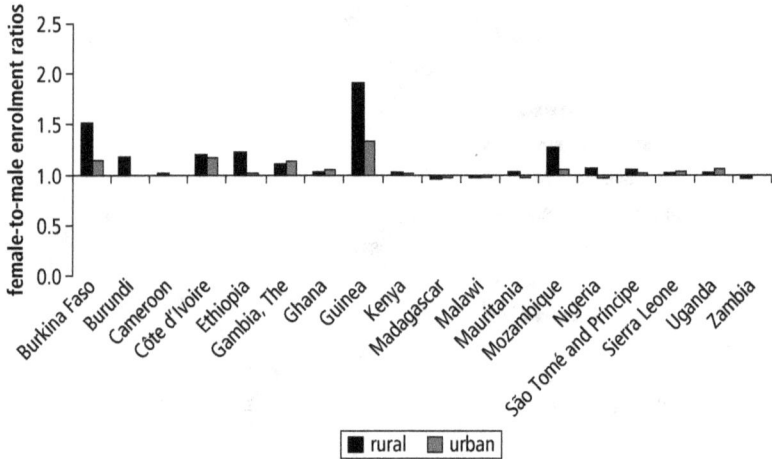

Source: World Bank SHIP.

Figure 1.12 Gender Differences in Enrollment Ratios Among Children Ages 7–12 by Consumption Quintiles, around 2000

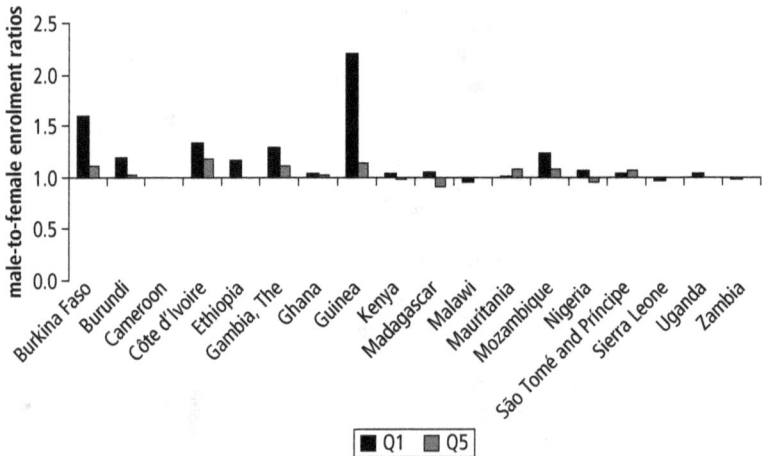

Source: World Bank SHIP.
Note: Q5 to Q1 refer to the top and bottom quintile of household consumption per capita.

Conclusions

This research sought to help fill a knowledge gap in the extent and nature of gender disparities in Africa's labor markets. Using a series of cross-country, comparable, standard and less standard indicators of labor market conditions derived from standardized, nationally representative survey data collected around 2000, this chapter provided an overview of gender disparities in labor market outcomes in 18 African countries. Despite the acknowledged shortcomings of the standardized surveys, which were not necessarily conducted during the same time period and which varied in quality, the results provided the following findings:

- Participation in productive employment in urban areas was appreciably lower for women, yet countries with more favorable employment outcomes for men also had higher employment ratios among women and less gender disparities in employment. The gender employment gap was also remarkable in rural areas in some countries. Gender disparities in employment were in general lower for youth.

- In most countries, unemployment was largely an urban phenomenon, affecting women disproportionately. However, the incidence of female unemployment was higher in the richest households, indicating that unemployment may not provide an adequate picture of labor market conditions in Africa.

- Women were overrepresented among the underemployed, and the incidence of female underemployment was lower among the richest households, confirming that underemployment may be a better measure of economic stress than unemployment.

- Low-paid work was an important issue in seven countries for which data were available, affecting both men and women. Among the self-employed, the incidence of low-paid work was higher among women.

- In most countries, women experienced a disadvantage in earnings, but there were large variations in the region in the severity of the disadvantage

- Overall in the region, there were fewer gender differences in self-employment, but women were almost two times more likely to be in the informal sector and about two times less likely to be in public and private wage employment.

- Women tended to be underrepresented in the industry and service sectors and overrepresented in agriculture.

- For both men and women, education did not seem to be associated with lower unemployment and higher employment; however, the higher the education level, the lower the incidence of low-paid jobs and underemployment. At the same time, more educated men and women were more likely to be in wage employment and less likely to be in self-employment and informal employment.

- The returns from education on earnings were important, and education also had a positive effect on gender wage equity.
- Gender disparities in education outcomes were important in rural areas for all levels of education. In urban areas, the gender gap was small at primary and secondary levels, but it became an issue at tertiary levels. A positive development is that education parity was progressing among younger generations.

These findings call attention to the fact that, for the region as a whole, women are at a disadvantage in the labor market, especially in urban areas. Yet, an overall expansion of decent job opportunities is likely to benefit women in both absolute and relative terms. Moreover, progress toward gender equity in education will likely contribute to improving women's position in Africa's labor markets. However, there are still other factors that may prevent women from participating in and benefiting from paid employment.

While the overall conclusion of this chapter is that gender inequality in the labor market is a major concern in Africa, the possibility of strengthening policy makers' understanding and willingness to respond to gender inequality issues will further depend on a deeper analysis of the root causes of the observed outcomes and on a better understanding of the impact of ongoing development policies.

Given governments' current focus on meeting the MDGs, a first challenge is to estimate the contribution of education parity—one of the education MDGs—on the reduction of gender disparities in the labor market. Another challenge is to better capture the contribution of potential gender discrimination and social norms on labor market outcomes—and how these outcomes might be influenced by globalization and greater competition. The minimum data requirements include comprehensive household surveys with detailed information on education and job characteristics, as well as qualitative data that could complement and enrich the quantitative analyses.

Annex

Table 1A.1 Frequencies for Missing Data by Country—Individuals, ages 15–64
(percent)

Country	Gender	Area of residence	Literacy status	Ever attended school	Education level	Primary Enrollment [7-12]	Labor Force	Main occupation	Status of occupation*	Employment sector*
Burkina Faso	0	0	0	0	1.3	0	0	0	0	0
Burundi	0	0	0	0	56.0	0	0	0	0	0
Cameroon	0	0	0	0	0.2	15.0	0	0	0	0
Côte d'Ivoire	0	0	2.7	0	0.2	0.5	3.8	3.8	100	0.2
Ethiopia	0	0	0.6	1.0	1.2	1.1	0	0	0	100
Gambia, The	0.1	0	100	6.8	7.8	0	23.6	23.6	1.7	0
Ghana	0	0	3.5	3.7	3.9	2.8	0	0	0	0.3
Guinea	0	0	0	0	9.5	0.5	0.6	0.6	0	5.8
Kenya	0	0	0	0	2.5	0	1.1	1.1	0	0
Madagascar	0	0	0.8	0	0	0	0.5	0.5	0	0
Malawi	0	0	3.4	3.0	4.2	0	0.1	0.1	5.9	0
Mauritania	0	0	5.8	100	5.8	1.8	0.5	0.5	0	0
Mozambique	0	0	1.4	1.2	1.4	0.3	0	0	0.5	100
Niger	0	0	0	0	83.1	100	100	100	100	100
Nigeria	0	0	0	0	0	0	0	0	1.0	100
São Tomé and Príncipe	0	0	0	0	10.5	0	0	0	0	0.5
Sierra Leone	0	0	0.4	0.2	1.6	0	0	0	0	0.1
Uganda	0	0	0	0	0.5	0	0	0	0.4	0
Zambia	0	0	100	0.2	13.3	0.4	0.7	0.7	0.6	0
Average	0	0	11.5	6.1	10.7	6.4	6.9	6.9	11.1	21.4

Source: SHIP data.
* For individuals who reported being "employed" as their main occupation.

Notes

1. http://web.worldbank.org/WBSITE/EXTERNAL/COUNTRIES/AFRICAEXT/ EXTPUBREP/EXTSTATINAFR/0,,contentMDK:21102610~menuPK:3084052~page PK:64168445~piPK:64168309~theSitePK:824043,00.html
2. Net enrollment ratio is the ratio of children of official school age (as defined by the national education system) who are enrolled in school to the population of the corresponding official school age. It is based on the International Standard Classification of Education 1997 (ISCED97). However, the measure of the net enrollment ratio used in this study differs from the ILO's standard definition because information on ISCED97 was not available.
3. Total labor force comprises people who meet the ILO definition of the economically active population. It includes both the employed and the unemployed. While national practices vary in the treatment of such groups as the armed forces and seasonal or part-time workers, the labor force generally includes the armed forces, the unemployed, and first-time job-seekers, but excludes homemakers and other unpaid caregivers and workers in the informal sector.
4. Sector I: agriculture and mining; Sector II: manufacturing, construction, and utilities; Sector III: commerce, banking and financial services, professional, public administration, transport. A last category, "other," was not assigned.
5. This figure is high because of the value of the earnings gap ratio in Burkina Faso. Average for the six other countries gives a ratio of 1.6.

References

Appleton, S., J. Hoddinott, and P. Krishnan. 1999. "The Gender Wage Gap in Three African Countries." *Economic Development and Cultural Change* 47 (2): 289–312.

Bigsten, A., and S. Horton. 1997. "Labor Markets in Sub-Saharan Africa." World Bank document to be included in *Poverty in Sub-Saharan Africa*, University of Gothenborg, Sweden.

Blackden, M., and Q. Wodon (eds.). 2006. "Gender, Time Use and Poverty in Sub-Saharan Africa." Working Paper 73, World Bank, Washington DC.

Brilleau, A., F. Roubaud, and C. Torelli. 2004. *L'Emploi, le Chômage et les Conditions d'Activité dans les Principales Agglomérations de Sept Etats Membres de l'UEMOA Principaux Résultats de la Phase 1 de l'Enquête 1-2-3 de 2001–2002.* DIAL (Développment, Institutions and Analyses de Long Terme) working paper 6, L'Union Economique et Monetaire Ouest Africaine (UEMOA), Ouagadougou.

ECA (Economic Commission for Africa). 2005. "Meeting the Challenges of Unemployment and Poverty in Africa." *Economic Report on Africa 2005.* Addis Ababa, Ethiopia.

Glick, P., and F. Roubaud. 2004. "Export Processing Zone Expansion in an African Country: What are the Labor Market and Gender Impacts?" Working paper 15. Développment, Institutions, and Analyses de Long Terme, Paris.

ILO (International Labour Organization). 2002. "Women and Men in the Informal Economy: A Statistical Picture." Gender and Employment Sector, ILO, Geneva.

———. 2004. *Global Employment Trends.* Geneva: ILO.

Kuepie, M., C. Nordman, and F. Roubaud. 2006. "Education and Labor Market Outcomes in Sub-Saharan West Africa." Working paper 16, Développment, Institutions, and Analyses de Long Terme, Paris.

Kabubo-Mariara, J. 2003. "Wage Determination and the Gender Wage Gap in Kenya: Any Evidence of Gender Discrimination?" Research Paper 132, African Economic Research Consortium, Nairobi, Kenya.

Lachaud, J. P. 1997. *Les Femmes et le Marché du Travail Urbain en Afrique Subsaharienne.* Paris: Editions l'Harmattan.

Sender, J., C. Cramer, and C. Oya. 2005. "Unequal Prospects: Disparities in the Quantity and Quality of Labor Supply in Sub-Saharan Africa." Social Protection Discussion Paper Series, Social Protection Unit, World Bank, Washington, DC.

Siphambe, H. K., and M. Thokweng-Bakwena. 2001. "The Wage Gap between Men and Women in Botswana's Formal Labor Market." *Journal of African Economies* 10 (2): 127–42.

UNESCO (United Nations Educational, Scientific, and Cultural Organization). 2005. *Repères pour l'Action: Education Pour Tous en Afrique.* UNESCO Office Dakar and Regional Bureau for Education in Africa, Dakar, Senegal.

UNICEF (United Nations International Children's Fund). 1999. "Women in Transition." Regional Monitoring Reports no. 6, UNICEF, Florence.

World Bank. 2006a. *Youth in Africa's Labor Market.* Washington DC: World Bank.

———. 2006b. "A Guide for Assessing Labor Market Conditions in Developing Countries." World Bank, Washington DC.

———. 2006c. "What Africa Needs to Do to Spur Growth and Create More Well-Paid Jobs." Federal Ministry for Economic Cooperation and Development, Policy Note 2, World Bank, Washington DC.

———. 2007. *Global Monitoring Report.* Washington DC: World Bank.

Part 2

Disparities in Employment, Pay, Education, and Other Dimensions: A Micro-analysis

Chapter 2

Exploring the Gender Pay Gap Through Different Age Cohorts: The Case of Ethiopia

Alexandre Kolev and Pablo Suárez Robles

A s part of its overall objective of reaching the United Nations Millennium Development Goals (MDGs), the Government of Ethiopia has made significant efforts toward universal primary education, gender equality, and the empowerment of women. While large gender disparities in education remain, Ethiopia has seen an enormous and rapid increase in enrollment in primary education that has contributed to reducing the gender imbalance (MoFED 2005). The emphasis on education and gender equality also reflects the instrumental importance of education in fostering progress towards other goals, such as raising labor compensation and supporting women's progress in the labor market. Research shows that women's earnings can influence their status and decision making power within the family, as well as their choices about labor force participation and fertility. Women's wages are especially important for the status of children because women tend to spend their earnings directly on the needs of children (UNICEF 1999).

However, there are still important policy questions facing Ethiopia, a country that has ratified the UN Convention on the Elimination of All Forms of Discrimination against Women. How significant is the gender pay gap? What lies behind the pay differentials between men and women? Is potential discrimination important? Is the wage gap equally important across age cohorts? In contrast to the abundance of literature on the gender pay gap in developed countries and the growing number of studies for emerging countries, few studies have

The paper on which this chapter is based was undertaken as part of a joint research project by the French Development Agency and the World Bank on gender disparities in Africa's labor markets. The authors thank Marc Gurgand, Blandine Ledoux, Christophe Nordman, and Caterina Ruggieri Laderchi for their help in writing this chapter.

actually attempted to address these important questions in the case of Africa (Weichselbaumer and Winter-Ebmer 2003).

Available evidence derived from survey data confirms the presence of large gender pay gaps in several African countries. For instance, the ratio of women's to men's earnings was estimated to range from 40 percent in Kenya (Kabubo-Mariara 2003), to 70 percent in Cameroon (Lachaud 1997), 80 percent in Botswana (Siphambe and Thokweng-Bakwena 2001), and 90 percent in Burkina Faso (Lachaud 1997). In the case of Ethiopia, Temesgen (2006) found that, in the manufacturing sector in 2002, women's hourly wages stood at 73 percent of men's wages. Similarly, in a study of the size and determinants of the gender wage gaps in three African countries, Appleton, Hoddinott, and Krishnan (1999) found that, in urban Ethiopia in 1990, women's earnings represented on average 78 percent of men's earnings. In most of these studies that attempt to explain the extent of the gender wage gap, the unexplained term resulting from the so-called "discrimination component," along with differences in educational endowment, account for a non-negligible share of the pay gap. Yet, their relative importance decreases when other factors, such as job tenure and job characteristics, are included as controlled variables in the wage equations (Fafchamps, Söderbom, and Benhassine 2006; Nordman and Roubaud 2005; Nordman and Wolff 2008, 2009).

The aim of this chapter is to cast new light on the gender pay gap in Ethiopia using the 2005 Ethiopian Labour Force Survey (LFS). This chapter complements existing studies by adopting a comprehensive approach in which the factors related to the gender pay gap in Ethiopia are analyzed for different age cohorts. To this end, we start estimating wage equations using two specifications (accounting and not-for-job characteristics), separately for men and women. We then apply a decomposition procedure proposed by Cotton (1988) and Neumark (1988) to disentangle the effects on the pay gap of human capital and job characteristics from an unexplained or discriminatory component.

The chapter is organized as follows. The next section presents the dataset, the concepts, and detailed summary statistics on gender disparities in employment, education, and pay for different age cohorts, segments of the labor market, and wage levels. The method chosen for estimating wage equations and decomposing gender wage gaps are explained in the third section, followed by results and conclusions.

Data and Concepts

This section presents the data used for the analysis of the gender wage gap and provides an explanation of the definitions and measures of key relevant labor market indicators. It concludes with basic descriptive statistics on employment and education broken down by gender.

The Ethiopia Labour Force Survey

To explain the differences in earnings by gender and analyze the factors related to the gender pay gap in Ethiopia, the LFS, collected in Ethiopia by the Central Statistical Agency (CSA) in 2005, was used. The LFS is a household survey designed to monitor the social and economic situation of the economically active population. It is intended to represent the active population as a whole in urban and rural areas.[1] Of the total 230,680 individuals successfully interviewed in the LFS, about 50 percent were located in urban areas, and weighting was used to obtain a representative sample by urban and rural areas. The individual record includes a broad range of information about age, gender, education, employment status, wage and nonwage activities, job characteristics, and earnings, providing sufficient opportunity for this study.

Definitions and Measurement Issues

The 2005 LFS contains self-classification information on productive activities such as work for payment, family gain, or profit for own consumption performed in the last seven days by individuals age 5 years and older. In this study, the measure of the labor force refers to all persons aged 15 and older either engaged in, or available to undertake, productive activities.[2]

Wage Employment. Included under the label "wage employment" are all individuals engaged in productive activities who worked as paid employees at least four hours in the last seven days. Also included are all those who were working less than four hours or were not working in the last seven days and who were paid for duration of absence or who had an assurance or an agreement for returning to work.

Wage employment represents a significant share of total employment in the LFS (about 25 percent) and is the basis for analysis of the gender pay gap. Coverage of wage employment is also broader than usually found in wage studies for Ethiopia and includes rural labor markets. Rural wage employment indeed represents a small, but not negligible, share of total wage employment (11 percent).

Formal and Informal Wage Employment. In the absence of an international consensus on how to measure the informal sector, it is important to clarify the concepts used in this study to define "formal" and "informal" wage employment. This chapter follows the recommendation of the World Bank (World Bank 2006) and uses a broad concept of the informal sector. In the survey, individuals who work for a wage or salary are asked to describe the employment status of their main occupation. Those who report working in the public sector as government or parastatal employees, as well as nongovernmental organization (NGO) employees and other private employees working in private organizations with 10 or more employees, or that have a license or a book account, are classified as "formally wage-employed."

In contrast, "informal wage employment" includes paid employees who work in a private organization that has fewer than 10 employees, is not licensed, and does not have a book account. It also includes employees for whom this information is missing and who are paid only in kind or are doing casual work. The latter, in fact, are very likely to be located in the unregulated sector.

Following this classification, wage employment is further broken down into three components: public formal wage employment (government and parastatal employees), formal private wage employment (employees in formal private organizations and NGOs), and informal private wage employment (employees in informal private organizations and domestic employees).

Earnings. The 2005 LFS provides a good opportunity to analyze the gender pay gap because it provides information on earnings, the time basis for the payment (hourly, daily, weekly, half monthly, monthly, or yearly), and the number of payments per month. This information was used in calculating the corresponding equivalent monthly earnings from the main occupation for each worker in wage employment used for this study. However, the use of earnings as a proxy for the returns from work is not without problems. As earnings are available exclusively for the wage-employed and from their main occupation only, this excludes the possibility of analyzing the returns from self-employment. Moreover, it does not take into account the returns from secondary employment.[3] Finally, non-wage benefits may be important in some cases (in particular, government and the parastatal might offer additional benefits in terms of pension benefits or job security), and because they are not included in the data, the true level of earnings may be underestimated. Notwithstanding these issues, earnings data remain essential to understanding the gender pay gap in Ethiopia.

Descriptive Statistics

This section provides basic descriptive statistics on employment and education broken down by gender, which illustrate gender disparities in the labor force and employment status, as well as in education characteristics among the wage-employed.

Labor Force and in Employment Status. Basic labor market indicators for men and women are reported in table 2.1 According to these data, the situation of women appears less favorable than that of men. Participation rate and employment ratio are lower for women, while female unemployment is almost two times higher than male unemployment. And a much higher proportion of the male population is in wage employment.

The characteristics of wage employment shown in table 2.2 indicate large gender variations in the nature and terms of wage employment. For men, public formal wage employment and private formal wage employment together constitute the biggest share of the wage-employed. Only 13 percent of wage-employed

Table 2.1 Selected Labor Market Indicators, 2005

	All (%)	Male (%)	Female (%)
Activity rate	73	82	65
Employment ratio	67	77	58
Wage-employment ratio	17	22	13
Unemployment rate	8	6	10
Inactivity rate	27	18	35

Source: LFS 2005.
Note: Percentages are of individuals aged 15 and older in the entire population, except for unemployment rate, which is the percentage of the economically active population aged 15 and older.

Table 2.2 Nature and Terms of Wage Employment in Total Wage Employment, 2005

	All (%)	Male (%)	Female (%)
Pubic formal wage employment	43	47	38
Private formal wage employment	35	40	28
Private informal wage employment	22	13	34
Permanent employment	43	48	36
Temporary employment	39	33	47
Contract employment	9	10	8
Casual or other employment	9	9	9

Source: LFS 2005.
Note: Individuals aged 15 and older.

men are in informal private jobs. For women, however, the proportion of the wage-employed in private informal jobs represents the second most frequent form of wage employment (34 percent) after public employment (38 percent). In relative terms, women are much more likely than men to work in informal jobs and less likely to work in permanent employment, suggesting that the conditions of work among wage-employed women may be less favorable than they are for men.

The Unadjusted Gender Pay Gap. Table 2.3 provides information on the crude gender pay gap for different wage levels, age cohorts, and segments of the labor market. On average, female wages represent about 55 percent of male wages, which is remarkably low, even from an African perspective. The unadjusted relative wage disadvantage for women is also more pronounced for younger women. As women get older, the pay differential with men tends to get lower. Table 2.3 further shows large variations in the gender pay gap at different points in the wage distribution. While female wages represent nearly 60 percent of male wages among the top quartile, they represent only about 30 percent of male wages among the bottom quartile. These findings are at odds with the

Table 2.3 Unadjusted Gender Monthly Wage Gap by Age and Wage Level, 2005 (percent)

Age groups				Wage percentiles			Sector of wage employment		
15+	15–24	25–34	35+	P25	P50	P75	Public	Formal private	Informal private
54.7	55.5	62.9	69.5	33.3	42.9	59.7	71.7	61.1	31.5

Source: LFS 2005.
Note: Women's earnings in terms of men's earnings.

results for developed countries, which show that, in line with the glass ceiling hypothesis, the gender wage gap tends to be more pronounced at the upper tail of the wage distribution. The gender disadvantage in terms of wage is also more pronounced in the private sector than in the public sector, especially in the informal private sector. It is nonetheless interesting to note that even in the public sector, women tend to earn on average 30 percent less than men.

Education Characteristics Among the Wage-Employed. Table 2.4, which presents the educational characteristics of the wage-employed for men and women, reveals a strong disadvantage for women. Illiteracy is two times higher among wage-employed women. More wage-employed men than women have acquired education at general level or beyond.[4] It is also worth noting that the gender educational gap in favor of wage-employed men is observed for all age groups and is remarkable among youth.[5] For both men and women, more highly educated workers tend to be disproportionately concentrated in better paid jobs. Public wage employment predominantly comprises workers with general or beyond education, and this is true for both men and women. As for private wage employment, there is an important dichotomy between the formal and informal sectors. While formal private wage employment includes workers with all levels of education (from illiteracy to beyond general education), informal private wage employment is predominantly workers with low education levels, especially for women. Yet, it is interesting to note that in private formal employment, there are more highly educated women than men, indicating that access to private formal jobs may be more competitive for women.

Methodology

This section introduces the estimation method used to analyze the determinants of wages for the overall sample of the wage-employed and for different age cohorts of wage employees. The decomposition technique of the gender wage gap implemented for the study's wage equations[6] is then explained.

Table 2.4 Levels of Education Among the Wage-Employed by Gender, 2005

	Illiterate		Primary education		General education		Beyond general education	
	Men (%)	Women (%)	Men (%)	Women (%)	Men (%)	Women (%)	Men (%)	Women (%)
All wage-employed (aged 15+)	14	30	34	29	28	24	24	18
Age cohorts								
15–24	19	35	42	36	25	17	14	11
25–34	10	21	31	23	34	33	25	23
35+	15	32	32	23	25	21	28	24
Wage quartiles								
Q1	36	62	49	33	14	5	1	1
Q2	14	36	48	43	33	18	6	3
Q3	5	14	30	31	41	41	24	15
Q4	2	1	9	6	24	34	65	59
Wage employment								
Public formal wage employment	7	13	23	18	30	34	39	35
Private formal wage employment	18	23	42	32	28	29	12	16
Private informal wage employment	29	54	50	38	18	7	4	1

Source: LFS 2005.

Estimation of Wage Equations

This study used the following augmented version of the traditional human capital semi-logarithmic earnings equation developed by Mincer (1974):

$$y_i = \beta_i + \varepsilon_i \qquad (2.1)$$

Where y is the log monthly earnings in the main occupation of individual i, which are observed only for paid employees; X is a vector of explanatory variables, including human capital variables (dummies for three levels of educational attainment,[7] potential work experience, which is defined by age minus years of schooling minus six, and its square to take into account its possible decreasing returns, and a dummy for training); another individual variable (a dummy for marital status); job characteristics (dummies for various sectors of activity, sectors of employment, terms of employment, and occupations); urban and regional dummies. ε is the error term, with an expected value of zero, and β is a set of coefficients to be estimated (including a constant term).

Heckman's Two-Step Estimation Procedure. Having specified the wage equation, we now use Heckman's two-step estimation procedure to estimate the determinants of earnings separately by gender for the overall sample of the wage-employed (aged 15+) and for three different age cohorts of wage earners (aged 15–24, 25–34, and 35+). This method allows correction for a possible sample selection bias, which may arise because the study's sample of wage-employed may not be random and may have specific characteristics.

According to Heckman (1979), selection bias can be thought of as a form of omitted variable bias. The omitted variables problem, which, indeed, Heckman has shown to be equivalent to the use of nonrandom samples, can be solved by including in the log monthly earnings equation (equation 2.1) a sample selection term constructed from an equation modeling the probability of being in wage employment.

In the first stage, maximum likelihood estimates of the probit model used to estimate the probability of selecting wage-employment (the selection equation) are separately performed for women and men.[8] A selection correction term (the inverse of the Mills ratio) is then included in the log monthly earnings equations, for women and men, respectively. The OLS (ordinary least squares) estimates of these augmented earnings equations are unbiased and consistent.

Decomposition of the Gender Wage Gap

To decompose the gender wage gap into human capital, job, and other characteristics, and the treatment or discrimination component, a decomposition procedure proposed by Cotton (1988) and Neumark (1988) was applied.

The Cotton-Neumark Decomposition Procedure. The Neumark decomposition procedure is defined as follows:

$$\ln\left(\overline{Y}_m\right) - \ln\left(\overline{Y}_f\right) = \hat{\beta}^*\left(\overline{X}_m - \overline{X}_f\right) + \overline{X}_m\left(\hat{\beta}_m - \hat{\beta}^*\right) + \overline{X}_f\left(\hat{\beta}^* - \hat{\beta}_f\right). \quad (2.2)$$

The first component on the right-hand side represents the part of the gender average earnings gap attributable to differences in characteristics evaluated at the hypothetical market that would prevail in a nondiscrimination case. The second and third components constitute the treatment or discrimination component and represent, respectively, the amount by which men's characteristics are overvaluated (men's treatment advantage) and the amount by which women's characteristics are undervaluated (women's treatment disadvantage) in the labor market.

While Neumark's approach is to estimate the nondiscriminatory wage structure β^* from an earnings function estimated over the pooled sample of men and women, another approach suggested by Cotton (1988) is to compute the nondiscriminatory wage structure by weighting the male and female wage structures by the respective proportions of men and women in the sample of wage-employed.

In this chapter, we followed a recent study on gender earnings disparities in Ethiopia (Temesgen 2006) and decided to use the Neumark decomposition procedure using the Cotton definition of the non-discriminatory wage structure. The Cotton-Neumark decomposition procedure is applied to decompose the gender wage gap for the overall sample of wage-employed and for three age cohorts of wage earners (15–24, 25–34, and 35+).

Treatment of the Sample Selection Correction. There is no obvious way to handle the selectivity bias correction within the decomposition of the raw gender gap. The method proposed by Heckman corrects for a possible sample selection bias. As a result, selection correction terms appear in the corresponding wage decompositions, and these are generally treated in two different ways. A first set of studies treats the correction terms as a separate component in the decomposition and dissociates the wage gap into an explained component, an unexplained (or discriminatory) component, and a selection effect. A second set of studies subtracts the selection effect from the observed wage gap in order to obtain a wage differential that is corrected for sample selection and that can be decomposed in two components only (an explained and a discriminatory component). The latter wage gap is then often interpreted as the differential in potential or offered wages, as opposed to observed wages. This study focuses on the observed wage gap and considers the impact of the selectivity correction term as a third component of the decomposition.

Results

The study then investigated the gender pay gap in Ethiopia using the 2005 LFS, with particular attention given to the way the wage gap may vary through age cohorts. First, the results of the wage equations are discussed and then the results of the wage decompositions are provided.

Estimations of the Wage Equations

Earnings equations are estimated separately for wage-employed men and women using Heckman's two-step estimation. The discussion focuses on the wage estimates corrected for sample selectivity, which is also the most common approach used in recent studies. We note, however, that selectivity corrections are rather sensitive to slight changes in specifications and modeling, as well as to different choices of identification variables.

Two specifications are used for each of the earnings equations. The first specification includes as explanatory variables, individual characteristics (such as education, potential work experience, training, marital status); job characteristics (sector, occupational group, conditions of employment); and spatial information (location). The second specification includes the same set of explanatory variables, but excludes job characteristics. The latter are indeed partly determined by the level of education, and their inclusion tends to underestimate the full impact of education on wages.[9] The first specification is interesting because it allows us to isolate the role of job characteristics on wages, but it provides only lower estimates of the effects of education on wages. In comparison, the second specification allows us to get upper estimates of the education effects that capture the broader impact of education on wages. This broader impact can be understood as the combination of a direct effect of education on wages, which is measured by the lower estimates of the wage effects of education (when holding job characteristics constant), and an indirect effect—which is not observed per se, but which corresponds to the impact of education on wages through its effect on job characteristics (in other words, the amount of that particular fraction of the effect of job characteristics on wages that is attributable to education). To simplify the presentation, we report only the results of the first specification, unless otherwise mentioned. The results are presented in the Annex table 2A.1 and tables 2A.2-1 to 2A.2-3.

Use of statistical tests revealed that the equality of coefficients across gender in overall wage employment and across age cohorts for both men and women could be globally rejected at a reasonable confidence level. This result indicates that estimating wages separately for men and women and for the different subsamples of wage-employed separately by gender may provide more satisfactory results than estimating a single wage equation obtained from the overall sample of the wage-employed. It also echoes the results of other studies that discuss the likely segmented nature of the urban labor market in Ethiopia. According to Bigsten, Mengistae, and Shimeles (2007), men and women do not apply for the same jobs, and this may be a result of a combination of factors, including education, as well as social norms.

The marginal effects of education on wages—the so-called private returns to education—using a calculation proposed by Kennedy (1981), are displayed in table 2.5 for the study's two specifications.[10] The returns are large, even for the lower estimates, and significant in all wage equations, except for men in informal private wage employment. The private returns to education are particularly important for women and for youth, and they are systematically larger for higher levels of educational attainment. Yet, it is worth noting that, in comparison with illiteracy, the private returns to primary education are always important and significant. Although not directly comparable, these findings are contrary to the results of other studies of urban Ethiopia that found that private returns to primary education are often insignificant.[11]

Looking at the estimation results for the overall sample of the wage-employed based on Heckman's procedure, it appears that the selectivity correction variable

Table 2.5 Lower and Upper Estimates of Private Returns to Education, 2005

	Primary education		General education		Beyond general education	
	Men (%)	Women (%)	Men (%)	Women (%)	Men (%)	Women (%)
All wage-employed (aged 15+)						
Lower estimates	26	39	66	89	130	136
Upper estimates	53	95	164	398	353	662
Age cohorts						
15–24						
Lower estimates	50	39	122	90	163	138
Upper estimates	81	64	222	249	394	435
25–34						
Lower estimates	22	29	44	58	102	93
Upper estimates	39	67	99	251	246	451
35+						
Lower estimates	14	31	37	72	91	122
Upper estimates	40	126	128	472	275	743
Wage quartiles						
Q1						
Lower estimates	33	41	72	83	135	122
Upper estimates	66	83	206	381	426	700
Q2						
Lower estimates	24	37	59	80	113	125
Upper estimates	61	96	166	442	330	678
Q3						
Lower estimates	23	34	53	84	117	126
Upper estimates	47	118	139	443	286	666
Wage employment						
Public formal						
Lower estimates	13	41	28	76	60	115
Upper estimates	34	81	109	199	215	291
Private formal						
Lower estimates	24	19	50	43	97	83
Upper estimates	46	26	106	83	254	196
Private informal						
Lower estimates	7[a]	45	38[a]	157	29[a]	294
Upper estimates	31	51	104	205	132	457

Source: LFS 2005.
Note: Lower estimates are based on the first specification (accounting for job characteristics), and upper estimates are based on the second specification (not accounting for job characteristics) of the log monthly earnings equations.
a. Log monthly earnings equation's coefficient not significant at 10% or less.

is significant for women only. The negative sign of the correction term for women means that unobserved characteristics that increase women's probability of participating in wage employment have a negative effect on their earnings.

In contrast, the effects of potential work experience and training on wages are positive, but stronger for men than for women. For both men and women, working in the public sector or the private formal sector, compared to the private informal sector, is associated with higher wages. The wage difference between the informal and formal sector (public or private) is particularly pronounced for women. Note, however, that the wage gain is highest in the public sector for women, while it is highest in the private formal sector for men, reflecting a rather less favorable situation for women in the private sector. Some gender differences also exist in the way occupation variables affect wages.

Conducting additional estimations for different subgroups of the wage-employed provides further notable findings. Noteworthy regarding the Heckman estimation results for different age cohorts is that the returns to education and the impact of training are much more important for the youngest age group (15–24), and this is equally true for men and women (see table 2.5). Note, moreover, that none of the selection terms appears significant.

Wage Decompositions

The estimates of the previous wage equations are then used to implement the decomposition procedure proposed by Cotton and Neumark to answer the following questions: What lies behind the gender pay gap in Ethiopia? Is potential discrimination important? Is the gap equally important throughout age cohorts?

Among the overall sample of the wage-employed (Annex table 2A.3), together with the differences in educational background, the differences between men and women in potential work experience and training contribute to an increase in the wage gap. Overall, from at least 20 percent (first specification) to at most 39 percent (second specification) of the gender wage gap can be attributed to differences in human capital characteristics (education, potential experience, and training).

When job characteristics are taken into account (sector of activity, sector of wage employment, and terms of employment and occupation), the contribution of the differences in human capital variables is reduced, and the contribution of the differences in job characteristics between men and women rise to nearly 25 percent of the wage gap. In other words, gender disparities in job allocation, which are partially driven by the gender differences in education characteristics, appear as a non-negligible source of the wage gap. Among the differences in job characteristics, the fact that more women work in the informal private sector and fewer are in the formal private and public sectors leads to the highest increase of the gap. Other important contributing job-related factors are the different employment shares of men and women in permanent employment and occupations.

Considering the importance of the effect of differences in job characteristics on the gender wage gap, it is worth exploring the determinants of these dispari-ties in more detail. Are they mostly driven by the differences in human capital characteristics? Does job discrimination against women play any role? Can the differences in individual work preferences between men and women explain some of the differences in job characteristics? Additional multivariate analyses performed for this study showed that besides the significant effect of education on job characteristics, gender is another significant factor that picks up either a form of sex-based segmentation or some gender-specific preferences.

The fact that job characteristics are systematically less favorable for women in Ethiopia, with more women in the informal sector and fewer in formal public and private jobs, could mean there is an implicit form of job discrimination that plays in fine against women's wages. Studies of Ethiopia's labor market show indeed that the informal sector is mostly residual, where activities are being pursued in the absence of other options. Most new participants in the informal sector come from the pool of the unemployed and first-time job seekers (World Bank 2006). When regular, full-time jobs that provide clear career prospects exist and are accessible to women, they usually contribute to women's empow-erment and offer alternative interests and achievements to domestic work or motherhood (Lim 2002). Yet, differences in job characteristics may also reflect gender-specific preferences. In the absence of flexible work arrangements in formal and better paid jobs, the burden of women's household responsibilities such as housework and childcare could be a strong incentive for women to engage in the informal sector, which offers less protection but potentially more flexibility. The 2006 Addis Labor Market Survey found, for instance, that among a sample of unemployed people located in Addis Ababa, women were more inclined than men to look for independent work closer to their home, probably as the result of their household responsibilities (World Bank 2006).

What is also notable is the importance of the unexplained component—the potential wage discrimination effect—which would make up on average 40 percent (based on the lower estimates) to 43 percent (based on the upper estimates) of the gender pay differential. However, the size of the unexplained component needs to be interpreted with caution, since it is usually sensitive to the specification of the wage equations and may also pick up the effects of factors that are imperfectly captured in the set of explanatory variables. In the study's specifications, real job experience is imperfectly measured by age minus years of schooling minus six. In particular, it does not take into account the fact that women may have on average longer career interruptions and may therefore earn, at a given age, less than men.

We further investigate the way the determinants of the gender wage gap, other than education characteristics, vary across different age cohorts (annex table 2A.4). The results show (first specification) that the differences in job characteristics, mostly the differences in the sector of wage employment (with women being disproportionately concentrated in the informal sector), explain a much higher proportion of the gender wage gap among the younger wage-employed individuals. In other words, the negative impact of job segmentation on female wages tends to be disproportionately high for young women. It is worth emphasizing here that the Ethiopian economy has experienced radical changes in recent years, with the collapse of the socialist regime, the rise of the private sector, and the increase in the informal economy. These changes have resulted in a more fragmented labor market, in which young women appear particularly disadvantaged in terms of earnings.

It should be noted that the unexplained component of the estimated wage gap—the potential discrimination effect—increases with age. This could be explained by very different factors, however. On the one hand, it could indicate a positive impact of changing gender attitudes in society, with less discriminatory practices in gender wages for new labor market entrants, together with a reduction in education inequality that has a positive effect on young women relative wages. On the other hand, it could well reflect the deleterious cumulative impact of gender discrimination on wage progression. Another possible reason is that, since we cannot properly measure interruptions in the career path of women in our data, we may have greater difficulties in capturing, for older and more experienced workers, the fact that pay advancement may be smaller for women. The results further show that the selection component is positive except for the age group 35 and older.

Conclusions

The authors seek to contribute to a better understanding of the factors related to the gender wage gap in Ethiopia, drawing special attention to different age cohorts. Using the Heckman's two-step estimation procedure for the wage equations and the Cotton-Neumark decomposition procedure for the estimated wage gaps, we were able to isolate the determinants of the pay differentials and to examine the way the contributing factors may vary for different age cohorts. Despite the acknowledged shortcomings of the decomposition, which is fairly sensitive to the quality of the information available and the estimation model used, the results provide some interesting insights. The main findings can be summarized as follows.

First, the data indicate that on average women's monthly wages represented in 2005 only about 55 percent of men's wages. There were also large variations across subgroups. The raw gender pay differential was found to be more pronounced for younger workers.

Second, the decomposition results showed that no more than 50 percent of the observed wage gap could be attributed to explained differences in characteristics, leaving a large fraction of the gap unexplained. Further evidence provided in this chapter points out that the unexplained component was probably much lower for youth. The extent to which the unexplained component was a sign of a potential wage discrimination effect was difficult to assess precisely, however. It depended on the specification and quality of information used, as well as on the estimation model applied. A related recommendation would be to pay careful attention to the measurement of key variables in the LFS, in particular work experience, job tenure, and career interruptions.

Third, a non-negligible proportion of the gender wage gap—at least 11 percent but no more than 23 percent on average—was explained by the differences in education endowments between men and women. The impact of education disparities on the gender wage gap was further found to vary across age groups.

Fourth, job characteristics were found to be systematically less favorable for women. When included in the analysis, the differences in job characteristics across gender explained an important share of the gender wage gap (about 25 percent on average). These differences in job characteristics were largely driven by the differences in education between men and women, but also by an unexplained gender factor that may well reflect a mix of sex-based segregation and gender differences in individual work preferences.

Overall, these findings indicate that unexplained factors dominate among the sources of the gender wage gap in Ethiopia, which could pick up some form of wage discrimination as well as unobserved differences in characteristics. The role of differences in education was also important, indicating that ongoing progress toward gender equity in education will likely contribute to improving women's relative wages, including through a more equitable distribution of job characteristics between men and women and indirectly through changes in attitude toward gender.

For promotion of gender equity in pay, a mix of interventions is needed. In the longer term, investment in education and greater gender equity appears essential. In the short-term, enforcement of anti-discrimination legislation, combined with an institutional framework that creates incentives to comply, could be an important way to support women's wage equity while enhancing the returns to girls' education.

Annex

Table 2A.1 Selectivity Corrected (Heckman Two-Step Method) Log Monthly Earnings Equations in Wage Employment by Gender, 2005

	Men		Women	
	Mean	Coefficient	Mean	Coefficient
Human capital characteristics				
Illiterate (reference category)	0.144	—	0.297	—
Primary education	0.339	0.2336*** (11.50)	0.286	0.3271*** (17.56)
General education	0.278	0.5077*** (19.47)	0.235	0.6343*** (23.20)
Beyond general education	0.240	0.8335*** (24.13)	0.183	0.8594*** (21.80)
Potential experience	20.326	0.0317*** (15.42) -	15.995	0.0231*** (9.39)
Squared potential experience	582.903	−0.0005*** (−13.69)	366.694	−0.0003*** (−5.47)
Training	0.419	0.2844*** (11.75)	0.269	0.1462*** (5.56)
Other individual characteristic				
Married	0.586	0.1547*** (10.58)	0.324	0.0509*** (2.75)
Job characteristics				
Primary sector activity (reference category)	0.086	—	0.037	—
Secondary sector activity	0.126	0.0428 (1.49)	0.097	−0.0690* (−1.67)
Tertiary sector activity	0.788	0.1359*** (5.63)	0.866	−0.0903** (−2.49)
Public sector	0.472	0.2676*** (12.57)	0.383	0.7110*** (30.60)
Formal private sector	0.397	0.3276*** (17.64)	0.280	0.5830*** (31.10)
Informal private sector (reference category)	0.131	—	0.337	—
Permanent employee	0.493	0.4621*** (17.56)	0.374	0.7387*** (24.16)
Temporary employee	0.338	0.0575** (2.46)	0.476	0.1544*** (6.08)
Contract employee	0.096	0.2519*** (8.83)	0.076	0.3688*** (10.90)
Casual or other worker (reference category)	0.073	—	0.074	—

continued

Table 2A.1 *continued*

	Men		Women	
	Mean	Coefficient	Mean	Coefficient
Occupation 1	0.335	0.5710*** (27.92)	0.300	0.4554*** (17.94)
Occupation 2	0.348	0.3545*** (22.05)	0.215	0.0335* (1.86)
Occupation 3 (reference category)	0.317	—	0.484	—
Location variables				
Urban	0.875	0.4351*** (12.89)	0.923	0.2634*** (7.39)
Addis Ababa (reference category)	0.285	—	0.325	—
Northeast	0.098	0.0215 (0.98)	0.077	0.0033 (0.13)
Southeast	0.221	−0.1446*** (−7.95)	0.194	−0.2092*** (−10.75)
Southwest	0.143	−0.2372*** (−11.31)	0.123	−0.2859*** (−12.65)
Northwest	0.253	−0.1963*** (−11.60)	0.281	−0.3192*** (−18.47)
Selection variable				
lambda	0.966	0.0581 (1.62)	1.149	−0.0464* (−1.78)
Constant	1.000	3.4933*** (38.12)	1.000	3.3676*** (42.21)
Number of observations	—	13170	—	8880
R-squared	—	0.5935	—	0.7408
ln monthly earnings	5.7751	—	4.9860	—
Monthly earnings	498.21	—	272.42	—

Source: Ethiopia Labour Force Survey 2005.
Note: Occupation 1 includes legislators, senior officials, managers, professionals, technicians and associate professionals, and clerks. Occupation 2 includes plant machine operators and assemblers; armed forces; craft and related trades persons; and service, shop, and market sales workers. Occupation 3 includes skilled agricultural, fishery, and elementary occupations.
Z statistics in parenthesis. * Significant at 10% level. ** Significant at 5% level. *** Significant at 1% level.
— = not applicable.

Table 2A.2-1 Selectivity Corrected (Heckman Two-Step Method) Log Monthly Earnings Equations in Wage Employment by Gender, 2005 (age group 15–24)

	Men		Women	
	Mean	Coefficient	Mean	Coefficient
Human capital characteristics				
Illiterate (reference category)	0.192	—	0.354	—
Primary education	0.416	0.4070*** (7.63)	0.359	0.3274*** (11.09)
General education	0.250	0.8018*** (11.03)	0.174	0.6443*** (13.16)
Beyond general education	0.143	0.9721*** (10.07)	0.113	0.8684*** (11.94)
Potential experience	7.933	0.0436** (2.48)	8.738	0.0179 (1.41)
Squared potential experience	81.914	0.0001 (0.09)	95.526	−0.0000 (−0.05)
Training	0.257	0.4657*** (7.75)	0.166	0.2117*** (4.44)
Other individual characteristic				
Married	0.123	0.1748*** (3.92)	0.122	0.1119*** (3.11)
Job characteristics				
Primary sector activity (reference category)	0.141	—	0.034	—
Secondary sector activity	0.147	0.3736*** (5.76)	0.061	−0.1191* (−1.74)
Tertiary sector activity	0.712	0.3312*** (6.22)	0.905	−0.0995* (−1.74)
Public sector	0.223	0.4133*** (7.98)	0.169	0.7798*** (19.85)
Formal private sector	0.563	0.3347*** (9.20)	0.298	0.5826*** (20.93)
Informal private sector (reference category)	0.214	—	0.533	—
Permanent employee	0.216	0.2521*** (4.33)	0.167	0.4688*** (9.68)
Temporary employee	0.547	−0.0136 (−0.31)	0.674	0.0594 (1.55)
Contract employee	0.115	0.1359** (2.34)	0.085	0.3009*** (5.99)
Casual or other worker (reference category)	0.122	—	0.073	—
Occupation 1	0.174	0.3445*** (6.02)	0.161	0.4092*** (9.24)

continued

Table 2A.2-1 *continued*

	Men		Women	
	Mean	Coefficient	Mean	Coefficient
Occupation 2	0.424	0.0881** (2.42)	0.202	0.0043 (2.42)
Occupation 3 (reference category)	0.402	—	0.637	—
Location variables				
Urban	0.813	0.3564*** (5.75)	0.920	0.2003*** (3.75)
Addis Ababa (reference category)	0.296	—	0.334	—
Northeast	0.085	−0.0272 (−0.49)	0.066	−0.0044 (−0.10)
Southeast	0.218	−0.1490*** (−3.55)	0.185	−0.2177*** (−7.24)
Southwest	0.142	−0.2745*** (−5.67)	0.115	−0.3117*** (−8.81)
Northwest	0.259	−0.2462*** (−6.22)	0.300	−0.4364*** (−17.09)
Selection variable				
lambda	1.259	0.0726 (1.29)	1.106	−0.0506 (−1.57)
Constant	1.000	3.1848*** (16.23)	1.000	3.5920*** (26.92)
Number of observations	—	2945	—	3694
R-squared	—	0.4347	—	0.6565
ln monthly earnings	5.1611	—	4.4616	—
Monthly earnings	263.25	—	146.12	—

Source: Ethiopia Labour Force Survey 2005.
Note: Occupation 1 includes legislators, senior officials, managers, professionals, technicians and associate professionals, and clerks. Occupation 2 includes plant machine operators and assemblers; armed forces; craft and related trades persons; and service, shop, and market sales workers. Occupation 3 includes skilled agricultural, fishery, and elementary occupations.
Z statistics in parenthesis. * Significant at 10% level. ** Significant at 5% level. *** Significant at 1% level.
— = not applicable.

Table 2A.2-2 Selectivity Corrected (Heckman Two-Step Method) Log Monthly Earnings Equations in Wage Employment by Gender, 2005 (age group 25–34)

	Men		Women	
	Mean	Coefficient	Mean	Coefficient
Human capital characteristics				
Illiterate (reference category)	0.096	—	0.209	—
Primary education	0.313	0.1983*** (4.43)	0.234	0.2566*** (6.06)
General education	0.337	0.3644*** (6.36)	0.330	0.4592*** (7.59)
Beyond general education	0.254	0.7047*** (9.82)	0.227	0.6623*** (8.43)
Potential experience	14.101	0.0026 (0.23)	14.623	0.0068 (0.54)
Squared potential experience	224.576	−0.0001 (−0.28)	244.785	−0.0003 (−0.74)
Training	0.453	0.3281*** (8.01)	0.347	0.1504*** (3.93)
Other individual characteristic				
Married	0.534	0.1293*** (5.99)	0.431	0.0317 (1.08)
Job characteristics				
Primary sector activity (reference category)	0.064	—	0.028	—
Secondary sector activity	0.117	0.0548 (1.07)	0.099	−0.1551** (−2.02)
Tertiary sector activity	0.819	0.2158*** (4.92)	0.872	−0.1886*** (−2.73)
Public sector	0.457	0.1819*** (5.08)	0.457	0.5667*** (14.47)
Formal private sector	0.417	0.3454*** (11.12)	0.322	0.5292*** (15.81)
Informal private sector (reference category)	0.126	—	0.221	—
Permanent employee	0.485	0.4922*** (11.08)	0.444	0.8550*** (16.42)
Temporary employee	0.341	0.1040*** (2.64)	0.400	0.2197*** (4.95)
Contract employee	0.103	0.3398*** (7.15)	0.083	0.4356*** (7.52)
Casual or other worker (reference category)	0.071	—	0.073	—
Occupation 1	0.342	0.5916*** (17.62)	0.385	0.4665*** (11.90)
Occupation 2	0.394	0.3726*** (13.92)	0.224	0.0588* (1.88)
Occupation 3 (reference category)	0.264	—	0.390	—

continued

Table 2A.2-2 *continued*

	Men		Women	
	Mean	Coefficient	Mean	Coefficient
Location variables				
Urban	0.886	0.4500*** (7.74)	0.930	0.3529*** (5.66)
Addis Ababa (reference category)	0.300	—	0.323	—
Northeast	0.095	0.0205 (0.55)	0.074	−0.0149 (−0.33)
Southeast	0.207	−0.1125*** (−3.58)	0.194	−0.1913*** (−5.78)
Southwest	0.153	−0.1744*** (−4.90)	0.141	−0.2522*** (−6.96)
Northwest	0.244	−0.0892*** (−3.12)	0.269	−0.2023*** (−6.60)
Selection variable				
lambda	0.839	0.1681** (2.50)	1.023	−0.0309 (−0.64)
Constant	1.000	3.7091*** (21.20)	1.000	3.6726*** (20.57)
Number of observations	—	4273	—	2894
R-squared	—	0.5312	—	0.7060
ln monthly earnings	5.8436	—	5.2435	—
Monthly earnings	487.85	—	306.92	—

Source: Ethiopia Labour Force Survey 2005.
Note: Occupation 1 includes legislators, senior officials, managers, professionals, technicians and associate professionals, and clerks. Occupation 2 includes plant machine operators and assemblers; armed forces; craft and related trades persons; and service, shop, and market sales workers. Occupation 3 includes skilled agricultural, fishery, and elementary occupations.
Z statistics in parenthesis. * Significant at 10% level. ** Significant at 5% level. *** Significant at 1% level.
— = not applicable.

Table 2A.2-3 Selectivity Corrected (Heckman Two-Step Method) Log Monthly Earnings Equations in Wage Employment by Gender, 2005 (age group 35+)

	Men		Women	
	Mean	Coefficient	Mean	Coefficient
Human capital characteristics				
Illiterate (reference category)	0.154	—	0.315	—
Primary education	0.320	0.1302*** (4.09)	0.234	0.2708*** (5.77)
General education	0.248	0.3141*** (6.71)	0.212	0.5464*** (6.72)
Beyond general education	0.277	0.6469*** (9.63)	0.239	0.8037*** (6.99)
Potential experience	30.927	0.0083** (2.31)	29.421	0.0156** (1.96)
Squared potential experience	1088.034	−0.0001*** (−3.09)	957.661	−0.0002 (−1.50)
Training	0.476	0.1373*** (2.99)	0.335	0.0907* (1.68)
Other individual characteristics				
Married	0.852	0.1348*** (5.92)	0.515	0.0560 (1.55)
Job characteristics				
Primary sector activity (reference category)	0.075	—	0.052	—
Secondary sector activity	0.122	−0.1728*** (−4.29)	0.152	0.0199 (0.27)
Tertiary sector activity	0.803	−0.0568* (−1.67)	0.796	0.0073 (0.11)
Public sector	0.607	0.2446*** (7.87)	0.637	0.7498*** (15.08)
Formal private sector	0.300	0.2968*** (9.97)	0.195	0.6289*** (13.75)
Informal private sector (reference category)	0.094	—	0.168	—
Permanent employee	0.636	0.6046*** (14.89)	0.617	0.9144*** (14.25)
Temporary employee	0.232	0.1426*** (3.68)	0.252	0.1942*** (3.62)
Contract employee	0.082	0.3273*** (7.26)	0.054	0.3681*** (4.91)
Casual or other worker (reference category)	0.050	—	0.078	—
Occupation 1	0.411	0.6433*** (23.56)	0.417	0.4522*** (8.59)
Occupation 2	0.276	0.4945*** (21.33)	0.227	0.0379 (1.01)
Occupation 3 (reference category)	0.313	—	0.356	—

continued

Table 2A.2-3 *continued*

	Men		Women	
	Mean	Coefficient	Mean	Coefficient
Location variables				
Urban	0.897	0.3293*** (3.39)	0.921	0.2209*** (2.62)
Addis Ababa (reference category)	0.269	—	0.315	—
Northeast	0.106	0.0213 (0.69)	0.096	0.0756 (1.50)
Southeast	0.233	−0.1132*** (−3.66)	0.209	−0.1867*** (−4.85)
Southwest	0.136	−0.2129*** (−5.82)	0.113	−0.2529*** (−5.34)
Northwest	0.256	−0.1941*** (−7.32)	0.266	−0.2239*** (−6.36)
Selection variable				
lambda	0.850	−0.1491 (−1.29)	1.182	−0.0762 (−0.86)
Constant	1.000	4.3733*** (20.62)	1.000	3.3443*** (13.78)
Number of observations	—	5,952	—	2,292
R-squared	—	0.6339	—	0.7439
In monthly earnings	6.0298	—	5.5061	—
Monthly earnings	621.91	—	432.41	—

Source: Ethiopia Labour Force Survey 2005.
Note: Occupation 1 includes legislators, senior officials, managers, professionals, technicians and associate professionals, and clerks. Occupation 2 includes plant machine operators and assemblers; armed forces; craft and related trades persons; and service, shop, and market sales workers. Occupation 3 includes skilled agricultural, fishery, and elementary occupations.
Z statistics in parenthesis. * Significant at 10% level. ** Significant at 5% level. *** Significant at 1% level.
— = not applicable.

Table 2A.3 The Cotton-Neumark Decomposition of the Gender Mean Log Monthly Earnings Differentials in Wage Employment

Gender mean observed log monthly earnings gap	0.7891
First specification (accounting for job characteristics)	
Difference due to:	
Explained	**46.14%**
Human Capital characteristics	20.14%
Of which:	
Education	10.97%
Experience	4.80%
Training	4.37%
Job characteristics	24.84%
Of which:	
Sector of activity	−0.45%
Sector of wage employment	11.42%
Terms of employment	7.76%
Occupation	6.12%
Other characteristics	1.16%
Unexplained	**39.98%**
Selectivity	**13.88%**
Second specification (not accounting for job characteristics)	
Difference due to:	
Explained	**45.06%**
Human Capital characteristics	38.95%
Of which:	
Education	22.64%
Experience	8.80%
Training	7.50%
Other characteristics	6.11%
Unexplained	**43.02%**
Selectivity	**11.93%**

Source: Ethiopia Labour Force Survey 2005.
Note: Positive sign indicates advantage to men and negative sign indicates advantage to women. The decomposition is computed using the results of the log monthly earnings equations estimated with the Heckman two-step procedure.

Table 2A.4 The Cotton-Neumark Decomposition of the Gender Mean Log Monthly Earnings Differentials in Wage Employment by Age Cohorts (15–24, 25–34, 35+)

Gender mean observed log monthly earnings gap	0.6995	0.6001	0.5237
First specification (accounting for job characteristics)			
Difference due to:			
Explained	**37.80%**	**22.89%**	**30.45%**
Human capital characteristics	15.40%	11.23%	12.97%
Of which:			
Education	14.60%	6.50%	10.49%
Experience	–3.40%	0.22%	–0.86%
Training	4.21%	4.51%	3.34%
Job characteristics	26.48%	13.28%	12.75%
Of which:			
Sector of activity	–1.29%	–0.56%	0.63%
Sector of wage employment	22.68%	6.64%	5.52%
Terms of employment	3.08%	4.13%	3.80%
Occupation	2.01%	3.07%	2.80%
Other characteristics	–4.08%	–1.63%	4.73%
Unexplained	**41.13%**	**48.37%**	**76.53%**
Selectivity	**21.08%**	**28.74%**	**–6.98%**
Second specification (not accounting for job characteristics)			
Difference due to:			
Explained	**27.25%**	**21.40%**	**40.74%**
Human capital characteristics	28.04%	21.04%	32.18%
Of which:			
Education	24.60%	12.89%	26.63%
Experience	–2.88%	0.76%	–2.13%
Training	6.33%	7.39%	7.68%
Other characteristics	–0.79%	0.37%	8.56%
Unexplained	**49.50%**	**63.43%**	**94.54%**
Selectivity	**23.25%**	**15.17%**	**–35.28%**

Source: Ethiopia Labour Force Survey 2005.
Note: Positive sign indicates advantage to men and negative sign indicates advantage to women. The decomposition is computed using the results of the log monthly earnings equations estimated with the Heckman two-step procedure.

Notes

1. The 2005 LFS covers all parts of the country except the Gambela region (including Gambela town) and the non-sedentary population of three zones of the Afar and six zones of the Somali regions.
2. See the World Bank (2006) Ethiopia report for a detailed discussion of the various concepts used by the CSA and the World Bank to classify employment. Our definition of the labor force is that used by the World Bank report and referring to the age group 15 years and more, while the CSA (2006) uses a different age threshold (10 and above).
3. The absence of returns from secondary employment data should not be a serious problem, however, because according to data from the Addis Labor Market Survey, wages from secondary jobs do not appear to be an important element of overall earnings (World Bank 2006).
4. "General education" includes grades 9–12 in the new system (general secondary education, grades 9–10; preparatory secondary education, grades 11–12) and grades 9–12 in the old system. "Beyond general education" includes new vocational education (grades 11–12), certificate, diploma (grades 11–13), degree completed or not, and above degree. And "primary education" includes primary education in the new system (basic education cycle, grades 1–4; general primary cycle, grades 5–8), non-formal education, and literacy campaign.
5. Note that recent progress toward universal primary education and gender equity in primary and secondary education cannot yet be observed in the age group 15–24.
6. For a comprehensive review of the various methods related to the analysis of the gender wage gap, see Beblo et al. (2003).
7. Primary, general, and beyond general education. The reference category is "illiterate."
8. The selection equation includes all explanatory variables included in equation 2.1, except job variables, and also three identification variables (the inverse of the dependency ratio, the number of children between 0 and 6 years, and the number of children between 7 and 14 years, per household member). These latter variables are expected to have a direct impact on the decision to participate in wage-employment, but not on earnings.
9. To test for the possible influence of education on job characteristics, the job characteristics were estimated on a set of explanatory variables that includes education variables and a dummy for gender. The estimates showed that job characteristics were indeed partly determined by the level of education. Gender was also shown to be a significant predictor, when education characteristics were held constant, which demonstrates the existence of a form of gender segmentation in job allocation.
10. According to Halvorsen and Palmquist (1980), some articles misinterpret the coefficients of dummy variables in semilogarithmic regression equations by assuming that the coefficient of a dummy variable, multiplied by 100, is equal to the percentage effect of that variable. This interpretation, which is correct for continuous variables, is not true for dummy variables and can result in substantial errors. The larger the coefficient of a dummy variable, the more important the difference is between the percentage effect and the coefficient. Given that our estimated coefficients of education dummy variables are large and, in order to correct for standard deviation, we

use the Kennedy correction method—which can be expressed as follows: let ρ be the direct (marginal) returns of our education variables in the semi-logarithmic wage equation—we then have:

$$\rho = \left(e^{r - \frac{S_r^2}{2}} - 1 \right) * 100$$

where r is the coefficient on education dummy and S_r is the estimated standard error.

11. In Appleton et al. (1995), the returns to primary education are found to be generally small and not statistically significant for men in both the private and public sectors and for women in the public sector. More recently, Appleton, Hoddinott, and Krishnan (1999) found that the returns to primary education are significant only for men in the public sector, when wage estimates are not corrected for sample selection. In another study looking at the changes in returns from education during structural adjustment in Ethiopia, Krishnan, Selassie, and Dercon (1998) showed that the private returns to primary education are significant only for men in the public sector in 1994 and 1997, and only for women in the private sector in 1990. Finally, in the World Bank (2006) report on Ethiopia, private returns to nonformal education and basic education (grades 1–4) are not significant.

References

Note: Source of study data: Ethiopia Labour Force Survey 2005, dataset version 1.0— May 2006, provided by the Central Statistical Authority of Ethiopia.

Appleton, S., J. Hoddinott, and P. Krishnan. 1999. "The Gender Wage Gap in Three African Countries." *Economic Development and Cultural Change* 47 (2): 289–312.

Appleton, S., J. Hoddinott, P. Krishnan, and M. Kerry. 1995. "Does the Labor Market Explain Low Female Schooling? Evidence From Three African Countries." Queen Elizabeth House Development Studies Working Paper 83, University of Oxford, United Kingdom.

Beblo, M., D. Beninger, A. Heinze, and F. Laisney. 2003. "Methodological Issues Related to the Analysis of Gender Gaps in Employment, Earnings and Career Progression." Final report, Project of the European Commission, Employment and Social Affairs DG, Mannheim, Germany.

Bigsten, A., T. Mengistae, and A. Shimeles. 2007. "Mobility and Earnings in Ethiopia's Urban Labor Markets: 1994–2004." Policy Research Working Paper Series 4168, World Bank, Washington, DC.

Cotton, J. 1988. "On the Decomposition of Wage Differentials." *The Review of Economics and Statistics* 70 (2): 236–43.

CSA (Central Statistical Agency). 2006. "Report on the 2005 National Labour Force Survey." *CSA Statistical Bulletin* 365, Addis Ababa, Ethiopia.

Fafchamps, M., M. Söderbom, and N. Benhassine. 2006. "Job Sorting in African Labor Markets." Working Paper Series 2006–02, Centre for the Study of African Economies, University of Oxford, United Kingdom.

Heckman, J. 1979. "Sample Selection Bias as a Specification Error." *Econometrica* 47 (1): 153–62.

Halvorsen, R., and R. Palmquist. 1980. "The Interpretation of Dummy Variables in Semilogarithmic Equations." *American Economic Review* 70 (3): 474–75.

Kabubo-Mariara, J. 2003. "Wage Determination and the Gender Wage Gap in Kenya: Any Evidence of Gender Discrimination?" Research Paper 132, African Economic Research Consortium, Nairobi, Kenya.

Kennedy, P. 1981. "Estimation with Correctly-Interpreted Dummy Variables in Semi-Logarithmic Equations." *American Economic Review* 71 (4): 801.

Krishnan, P., Selassie T. G., Dercon, S. 1998. "The Urban Labor Market during Structural Adjustment: Ethiopia 1990–1997." Working Paper 73, The Centre for the Study of African Economies.

Lachaud, J. P. 1997. *Les Femmes et le Marché du Travail Urbain en Afrique Subsaharienne.* Paris: Editions l'Harmattan.

Lim, L. L. 2002. "Female Labor Force Participation." Background paper for the United Nations Population Division, Expert Group Meeting on Completing the Fertility Transition, March 2002.

Mincer, J. 1974. *Schooling, Experience and Earnings.* New York: National Bureau of Economic Research.

MoFED (Ministry of Finance and Economic Development). 2005. "Ethiopia: The Millennium Development Goals (MDGs) Needs Assessment." Synthesis Report, Development Planning and Research Department, MoFED, Addis Ababa, Ethiopia.

Neumark, D. 1988. "Employer's Discriminatory Behavior and the Estimation of Wage Discrimination." *Journal of Human Resources* 23 (3): 279–95.

Nordman, C. J., and F. Roubaud. 2005. "Reassessing the Gender Wage Gap: Does Labor Force Attachment Really Matter? Evidence from Matched Labor Force and Biographical Surveys in Madagascar." Document de Travail, Institut Recherche Développment, Développment, Institutions and Analyses de Long Terme, Paris.

Nordman, C. J., and F. C. Wolff. 2008. "Islands Through the Glass Ceiling? Evidence of Gender Wage Gaps in Madagascar and Mauritius." Working Paper DT/2008/02, Développment, Institutions and Analyses de Long Terme, Paris.

———. 2009. "Gender Differences in Pay in African Manufacturing Firms." Working Paper hal-00421227_v1, HAL.

Siphambe, H. K., and M. Thokweng-Bakwena. 2001. "The Wage Gap Between Men and Women in Botswana's Formal Labor Market." *Journal of African Economies* 10 (2): 127–42.

Temesgen, T. 2006. "Decomposing Gender Wage Differentials in Urban Ethiopia: Evidence from Linked Employer-Employee (LEE) Manufacturing Survey Data." *Global Economic Review* 35 (1): 43–66.

UNICEF (United Nations Children's Fund). 1999. "Women in Transition." The MONEE Project Regional Monitoring Report 6, ICDC, Florence, Italy.

Weichselbaumer, D., and R. Winter-Ebmer. 2003. "A Meta-Analysis of the International Gender Wage Gap." Discussion Paper 906, Institute for the Study of Labor, Bonn, Germany.

World Bank. 2006. *Urban Labor Markets in Ethiopia: Challenges and Prospects*. Vol.I: Synthesis Report; Vol. II: Background Papers. Poverty Reduction and Economic Management Unit, Africa Region. Washington, DC: World Bank.

Chapter 3

Gender Disparities in the Malagasy Labor Market

Christophe J. Nordman, Faly Rakotomanana,
and Anne-Sophie Robilliard

G ender differences in terms of labor market performance are common
around the world. In the case of least-developed countries, understanding the roots of inequalities between the sexes and reducing the gender
gap are important goals because gender disparities have a potential negative
effect on both broad-based growth and poverty reduction. Policies designed to
reduce gender discrimination are indeed among the most often recommended
solutions to reduce poverty: Goal 3 of the United Nations Millennium Development Goals (MDG) is specifically aimed at reducing gender inequalities, and
the promotion of women's empowerment is among the aims of Poverty Reduction Strategy Papers (PRSP) of many poor countries.

In developed countries, the gender wage gap has been the subject of an important area of labor economics research. More specifically, starting with the seminal methodological contributions of Oaxaca (1973) and Blinder (1973), many
attempts have been made to estimate the extent to which the average gender
wage gap is a result of differences in human capital attributes, such as schooling
and work experience, versus differences between genders in wages paid for given
attributes (Blau and Kahn 2000; Weichselbaumer and Winter-Ebmer 2005). The
part of the gender wage gap that is not explained by differences in observed
endowments across genders (the unexplained portion of the gap) is often interpreted as the result of discrimination (see Annex 3A for a definition).

For Africa, research on gender disparities in labor market outcomes is relatively recent and has followed similar methodological approaches. A wide
consensus has developed on the presence of important earnings inequalities

The authors thank Jorge Arbache, Elena Bardasi, Mayra Buvinic, Ewa Filipiak, Markus Goldstein,
Alexandre Kolev, David Stifel, Stefano Paternostro, and an anonymous referee for helpful suggestions on first drafts of this study.

between men and women, both for salaried and self-employed workers.[1] For instance, in Guinea, Glick and Sahn (1997) find that differences in characteristics account for 45 percent of the male-female gap in earnings from self-employment and 25 percent of the differences in earnings from public-sector employment, while, in the private sector, women actually earn more than men. Armitage and Sabot (1991) also find such gender inequality in the public sector of Tanzania, but they observed no gender "discrimination" in Kenya's labor market. The latter result is true both for the public and private sectors of the Kenyan economy. Similarly, Glewwe (1990) finds no residual gender wage gap once individual characteristics are accounted for in Ghana; on the contrary, women seem better off than men in the public sector. More recently, Siphambe and Thokweng-Bakwena (2001) show that, in the public sector of Botswana, most of the wage gap is a result of differences in characteristics between men and women. On the other hand, in the private sector, most of the wage gap remains unexplained by workers' endowments. Likewise, in Uganda and Côte d'Ivoire, Appleton, Hoddinott, and Krishnan (1999) find evidence that the public sector practices less wage discrimination than the private sector. However, from their data on Côte d'Ivoire, Ethiopia, and Uganda, they conclude that there is no common cross-country pattern in the relative magnitudes of the gender wage gaps in the public and private sectors.[2]

There is, however, an important specificity of African countries' labor markets that makes it hazardous to interpret the unexplained part of the gender pay gap as solely a result of discriminatory practices against women. This specificity is the large share of the labor force that is employed in nonwage activities in these countries. In addition, religion, ethnic issues, and social norms are likely to also play a non-negligible role in gender disparities in labor market outcomes.

In the Malagasy case, the deterioration of the labor market as well as the partial freeze on public sector recruitment since the mid-1980s may have accentuated the circumstances (that is, labor market entry and exit) that could give rise to gender inequalities in the labor market. Indeed, the decrease in jobs for women in the public sector was particularly significant, while this sector offered the most rewarding labor market segment (Razafindrakoto and Roubaud 1999; Roubaud 2002). In this context, the predominance of informal activity for women, as well as the decreasing role of the public sector in providing stable jobs, may have given rise to increased poverty and, consequently, to significant selection effects at the formal labor market entry.

This study casts new light on these issues by using household surveys—Enquête Périodique auprès des Ménages (EPM)—carried out in 2001 and 2005 in Madagascar. Previous studies of this country were conducted by Nicita and Razzaz (2003), Nordman and Roubaud (2009), and Nordman and Wolff (2009b, 2009c). Nicita and Razzaz investigated the gender wage gap in relation to an analysis of the growing potential of a particular economic sector, the textile industry. From their earnings differential decomposition, they first show that both the endowments and the unexplained part of the wage difference favor male workers, although the latter dominates the former.[3] Second, education and potential experience are similarly important in determining the wage differential. Third, level of education and being resident in urban Antananarivo slightly reduce the unexplained part of the wage differential. However, an important limitation of their study is that, as a result of lack of information, they proxy total experience by age and include very few regressors in their wage equations by sex. As pointed out by some authors (for example, Nordman and Roubaud 2009; Weichselbaumer and Winter-Ebmer 2005), this method has the consequence of greatly amplifying the unexplained share of the gender pay gap.

By contrast, using linked worker-firm data from the manufacturing sectors, thereby enabling perfect control of the employer effects on earnings, Nordman and Wolff (2009b, 2009c) show that the magnitude of the adjusted gender wage gap is almost insignificant. Yet no general conclusion on Madagascar can be drawn from this analysis, because it only concerns the formal sector of the economy, whereas informal activity largely dominates the Malagasy labor market.

Nordman and Roubaud (2009) adopt a different approach by matching two original urban surveys conducted in Madagascar in 1998—a labor force survey and a biographical survey. They build a dataset that enables them to combine the original information gathered from each survey, particularly the earnings from current employment and the workers' entire professional trajectories. Their results lead to a reassessment of the returns to human capital for both men and women. They show that using more precise labor force attachment variables greatly increases the portion of the gender gap explained by observable characteristics.

This study extends the analysis of the previous authors to the entire country (rural and urban), though with more data constraints concerning the workers' and employers' observed characteristics, notably the lack of precise labor force attachment variables. However, the originality of our study lies in the longer time perspective of gender differences in labor market performance that is made possible by the availability of the two cross-sectional household surveys (2001 and 2005). During this period, the Madagascar economy experienced several large-scale shocks: in addition to recurrent weather problems, the country experienced a 2002 political crisis that resulted in a major disruption of economic activity caused by general strikes and roadblocks on major national roads. More recently, the Madagascar economy faced a strong currency depreciation and rise in international oil and rice prices in 2004 and 2005, as well as the final phase-out of the Multi-Fibre Arrangement, the tariff agreement on textile and clothing that had boosted local industry by giving preferential access to European and American markets in 2005 (Cling,

Razafindrakoto, and Roubaud 2007). These shocks may have affected men and women differently and, as a result, changed their relative positions in the labor market. This study addresses that question by examining two aspects of gender differences in labor market outcomes: (1) employment status and (2) wages and earnings.

The study's results for labor allocation show that the structure of employment changed between 2001 and 2005. We find a strong positive impact of education on the probability of getting a paid job for both men and women. This effect also increases with education level. For men and women alike, education has the strongest positive impact on the probability of accessing the public sector, followed by private formal wage employment and, finally, informal self-employment. Interestingly, education seems to be more favorable to having a self-employed job in the informal sector rather than a salaried job in this sector.

Regarding gender inequality in earnings,[4] the results show that the average gender wage gap (that is, for wage workers, including farm salaried workers) is relatively small and stable over time. In non-farm self-employment, however, the gap is much higher, and it declined between 2001 and 2005. Earnings equations estimates indicate that human capital is an important determinant of earnings for both men and women and across sectors of employment. Decompositions of the gender wage gap show that differences in individual characteristics of men and women account for almost 70 percent of the gap in 2001. However, this share is down to less than 40 percent in 2005. When job characteristics of men and women are also taken into account, differences in characteristics explain more than 60 percent of the gap, and the share remains stable over time. Across wage employment sectors, the gender gap appears to be lowest in the public sector and highest in the informal sector. Using full sectoral decomposition techniques also shows that gender-specific sectoral location explains a significant share of the gender wage gap in both years. This result is mainly driven by the fact that the proportion of women is higher in the self-employed sector, where earnings are lower. Augmented earnings equations estimates carried out for the non-farm self-employment sector suggest that the gap in this sector is driven by the very unequal distribution of micro-firm attributes between men and women. This result points to a potential source of earnings differential often ignored in the gender earnings gap literature—access to physical capital.

The remainder of this chapter is divided as follows. The second section briefly presents the background of the Malagasy labor market and its main characteristics. The next section discusses the data, concepts, and methods used in this study, followed by comments on the results and a conclusion drawing together the main study findings.

Characteristics of the Malagasy Labor Market

Workforce participation in Madagascar is high. Table 3.1 provides some basic labor market indicators for 2001 and 2005.[5] These numbers show that 86.9 percent of the population reports some form of productive activity in 2005, an increase of 4.4 percentage points from 2001. This growth in activity was driven by greater participation of women, with female activity rate growing from 77.7 percent to 84.6 percent, relative to male activity rate rising from 87.5 percent to 89.4 percent. Open unemployment is structurally low, though it may be problematic in urban areas and is found to be higher for women than for men.

More than 85 percent of workers in Madagascar were employed in nonwage activities in 2005, and this share of nonwage to total employment rose by 3.4 percent between 2001 and 2005. Unsurprisingly, the informal sector dominates the labor market in Madagascar. A conservative estimate places 64.5 percent of the 1.2 million wage workers in the informal sector. Considering the total workforce, including nonwage workers, approximately 95 percent of the 8.3 million working age adults are informally employed.

Despite relatively equal access to the general workforce, men have greater access to "good" jobs than women, that is, non-agricultural wage employment. Men and women have similar nonwage agricultural earnings, but men fare better than women in terms of earnings in every other employment category. Women tend to be employed more often in agriculture and the informal sector, where earnings are relatively low, while men tend to have higher rates of employment in the formal sector, where earnings are relatively high. Further, for those women who are employed in the formal sector and other higher-wage jobs, their earnings fall below those of men in the same sectors on average.

The Malagasy labor market is characterized by the coexistence of different types of employment sectors with different entry, exit, and wage setting rules. However, according to Stifel, Rakotomanana, and Celada (2007), there is no evidence of labor market segmentation between the private formal and informal

Table 3.1 Selected Labor Market Indicators in Madagascar

	All (%)		Male (%)		Female (%)	
	2001	2005	2001	2005	2001	2005
Activity rate	82.5	86.9	87.5	89.4	77.7	84.6
Employment ratio	81.5	84.7	86.8	87.8	76.5	81.7
Wage employment ratio	18.2	14.6	22.6	17.5	13.5	11.6
Unemployment rate	1.2	2.6	0.9	1.8	1.6	3.5

Sources: Madagascar EPM 2001, 2005; authors' calculations.
Note: Individuals aged 15 and older.

wage sectors. Differences in earnings between those employed in the private formal and informal sectors appear to be driven by differences in endowments, not by differences in returns to education and labor market experience. The exception is that the gap between men's earnings (higher) and women's earnings (lower) is larger in the informal sector than the formal sector. However, there does appear to be some segmentation between the private and public sectors, as there are higher returns to education in the latter.

Data, Definitions, and Methods

This section first describes the data and concepts used in this study before discussing the methodology of earnings equations and gender earnings decompositions, an essential aspect of this study's investigation of the gender disparities in the labor market.

Data and Definitions

This study is based primarily on an analysis of the 2001 and 2005 EPM. The EPMs are nationally representative, integrated household surveys of 5,080 households (23,167 individuals) and 11,781 households (55,995 individuals) in 2001 and 2005, respectively. Our study is carried out on the subsample of individuals age 15 years and older. In 2005, women represented 51.3 percent of this sample of individuals.

The multipurpose questionnaires include sections on education, health, housing, agriculture, household expenditure, assets, non-farm enterprises, and employment. Employment and earnings information are available in the employment, non-farm enterprise, and agriculture sections.

The choice of these databases to analyze gender disparities on the Malagasy labor market can be justified on the following grounds:

- The EPM is the only survey that provides information on labor market conditions and is representative at the national and regional level without any restriction on the type of jobs (paid or unpaid, wage or non-wage), the sectors (agricultural or not), and the institutional sector (public or private, formal or informal).

- Another advantage of the EPM data bases lies in their multipurpose characteristic, that is, having access to a large set of data in different domains stemming from the same survey allows analysis of a wide range of issues within a comprehensive and coherent framework. It improves the quality of analysis carried out on determinants of labor participation, such as individual characteristics (age, gender, education) and household living conditions (household size and structure, consumption, and wealth).

- The EPM questionnaires in 2001 and 2005 are very similar, thus enabling consistent analysis of the evolution of labor market indicators.

Among the 15 sections of the questionnaire, the employment section more specifically covers the supply side of the labor market, with information on the main variables used in this study: employment status, sector of employment, wage labor earnings, hours worked, as well as other data on employment conditions. The section on non-farm enterprises (NFE) provides information on earnings for self-employed workers as well as some characteristics of NFEs. The other variables used in this study are derived from the section on the demographic composition of the household as well as from the section on education.

Gender differences in labor market performance can be understood through the analysis of two types of labor market outcomes: employment status and earnings. As noted, more than 85 percent of workers in Madagascar are employed in non-wage activities. Although the EPMs are designed to measure both wage and non-wage earnings, non-wage earnings are typically generated at the household level, making it difficult to analyze them in relation to individual characteristics such as gender. Another issue is that non-wage earnings are usually derived not only from human capital but also from physical capital. However, the data at hand do not allow separating labor from capital income. We therefore chose to estimate modified earnings equations for independent workers, taking into account the value of capital.

The construction of the earnings variable is based on the following rules:

- For wage workers, earnings data were collected at the individual level and wage earnings are defined as the sum of net wages paid; other advantages (rent, clothes, transport or gas, and so on), and food provided by the employer earned as compensation for the main activity (secondary activities are excluded from the analysis).[6]

- For self-employed workers, earnings were collected in two different sections, depending on whether the self-employment activity is related to the operation of a farm or a non-farm enterprise.

- In the case of non-farm self-employment, earnings are defined as the net income of non-farm enterprises (sales minus paid wages, non-wage costs, and taxes). This information was collected at the firm level, but family members involved in the activity are listed. In the case of multiple family member participation, however, it is not possible to attribute individual earnings to each member involved. The income was therefore attributed exclusively to the head of the enterprise, and other household members were treated as unpaid family workers.

- Because agricultural incomes cannot be assigned similarly to a single household member, these earnings were excluded from the analysis. In the participation equation, agricultural self-employment is treated as a specific category.

- All earnings are divided by the number of hours worked in the corresponding activity.

Given that, as mentioned, wages and earnings from self-employment are different types of income and are measured using different rules and different parts of the questionnaire, the study separately analyzes gender earnings differences for wage employment (including farm salaried workers) and non-farm self-employment.

Methods

The empirical analysis was carried out separately for the two years (2001 and 2005). We rely on different approaches, first tackling the question of employment status and sector allocation across gender (see next section). After a preliminary discussion using descriptive statistics, we made use of multinomial logit models that allow disentangling the determinants of labor allocation across different institutional sectors: public employment, private formal wage employment, private informal wage employment, private informal self-employment and agricultural self-employment.[7]

The analysis of gender differences then focuses on another main labor market outcome, namely earnings. Average earnings are first compared across gender. We then rely on estimations of Mincer-type earnings functions for men and women to decompose the earnings gap. The objective is to determine the extent to which the average gender wage gap is due to differences in human capital attributes, such as schooling and work experience, versus differences between genders in wages paid for given attributes (Blau and Kahn 2000).

The specifications of the earnings equations and an additional discussion on sample selection issues related to paid-work participation and sector choice are reported in Annex 3.A. This annex also presents the most common approach to identifying sources of gender earnings gaps (Oaxaca-Blinder and Neumark decompositions), together with a full sectoral decomposition that explicitly takes into account the sectoral structures between genders in the measure of the gender earnings gaps (Appleton, Hoddinott, and Krishnan 1999).

Results

Two aspects of labor market performances of men and women in 2001 and 2005, employment status and earnings,[8] are examined in turn.

Employment Status

Before turning to the determinants of employment status across sectors and gender, global statistics of labor allocation in Madagascar are discussed.

Labor Allocation Across Sectors. Statistics of employment status are reported in Annex tables 3C.1, 3C.2, and 3C.3. The main results are summarized in figure 3.1 below.

Overall, the structure of employment has changed between 2001 and 2005, mainly as a result of the increase in the proportion of family workers (37.4 percent to 47.7 percent) and the slight concomitant decrease in the share of self-employed workers (44.3 percent to 37.8 percent). This change in the structure of employment is mostly explained by the shift in women's labor allocation, which proportion in the category of family workers substantially increased from 53.5 percent to 70.6 percent in four years. The expansion goes along with the decline in the share of women in the category of self-employed workers. In fact, according to these figures, the nature of employment differs greatly between men and women:

- Women are much more often family workers than men (70.6 percent versus 25.1 percent in 2005), and less often declare themselves as self-employed (17.8 percent versus 57.4 percent of men in 2005).

- Only 3.5 percent of women are employed in the formal sector, versus 6.7 percent of men.

Figure 3.1 Distribution of Individuals Aged 15 and Older Across All Sectors of Employment in Madagascar

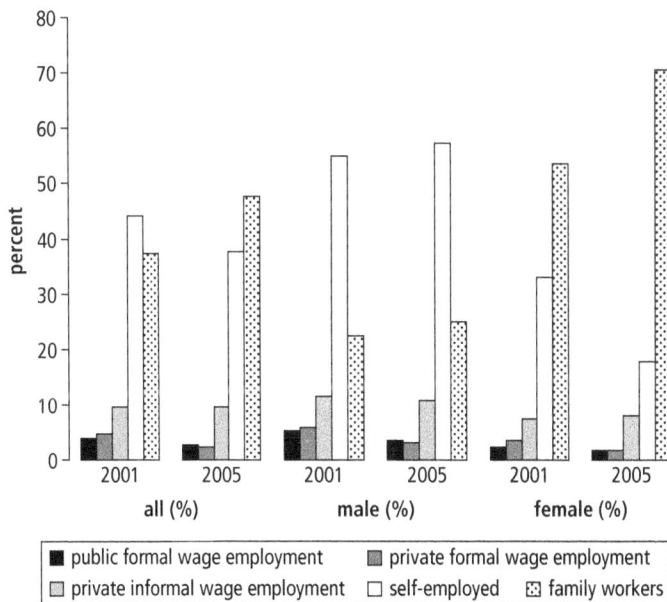

Sources: Madagascar EPM 2001, 2005; authors' calculations.

The evolution in employment status can be explained in part by some of the shocks experienced by the Malagasy labor market between 2001 and 2005. More specifically, the final phase-out of the Multi-Fibre Arrangement in 2005—which ended the preferential access of Malagasy products to European and American markets and opened the Malagasy garment industry to competition from Asian countries—generated massive layoffs in the textile sector and caused self-employment in that sector to diminish.

The distribution of labor greatly differs between rural and urban areas as well, as shown in figure 3.2. First, private formal and informal wage workers are scarce in rural areas, while their proportion is much higher in towns. Employment structure in rural locations is thus essentially made up of self-employed workers (39 percent in 2005) and family workers (51 percent in 2005). Men are much more likely to be self-employed than women in rural areas (61 percent versus 17 percent, respectively, in 2005), and women are found predominant in the category of family workers (75 percent versus 27 percent in 2005).[9]

Determinants of Labor Allocation Across Sectors. The estimation method for determinants of labor allocation across sectors using multinomial logit models is explained as follows. First, gender-specific multinomial logit models of labor allocation were carried out using three broad categories: (1) "inactive, unemployed, family worker" (thus defining a category of "unpaid" individuals in the labor market); (2) "non-farm paid employment" (including public and private formal and informal wage employment and non-agricultural self-employment); and (3) "agricultural self-employment." The results of these estimations are reported in Annex table 3C.4.

A second model refines the second modality of the preceding model (non-farm paid employment) in order to account for differentiated determinants of labor allocation, in particular for "public employment," "private formal wage employment," "private informal wage employment," and "private informal self-employment." The "agricultural self-employment" category is left unchanged. Annex tables 3C.5 and 3C.6 report the coefficient estimates of this multinomial logit model with six modalities. All the coefficients must be interpreted in relation to the reference category, which is "unpaid" individuals.[10]

The list of covariates includes a set of human capital variables and individual demographics deemed to influence labor supply. Household characteristics are also accounted for, as well as three variables reflecting physical capital endowments. These variables, namely the log of other household members' earnings per capita and the log of the amount of land and value of livestock owned by the individual's household, are indeed good candidates to affect both the opportunity cost of labor and labor allocation across sectors.

Annex table 3C.4 shows the following results. First, unsurprisingly, education has differentiated effects on the sector "choice." While schooling attainment

Figure 3.2 Distribution of Individuals Aged 15 and Older Across All Sectors of Employment in Urban and Rural Areas

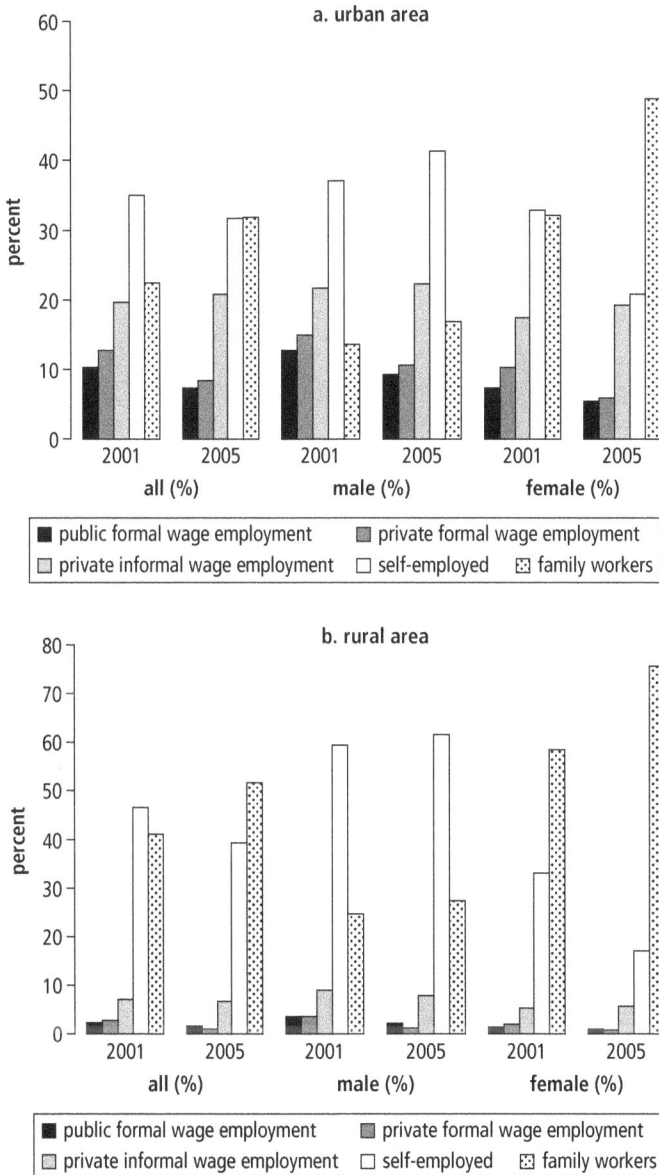

a. urban area

b. rural area

Sources: Madagascar EPM 2001, 2005; author's calculations.

positively affects the likelihood of being in paid work for both men and women (the result being also robust to both years), the reverse is true for agricultural self-employment, which is often negatively associated with higher levels of schooling, in particular for males. For women, however, this negative association is actually not observed in particular for low levels of education. For instance, reaching the first cycle of secondary education is positively associated with access to agricultural self-employment for women in 2005.

Second, other human capital indicators, such as potential experience in the labor market and past vocational training, are positively associated with access to paid employment (with a decreasing marginal effect for experience). Experience in the labor market is also positively related to agricultural self-employment for men and women as compared to unpaid individuals. Nonetheless, vocational training is significantly negatively associated with a job in agriculture for men in both years.

Marital status (married versus single or divorced or widowed) presents an interesting pattern. For men, being married is associated with a greater likelihood of having access to a farm and non-farm paid employment, whatever the considered sector. The reverse is observed for women, whose marriage appears to be negatively associated to access to a paid job.

Finally, additional household and property (land and livestock) variables are always highly significant. The variable indicating the sum of other household members' earnings is positively associated with the probability of having access to paid employment. Conversely, its effect is always negative on the "choice" of an agricultural self-employed job. A possible explanation for these findings is that this variable may be capturing an income effect of the household, that is, reflecting the fact that workers in wealthier households are mostly found in non-farm paid employment rather than in agricultural self-employment. Similarly, the opposite—and expected—effect was found for the land value variable: the higher the land value owned, the higher the probability of having a self-employed agricultural job. Interestingly, the magnitude of this effect is stronger for men than for women, especially in 2005. The same comment can be made for the variable of livestock value in 2001, which exhibits positive coefficients for self-employed agricultural jobs and negative coefficients for paid jobs. However, the coefficient shifts signs for women in 2005, indicating a negative association between the value of the livestock and the probability to have a self-employed job in agriculture. In the meantime, the coefficient loses significance for men self-employed in agriculture. This might reflect the improvement in the profitability of cropping activities that could have resulted in a shift away from cattle.

We now turn to more detailed estimates reported in Annex tables 3C.5 (men) and 3C.6 (women). For men and women alike, education has the strongest positive impact on the probability of accessing the public sector, followed by private formal wage employment and, finally, informal self-employment. This finding is robust to both years considered. Interestingly, then, education seems to be more favorable to having a self-employed job in the informal sector rather than a salaried job in this sector. This may reflect the fact that schooling is necessary to acquire managerial skills, even in informal activities. Note that the main difference across sexes is that education has a much stronger impact for women, especially in the formal sector of the economy, and that schooling is negatively associated with an informal wage employment in 2001 for women; whereas, for men, the impact is insignificant.

The other human capital variables (vocational training, experience) exhibit expected signs (positive and concave profile for experience), with the exception of vocational training in agricultural self-employment, where it is insignificant for women and even found to have a negative effect for men. Concerning marital status: being married is again positively associated with being in paid employment for men, and negatively so for women.

Finally, other household members' earnings are significantly and positively associated with having wage employment, while this variable is negatively related to self-employed jobs. This result is robust to both years and sexes (with the exception of women's informal self-employment). Also, the effect of the land value owned is consistent with expectation and across years and sexes: its effect is significantly negative for non-agricultural jobs and positive for agricultural self-employment. The same comment can be made for the livestock value, with the exception that its effect is not systematically positive for self-employed agricultural jobs in 2005 (notably, significantly negative for women).

Decomposing the Gender Earnings Gap

We now turn to explaining workers' earnings in their jobs, thus disentangling the various determinants of earnings differentials across sectors and sexes. Before discussing the gender earnings gaps decompositions, it is necessary to provide simple descriptive statistics of the gender earnings gap across years. This is followed by an analysis of the determinants of earnings for wage and non-wage employment (excluding agriculture) across gender and for the two years of the survey. The results of the various gender earnings gap decompositions will then be explained.

Both monthly and hourly gender earnings gaps were reported. Taking into account the hours worked by gender is important to get a proper view of the gender pay gap because important gender-specific time allocation choices also exist. This is apparent in table 3.2, which shows that men work on average longer wage hours than women. This holds true across wage employment sectors. Individuals engaged in non-farm self-employment appear to be working longer hours than those in other sectors, and the gender difference is smaller.[11]

Earnings gaps are here computed as the difference in average earnings of men and women expressed as a percentage of average men earnings.[12] The results in table 3.3 indicate that, for wage employment, the aggregate monthly earnings

Table 3.2 Monthly Hours Worked in Madagascar

	2001		2005	
	Males	Females	Males	Females
Wage employment				
Full sample (aged 15+)	185.9	162.7	198.2	168.1
Public formal wage employment	170.3	146.9	181.5	151.9
Private formal wage employment	189.9	179.8	218.1	197.2
Private informal wage employment	191.0	159.1	198.2	165.6
Non-farm self-employment				
Full sample (aged 15+)	230.0	213.3	203.3	187.2

Sources: Madagascar EPM 2001, 2005; authors' calculations.

Table 3.3 Gender Earnings Gaps in Madagascar
(percent)

	2001		2005	
	Monthly	Hourly	Monthly	Hourly
Wage employment				
Full sample (aged 15+)	42.8	26.4	49.5	24.6
Age groups				
15–24	11.0	6.7	20.6	−1.4
25–34	29.7	14.3	50.1	22.1
35+	52.7	28.5	53.4	29.8
Employment sectors				
Public formal wage employment	7.4	−3.8	35.0	13.1
Private formal wage employment	25.5	19.2	15.8	7.8
Private informal wage employment	52.2	27.4	45.5	18.3
Non-farm self-employment				
Full sample (aged 15+)	99.0	83.1	93.3	69.6
Age groups				
15–24	97.8	107.1	88.9	66.0
25–34	78.6	63.6	70.2	41.3
35+	117.5	93.1	105.6	85.0

Sources: Madagascar EPM 2001, 2005; authors' calculations.
Note: Gaps are computed as the difference in average earnings of men and women expressed as a percentage of average men earnings.

gap increased from 42.8 percent to 49.5 percent between 2001 and 2005, while the aggregate hourly earnings gap decreased slightly. The lower hourly earnings gap is consistent with the fact that men work longer hours in the wage and non-farm self-employment sectors. Moreover, the concomitant increase in the monthly earnings gap and decrease in hourly earnings gap between the two years reflects the fact that the gender gap in hours worked increased between 2001 and 2005 in the formal sectors and in the non-farm self-employment sector (table 3.2). More specifically, the growth in hours worked has been greater for men in all sectors except the informal wage sector.

Although lower than the monthly earnings gap, the gender gap in *hourly* earnings is still significant in Madagascar. It was equal to 26.4 percent (respectively 24.6 percent) in 2001 (respectively 2005) for wage employment and to 83 percent (respectively 69 percent) in 2001 (respectively 2005) for non-farm self-employment.

Data from table 3.3 also suggest that the earnings gap varies across cohorts: it is higher for older workers than for younger ones. In 2005, the hourly earnings gap actually slightly negative (that is, to the advantage of females) for the age 15–24 cohort.

Finally, the size of the gap differs across wage sectors. For both years, it is highest in the informal wage sector. In 2001, it is smaller in the public sector and actually negative when hours worked are accounted for. In 2005, the smallest gap was in the private formal sector. For non-farm self-employed workers, the gap appears much higher but slightly decreases between the two years.

Whether these gaps are a result of differences in endowments between men and women (the "explained" share of the gap) or to differences in returns to endowments (the "unexplained" portion of the gap, which may be attributed in part to discrimination) is an empirical question that is addressed using the decomposition techniques presented in Annex 3A. These techniques rely on the estimation of earnings equations, which are presented in the following section.

Earnings Determinants. In order to eliminate the effect of the number of hours worked on earnings, hourly earnings are used to analyze gender differences.[13] Earnings equations are estimated separately for men and women over the sample of individuals with positive earnings.

Wage Employment. The sample of wage workers includes all wage workers and excludes self-employed workers, unpaid family workers, as well as agricultural workers. The sample contains 1,845 men and 1,089 women in 2001 and 2,390 men and 1,474 women in 2005. Annex table 3D.1 reports ordinary least squares (OLS) as well as selectivity corrected earnings equations for 2001 and 2005. Selection into labor force participation is accounted for using the methods advocated in Annex table 3A.2.

The question of selection will be discussed before turning to the main results. As indicated by the coefficients on the selection correction terms (Mills ratios) in the Heckman versions of the different models,[14] selection into labor force participation does not appear to be an issue here: the correction terms are never significantly different from zero for men and for women for both years. In other words, the mechanism of allocation between the two groups (individuals for whom individual earnings can be computed versus other individuals) does not affect earnings significantly. As a result, the different coefficients on the human capital variables are only marginally modified from OLS to Heckman equations. The focus is now on the OLS estimates.

Annex table 3D.1 shows evidence of significant and positive returns to human capital variables for both sexes and years. The coefficients on the three education dummies highlight an increasing premium to schooling attainment in reference to the category of workers with no schooling or incomplete primary education. There are some differences across gender and years, however. First, in 2001, education returns are always larger for men than for women, in particular at low and high levels of schooling attainment. This pattern holds true in 2005, except that education of female workers who had achieved the first cycle of secondary schooling is given more value than that of their male counterparts. The experience-earnings profile is found to be slightly concave for both men and women (that is, increasing, but less and less as workers age), with slightly greater returns for men in 2001. In 2005, the reverse pattern for experience is observed, however, with greater return for women. This difference between 2001 and 2005 may in part reflect the increased labor market participation of women over this period, which may have accrued the market value of experience of those women already working relative to new entrants. Indeed, a strong increase of inexperienced workers in the labor market would presumably have the consequence of enhancing the average returns to experience.

Among the other regressors introduced in the earnings functions, vocational training received in school appears to be an important determinant of earnings for both men and women. Training is indeed likely to increase workers' productivity. For this reason, Weichselbaumer and Winter-Ebmer (2005) have shown that omitting it in wage equations by gender can result in serious biases in the calculation of the unexplained component of the gender wage gap.[15] The fact of being married positively affects the earnings of men in 2005 only while it has no impact on earnings elsewhere. In developed country data, marriage is usually found to have a positive impact on earnings, at least for men (Korenman and Neumark 1991). However, the insignificant impact of marriage for females is also an expected result when such a cross-sectional dataset is used (Korenman and Neumark 1992).[16]

Earnings equations were estimated for each of the three wage employment sectors using both OLS and Lee's method to correct for sectoral selection (Annex tables 3D.2 to 3D.4). A first result worth noting is that correcting for selectivity into the public sector is significant for men only (table 3D.2), while sectoral selection does not appear to affect the distribution of earnings in the two other wage employment sectors (private formal and informal). The only exception is for women in the informal wage sector in 2005 (table 3D.4). The significant negative effect of the selection term in this equation means that women's unobserved characteristics that positively affect their probability of participating in the informal wage sector in 2005 also influence their earnings levels, but negatively.

In the public sector, once sectoral selection is accounted for, the returns to education are almost null for both men and women. This may be the result of high entry costs into the public sector, where earnings differentials have no direct relationship with educational attainment. In other words, earnings in this sector are probably determined by a number of factors orthogonal to productive ability, so that the returns to education have a different interpretation in this sector than in the private ones.[17] Still, we rely on the OLS estimates in the following analysis (decompositions) given that sample selection does not appear to be an issue for women, and so as to preserve perfect comparability across the other sectors of the analysis where selection appears to be mostly insignificant.

Turning to the OLS estimates in the formal public and private sectors, one sees that returns to education are higher for men in 2001, while the reverse is true in 2005, which is consistent with the previous finding using aggregate equations. In the informal wage sector, returns are greater for men in both years, especially at low and high levels of educational attainment.

Non-Farm Self-Employment. For the non-farm self-employed (Annex table 3D.5), the specification of the earnings equations is slightly different. Indeed, there are many other aspects deemed to influence self-employed workers' earnings other than their demographic characteristics and human capital endowments. We believe it is important to account for the micro-firm attributes, because they arguably constitute crucial determinants of the dispersion of earnings in self-employment. For that purpose, two variables were included: the first one indicates the eventual number of employees in the informal production unit, while the second is a measure of the value of physical capital used in the workers' activity.[18] Two comments are in order.

First, the two measures of the microfirm attributes are highly significant and exert a positive effect on the selfemployed earnings differentials. This is an expected effect as they act as production factors in the earnings determination. Interestingly enough, greater microfirm attribute returns were observed for men in 2001 and for women in 2005.

Second, returns to self-employed workers' education are significant and positive even after taking into account the micro-firm effects on earnings. However, returns are systematically higher for women in 2001, while in 2005 they are higher for men at the intermediate level of schooling.

To summarize, the results on earnings determination across gender point to a number of stylized facts:

- Not surprisingly, human capital variables, particularly education, are strong predictors of earnings for both men and women and across years.
- This holds true across sectors of activity. In particular, returns to education are high in the non-farm self-employment sector, notably for higher levels of education and for women in both years.

- However, returns vary markedly across sectors and years and no clear sectoral or dynamic pattern emerges from the study data.
- In line with similar work on Africa using different data sources (for example, Kuepie, Nordman, and Roubaud 2009; Nordman and Wolff, 2009a, 2009b; Söderbom et al. 2006), the study results suggest that marginal returns to education are non-constant with a convex profile, that is, increasing with the level of education.[19]
- The experience-earnings profile is found to be slightly concave for wage employment for both men and women, with somewhat greater returns for men in 2001, while the reverse is observed in 2005.
- Earnings functions for non-farm self-employed workers provide evidence that the quantity of labor and the amount of physical capital used in their activity are important determinants of their earnings. The study finds greater returns to these production factors for men in 2001, while a reverse pattern to the advantage of women is observed in 2005.

The results presented in this section are interesting in that they highlight gender-specific earnings determination processes. In particular, these estimates point to possible explanations of the differences in the earnings levels of men and women. As mentioned previously, the gender gap may be a result of differences in the rewards for human capital attributes, but also may result from differences in average human capital characteristics across gender. The earnings equation analysis conducted above indicates that returns to attributes differ between genders, but the analysis is unable to provide a synthetic decomposition of these different effects. This decomposition will be carried out in the following section.

Gender Earnings Gaps Decomposition. Gender earnings gap decompositions are presented in turn for wage and non-wage employment based on the OLS earnings equations estimates presented in the previous section.

Wage Employment. Annex table 3E.1 reports the decomposition of the gender gap for wage earnings in 2001 and 2005 based on OLS estimations of the earnings equations. Indeed, given that sample selection did not appear to be a major issue in the previous section, the OLS estimations are preferred.[20] Two specifications are considered for the earnings equations. The first corresponds to the specification presented in the previous section, where explanatory variables are limited to human capital endowments (education, experience, and training), sociodemographics (marital status, ethnic group, religion), and geographical dummies indicating place of residence. In the second specification, variables describing job characteristics are added. They include dummies characterizing the type of occupation (executive, skilled worker, or unskilled worker) and the nature of employment (permanent or temporary). Since it is debatable whether job characteristics such as occupation should be taken into account in earnings equations, we chose to introduce them in a separate decomposition. Indeed, controlling for occupation in earnings equations by sex amounts to considering the possibility of occupational segregation across gender and, for instance, the existence of high-paying occupations for men and low-paying occupations for women. The difficulty, however, is to establish whether these occupational outcomes are the result of discrimination practices of the employer or of gender-specific occupational choices.

In 2001, differences in socio-demographic characteristics, human capital endowments, and geographical location explain 68.6 percent of the raw hourly earnings gap using Neumark's decomposition rule. Human capital endowments explain up to 51.3 percent. Among human capital variables, it is the difference in educational attainment that explains most of the gap (about 30 percent). This result stems from the fact that education returns are positive and that men have on average more education than women. The distribution of experience and training between genders also contributes positively to explaining the earnings gap, but at a much lower level than education.

Surprisingly, including job characteristics, such as occupation and terms of employment, actually leads to a small decrease of the explained share of the gap from 68.6 percent to 66.5 percent using Neumark's decomposition. As pointed out earlier, it is unclear whether the employment status is an outcome of employer practice or of individual choice and productivity differences. In other words, the share explained by job characteristics could be at least in part attributable to occupational segregation.

In 2005, the decomposition varies according to the specification of the earnings equation. Not taking into account occupation, the explained share of the gap amounts to 37.5 percent. This is an important decrease compared to the same decomposition computed for 2001, where the explained share of the gap attains 68.6 percent. This fall in the explained share is principally explained by the significant decrease in the explanatory power of human capital variables in 2005, in particular, education and professional experience. These two variables explain, indeed, only 11.2 percent and 9.9 percent, respectively, of the gender earnings gap in 2005, whereas the respective proportions are 30.1 percent and 13.7 percent in 2001.

Introducing job characteristics increases the explained share up to 61.7 percent in 2001, a figure similar to that obtained for 2001. Among other observables, job characteristics explain 41.2 percent of the gap, hence much more than in 2001 where this proportion is only 23.8 percent.

The other significant contribution to explaining the earnings gap comes from the distribution of human capital endowments: the gender difference in endowments contributes to 14.9 percent of the gap. However, among human capital variables, education no longer is the main contributor.

Wage Employment By Sector. The Malagasy labor market is characterized by the coexistence of different types of wage employment sectors with different entry, exit, and wage-setting rules. As noted earlier, the hourly gender gap appears negative (that is, in favor of women) in the public sector in 2001 and relatively high in the informal wage employment sector for both years. Several results emerge from the decomposition of earnings by sector and for each surveyed year (Annex table 3E.2).

First, in any given wage employment sector, the gap is lower than the average gap over all wage employment sectors (except for informal wage employment in 2001), a possible indication of nonrandom gender allocation between wage employment sectors.

Second, the share of explained gap varies across sectors and years. In particular, looking at the decompositions without job characteristics, the patterns are somewhat different across the two years, especially for the formal sectors. For instance, while human capital endowments positively explain the gender gap in 2001 in the public sector, the pattern is reversed in 2005 as the contribution of human capital to the gender gap shifts sign and becomes negative. In other words, women have more favorable human capital characteristics in 2005 than in 2001 in the public sector (on average, women in the public sector are actually more educated than men in 2005). As for the informal wage sector, the explained share of the gap falls dramatically between the two years. This fall in the explained share probably reveals a greater heterogeneity in earnings or greater unobserved heterogeneity among the sample of workers in this sector in 2005, or both. This result, of course, may be interpreted in light of the several shocks endured by the labor market between 2002 and 2005, a period where the explanatory power of traditional human capital attributes as determinants of earnings has declined.

Third, job characteristics contribute positively to explaining the gaps in most sectors, and the explained share of the gaps generally increases with the inclusion of job characteristics in the earnings equations. The only exceptions are the informal wage sector in 2001, where job characteristics add nothing to the explanation of the gap and, more importantly, the formal wage sector in 2005, where the explained portion actually decreases from 43.7 percent to 21.0 percent once occupations and terms of employment are accounted for. This finding is somewhat difficult to explain and may be a result of the fact that occupational distribution across gender is already partly the result of differences in educational attainment, therefore possibly creating colinearity issues in the earnings equations that include both human capital and job characteristics. More confidence can then be put into the decompositions that do not include job characteristics, especially where the results are difficult to interpret.

Full Decomposition. As mentioned in the previous section, the fact that the gap in any given wage employment sector is usually lower than the aggregate gap suggests that gender location between sectors is not random. This of course is expected, since observable characteristics determine sectoral allocation. For instance, more educated individuals tend to work in formal sectors, and this characteristic is not distributed evenly between genders. However, this gender-specific sectoral location could possibly also be the result of different effects of observable characteristics on sectoral location, a reflection either of choice or discrimination. In order to examine the contribution of different sectoral structures between men and women in Madagascar, we apply to our data sets a full decomposition approach developed by Appleton, Hoddinott, and Krishnan (1999), with the results shown in table 3.4.

As explained in Annex 3A.3-2, the first three terms of this full decomposition (A, B, and C) are similar to those found in the decompositions discussed previously (Neumark's) and account for the within-sector earnings gaps. The last three terms (D, E, and F) measure the difference in earnings resulting from differences in distribution of male and female workers in the different sectors. More precisely, the last two terms account for differences in earnings resulting from the deviations between predicted and actual sectoral compositions of men and women not accounted for by differences in characteristics.

Results from table 3.4 indicate that within-sector differences in earnings contribute to 71.6 percent of the gender gap in 2001. In 2005, this share is smaller but still represents 65.7 percent of the gap. Differences in character-istics account for more than half of that share in 2001, but account only for 15 percent in 2005. Given that the "non-discriminatory" wage structure is esti-mated on the pooled sample of men and women, it is possible to compare the "distance" between this non-discriminatory wage structure and the returns to individual characteristics for men on one hand (this term is interpreted as

Table 3.4 Full Decomposition of the Gender Wage Gap (OLS estimates)

	2001	%	2005	%
Raw wage gap	0.232	100	0.220	100
Difference due to within-sector differences in earnings attributable to				
A. Characteristics	0.090	38.7	0.020	8.9
B. Deviation in male returns	0.029	12.5	0.051	23.0
C. Deviation in female returns	0.047	20.4	0.074	33.8
Subtotal	**0.166**	**71.6**	**0.145**	**65.7**
Difference due to differences between sectoral location attributable to				
D. Characteristics	0.079	34.1	0.069	31.2
E. Deviation in effect of characteristics on male location	−0.004	−1.9	0.002	1.1
F. Deviation in effect of characteristics on female location	−0.009	−3.9	0.005	2.0
Subtotal	**0.066**	**28.3**	**0.076**	**34.3**

Sources: Madagascar EPM 2001, 2005; authors' calculations.

"nepotism"[21]), and the distance between this non-discriminatory wage structure and returns to individual characteristics for women (the so-called "pure
discrimination") on the other hand. The study results suggest that both "nepotism" and "pure discrimination," using the terminology of Neumark (1988, see
Annex 3A.4-1), contribute to the unexplained component of the gap, however,
with a bigger share explained by the latter: the contribution of the deviation in
females' return (C) to the unexplained share of the gender gap appears indeed
higher than the contribution of the deviation in males' return (B).

However, the results also show that gender-specific sectoral location explains
a significant share of the gender-earnings gap in both years. This is highlighted
by the positive sums of the last three terms (D + E + F) for both years, which
suggest that the differences in sectoral location are more favorable to men
than to women. The gender earnings gap would have been 28.3 percent and
34.3 percent smaller, respectively, for 2001 and 2005, if men and women had
been "equally" distributed across the three sectors. These results are driven by
the fact that the proportion of women is higher in both years in the informal
wage employment sector where earnings are lower. Moreover, the increase in the
sectoral location effect between the two years (from 28 percent to 34 percent)
reflects the greater proportion of women in the lower-paying wage sector in
2005 compared to 2001 (67 percent versus 59 percent of female wage workers).

Finally, the decomposition of the contribution of the sectoral location further
indicates that characteristics explain an important part of sectoral location both
in 2001 and in 2005. In other words, the study results suggest that sectoral location differences are mostly attributable to differences in characteristics and not
to difference in returns. This is apparent in the very small values of terms E and
F in table 3.4. On the contrary, differences in returns account for an important
share of the difference in within-sector earnings, both through "nepotism" (B) and
"discrimination" (C). This stylized fact holds true across years, although the unexplained share of gap (B + C) appears to have increased between 2001 and 2005.

Non-Farm Self-Employment. As noted above, the gender gap in the non-farm
self-employment sector is much higher than in the wage employment sectors
in both years. This stems in part from the way earnings from self-employment
are computed, because income of nonfarm enterprises was attributed entirely
to the head of the enterprise. Male-owned enterprises are more likely to have
at least one additional worker (the wife of the firm owner) than female-owned
enterprises. Indeed, descriptive statistics confirm that microfirms owned by
women are on average much smaller than those owned by men. What follows
takes into account these differences in the decomposition of the earnings gap
by including firm characteristics as determinants of the earnings equations.

As noted in the introduction, interpreting the unexplained part of the gender
earnings gap solely by discriminatory practices against women is even more

hazardous for non-wage activities than for wage work, since "classical" discrimination by employers should not be weighted on self-employed workers. However, these workers could face discriminatory practices in access to physical capital or from their clients.

Two specifications are considered for the earnings functions: the first includes individual and firm level productive characteristics, while in the second, dummies indicating the branch of activity are added. The decomposition results presented in Annex table 3E.3 reveal two things.

First, observable characteristics—both at individual and firm levels—explain most of the observed gap. Including the branch of activity results in a dramatic decrease in the unexplained share of the gap, from 42.9 percent to 21.3 percent in 2001 and from 41.0 percent to 15.8 percent in 2005. Second, differences in human capital endowment explain some of the gender gap, but much less than firm-level characteristics: using the first specification, firm-level characteristics in 2001 explain 47.1 percent of the gap vs. 16.3 percent for human capital endowment; in 2005, the respective contributions are 26.9 percent vs. 18.8 percent. Both the number of employees and the amount of capital invested in the firm appear to explain a significant part of the gap.

These results suggest that including firm-level characteristics is important to properly decompose the gender earnings gap in the non-farm self-employment sector. They also point to a potential source of "discrimination" often ignored in the gender earnings gap literature, which is access to physical capital (whether through gender-biased inheritance rules or through discrimination in credit lending practices).[22]

Summary and Concluding Remarks

This chapter examined two aspects of labor market performance of men and women in Madagascar in 2001 and 2005: (1) participation and sectoral allocation and (2) earnings. Several results that emerged are as follows.

Regarding labor allocation, participation of women in the Malagasy labor market appears to be high, and it increased between 2001 and 2005. Overall, the structure of employment changed between 2001 and 2005. The evolution in employment status can be explained in part by some of the shocks experienced by the Malagasy labor market between 2001 and 2005, namely massive layoffs and reduction of subcontracted self-employment in the textile sector.

The study found a strong positive impact of education on the probability of getting a paid job, for both men and women. This effect also increases with education level. For men and women alike, education has the strongest positive impact on the probability of accessing the public sector, followed by private formal wage employment and, finally, informal self-employment. Interestingly, education seems to be more favorable to obtaining a self-employed job in the informal sector, rather than a salaried job in this sector. This result is consistent with the concept of dynamic entrepreneurship in the informal self-employment sector (Maloney 2004), where entrepreneurial skills would be needed, as opposed to the informal salaried sector, which would be more reflective of hidden unemployment or a stepping stone toward better labor market opportunities in the future.

Regarding gender inequality in earnings, the results show that the average gender wage gap (that is, for wage workers, including farm employment) is relatively small and stable over time. In non-farm self-employment, however, the gap is much higher and declined between 2001 and 2005. Earnings equations estimates indicate that human capital is an important determinant of earnings for both men and women and across employment sectors. However, returns to human capital vary markedly across sectors and years, and no clear sectoral or dynamic pattern emerges from the data.

Decomposition of the gender wage gap shows that differences in individual characteristics of men and women account for almost 70 percent of the gap in 2001. However, this share is down to less than 40 percent in 2005. When also taking into account job characteristics of men and women, differences in individual endowments and job characteristics across gender explain more than 60 percent of the gap, and this share remains stable over time.

Across wage employment sectors, the gender gap appears to be lowest in the public sector and highest in the informal sector. Using full sectoral decomposition techniques, the study provides evidence that gender-specific sectoral location explains a significant share of the gender wage gap in both years. This result is mainly driven by the fact that the proportion of women is higher in the self-employed sector, where earnings are lower. In long-term perspective, the main characteristic of the Malagasy labor market evolution was the partial freeze on public sector recruitment from the mid-1980s, which went hand in hand with a drop in the numbers of wage earners and an underlying rise in job precariousness. The decrease in jobs in the public sector was particularly significant for women (Antoine et al. 2000), which then probably worsened women's economic position as more women moved from the public to the private sector.

Augmented earnings equations estimates carried out for the non-farm self-employment sector suggest that the gap in this sector is driven by the very unequal distribution of microfirm attributes between men and women. This result points to a potential source of "discrimination" often ignored in the gender gap literature, which is access to physical capital, whether through gender-biased inheritance rules or discrimination in credit lending practices.

Between 2001 and 2005, Madagascar experienced several large-scale shocks. Although these shocks had different effects on labor market participation of men and women, the gender wage gap remained relatively small and stable over time. The contribution of differences in returns to attributes, however, did increase. This increase could be related to increased competition for fewer available wage jobs. This evolution did not result in an increase in the gender wage gap, because most productive characteristics of male and female wage workers converged between the two years.

From a policy perspective, given the multifaceted aspect of gender disparities in the Malagasy labor market, efforts to reduce the gender earnings gap will entail various types of policy changes:

- First, differences in human capital endowments must be reduced: If human capital characteristics of women and men were similar, the gender earnings gap would be reduced by at least a third. This would entail further efforts to enhance girls' schooling achievements, particularly at higher levels.

- However, differences in individual characteristics do not explain the full difference between men's and women's earnings. Although the unexplained share of the difference cannot be fully attributed to discrimination, further reduction of the gender gap would probably entail policies aimed at promoting women's access to quality jobs in the public and formal wage sectors, as well as policies to foster equal pay for equal jobs.

- Finally, the very large gaps observed in the non-farm self-employment sector—and the fact that these gaps are in large part explained by differences in microfirm characteristics—suggest that efforts must be made to allow women informal entrepreneurs to access physical capital. This source of earning differential is often ignored in the gender gap literature. Whether it arises because of gender-biased inheritance rules, through discrimination in credit lending practices, or just because of different individual reinvestment choices is an empirical question that should be further investigated. From a policy perspective, this result suggests that micro-credit directed specifically at groups of women should be a part of any policy package designed to reduce gender differences.

Finally, from a methodological perspective, some comments are in order. The earnings models used in the decomposition analysis of this study account for no more than 40 percent of the variation in the earnings of men and women. This means that an important variation in earnings remains unexplained by the observed workers' characteristics. The models might then be better fitted to the data by including other variables deemed to influence earnings. Typically, the data used come from household surveys. For a long time, researchers have been unable to document the potential effect of job and firm characteristics—other than industry and firm size—on the wages of men and women. Still, this study provides a first attempt to account for other determinants of individual earnings, in particular micro-firm attributes of the self-employed workers. But for wage workers, linked employer-employee surveys would allow researchers and policy makers to move beyond the individual worker to consider the importance of the workplace in wage determination. There is much to learn about the demand-side factors that may influence employers' decisions concerning hiring and promotions or use gender to predict future work commitment.

Annex 3A Concepts and Methods

3A.1 Concepts (Council of Economic Advisers 1998)

Gender discrimination may take a variety of forms, from practices that reduce the chances that a woman will be hired to differences in pay for men and women who work side by side doing the same tasks equally well. There are a variety of theories about how and why women face discrimination in the labor market. An employer may dislike female employees or underestimate their abilities, customers may dislike female employees or underestimate their abilities, or male co-workers may resent working with women. These attitudes may not be directed toward all workers, but may only focus on women in higher status occupations. For example, male employees may not object to having women work for them but may object when women are their superiors. In addition, employers may engage in what is called "statistical discrimination," meaning that they assume an individual woman has the average characteristics of all women. For example, because women on average have higher turnover rates than men, an employer may assume that a given female job candidate is more likely to leave the firm than a similar male candidate.

Following the seminal contributions of Oaxaca (1973) and Blinder (1973), the measure of the degree of discrimination faced by women is often based on a decomposition of the gender pay gap between an "explained" gap and an "unexplained" gap. The explained gap is the gap that can be attributed to differences between male and female labor-related attributes (education, experience, etc.) while the unexplained portion of the pay gap is often interpreted as the result of discrimination. In this view, once differences between men and women in the relevant determinants of wages are taken into account, any remaining difference in pay must be because of discrimination. But this explanation may be too simplistic. To the extent that discrimination affects women's education, job, and family choices, the "unexplained" differential will understate the true effect of discrimination. And, to the extent that an analyst cannot adequately measure all the determinants of wages using available data, there may be significant unmeasured labor market skills that differ between men and women. For example, if women's labor market experience is less likely to be continuous (for example, because of childbearing), then just controlling for years of work may not fully control for the differential effects of experience on male and female wages. In this case, the "unexplained" differential will overstate the true effect of discrimination, because it includes the effect of relevant unmeasured factors that influence the relative productivity of male and female employees.

We now discuss the econometric methods used for earnings determination and decomposition in this study. First, the chosen specifications for earnings determination are presented, then the sample selection issue is discussed in the context of sectoral choice, and, finally, different decomposition techniques traditionally used for analyzing the gender earnings gaps are presented.

3A.2 Earnings Determination

Let the earning function take the form:

$$\ln w_i = \beta x_i + \varepsilon_i \qquad (3A.1)$$

where $\ln w_i$ is the natural logarithm of the observed hourly earnings for individual i, x_i is a vector of observed characteristics, β is a vector of coefficients, and ε_i is a disturbance term with an expected value of zero.

We estimate the log earning functions separately for men and women, and also for the different sectors. There is no universally accepted set of conditioning variables that should be included for describing the causes of gender labor market outcome differentials. Yet, the consensus is that controls for productivity-related factors, such as education, labor market experience, and marital status, should be included. However, it is debatable whether job characteristics, occupation, and industry should be taken into account: if employers differentiate between men and women through their tendency to hire into certain occupations, then occupational assignment is an outcome of employer practices rather than an outcome of individual choice or productivity differences.[23]

Also incorporated in the earnings functions are a few dummy variables aimed at capturing the worker's specific human capital (vocational training received in school), religion (Catholic versus other religion), ethnicity (Merina, the dominant ethnic group, versus other ethnic groups), and place of residence (a dummy for urban versus rural, and six indicators of provinces of residence). These last dummies are expected to capture spatial specificities in earnings determination: first, they capture price differences across regions, which are significant given that weak infrastructures prevent the integration of regional markets for goods and labor; second, there are also important differences across regions in terms of economic and social development; and third, labor market regulations are different across regions given that regulating institutions are in part decentralized.

Education, a main variable in this study, is split into four dummies indicating the schooling level attained by workers, namely no schooling or incomplete primary education; beyond primary education (that is, primary achieved but first cycle of secondary education incomplete); beyond first cycle of secondary education (that is, incomplete second cycle of secondary school); and beyond secondary education (or higher education). Recent empirical literature on the returns to education in Africa has indeed shown that the marginal returns to schooling are nonlinear,[24] with a convex profile, that is, increasing with the level of education. Using a series of dummy variables instead of a continuous variable for the years of schooling better allows for this nonlinearity in the returns to education.

In this chapter, it is not possible to account for the workers' actual experience in the labor market, but only for potential experience that can be viewed as reflecting the "gross" time that individuals have spent while in the labor force (measured as age minus years of schooling minus six—the legal age at school entry). This is a possible limitation of this study, because, as argued in the empirical literature, differences in labor force attachment across gender are important to explain the extent of the gender wage gap. Indeed, measures of women's work experience are particularly prone to error, given women's discontinuity in labor market participation (for child care, for instance). Using proxy measures such as potential experience may lead to overestimating the amount of experience for women, while it might be a good approximation of true experience for men with higher labor force attachment. Nordman and Roubaud (2009) show for Madagascar, however, that the corresponding potential bias in the estimates of the returns to experience depends on the institutional sector and on whether other labor force attachment variables can also be controlled for (the number of work interruptions, unemployment periods, spells of inactivity, and so on). In the absence of such measures, potential experience might be a better proxy than the solely used actual experience, since including this variable may introduce an additional endogeneity problem in the estimation of the earnings function.[25]

The study also estimates earnings functions for the category of self-employed workers.[26] Apart from the probability of greater measurement errors, estimating earnings with standard human capital wage functions for these workers is problematic as a result of other factors not being taken into account in the equation, such as the amount of capital or access to credit, which are likely to have a significant impact on their incomes. This is the reason why, for modeling their earnings, additional regressions were performed, including the log of value of capital and number of potential employees used in their activity.

3A.3 Sample Selection

Concerns arise over possible sample selection bias in the estimations. Strictly speaking, there are two sources of selectivity bias involved. One arises from the fact that wage earners are only observed when they work, and not everyone is working. The second comes from the selective decision to engage in public wage employment rather than private wage employment or the informal sector. We use Heckman's two-step procedure to address the first issue. In the first stage, probit estimates of the probability of participation are separately performed for men and women. Then the appropriate estimated correction term (Inverse Mills Ratios, IMR) is included in the second-stage earnings equations, for men and women, respectively. The inclusion of the correction term ensures that the OLS gives consistent estimates of the augmented earnings functions.

One way to account for the second issue is to determine whether the returns to characteristics of a wage-earner differ from one institutional sector to another. However, given the overrepresentation of men in the public sector in both years 2001 and 2005, the decision to work in a particular sector may not be determined exogenously. Apart from the observed characteristics discussed above, this decision may correlate with unobserved characteristics. We use Lee's two-stage approach to take into account the possible effect of endogenous selection in different sectors on earnings (Lee 1983). In the first stage, multinomial logit models of individual i's participation in sector j are used to compute the correction terms λ_{ij} from the predicted probabilities P_{ij}. The appropriate correction term is then included in the respective earnings equation as an additional regressor in the second stage.[27]

Lee's method has been criticized recently because it relies on a strong assumption regarding the joint distribution of error terms of the equations of interest (see Bourguignon, Fournier, and Gurgand 2007). However, the existing alternative methods we tried, such as Dubin and McFadden's or Dahl's, did not appear more efficient given the limited size of our sectoral subsamples.[28] Another potential problem is that the multinomial logit may suffer from the Independence of Irrelevant Alternatives (IIA) assumption, which, in most cases, is questionable. We perform Hausman-type tests proposed by Hausman and McFadden (1984) which all provide evidence that the IIA assumption is not violated for both the male and female samples.

A multinomial logit model with five categories is then specified. It includes nonparticipation in paid employment (as the base category), public wage employment, private formal wage employment, private informal wage employment, and self-employed workers. In both Heckman's and Lee's procedures, identification is achieved by the inclusion of three additional individual variables in the first stage selection equations, which are omitted in the second stage earnings regressions: the log income of other household members, the log of the surface of land potentially owned by the worker, and the log of the individual's value of potential livestock. The assumption is that these variables have arguably no reason to influence earnings level because these incomes stem from non-agricultural activities. For women and men alike, these instruments do appear to be strong predictors of both participation and sector choice. Relying on the distributional assumptions of the selection correction models, we tested the appropriateness of this identification strategy using Wald tests of joint significance of the identifying variables in the first stage and insignificance in the second stage of the analysis for men and women in the different sectors. The tests highlight the appropriateness of their choice as excluding conditions.[29]

3A.4 Gender Earnings Gap Decomposition Techniques

3A.4-1 Oaxaca and Neumark's Traditional Earnings Decompositions. The most common approach to identifying sources of gender wage gaps is the Oaxaca-Blinder decomposition. Two separate standard Mincerian log earnings equations are estimated for men and women. The Oaxaca decomposition is:

$$\overline{\ln w_m} - \overline{\ln w_f} = \beta_m(\bar{x}_m - \bar{x}_f) + (\beta_m - \beta_f)\bar{x}_f \qquad (3A.2)$$

where w_m and w_f are the means of men's and women's earnings, respectively; x_m and x_f are vectors containing the respective means of the independent variables for men and women; and β_m and β_f are the estimated coefficients. The first term on the right-hand side captures the earnings differential due to different characteristics of men and women. The second term is the earnings gap attributable to different returns to those characteristics or coefficients.

It can be argued that, under discrimination, men are paid competitive wages but women are underpaid. If this is the case, the male coefficients should be taken as the non-discriminatory wage structure, as in equation 3A.2. Conversely, if employers pay women competitive wages but pay men more (nepotism), then the female coefficients should be used as the nondiscriminatory wage structure. Therefore, the issue is how to determine the wage structure β^* that would prevail in the absence of discrimination. This choice poses the well-known index number problem, given that we could use either the male or the female wage structure as the nondiscriminatory benchmark. While, a priori, there is no preferable alternative, the decomposition can be quite sensitive to the selection made. The literature has proposed different weighting schemes to deal with the underlying index problem (Cotton 1988; Oaxaca 1973; Reimers, 1983). We use that of Neumark (1988), who proposes a general decomposition of the gender wage differential such that:

$$\overline{\ln w_m} - \overline{\ln w_f} = \beta^*(\bar{x}_m - \bar{x}_f) + [(\beta_m - \beta^*)\bar{x}_m + (\beta^* - \beta_f)\bar{x}_f] \qquad (3A.3)$$

This decomposition can be reduced to Oaxaca's two special cases if it is assumed that there is no discrimination in the male wage structure, that is, $\beta^* = \beta_m$, or if it is assumed that $\beta^* = \beta_f$. Neumark shows that β^* can be estimated using the weighted average of the wage structures of men and women, and Neumark advocates using the pooled sample to estimate β^*. The first term is the gender wage gap attributable to differences in characteristics. The second and the third terms capture the difference between the actual and pooled returns for men and women, respectively.

While the improvement proposed by Neumark's decomposition is attractive, it fails to account for differences in sectoral structures between gender groups. This is why we also turn to Appleton, Hoddinott, and Krishnan's (1999) sectoral decomposition.

3A.4-2 A Full Sectoral Decomposition. This decomposition technique takes into account sectoral structures between genders. Appleton, Hoddinott, and Krishnan (1999) adopt a similar approach to that of Neumark and decompose the gender earnings gap into three components. Since this technique is based on Neumark's decomposition, it does not suffer from the index number problem encountered by previous authors who attempted to account for differences in occupational choices (Brown, Moon, and Zoloth 1980). Let $\bar{W}_m$ and $\bar{W}_f$ be the means of the natural logs of male and female earnings, and $\bar{P}_{mj}$ and $\bar{P}_{fj}$ be the sample proportions of men and women in sector j, respectively. Similarly to Neumark (1988), Appleton, Hoddinott, and Krishnan (1999) assume a sectoral structure that would prevail in the absence of gender differences in the impact of characteristics on sectoral choice ($\bar{P}_j^*$, the proportion of employees in sector j under this common structure). They then decompose the difference in proportions employed in three sectors such that

$$\bar{W}_m - \bar{W}_f = \sum_{j=1}^{3} \bar{P}_j^*(\bar{W}_{mj} - \bar{W}_{fj}) + \sum_{j=1}^{3} \bar{W}_{mj}(\bar{P}_{mj} - \bar{P}_j^*) + \sum_{j=1}^{3} \bar{W}_{fj}(\bar{P}_j^* - \bar{P}_{fj}) \quad (3A.4)$$

A multinomial logit model is used to specify the selection process of an individual into the different sectors. If q_i is a vector of i's relevant characteristics, the probability of a worker i being in sector j is given by

$$P_{ij} = \exp(\gamma_{ij} q_i) / \sum_{j=1}^{3} \exp(\gamma_{ij} q_i) \quad \text{with } i = m,f$$

If the distribution of men and women across sectors is determined by the same set of coefficients γ_j^*, then the probability of a worker with characteristics q_i being in sector j is

$$P_{ij}^* = \exp(\gamma_j^* q_i) / \sum_{j=1}^{3} \exp(\gamma_j^* q_i)$$

Hence, by estimating pooled and separate multinomial logit models for men and women, it is possible to derive the average probability for male and female workers in the different sectors. These mean probabilities are denoted by $\bar{P}_{ij}^*$.

The relationship between γ^* and γ_i is similar to that of β^* and β_j in Neumark's decomposition. Embedding the self-selection process in equation (3A.4), the full decomposition can be written as follows:

$$
\begin{aligned}
\overline{W}_m - \overline{W}_f = {} & \sum_{j=1}^{3} \overline{P}_j^*(\overline{x}_{mj} - \overline{x}_{fj})\beta_j + \sum_{j=1}^{3} \overline{P}_j^*\overline{x}_{mj}(\beta_{mj} - \beta_j) \\
& + \sum_{j=1}^{3} \overline{P}_j^*\overline{x}_{fj}(\beta_j - \beta_{fj}) + \sum_{j=1}^{3} \overline{W}_{mj}(\overline{P}_{mj}^* - \overline{P}_j^*) \\
& + \sum_{j=1}^{3} \overline{W}_{fj}(\overline{P}_j^* - \overline{P}_{fj}^*) + \sum_{j=1}^{3} \overline{W}_{mj}(\overline{P}_{mj} - \overline{P}_{mj}^*) \\
& + \sum_{j=1}^{3} \overline{W}_{fj}(\overline{P}_{fj}^* - \overline{P}_{fj}) \qquad\qquad\qquad (3A.5)
\end{aligned}
$$

The first three terms are similar to Neumark's decompositions of within-sector earnings gaps. The fourth and fifth terms measure the difference in earnings resulting from differences in distribution of male and female workers in different sectors. The last two terms account for differences in earnings resulting from the deviations between predicted and actual sectoral compositions of men and women not accounted for by differences in characteristics.

Annex 3B Summary Statistics of the Variables Used in the Econometric Analysis

Table 3B.1 Summary Statistics of the Variables Used in the Labor Allocation Models

	2001		2005	
	Males (%)	Females (%)	Males (%)	Females (%)
Less than primary education	55.8	60.7	68.3	72.5
Beyond primary education	23.2	23.3	21.0	20.4
Beyond first cycle of secondary education	14.7	12.0	8.6	6.0
Beyond secondary education	6.3	4.0	2.1	1.2
Potential experience	22.5	22.7	24.3	24.1
Training	13.5	8.0	7.0	5.6
Married	60.0	54.4	60.8	57.9
Non-Christian	8.9	8.8	16.7	15.5
Merina	37.0	36.6	23.1	22.0
Urban	59.0	62.7	49.4	51.0
Observations	6,409	7,197	14,635	15,624

Sources: Madagascar EPM 2001, 2005; authors' calculations.
Note: Individuals aged 15 and older.

Table 3B.2 Summary Statistics of the Variables Used in the Earnings Equations

	Wage workers (%)				Non-farm self-employed workers (%)			
	2001		2005		2001		2005	
	Males	Females	Males	Females	Males	Females	Males	Females
Less than primary education	39.9	46.3	48.0	52.1	59.2	66.2	67.0	79.1
Beyond primary education	24.5	26.3	24.3	24.9	23.4	23.4	22.8	15.9
Beyond first cycle of secondary education	24.4	19.0	20.4	15.3	13.2	8.9	8.4	4.2
Beyond secondary education	11.2	8.4	7.3	7.7	4.2	1.5	1.8	0.8
Potential experience	23.1	21.4	23.8	22.7	n.a.	n.a.	n.a.	n.a.
Training	25.5	18.7	20.0	16.4	n.a.	n.a.	n.a.	n.a.
Married	74.2	47.8	75.0	53.1	86.7	56.5	90.1	54.8
Non-Christian	8.4	7.9	7.6	5.2	10.2	6.9	9.4	11.4
Merina	51.5	54.0	52.1	52.4	39.0	29.6	43.2	29.5
Urban	44.0	50.0	50.0	49.5	28.8	33.5	31.9	25.6
Number of employees	n.a.	n.a.	n.a.	n.a.	2.1	1.4	1.2	1.1
Value of capital	n.a.	n.a.	n.a.	n.a.	311 311	74 799	318 901	47 500
Observations	1,845	1,089	2,390	1,474	632	619	1,630	1,573

Sources: Madagascar EPM 2001, 2005; authors' calculations.
Note: Individuals aged 15 and older.
n.a. = not applicable for wage workers;
n.a. = not available for non-wage earners.

Annex 3C Determinants of Sectoral Allocation

Table 3C.1 Nature and Terms of Employment in Total Employment in Madagascar

	All (%)		Male (%)		Female (%)	
	2001	2005	2001	2005	2001	2005
Type of employment						
Public formal wage employment	3.9	2.7	5.3	3.6	2.4	1.8
Private formal wage employment	4.7	2.4	5.8	3.1	3.5	1.7
Private informal wage employment	9.6	9.5	11.5	10.8	7.5	8.1
Self-employed	44.3	37.8	55.0	57.4	33.0	17.8
Family workers	37.4	47.7	22.4	25.1	53.5	70.6
Activity sector						
Primary production activity	73.9	80.4	72.5	79.8	75.3	81.1
Manufacturing	5.6	2.3	5.6	2.9	5.6	1.7
Electricity, gas, and water supply	1.1	0.2	2.0	0.3	0.1	0.0
Construction	0.7	1.3	0.7	2.5	0.6	0.1
Trade	6.1	5.3	3.9	3.9	8.5	6.8
Hotel and restaurants	1.2	0.7	0.8	0.7	1.5	0.8
Transport, storage, and communications	1.8	0.9	3.4	1.7	0.0	0.0
Financial and business activities	0.1	0.1	0.1	0.1	0.0	0.0

Public administration	3.7	2.5	4.4	3.2	2.9	1.7
Other services	5.6	3.6	5.7	2.3	5.4	4.9
Education and health	0.4	0.3	0.8	0.7	0.0	0.0
Other	0.0	2.4	0.0	2.0	0.0	2.9
Occupation category						
Managers	3.2	1.5	4.3	2.0	1.9	0.9
Skilled employed	5.8	5.1	7.3	6.8	4.2	3.3
Unskilled employed	9.4	8.1	11.1	8.7	7.5	7.4
Self-employed	44.3	37.8	55.0	57.4	33.0	17.8
Family workers	37.4	47.7	22.4	25.1	53.5	70.6
Type of contract						
Permanent employment	82.6	85.2	82.9	86.2	82.2	84.2
Temporary employment	17.4	14.8	17.1	13.8	17.8	15.8

Sources: Madagascar EPM 2001, 2005.
Note: Individuals aged 15 and older.

Table 3C.2 Nature and Terms of Employment in Total Employment in Urban Areas

	All (%)		Male (%)		Female (%)	
	2001	2005	2001	2005	2001	2005
Type of employment						
Public formal wage employment	10.2	7.4	12.7	9.2	7.3	5.4
Private formal wage employment	12.7	8.3	14.9	10.5	10.2	5.8
Private informal wage employment	19.7	20.8	21.7	22.3	17.5	19.2
Self-employed	35.1	31.7	37.1	41.3	32.9	20.9
Family workers	22.4	31.9	13.7	16.8	32.2	48.8
Activity sector						
Primary production activity	37.4	45.8	36.4	43.5	38.5	48.3
Manufacturing	12.9	7.1	13.2	8.6	12.6	5.3
Electricity, gas, and water supply	2.8	0.6	5.1	1.1	0.2	0.1
Construction	1.5	4.0	1.9	7.4	1.0	0.2
Trade	14.1	14.5	9.5	10.9	19.4	18.4
Hotel and restaurants	2.6	2.4	1.4	2.3	3.9	2.4
Transport, storage, and communications	4.4	3.0	8.1	5.5	0.1	0.2

Financial and business activities	0.4	0.2	0.5	0.3	0.2	0.2
Public administration	9.6	6.6	10.6	8.0	8.4	5.0
Other services	13.3	6.8	11.2	5.1	15.7	8.7
Education and health	1.1	0.7	2.1	1.4	0.1	0.0
Other	0.0	8.3	0.0	5.8	0.0	11.2
Occupation category						
Managers	8.4	4.7	10.8	5.8	5.4	3.4
Skilled employed	14.9	15.5	18.3	19.8	11.1	10.7
Unskilled employed	19.3	16.3	20.1	16.3	18.4	16.2
Self-employed	35.2	31.7	37.1	41.3	32.9	20.9
Family workers	22.4	31.9	13.7	16.8	32.2	48.8
Type of contract						
Permanent employment	78.8	86.7	79.3	87.7	78.1	85.6
Temporary employment	21.2	13.3	20.7	12.3	21.9	14.4

Sources: Madagascar EPM 2001, 2005.
Note: Individuals aged 15 and older.

Table 3C.3 Nature and Terms of Employment in Total Employment in Rural Areas

	All (%)		Male (%)		Female (%)	
	2001	2005	2001	2005	2001	2005
Type of employment						
Public formal wage employment	2.4	1.5	3.5	2.1	1.3	0.9
Private formal wage employment	2.8	0.9	3.6	1.1	2.0	0.7
Private informal wage employment	7.1	6.7	8.9	7.8	5.2	5.6
Self-employed	46.6	39.3	59.5	61.6	33.1	17.1
Family workers	41.1	51.6	24.6	27.3	58.5	75.7
Activity sector						
Primary production activity	82.8	89.0	81.7	89.3	83.9	88.8
Manufacturing	3.9	1.1	3.7	1.4	4.0	0.8
Electricity, gas, and water supply	0.7	0.0	1.3	0.1	0.1	0.0
Construction	0.5	0.6	0.4	1.2	0.5	0.1
Trade	4.2	3.1	2.5	2.1	6.0	4.1
Hotel and restaurants	0.8	0.3	0.7	0.3	0.9	0.4
Transport, storage, and communications	1.2	0.4	2.3	0.7	0.0	0.0

Financial and business activities	0.0	0.0	0.0	0.0	0.0	0.0
Public administration	2.2	1.4	2.8	1.9	1.6	0.9
Other services	3.7	2.8	4.3	1.6	3.0	4.0
Education and health	0.2	0.2	0.5	0.5	0.0	0.0
Other	0.0	1.0	0.0	1.0	0.0	0.9
Occupation category						
Managers	1.9	0.7	2.6	1.0	1.0	0.4
Skilled employed	3.5	2.5	4.6	3.4	2.4	1.5
Unskilled employed	6.9	6.0	8.8	6.7	5.0	5.3
Self-employed	46.6	39.3	59.5	61.6	33.1	17.1
Family workers	41.1	51.6	24.6	27.3	58.5	75.7
Type of contract						
Permanent employment	83.5	84.8	83.8	85.8	83.1	83.9
Temporary employment	16.5	15.2	16.2	14.2	16.9	16.1

Sources: Madagascar EPM 2001, 2005.
Note: Individuals aged 15 and older.

Table 3C.4 Determinants of Labor Allocation Across Paid Employment and Agricultural Self-Employment (Multinomial Logit Models)

	2001				2005			
	Males		Females		Males		Females	
	Paid employment	Agricultural self-employment	Paid employment	Agricultural self-employment	Paid employment	Agricultural self-employment	Paid employment	Agricultural self-employment
Beyond primary education	0.496***	-0.477***	0.389***	0.079	0.526***	0.007	0.446***	0.261**
(Reference category: no schooling or primary incomplete)	(4.56)	(-3.43)	(4.79)	(0.61)	(5.91)	(0.07)	(6.63)	(2.36)
Beyond first cycle of secondary education	0.561***	-1.175***	0.593***	-0.502*	0.685***	-0.626***	1.034***	-0.214
	(4.20)	(-5.68)	(5.85)	(-1.95)	(5.66)	(-4.130)	(10.76)	(-0.81)
Beyond secondary education	0.899***	-1.405***	0.636***	-0.852	1.173***	-0.631*	1.677***	-0.697
	(4.72)	(-3.44)	(4.16)	(-1.41)	(5.01)	(-1.82)	(9.01)	(-0.66)
Potential experience	0.222***	0.192***	0.186***	0.161***	0.273***	0.250***	0.199***	0.247***
	(20.40)	(15.77)	(22.46)	(15.14)	(30.16)	(31.24)	(28.72)	(28.75)
Potential experience squared	-0.004***	-0.003***	-0.003***	-0.002***	-0.004***	-0.003***	-0.003***	-0.003***
	(-20.14)	(-15.01)	(-19.65)	(-12.70)	(-27.67)	(-27.84)	(-24.79)	(-24.63)
Training	0.821***	-0.589***	1.139***	0.303	1.084***	-0.530***	1.077***	-0.180
	(6.21)	(-2.92)	(10.82)	(1.28)	(8.46)	(-3.38)	(12.04)	(-1.02)
Married	2.137***	3.379***	-0.817***	-0.921***	2.221***	3.689***	-1.398***	-2.864***
	(20.59)	(26.37)	(-11.34)	(-10.05)	(28.20)	(48.48)	(-23.32)	(-36.73)

	(1)	(2)	(3)	(4)	(5)	(6)	(7)	(8)
Non-Christian	0.259* (1.80)	−0.134 (−0.76)	0.058 (0.55)	0.067 (0.44)	−0.053 (−0.54)	0.084 (0.94)	−0.061 (−0.74)	0.004 (0.04)
Merina	0.350*** (2.64)	0.127 (0.66)	0.085 (0.87)	0.064 (0.35)	0.296** (2.46)	0.042 (0.31)	0.085 (0.93)	−0.251 (−1.635)
Urban	0.279*** (2.77)	−1.151*** (−10.35)	0.359*** (4.38)	−0.818*** (−8.41)	0.241*** (3.32)	−0.385*** (−5.52)	0.051 (0.86)	−0.267*** (−3.84)
Other household members earnings per capita (log)	0.022*** (4.81)	−0.075*** (−10.99)	0.021*** (5.79)	−0.037*** (−6.75)	0.046*** (10.85)	−0.072*** (−12.92)	0.043*** (13.69)	−0.043*** (−7.241)
Land area (log)	−0.048*** (−5.18)	0.060*** (6.72)	−0.055*** (−6.68)	0.051*** (6.91)	−0.093*** (−12.71)	0.313*** (18.54)	−0.087*** (−16.97)	0.188*** (11.31)
Livestock value (log)	−0.020*** (−4.45)	0.024*** (5.09)	−0.024*** (−6.50)	0.013*** (3.11)	−0.034*** (−10.04)	−0.003 (−0.982)	−0.030*** (−11.14)	−0.021*** (−6.412)
Constant	−4.012*** (−20.27)	−4.590*** (−17.24)	−3.570*** (−23.12)	−2.952*** (−12.40)	−4.382*** (−25.38)	−6.744*** (−32.25)	−3.265*** (−25.26)	−5.365*** (−23.78)
Observations	6,409		7,197		14,635		15,624	
Pseudo R-squared	0.49		0.20		0.55		0.27	

Sources: Madagascar EPM 2001, 2005.
Note: Individuals aged 15 and older. The multinomial logits are performed for each sex. The reference category is "Inactive – Unemployed – Family workers." Dummies for location are also included in the models.
Robust t statistics in parentheses.
* significant at 10%, ** significant at 5%, *** significant at 1%.

Table 3C.5 Determinants of Labor Allocation Across Sectors for Males (Multinomial Logit Models)

	2001					2005				
	Public employment	Private formal wage employment	Private informal wage employment	Private informal self-employment	Agricultural self-employment	Public employment	Private formal wage employment	Private informal wage employment	Private informal self-employment	Agricultural self-employment
Beyond primary education	1.528*** (7.79)	0.901*** (5.63)	0.174 (1.41)	0.410*** (2.89)	−0.418*** (−3.00)	1.410*** (8.75)	1.287*** (7.71)	0.169* (1.68)	0.610*** (5.42)	0.060 (0.63)
Beyond first cycle of secondary education	2.233*** (10.58)	1.151*** (6.36)	0.016 (0.10)	0.342** (1.97)	−0.997*** (−4.76)	2.696*** (15.20)	1.881*** (9.85)	−0.022 (−0.15)	0.467*** (2.93)	−0.372** (−2.37)
Beyond secondary education	3.169*** (11.89)	1.716*** (7.30)	−0.024 (−0.10)	0.501** (1.99)	−1.091*** (−2.65)	3.918*** (13.17)	2.860*** (9.35)	−0.172 (−0.57)	0.903*** (2.91)	−0.088 (−0.24)
Potential experience	0.341*** (15.12)	0.234*** (13.35)	0.203*** (15.14)	0.207*** (13.46)	0.195*** (15.91)	0.382*** (19.94)	0.344*** (16.79)	0.248*** (22.89)	0.263*** (21.31)	0.252*** (31.32)
Potential experience squared	−0.005*** (−13.21)	−0.004*** (−12.52)	−0.003*** (−15.11)	−0.003*** (−13.13)	−0.003*** (−15.08)	−0.005*** (−16.79)	−0.005*** (−14.19)	−0.004*** (−21.06)	−0.004*** (−19.27)	−0.003*** (−27.86)
Training	1.227*** (7.21)	1.182*** (7.55)	0.547*** (3.63)	0.674*** (4.14)	−0.561*** (−2.77)	1.724*** (10.68)	1.427*** (8.26)	0.948*** (6.65)	0.754*** (4.78)	−0.492*** (−3.09)
Married	2.708*** (12.17)	2.166*** (13.62)	1.917*** (15.47)	2.336*** (15.93)	3.357*** (26.26)	2.582*** (15.15)	2.247*** (13.36)	1.868*** (20.11)	2.735*** (23.79)	3.686*** (48.43)

Non-Christian	-0.098 (-0.41)	0.050 (0.24)	0.294* (1.86)	0.337* (1.84)	-0.154 (-0.87)	-0.293 (-1.55)	-0.353 (-1.63)	-0.088 (-0.76)	0.133 (1.08)	0.092 (1.03)
Merina	-0.354* (-1.81)	0.249 (1.42)	0.433*** (2.87)	0.578*** (3.37)	0.103 (0.54)	-0.222 (-1.21)	0.062 (0.33)	0.279** (2.08)	0.610*** (4.09)	0.066 (0.48)
Urban	0.122 (0.70)	0.547*** (3.34)	0.238** (2.01)	0.227* (1.67)	-1.163*** (-10.43)	0.046 (0.35)	0.880*** (5.32)	0.083 (0.99)	0.434*** (4.49)	-0.361*** (-5.16)
Other household members earnings per capita (log)	0.012* (1.77)	0.012* (1.91)	0.044*** (8.37)	-0.009 (-1.52)	-0.077*** (-11.21)	0.021*** (3.06)	0.038*** (5.28)	0.073*** (15.74)	-0.004 (-0.78)	-0.079*** (-14.02)
Land area (log)	-0.045*** (-2.59)	-0.071*** (-4.34)	-0.043*** (-3.80)	-0.044*** (-3.39)	0.061*** (6.80)	-0.091*** (-8.21)	-0.103*** (-9.00)	-0.094*** (-11.90)	-0.083*** (-9.13)	0.314*** (18.57)
Livestock value (log)	-0.011 (-1.39)	-0.019*** (-2.62)	-0.019*** (-3.56)	-0.025*** (-4.03)	0.024*** (5.13)	-0.030*** (-5.12)	-0.045*** (-6.67)	-0.031*** (-7.94)	-0.038*** (-8.57)	-0.004 (-1.08)
Constant	-8.891*** (-20.92)	-6.199*** (-19.90)	-4.282*** (-18.50)	-5.466*** (-19.60)	-4.641*** (-17.34)	-9.329*** (-25.97)	-8.361*** (-23.57)	-4.066*** (-20.93)	-6.642*** (-27.06)	-6.934*** (-32.67)
Observations				6,409					14,635	
Pseudo R-squared				0.37					0.47	

Sources: Madagascar EPM 2001, 2005.
Note: Individuals aged 15 and older. The reference category is "Inactive – Unemployed – Family workers." Dummies for location are also included in the models. Robust t statistics in parentheses.
* significant at 10%, ** significant at 5%, *** significant at 1%.

131

Table 3C.6 Determinants of Labor Allocation Across Sectors for Females (Multinomial Logit Models)

	2001					2005				
	Public employment	Private formal wage employment	Private informal wage employment	Private informal self-employment	Agricultural self-employment	Public employment	Private formal wage employment	Private informal wage employment	Private informal self-employment	Agricultural self-employment
Beyond primary education	1.644*** (6.87)	0.912*** (5.09)	−0.228* (−1.89)	0.544*** (5.07)	0.100 (0.77)	2.272*** (9.90)	1.433*** (6.61)	−0.092 (−0.99)	0.572*** (6.22)	0.279** (2.53)
Beyond first cycle of secondary education	2.913*** (11.72)	1.450*** (7.47)	−0.433*** (−2.62)	0.471*** (3.24)	−0.434* (−1.69)	4.214*** (17.72)	2.646*** (11.31)	−0.043 (−0.28)	0.718*** (4.94)	−0.101 (−0.38)
Beyond secondary education	3.486*** (11.41)	1.645*** (6.75)	−0.421* (−1.68)	−0.341 (−1.12)	−0.722 (−1.20)	5.553*** (16.91)	3.641*** (11.39)	0.421 (1.47)	0.408 (1.03)	−0.439 (−0.42)
Potential experience	0.388*** (12.71)	0.216*** (11.95)	0.160*** (12.49)	0.167*** (14.94)	0.160*** (15.05)	0.306*** (13.73)	0.248*** (10.39)	0.198*** (18.81)	0.185*** (20.47)	0.245*** (28.63)
Potential experience squared	−0.006*** (−10.18)	−0.003*** (−9.77)	−0.003*** (−11.57)	−0.002*** (−12.72)	−0.002*** (−12.58)	−0.004*** (−10.13)	−0.004*** (−8.02)	−0.003*** (−16.88)	−0.002*** (−17.27)	−0.003*** (−24.49)
Training	1.820*** (10.07)	1.445*** (9.07)	0.694*** (4.22)	1.019*** (7.16)	0.311 (1.33)	1.853*** (11.38)	1.635*** (9.15)	0.638*** (4.74)	0.981*** (8.07)	−0.191 (−1.08)
Married	−1.058*** (−5.95)	−1.268*** (−8.49)	−1.157*** (−10.60)	−0.327*** (−3.40)	−0.902*** (−9.84)	−1.139*** (−6.87)	−1.302*** (−7.30)	−1.592*** (−18.92)	−1.243*** (−15.68)	−2.852*** (−36.61)

Non-Christian	-0.707** (-2.14)	-0.196 (-0.83)	0.265* (1.77)	0.080 (0.57)	0.068 (0.45)	-0.520 (-1.55)	-0.433 (-1.25)	-0.307** (-2.38)	0.144 (1.42)	0.008 (0.09)
Merina	-0.009 (-0.04)	0.186 (1.02)	0.252* (1.70)	-0.098 (-0.72)	0.062 (0.34)	-0.353* (-1.66)	0.104 (0.48)	0.079 (0.63)	0.195 (1.56)	-0.246 (-1.60)
Urban	0.338 (1.41)	0.471** (2.24)	0.359*** (2.75)	0.352*** (3.25)	-0.822*** (-8.45)	-0.005 (-0.03)	0.191 (0.98)	-0.192** (-2.33)	0.251*** (3.13)	-0.262*** (-3.78)
Other household members earnings per capita (log)	0.021** (2.29)	0.031*** (3.81)	0.052*** (8.73)	-0.002 (-0.41)	-0.037*** (-6.79)	0.016* (1.83)	0.042*** (4.48)	0.084*** (18.52)	0.008* (1.95)	-0.044*** (-7.28)
Land area (log)	-0.062** (-2.39)	-0.058*** (-2.64)	-0.062*** (-4.61)	-0.044*** (-4.06)	0.051*** (6.97)	-0.084*** (-6.37)	-0.104*** (-7.80)	-0.082*** (-11.79)	-0.091*** (-13.05)	0.187*** (11.29)
Livestock value (log)	-0.012 (-1.21)	-0.036*** (-3.31)	-0.017*** (-2.83)	-0.030*** (-6.08)	0.013*** (3.10)	-0.023*** (-2.95)	-0.029*** (-3.38)	-0.029*** (-7.47)	-0.031*** (-8.49)	-0.021*** (-6.41)
Constant	-10.069*** (-19.24)	-5.864*** (-17.05)	-3.930*** (-16.54)	-4.534*** (-20.58)	-2.971*** (-12.44)	-9.331*** (-22.56)	-6.876*** (-19.04)	-3.156*** (-17.83)	-4.766*** (-25.17)	-5.380*** (-23.79)
Observations	7,197					15,624				
Pseudo R-squared	0.19					0.26				

Sources: Madagascar EPM 2001, 2005.

Note: Individuals aged 15 and older. The reference category is "Inactive – Unemployed – Family workers." Dummies for location are also included in the models. Robust *t* statistics in parentheses.

* significant at 10%, ** significant at 5%, *** significant at 1%.

Annex 3D Wage Employment Earnings Equations

Table 3D.1 Log Hourly Earnings Equations for Wage Employment

| | 2001 | | | | 2005 | | | |
| | Men | | Women | | Men | | Women | |
	OLS	Heckman	OLS	Heckman	OLS	Heckman	OLS	Heckman
Beyond primary education	0.548*** (6.50)	0.527*** (6.09)	0.267*** (3.19)	0.254*** (3.03)	0.319*** (6.13)	0.323*** (6.28)	0.256*** (3.60)	0.257*** (3.62)
Beyond first cycle of secondary education	0.778*** (8.38)	0.727*** (7.81)	0.762*** (7.87)	0.735*** (7.69)	0.568*** (8.57)	0.583*** (8.65)	0.683*** (8.52)	0.701*** (8.52)
Beyond secondary education	1.369*** (14.97)	1.295*** (11.59)	1.111*** (9.52)	1.053*** (8.36)	1.217*** (11.69)	1.239*** (11.78)	1.170*** (10.58)	1.211*** (10.33)
Potential experience	0.033*** (2.77)	0.027** (1.97)	0.026*** (3.03)	0.019* (1.76)	0.027*** (3.87)	0.031*** (3.92)	0.038*** (5.14)	0.043*** (5.14)
Potential experience squared	-0.000** (-2.00)	-0.000 (-1.26)	-0.000** (-2.06)	-0.000 (-0.97)	-0.000** (-2.19)	-0.000** (-2.39)	-0.000*** (-3.66)	-0.001*** (-3.85)
Training	0.223*** (3.59)	0.187*** (2.60)	0.348*** (3.62)	0.301*** (3.07)	0.381*** (6.68)	0.402*** (6.69)	0.228*** (2.90)	0.260*** (3.09)
Married	0.121 (1.17)	0.117 (1.13)	0.038 (0.61)	0.075 (1.01)	0.23*** (4.27)	0.237*** (4.33)	0.037 (0.71)	0.020 (0.36)

Non-Christian	-0.027	-0.034	-0.077	-0.082	-0.134*	-0.136*	-0.253*	-0.262**
	(-0.36)	(-0.45)	(-0.98)	(-1.03)	(-1.80)	(-1.84)	(-1.92)	(-1.99)
Merina	0.023	0.016	0.166*	0.145	-0.019	-0.019	-0.055	-0.051
	(0.22)	(0.15)	(1.69)	(1.44)	(-0.31)	(-0.30)	(-0.76)	(-0.71)
Urban	0.141**	0.111*	0.136**	0.109	0.177***	0.196***	0.281***	0.294***
	(2.51)	(1.76)	(1.98)	(1.42)	(4.16)	(4.65)	(5.28)	(5.40)
Mill's ratio		-0.126		-0.129		0.055		0.079
		(-1.32)		(-1.07)		(1.23)		(1.16)
Constant	4.704***	4.939***	4.667***	4.931***	4.990***	4.885***	4.870***	4.727***
	(31.58)	(19.79)	(32.46)	(17.05)	(47.29)	(35.57)	(41.54)	(27.13)
Observations	1,845	1,845	1,089	1,089	2,390	2,390	1,474	1,474
R-squared	0.33	0.33	0.34	0.34	0.32	0.32	0.32	0.32

Sources: Madagascar EPM 2001, 2005.
Note: Individuals aged 15 and older. OLS = ordinary least squares. Robust t statistics in parentheses.
* significant at 10%; ** significant at 5%; *** significant at 1%. Dummies for location are also included in the models.

Table 3D.2 Log Hourly Earnings Equations for Public Wage Employment

	2001				2005			
	Men		Women		Men		Women	
	OLS	Lee	OLS	Lee	OLS	Lee	OLS	Lee
Beyond primary education	0.407** (2.01)	−0.237 (−0.88)	−0.391 (−1.65)	−0.368 (−0.73)	0.509*** (3.66)	0.159 (1.41)	0.652** (2.36)	0.447 (1.37)
Beyond first cycle of secondary education	0.600** (2.37)	−0.200 (−0.52)	0.276** (2.01)	0.062 (0.10)	0.506*** (3.34)	0.077 (0.41)	0.923*** (3.21)	0.639 (1.21)
Beyond secondary education	1.074*** (5.25)	0.152 (0.29)	0.613*** (3.40)	0.442 (0.61)	1.151*** (6.57)	0.523** (2.23)	1.348*** (4.36)	0.992 (1.53)
Potential experience	0.044 (0.96)	−0.020 (−0.49)	−0.001 (−0.04)	−0.014 (−0.21)	0.019 (1.30)	−0.001 (−0.04)	0.017 (0.72)	0.020 (0.66)
Potential experience squared	−0.000 (−0.60)	0.000 (0.55)	0.000 (0.38)	0.000 (0.30)	0.000 (0.17)	0.000 (0.90)	0.000 (0.53)	0.000 (0.28)
Training	0.178 (1.09)	−0.204 (−1.40)	0.167 (1.43)	0.111 (0.49)	0.251** (2.19)	0.023 (0.23)	0.245* (1.93)	0.020 (0.12)
Married	−0.259 (−0.59)	−0.306 (−1.48)	0.247** (2.34)	0.269 (1.42)	−0.131 (−0.72)	−0.064 (−0.53)	0.264 (1.63)	0.140 (1.31)

Non-Christian	−0.058	0.029	−0.039	0.072	−0.036	0.078	0.109	0.215
	(−0.38)	(0.21)	(−0.21)	(0.24)	(−0.22)	(0.64)	(0.40)	(1.16)
Merina	0.099	0.258*	0.328	0.316	0.016	0.105	0.051	0.082
	(0.42)	(1.67)	(1.44)	(0.93)	(0.11)	(1.17)	(0.32)	(0.70)
Urban	0.229**	0.123	0.251**	0.131	0.269***	0.178**	0.139	0.121
	(2.23)	(0.91)	(2.31)	(0.68)	(2.89)	(2.39)	(1.11)	(1.00)
Mill's ratio		0.727*		0.183		0.379**		0.135
		(1.76)		(0.43)		(2.38)		(0.45)
Constant	4.919***	7.930***	5.397***	6.095***	5.534***	6.727***	4.657***	5.283***
	(7.83)	(4.63)	(24.39)	(3.01)	(19.42)	(11.10)	(11.72)	(3.92)
Observations	434	434	212	212	586	586	273	273
R-squared	0.17	0.22	0.27	0.20	0.20	0.21	0.34	0.31

Sources: Madagascar EPM 2001, 2005.
Note: Individuals aged 15 and older. OLS = ordinary least squares. Robust *t* statistics in parentheses.
* significant at 10%; ** significant at 5%; *** significant at 1%. Dummies for location are also included in the models.

Table 3D.3 Log Hourly Earnings Equations for Formal Wage Employment

| | 2001 | | | | 2005 | | | |
| | Men | | Women | | Men | | Women | |
	OLS	Lee	OLS	Lee	OLS	Lee	OLS	Lee
Beyond primary education	0.568*** (3.22)	0.384*** (3.25)	0.084 (0.66)	0.316** (2.55)	0.243* (1.72)	0.101 (0.74)	0.258* (1.76)	0.192 (1.13)
Beyond first cycle of secondary education	0.753*** (6.45)	0.603*** (4.79)	0.307** (2.21)	0.599*** (3.84)	0.293** (2.32)	0.242 (1.60)	0.304** (2.00)	0.382 (1.53)
Beyond secondary education	1.473*** (9.43)	1.330*** (8.06)	0.825*** (5.22)	1.192*** (6.53)	0.866*** (5.22)	0.753*** (3.72)	0.905*** (4.82)	0.867** (2.39)
Potential experience	0.014 (0.76)	0.022 (1.41)	0.032*** (3.08)	0.035** (2.13)	0.015 (0.97)	0.027 (1.52)	0.038** (2.00)	0.029 (1.03)
Potential experience squared	-0.000 (-0.06)	-0.000 (-0.68)	-0.000* (-1.67)	-0.000 (-1.17)	-0.000 (-0.90)	-0.001 (-1.63)	-0.000 (-1.12)	-0.000 (-0.65)
Training	0.152* (1.79)	0.171* (1.81)	0.181* (1.91)	0.224** (2.10)	0.325*** (2.95)	0.153* (1.65)	0.212* (1.81)	0.282* (1.67)
Married	0.269** (2.01)	0.117 (0.99)	-0.247*** (-3.02)	-0.156 (-1.44)	0.285** (2.05)	0.165 (1.61)	-0.278** (-2.48)	-0.274** (-2.22)

Non-Christian	0.197	0.166	−0.097	−0.018	0.021	−0.075	0.391	0.066
	(1.37)	(1.03)	(−0.63)	(−0.12)	(0.14)	(−0.59)	(1.27)	(0.26)
Merina	0.032	−0.035	0.183	0.093	0.090	0.190*	0.044	0.339**
	(0.17)	(−0.36)	(1.43)	(0.73)	(0.65)	(1.81)	(0.34)	(2.05)
Urban	0.045	0.057	0.059	0.044	−0.035	−0.183	0.362***	0.387**
	(0.44)	(0.43)	(0.75)	(0.38)	(−0.30)	(−1.38)	(2.90)	(2.41)
Mill's ratio		0.018		0.022		0.172		−0.114
		(0.08)		(0.10)		(1.11)		(−0.40)
Constant	4.896***	5.111***	5.125***	4.891***	5.420***	5.826***	5.310***	4.930***
	(23.89)	(7.46)	(27.70)	(7.58)	(18.88)	(10.31)	(19.46)	(5.24)
Observations	532	532	302	302	395	395	209	209
R-squared	0.32	0.29	0.28	0.32	0.23	0.25	0.38	0.26

Sources: Madagascar EPM 2001, 2005.
Note: Individuals aged 15 and older. OLS = ordinary least squares. Robust t statistics in parentheses.
* significant at 10%; ** significant at 5%; *** significant at 1%. Dummies for location are also included in the models.

Table 3D.4 Log Hourly Earnings Equations for Informal Wage Employment

| | 2001 | | | | 2005 | | | |
| | Men | | Women | | Men | | Women | |
	OLS	Lee	OLS	Lee	OLS	Lee	OLS	Lee
Beyond primary education	0.442*** (4.10)	0.418*** (5.97)	0.101 (1.08)	0.198*** (2.69)	0.139** (2.50)	0.176*** (3.79)	-0.015 (-0.18)	0.064 (1.03)
Beyond first cycle of secondary education	0.616*** (5.61)	0.534*** (6.35)	0.627** (2.32)	0.522*** (4.40)	0.407*** (4.50)	0.414*** (5.94)	0.348*** (3.05)	0.263*** (2.87)
Beyond secondary education	1.136*** (8.44)	1.084*** (8.42)	0.803*** (3.16)	0.818*** (3.38)	1.057*** (5.22)	1.056*** (7.09)	0.782*** (3.80)	0.920*** (3.74)
Potential experience	0.027* (1.88)	0.028*** (3.34)	0.010 (0.82)	0.028** (2.52)	0.020** (2.41)	0.030*** (4.60)	0.027*** (3.28)	0.021*** (2.98)
Potential experience squared	-0.000* (-1.70)	-0.000*** (-2.63)	-0.000 (-0.51)	-0.000** (-2.12)	-0.000 (-1.52)	-0.000*** (-3.75)	-0.000*** (-2.75)	-0.000*** (-2.62)
Training	0.249** (2.47)	0.136* (1.90)	0.561* (1.92)	0.224** (1.98)	0.321*** (4.66)	0.254*** (4.69)	0.075 (0.64)	0.219** (2.55)
Married	0.110 (0.84)	0.192** (2.55)	0.106 (1.17)	0.001 (0.02)	0.223*** (3.39)	0.209*** (4.38)	0.073 (1.23)	0.031 (0.62)

Non-Christian	-0.022	-0.038	0.027	0.012	-0.148*	-0.082	-0.393***	-0.367***
	(-0.25)	(-0.50)	(0.29)	(0.12)	(-1.72)	(-1.23)	(-2.95)	(-3.83)
Merina	0.020	-0.052	-0.014	0.058	-0.011	0.133**	-0.036	0.048
	(0.18)	(-0.55)	(-0.10)	(0.43)	(-0.18)	(2.32)	(-0.39)	(0.60)
Urban	0.157**	0.133	0.080	0.098	0.147***	0.151***	0.283***	0.163***
	(2.02)	(1.52)	(0.68)	(0.96)	(3.12)	(3.64)	(4.58)	(3.18)
Mill's ratio		0.029		-0.161		-0.033		-0.129**
		(0.25)		(-1.07)		(-0.82)		(-2.08)
Constant	4.832***	4.860***	4.944***	4.501***	5.128***	4.816***	5.033***	4.879***
	(25.53)	(18.45)	(22.53)	(11.59)	(42.58)	(41.54)	(35.08)	(29.21)
Observations	868	868	555	555	1,409	1,409	992	992
R-squared	0.29	0.24	0.25	0.21	0.24	0.21	0.19	0.13

Sources: Madagascar EPM 2001, 2005.
Note: Individuals aged 15 and older. OLS = ordinary least squares. Robust *t* statistics in parentheses.
* significant at 10%; ** significant at 5%; *** significant at 1%. Dummies for location are also included in the models.

Table 3D.5 Log Hourly Earnings Equations for Non-Farm Self-Employment

| | 2001 | | | | 2005 | | | |
| | Men | | Women | | Men | | Women | |
	OLS	Heckman	OLS	Heckman	OLS	Heckman	OLS	Heckman
Enterprise characteristics								
Log (number of employees)	0.427*** (3.27)	0.427*** (3.25)	0.418** (2.55)	0.421** (2.57)	0.750*** (6.25)	0.750*** (6.25)	0.913*** (4.03)	0.910*** (4.01)
Log (value of physical capital)	0.058*** (3.93)	0.058*** (3.90)	0.031** (2.20)	0.030** (2.16)	0.029*** (3.67)	0.029*** (3.66)	0.032*** (3.95)	0.031*** (3.91)
Individual characteristics								
Beyond primary education	0.407** (2.26)	0.405* (1.95)	0.534*** (3.50)	0.450** (2.13)	0.135 (1.30)	0.202 (1.32)	0.428*** (4.24)	0.291 (1.17)
Beyond first cycle of secondary education	0.815*** (4.39)	0.814*** (4.27)	1.006*** (4.22)	0.957*** (3.83)	0.558*** (3.53)	0.534*** (3.28)	0.284 (1.55)	0.140 (0.48)
Beyond secondary education	0.720*** (3.16)	0.720*** (3.16)	2.052* (1.94)	2.139** (2.00)	1.035*** (3.74)	0.911*** (2.63)	1.550*** (3.06)	1.202 (1.54)
Married	−0.095 (−0.52)	−0.102 (−0.26)	0.070 (0.53)	0.071 (0.54)	−0.225* (−1.83)	0.262 (0.32)	0.174** (2.28)	0.083 (0.51)

	(1)	(2)	(3)	(4)	(5)	(6)	(7)	(8)
Non-Christian	-0.272	-0.273	0.188	0.229	-0.012	-0.060	-0.032	-0.056
	(-1.00)	(-1.01)	(0.81)	(0.99)	(-0.11)	(-0.45)	(-0.25)	(-0.42)
Merina	0.332	0.329	0.164	0.159	0.020	0.171	0.035	0.131
	(1.57)	(1.37)	(0.73)	(0.71)	(0.16)	(0.61)	(0.24)	(0.61)
Urban	0.219*	0.218	0.319***	0.240	0.300***	0.426*	0.375***	0.472***
	(1.78)	(1.54)	(2.60)	(1.39)	(3.68)	(1.86)	(4.82)	(2.70)
Mill's ratio		-0.012		-0.549		0.620		1.142
		(-0.02)		(-0.57)		(0.60)		(0.59)
Constant	4.538***	4.567***	4.206***	5.333***	5.552***	3.994	4.873***	2.794
	(14.69)	(3.05)	(16.08)	(2.67)	(31.55)	(1.53)	(30.36)	(0.80)
Observations	632	632	619	619	1,630	1,630	1,573	1,573
R-squared	0.22	0.22	0.21	0.21	0.15	0.15	0.17	0.17

Sources: Madagascar EPM 2001, 2005.
Note: Individuals aged 15 and older. OLS = ordinary least squares. Robust t statistics in parentheses.
* significant at 10%; ** significant at 5%; *** significant at 1%. Dummies for location are also included in the models.

Annex 3E Earnings Gap Decompositions for Wage Workers

Table 3E.1 Neumark's Decomposition of the Gender Log Hourly Earnings Gap (OLS estimates)

	2001	2005
Gender log hourly earnings gap to be decomposed	0.234	0.220
First specification (not accounting for job characteristics)		
Difference due to		
Explained (%)	**68.6**	**37.5**
Human capital characteristics	51.3	26.5
Of which		
Education	30.1	11.2
Experience	13.7	9.9
Training	7.6	5.4
Unexplained (%)	**31.4**	**62.5**
Total (%)	**100**	**100**
Second specification (accounting for job characteristics)		
Difference due to		
Explained (%)	**66.5**	**61.7**
Human capital characteristics	32.1	14.9
Of which		
Education	17.7	5.0
Experience	9.0	7.3
Training	5.4	2.6
Job characteristics	23.4	39.1
Of which		
Occupation	23.8	41.2
Terms of employment	−0.4	−2.1
Unexplained (%)	**33.5**	**38.3**
Total (%)	**100**	**100**

Sources: Madagascar EPM 2001, 2005; authors' calculations.
Note: OLS = ordinary least squares.

Table 3E.2 Neumark's Decomposition of the Gender Log Hourly Earnings Gap by Wage Employment Sector (OLS estimates)

	2001			2005		
	Public wage employment	Formal wage employment	Informal wage employment	Public wage employment	Formal wage employment	Informal wage employment
Gender log hourly earnings gap to be decomposed	−0.039	0.176	0.242	0.123	0.075	0.168
First specification (not accounting for job characteristics)						
Difference due to						
Explained (%)	**−29.5**	**17.5**	**65.6**	**9.3**	**43.7**	**11.0**
Human capital characteristics	34.1	20.0	45.8	−24.4	−2.4	10.1
Of which						
Education	1.0	−13.3	28.0	−19.9	−64.8	2.0
Experience	34.3	32.4	5.5	−11.0	71.8	4.8
Training	−1.2	0.9	12.3	6.6	−9.4	3.3
Unexplained (%)	**129.5**	**82.5**	**34.4**	**90.7**	**56.3**	**89.0**
Total (%)	**100**	**100**	**100**	**100**	**100**	**100**

continued

Table 3E.2 Neumark's Decomposition of the Gender Log Hourly Earnings Gap by Wage Employment Sector (OLS estimates) *continued*

	2001			2005		
	Public wage employment	Formal wage employment	Informal wage employment	Public wage employment	Formal wage employment	Informal wage employment
Second specification (accounting for job characteristics)						
Difference due to						
Explained (%)	**−48.7**	**29.8**	**65.4**	**45.3**	**21.0**	**35.1**
Human capital characteristics	17.4	10.9	34.6	−16.2	2.6	7.6
Of which						
Education	−8.8	−9.7	19.0	−12.9	−46.3	1.1
Experience	27.2	20.1	4.5	−6.9	54.5	4.7
Training	−1.0	0.4	11.1	3.6	−5.5	1.8
Job characteristics	43.2	11.0	15.3	40.9	−7.8	27.6
Of which						
Occupation	5.2	9.8	18.2	36.9	−9.0	32.9
Terms of employment	38.0	1.2	−3.0	4.0	1.3	−5.4
Unexplained (%)	**148.7**	**70.2**	**34.6**	**54.7**	**79.0**	**64.9**
Total (%)	**100**	**100**	**100**	**100**	**100**	**100**

Sources: Madagascar EPM 2001, 2005, authors' calculations.
Note: OLS = ordinary least squares.

Table 3E.3 Neumark's Decomposition of the Gender Mean Log Hourly Earnings Gap in the Non-Farm Self-Employment Sector (OLS estimates)

	2001	2005
Gender log hourly earnings gap to be decomposed	0.605	0.528
First specification (not accounting for branch of activity)		
Difference due to		
Explained (%)	**57.1**	**59.0**
Human capital characteristics	16.3	18.8
Of which		
Education	16.3	18.8
Enterprise characteristics	47.1	26.9
Of which		
Log (nb of employees)	27.2	11.1
Log (value of capital)	19.9	15.7
Unexplained (%)	**42.9**	**41.0**
Total (%)	**100**	**100**
Second specification (accounting for branch of activity)		
Difference due to		
Explained (%)	**78.7**	**84.2**
Human capital characteristics	8.7	17.4
Of which		
Education	8.7	17.4
Enterprise characteristics	77.0	56.3
Of which		
Log (nb of employees)	34.3	11.1
Log (value of capital)	9.5	12.7
Sector	33.2	32.6
Unexplained (%)	**21.3**	**15.8**
Total (%)	**100**	**100**

Sources: Madagascar EPM 2001, 2005; authors' calculations.
Note: OLS = ordinary least squares.

Notes

1. See, notably, Glewwe (1990) for Ghana; Cohen and House (1993) for Sudan; Milne and Neitzert (1994) and Agesa (1999) for Kenya; Glick and Sahn (1997) for Guinea; Lachaud (1997) for Burkina Faso and Cameroon; Armitage and Sabot (1991) for Kenya and Tanzania; Appleton, Hoddinott, and Krishnan (1999) for Uganda, Côte d'Ivoire, and Ethiopia; Isemonger and Roberts (1999) for South Africa; Siphambe and Thokweng-Bakwena (2001) for Botswana; Kabubo-Mariara (2003) for Kenya; Nordman (2004) for Tunisia; Temesgen (2006) for Ethiopia; Kolev and Suárez Robles (2010)

for Ethiopia; Nordman and Wolff (2009a) for Morocco; Nordman and Wolff (2009b) for Madagascar and Mauritius; and Nordman and Roubaud (2009) for Madagascar.

2. In Uganda, the authors find that the wage gaps in the public and private sector are comparable. In Ethiopia, there is a much wider gap in the private sector than in the public sector. In Côte d'Ivoire, the reverse is true.

3. In 1999, the gross unadjusted wage differential was about 51 percent in favor of men. The results of the decomposition attribute about 14 percent to differences in endowments. The unexplained part accounts for about 59 percent of the wage differential, while the remaining 27 percent is a result of selectivity.

4. The study considered earnings resulting from primary activities only.

5. See Stifel, Rakotomanana and Celada (2007) for more details on labor market conditions in Madagascar based on an analysis of EPM 2001 and 2005.

6. The authors chose to exclude secondary wage activities from the analysis for reasons of homogeneity of the study's earnings measures. The gender dimension of multiple jobs holdings is left for further research.

7. In a previous version of this study, the determinants of hours worked in productive activities and housework production across gender were analyzed. Because of important heterogeneity issues in the estimation of hours worked, the authors preferred to drop this section, which was arguably difficult to make sense of. The related results remain available from the authors upon request.

8. Summary statistics of the various variables used in these econometric analyses are reported in Annex tables 3B.1 and 3B.2.

9. Additional statistics reporting the distribution of workers across activity sectors and occupations can be found in Annex tables 3C.1 to 3C.3.

10. The authors performed Hausman-type tests proposed by Hausman and McFadden (1984,) which provided evidence that the Independence of Irrelevant Alternatives (IIA) assumption is not violated for both male and female samples, with the exception of males in public wage employment.

11. Data on housework hours collected in the 2005 survey indicate that, in total, women work many more hours than men: 38.8 weekly hours on average versus 18.9 for men. In previous analyses (not shown but available upon request), we disentangled the determinants of housework hours across gender. It was found that being married strongly affects the number of hours worked at home for both men and women, but with an opposite effect. Married men work fewer hours at home, whereas the reverse is true for married women. This result is robust across urban and rural areas. Another interesting pattern is revealed by the coefficient estimates of the number of children at different ages. While the number of young children (below age 5) does not seem to affect men's labor intensity at home, it does so positively for women, as could be expected. The reverse pattern is observed, however, when children age 5 to 14 are considered. Then, men's hours of housework are sensitive (negatively) to the number of their children, while those of women are not.

12. In the decomposition techniques that follow, the gap is defined instead as the difference in log earnings of men and women. This difference is identical to the coefficient of a female dummy in a regression of log earnings carried out over a pooled sample of wage workers with no other control variables.

13. Although monthly earnings are frequently used in this type of analysis, it may be problematic when the number of hours worked per month varies significantly across sexes, as is the case here, and if variations in hours reflect discriminatory practices and/or individual choices. Using hourly earnings is a way to avoid this problem and is equivalent to comparing gross wage rate across individuals, that is, referring to the same quantity of work.

14. See Annex 3A, section 3A.3.

15. However, as other human capital variables, training is not immune to the common criticism that it might be the result of individual choices and hence be correlated with individual ability.

16. Economic theories of fertility and marriage suggest that marital status and number of children may be endogenous with respect to wages: women may be selected or may self-select into different marital or fertility states on the basis of unmeasured characteristics that are correlated with wages. Then, individual heterogeneity may lead to biased estimates of the "direct" effects of marriage and motherhood on wages. Therefore, one should be careful in inferring any causal relationship between marriage, motherhood, and wages with such a cross-sectional dataset.

17. Alternatively, we cannot exclude the possibility that our model in the public sector is poorly identified because of the difficulty of finding valid identifying instruments for the sectoral selection (see Annex 3A, section 3A.2 for details).

18. Other potential sources of earnings differentials across self-employed workers were introduced in the regressions (such as access to credit or the rate of salaried workers in the informal production unit) and failed to provide meaningful results.

19. This result is obtained by replacing the dummy variables indicating educational level achievements with a continuous variable for years of education, as well as a quadratic term (years of education squared). We find that the sign of the quadratic term is positive, an indication of a convex profile of returns to education.

20. A similar rationale for this choice is given by Appleton, Hoddinott, and Krishnan (1999) in their paper analyzing the gender gap in three African countries. They state "[We focus ... on uncorrected estimates] partly for comparability with existing studies but also because of methodological controversies surrounding the selectivity corrections."

21. Neumark (1988) refers to "nepotism" as this deviation in returns represents the distance between actual men's returns and lower returns that would be associated with competitive wages (the non-discriminatory benchmark of the pooled sample). See Annex 3A, section 3A.3-1 for more details.

22. An argument against the discrimination hypothesis is that lower access to firm's physical capital may be caused by individual reinvestment choices. For example, female household heads traditionally spend more money on their children and household than do male household heads.

23. Conversely, one can argue that analyses that omit occupation and industry may underestimate the importance of background and choice-based characteristics on labor market outcomes (Altonji and Blank 1999).

24. Constant rates of return to education are more and more challenged in both developed and developing countries (Card 1999), especially in Africa (see Bigsten et al. 2000; Kuepie, Nordman, and Roubaud 2009; Schultz 2004; Söderbom et al. 2006).

25. Regan and Oaxaca (2006) show that using potential versus actual experience in earnings models is best viewed as a model misspecification problem, rather than a classical errors-in-variable framework. Instrumental variable techniques are the traditional approach taken to correct classical measurement error. Then, as underlined by Regan and Oaxaca (2006), instrumenting potential experience would not solve the model specification problem.

26. Remember that, in this study, self-employed workers are independent individuals working in informal non-agricultural activities.

27. The presence of the additional constructed selectivity correction terms renders the standard errors incorrect. Standard errors are then bootstrapped to provide asymptotically consistent values.

28. Indeed, based on Monte-Carlo simulations, Bourguignon, Fournier, and Gurgand (2007) conclude that Lee's method is well adapted to very small samples.

29. Note that these tests are made possible because, under the normality assumption, the inverse Mills ratio in sample selection models is a nonlinear function of the variables included in the first-stage probit and multinomial equations. Hence, the selection models are still identified, even without exclusion restrictions due to this nonlinearity (Olsen 1980).

References

Agesa, Richard U. 1999. "The Urban Gender Wage Gap in an African Country: Findings from Kenya." *Canadian Journal of Development Studies* 20 (1): 59–76.

Altonji, Joseph G., and Rebecca Blank. 1999. "Race and Gender in the Labor Market." In *Handbook of Labor Economics* (vol. 3c) ed. O. Ashenfelter and D. Card, 3144–259. North-Holland: Elsevier Science B.V.

Antoine, Philippe, Philippe Bocquier, Nicolas Razafindratsima, and François Roubaud. 2000. *Biographies de Trois Générations dans l'Agglomération d'Antananarivo*, Ceped, Collection Documents et Manuels no. 11, Paris.

Appleton, Simon, John Hoddinott, and Pramila Krishnan. 1999. "The Gender Wage Gap in Three African Countries." *Economic Development and Cultural Change* 47 (2): 289–312.

Armitage, Jane, and Richard Sabot. 1991. "Discrimination in East African's Urban Labor Market." In *Unfair Advantage: Labor Market Discrimination in Developing Countries*, ed. Nancy Birdsall and Richard Sabot. Washington DC: The World Bank.

Bigsten, A., A. Isaksson, M. Söderbom, P. Collier, A. Zeufack, S. Dercon, M. Fafchamps, J. W. Gunning, F. Teal, S. Appleton, B. Gauthier, A. Oduro, R. Oostendorp, and C. Patillo. 2000. "Rates of Return on Physical and Human Capital in Africa's Manufacturing Sector." *Economic Development and Cultural Change* 48: 801–27.

Blau, Francine, and Lawrence Kahn. 2000. "Gender Differences in Pay." *Journal of Economic Perspectives* 14: 75–99.

Blinder, Alan S. 1973. "Wage Discrimination: Reduced Form and Structural Estimates." *The Journal of Human Resources* 8 (4): 436–55.

Bourguignon, François, Martin Fournier, and Marc Gurgand. 2007. "Selection Bias Correction Based on the Multinomial Logit Model: Monte-Carlo Comparisons." *Journal of Economic Surveys* 21(1): 174–205.

Brown, Randall S., Marilyn Moon, and Barbara S. Zoloth. 1980. "Incorporating Occupational Attainment in Studies of Male-Female Earnings Differentials." *The Journal of Human Resources* 15 (1): 3–28.

Card, David. 1999. "The Causal Effect of Education on Earnings." In *Handbook of Labor Economics*, vol. 3A, ed. O. Ashenfelter and D. Card, 1801–63. Amsterdam: Elsevier/North Holland.

Cling, Jean-Pierre, Mireille Razafindrakoto, and François Roubaud. 2007. "Export Processing Zones in Madagascar: The Impact of the Dismantling of Clothing Quotas on Employment and Labour Standards." Working Paper DT/2007/6, Développment, Institutions and Analyses de Long Terme, Paris.

Cohen, Barney, and William J. House. 1993. "Women's Urban Labour Market Status in Developing Countries: How Well Do They Fare in Khartoum, Sudan?" *Journal of Development Studies* 29 (3): 461–83.

Cotton, J. 1988. "On the Decomposition of Wage Differentials." *Review of Economics and Statistics* 70 (2): 236–43.

Council of Economic Advisers. 1998. "Explaining Trends in the Gender Wage Gap." Council of Economic Advisors, The White House, Washington, D.C. http://clinton4.nara.gov/WH/EOP/CEA/html/gendergap.html#disc

Glewwe, Paul. 1990. "Schooling, Skills and the Return to Education: an Econometric Exploration Using Data from Ghana." Living Standards Measurement Working Paper 76, World Bank, Washington DC.

Glick, Peter, and David E. Sahn. 1997. "Gender and Education Impacts on Employment and Earnings in West Africa: Evidence from Guinea." *Economic Development and Cultural Change* 45 (4): 793–823.

Hausman, Jerry. A., and Daniel McFadden. 1984. "Specification Tests for the Multinomial Logit Model." *Econometrica* 52 (5): 1219–40.

Isemonger, A. G., and Neil Roberts. 1999. "Post-Entry Gender Discrimination in the South African Labour Market." *Journal for Studies in Economics and Econometrics* 23 (2): 1–25.

Kabubo-Mariara, Jane 2003. "Wage Determination and the Gender Wage Gap in Kenya: Any Evidence of Gender Discrimination?" Research Paper 132, African Economic Research Consortium, Nairobi, Kenya.

Kolev, Alexandre, and Pablo Suárez Robles. 2010. "Exploring the Gender Pay Gap Through Different Age Cohorts: The Case of Ethiopia." In *Gender Disparities in Africa's Labor Market*, ed. J. Arbache, A. Kolev, E. Filipiak, 57–86. Washington, DC: World Bank.

Korenman, Sanders, and David Neumark. 1991. "Does Marriage Really Make Men More Productive?" *The Journal of Human Resources* 26 (2): 282–307.

———. 1992. "Marriage, Motherhood, and Wages." *The Journal of Human Resources* 27 (2): 233–55.

Kuepie, Mathias, Christophe J. Nordman, François Roubaud. 2009. "Education and Earnings in Urban West Africa." *Journal of Comparative Economics* 37 (3): 491–515.

Lachaud, Jean-Pierre. 1997. *Les Femmes et le Marché du Travail Urbain en Afrique Subsaharienne.* Paris: l'Harmattan.

Lee, Lung-Fei. 1983. "Generalized Econometric Models with Selectivity." *Econometrica* 51 (2): 507–12.

Maloney, W. 2004. "Informality Revisited." *World Development* 32 (7): 1159–78.

Milne, William, and Monica Neitzert. 1994. "Kenya." In *Labor Markets in an Era of Adjustment: Issues Papers* 1, ed. Susan Horton, Ravi Kanbur, and Dipak Mazumdar, 405–57. EDI Development Studies. Washington DC: World Bank.

Neumark, David. 1988. "Employers' Discriminatory Behavior and the Estimation of Wage Discrimination." *The Journal of Human Resources* 23: 279–95.

Nicita, Alessandro, and Susan Razzaz. 2003. "Who Benefits and How Much? How Gender Affects Welfare Impacts of a Booming Textile Industry." Policy Research Working Paper 3029, World Bank, Washington, DC.

Nordman, Christophe J. 2004. "Discrimination Salariale, Capital Humain et Structure des Tâches Selon le Genre : l'Apport de Données Liées Employeurs-Employés au Maroc et en Tunisie." In *Marché du travail et genre: Maghreb-Europe*, ed. Margaret Maruani, Danielle Meulders, Catherine Sofer, et al., Chapter 2. Brussels Economic Series. Brussels: Éditions du Dulbéa.

Nordman, Christophe J., and François Roubaud. 2009. "Reassessing the Gender Wage Gap in Madagascar: Does Labour Force Attachment Really Matter?" *Economic Development and Cultural Change* 57 (4): 785–808.

Nordman, Christophe J., and François-Charles Wolff. 2009a. "Is there a Glass Ceiling in Morocco? Evidence from Matched Worker-Firm Data." *Journal of African Economies* 18 (4): 592–633.

———. 2009b. "Islands Through the Glass Ceiling? Evidence of Gender Wage Gaps in Madagascar and Mauritius." In *Labor Markets and Economic Development*, ed. Ravi Kanbur and Jan Svejnar, 521–44. Routledge Studies in Development Economics. London and New York: Routledge.

———. 2009c. "Gender Differences in Pay in African Manufacturing Firms." In *Gender Disparities in Africa's Labor Market*, ed. J.Arbache, A. Kolev, and E. Filipiak, 155–92. Washington, DC: World Bank.

Oaxaca, Ronald. 1973. "Male-Female Wage Differentials in Urban Labor Markets." *International Economic Review* 14 (3): 693–709.

Olsen, Randall J. 1980. "A Least Squares Correction for Selectivity Bias." *Econometrica* 148 (7): 815–20.

Razafindrakoto, Mireille, and François Roubaud. 1999. "La Dynamique du Marché du Travail dans l'Agglomération d'Antananarivo entre 1995 et 1999 : La Croissance Économique Profite-t-elle aux Ménages?" *Economie de Madagascar* 4: 103–37.

Regan, Tracy L., and Ronald L. Oaxaca. 2006. "Work Experience as a Source of Specification Error in Earnings Models: Implications for Gender Wage Decompositions." Discussion Papers 1920, Institute for the Study of Labor, Bonn, Germany.

Reimers, Cordelia W. 1983. "Labour Market Discrimination Against Hispanic and Black Men." *The Review of Economics and Statistics* 65 (4): 570–79.

Roubaud, François. 2002. "Madagascar après la Tourmente : Regards sur Dix Ans de Transitions Politique et Économique." *Afrique Contemporaine* 202/203 (special issue, April–September): 3–163.

Schultz, T. Paul. 2004. "Evidence of Returns to Schooling in Africa from Household Surveys: Monitoring and Restructuring the Market for Education." *Journal of African Economies* 13: 95–148.

Siphambe, Happy Kufigwa, and Malebogo Thokweng-Bakwena. 2001. "The Wage Gap Between Men and Women in Botswana's Formal Labour Market." *Journal of African Economies* 10 (2): 127–42.

Söderbom, Mans, Francis Teal, A. Wambugu, and G. Kahyarara. 2006. "Dynamics of Returns to Education in Kenyan and Tanzanian Manufacturing." *Oxford Bulletin of Economics and Statistics* 68: 261–88.

Stifel, D., F. H. Rakotomanana, and E. Celada. 2007. "Assessing Labor Market Conditions in Madagascar, 2001–2005." Africa Region Working Paper Series 105, World Bank, Washington, DC.

Temesgen, Tilahun. 2006. "Decomposing Gender Wage Differentials in Urban Ethiopia: Evidence from Linked Employer-Employee (LEE) Manufacturing Survey Data." *Global Economic Review* 35 (1): 43–66.

Weichselbaumer, Doris, and Rudolf Winter-Ebmer. 2005. "A Meta-Analysis of the International Gender Wage Gap." *Journal of Economic Surveys* 19 (3): 479–511.

Chapter **4**

Gender Differences in Pay in African Manufacturing Firms

Christophe J. Nordman and François-Charles Wolff

M any empirical studies have found that women and men face unequal treatment in the workplace, especially in terms of wages. Almost all developed countries' labor markets are characterized by a significant gender wage gap, the explanations for which may be related to differences in the level of human capital between male and female employees or to discrimination from employers against the female workforce, among other factors (see Blau and Kahn 2000). More recently, several studies using data from France, Spain, and Sweden have shown that the gender wage gap is unlikely to remain constant throughout the wage distribution (Albrecht, Björklund, and Vroman 2003; Barnet-Verzat and Wolff 2008; de la Rica, Dolado, and Llorens 2008; Jellal, Nordman, and Wolff 2008).

In contrast to developed countries, little is known about gender wage differences in developing countries, especially with respect to the possible varying magnitude of the gender gap across the wage distribution. Gender-specific analyses using African data remain scarce, as can be inferred from the meta-analysis of Weichselbaumer and Winter-Ebmer (2005). Results from previous studies on African countries indicate, however, that there is a wide consensus on the presence of substantial wage inequalities between men and women, both among salaried and self-employed workers.[1] This is somewhat worrisome because reducing gender inequality is usually recommended as an efficient tool in the fight against poverty in poor countries. Furthermore, decreasing gender inequality is part of the third United Nations Millennium Development Goal.

Our purpose in this chapter is to add new comparative evidence on the magnitude of the gender wage gap in the African manufacturing sectors. In a context where wages usually remain low, it may be that employers tend to limit

The authors thank Jorge Arbache and several reviewers for their useful comments and Antoine Leblois for valuable research assistance.

the use of discrimination against women. To investigate the potential differences in the gender wage gap more closely, we conduct a comparative analysis of seven African countries using the recent Investment Climate Assessment (ICA) surveys, carried out in the framework of the World Bank's Africa Regional Program on Enterprise Development (RPED).[2] These surveys gather information both on the characteristics of manufacturing firms and on a sample of their workers, meaning that they provide matched employer-employee data.

To study gender inequalities in pay, researchers rely on either household data with information on individual earnings or on such matched employer-employee data. In the former, it is theoretically possible to account for the selectivity issue, since many women do not take part in the labor market and some of them work in informal sector jobs. However, correction of the selectivity issue is often problematic as it raises methodological controversies regarding the choice of the appropriate instruments to identify selection.[3] In addition, in such household surveys, there is usually no detailed description of the respondent's job and workplace. This is a crucial feature when measuring experience, for instance. While numerous studies rely on potential experience, this covariate is likely to be affected by measurement error (Heywood 1988; Nordman and Roubaud 2009). The use of actual experience when it is available in the data, as is the case in this chapter, seems much more appropriate when studying gender wage differences.

Clearly, heterogeneity at the firm level is likely to bias the estimates of the gender wage gap if firms' characteristics influence wages of men and women differently.[4] The use of matched employer-employee data allows estimation of fixed effects models, which controls for both observed and unobserved characteristics of the workplace. Although employer-employee data are not representative of the population of interest at the country level, the matched data may offer more opportunities than household data to analyze gender differences in pay if we consider that the firms' characteristics matter in the wage formation process.[5]

Recent findings from Morocco indicate that it matters to account for firm fixed effects in wage regression when explaining gender differences in pay (Nordman and Wolff 2009a). In African manufacturing, Fafchamps, Söderbom, and Benhassine (2006) note that the gender wage gap may arise as a result of gender-specific sorting of workers across firms that pay different wages. This last explanation relates to the presence of gender segregation across firms. If there are high-paying firms that hire more men than women, and if there are, at the same time, low-paying firms hiring more women than men, then firms' characteristics will deeply influence the gender differences in wages. Controlling for firm heterogeneity, therefore, should reduce the magnitude of the gender wage gap. In the same vein, Hellerstein, Neumark, and Troske (2002) study whether competitive market forces act to reduce discrimination. They show that, among plants with high levels of product market power, those that employ relatively more women are more profitable, while the relationship is not significant for plants with low levels of market power. This result is consistent with sex discrimination in wages in markets where plants have product market power.

This discussion suggests that, ideally, employer-employee data are needed to study the gender pay gap, since such matched data allow purging the effect of firm heterogeneity on wage differentials (Meng 2004; Meng and Meurs 2004). Having matched data from manufacturing firms in African countries allows the study's empirical work to control for observed and unobserved heterogeneity at the firm level by estimating fixed effect wage models. In so doing, the study shows how controls of the firm wage policies in wage equations affect the estimated magnitude of the gender wage gap.[6] Furthermore, using information at the firm level (for example, the proportion of female employees in each enterprise), the study explicitly accounts for the possibility of gender segregation across firms, which may explain the varying magnitude of the gender gap across countries.

The seven African countries selected for econometric analysis in this study—Benin, Kenya, Madagascar, Mauritius, Morocco, Senegal, and Uganda—are particularly interesting to compare. For instance, while Mauritius is perhaps the most interesting economic development success story of the 1980s,[7] Benin, Kenya, Madagascar, Senegal, and Uganda, by contrast, remain some of the poorest countries in the world. According to the 2007–08 Human Development Index (HDI) ranking of the United Nations Development Programme (UNDP), Mauritius stands 65th, while Benin (163), Kenya (148), Madagascar (143), Senegal (156), and Uganda (154) are far down in the ranking of 177 countries. In this respect, Morocco at 126 is in an intermediate position.

A comparative case study of these countries is worthwhile in order to assess whether gender inequalities in pay are somehow linked to level of economic development. The fact that these countries have distinct economic performances and labor market features may be helpful in understanding the roots of gender wage differences. Empirical analysis for this study first estimates the gender wage gap using ordinary least squares (OLS) earnings regressions and decomposing the gender gap in two components, one taking into account differences in individual labor market characteristics, and the other, the differences in the returns to these characteristics. Then, using quantile regressions, the analysis tests whether the gender gap remains constant across the wage distribution. Finally, the study focuses more closely on the role of firm characteristics and job segregation across firms as potential factors explaining the gender wage gap. The study aims to answer the question: Do firm characteristics matter when explaining wage differences between male and female employees in the African manufacturing sectors?

The remainder of this chapter is organized as follows. The next section describes the ICA surveys and presents descriptive statistics on workers, firms, and wages. Then the study's different econometric results based on OLS and quantile regressions, fixed effect models, and decomposition techniques are presented, followed by an executive summary and concluding comments.

Data and Descriptive Statistics

This section presents the surveys used in this study, describes the different samples of firms and workers, and provides a descriptive analysis of gender wage differences in the seven selected African countries.

The ICA Surveys

The matched employer-employee data for Benin, Kenya, Madagascar, Mauritius, Senegal, and Uganda come from the ICA surveys conducted by the World Bank from to 2003 to 2005 in the framework of the RPED. The data for Morocco come from the Firm Analysis and Competitiveness Survey (FACS) conducted in 2000 by the World Bank and the Moroccan Ministry of Trade and Industry.[8]

The basis for these surveys is the notion that the workplace is the microdata unit where labor supply and labor demand meet. In that spirit, the ICA surveys and FACS collect data on both firm characteristics and a sample of employees in each workplace. The questionnaires addressed to both employers and employees are specifically adapted for each country, but they enable cross-country comparisons because the questions are very similar across countries.

In these countries, the firms were randomly selected among the population of formal establishments using a stratification based on sector, size, and localization. Hence, they are not mainly located in capital cities, but they do represent the various regions of each country. In each firm, up to 10 employees were randomly sampled following Mairesse and Greenan (1999). Some sampling frames at the firm level contained constraints on the size of the firms to be investigated, for instance no firm with less than 10 employees in Kenya, Madagascar, and Morocco, while some did not constrain firm size (Benin, Mauritius, Senegal, and Uganda).[9] Across countries, firms belong to more or less 10 manufacturing sectors[10] that regroup into broadly eight activities: (1) agro industry; (2) chemicals and related products; (3) materials for construction; (4) furniture; (5) metallic products; (6) industry of paper, paper products, and plastics products; (7) textiles and leather; and (8) wood.

Description of the Samples

The survey questionnaires allow us to construct identical human capital indicators for workers in the selected countries. For each respondent, number of years of completed schooling, number of years of actual experience out of the current firm, and number of years of tenure in the current firm are computed. These different covariates, which provide good controls for the potential productivity advantage in the labor markets, are then introduced into the wage regressions. Also used were two demographic variables, that is, a dummy for gender and a dummy indicating whether the individual is married or not.

Figure 4.1 shows large differences in the sex composition of the various samples. The proportion of women in each sample are: Benin (14.5 percent), Kenya (19 percent), Madagascar (37 percent), Mauritius (44 percent), Morocco (40 percent), Senegal (17.5 percent), and Uganda (19 percent). Then, for Benin, Senegal, Kenya, and Uganda, first, the much lower proportion of female employees should be noted, which indicates the presence of women with unusual observed and unobserved human capital characteristics.

The low proportion of women in the samples for some countries, which makes them a special case with particular human capital characteristics, is evidence of a selection effect on the labor market. Large inequalities in access to the manufacturing sector are present, and they certainly partly explain the cross-country differences observed in the magnitude of the wage gap. While the study's descriptive statistics suggest that access to manufacturing jobs is

Figure 4.1 Gender Composition of the Employee Samples

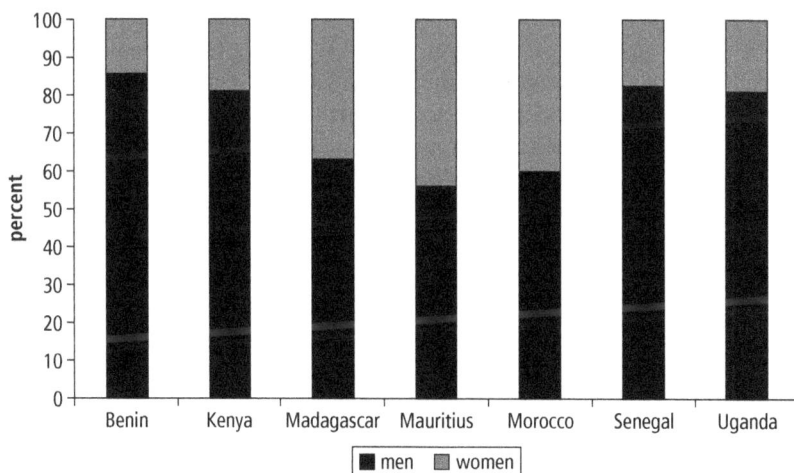

Sources: Investment Climate Surveys for Benin (2004), Kenya (2003), Madagascar (2005), Mauritius (2005), Senegal (2003), Uganda (2003); FACS for Morocco (2000); authors' calculations.

much more difficult for women living in Benin, Kenya, Senegal, and Uganda, the use of matched employer-employee data offers no solution to account for this selection effect.

According to Annex table 4A.1, Kenyan, Malagasy, and Ugandan workers are the most educated, with an average of more than 11 years of completed schooling. The least educated workers are those of Benin at 9.5 years and Morocco at 8.6 years, while Mauritian at 10 and Senegalese workers at 10.5 years are in intermediate positions. Given Kenya's, Madagascar's, and Uganda's respective levels of economic development compared to that of Mauritius and Morocco, this ranking is surprising. Indeed, Sub-Saharan African countries are often believed to be less endowed in human capital compared to their North African neighbors, and notably relative to the newly industrialized Mauritius Island.

A first explanation is that an overwhelming proportion of poorly educated individuals actually work in the informal sectors of the countries under consideration.[11] The latter are thus not in the sample design of the ICA surveys, because this study used data stemming from formal manufacturing firms and their workers. The formal private sectors in Benin, Kenya, Madagascar, Senegal, and Uganda are highly selective, thus are reserved for the most educated workers. This is probably less true for Morocco and Mauritius, where uneducated workers are also found in significant proportions in garment firms, for example.[12]

Another interesting pattern of the study samples, which may explain some differences in educational achievement across countries, is the sex distribution of education. While "only" two country samples exhibit a greater ratio of men's years of education to that of women (Mauritius, 103 percent, and Morocco, 103.5 percent), the other samples reveal an education gap in favor of women at the following percentages: Benin (94.6 percent), Kenya (94.8 percent), Madagascar (94.2 percent), Senegal (78.4 percent), and Uganda (95.8 percent). In this respect, the Senegalese case is the most revealing of the specificity of our samples, as female employees in this country benefit on average from almost three more years of education than their male counterparts (12.82. versus 10.05).[13]

In all countries, male workers offset their potential disadvantage in terms of education with greater average number of years of experience in the labor market. This is reflected both by the gender ratios of men's to women's experience in the current job: Benin (115), Kenya (213), Madagascar (155.4), Mauritius (137.7), Morocco (147.6), Senegal (163.2), and Uganda (161.4); and the sex ratios of tenure in the incumbent firm: respectively, 107, 129.4, 109.8, 135.2, 134.8, 124.9, and 107.1 percent. On average, Mauritian workers are the most experienced (15.1 years of total actual experience), followed by Kenyans and Senegalese (about 12.0 years), Malagasies (11.0 years), Beninese (9.5 years), and, finally, Moroccans and Ugandans (8.9 years).

The proportions of workers at the top of the occupational distribution (owners, managers, professionals) are roughly similar across Madagascar and

Mauritius. In Benin, Morocco, and Uganda, greater proportions of workers were observed in higher occupations, while employees in Kenya and Senegal are in intermediate positions. In all cases studied (with the exception of Benin), men, who are more likely to be owners or managers, have better occupations than women. Women, on the contrary, compete well with men in professional occupations (with university degree), which is in concert with the previous finding of a greater education level for women in five out of seven samples. Interestingly, women are always found in greater proportions than men in the category of health, office, and sales workers. Finally, unskilled production workers are prevalent in Madagascar (44 percent), followed by Senegal (32 percent), Morocco and Uganda (about 29 percent), Mauritius (26 percent), Kenya (22 percent), and Benin (20 percent).

Firm samples comprise 194 enterprises for Benin, 248 for Kenya, 281 for Madagascar, 189 for Mauritius, 842 for Morocco, 249 for Senegal, and 264 for Uganda. As shown in Annex table 4A.2, the average total employees in the firm samples ranges from 39 salaried workers in Benin to 227 in Kenya. In firm size, the Beninese sample stands out compared to the other countries, as it contains a significant proportion of small-sized enterprises, 30 percent of the firms having fewer than 11 employees.[14] Similar average proportions of women in each firm are found (about 15 percent) for Benin, Kenya, Senegal, and Uganda, while this share is more than twice as high for Moroccan, Malagasy, and Mauritian firms. More firms are owned by women in Madagascar: 20 percent versus less than 10 percent in the other samples. This may affect the measure of the gender wage gap if female owners are less likely to offer lower wages to women than male ones.

Ugandan firms display a higher share of managers and executives compared to the other countries (28 percent versus 17, 16, and 15 percent, respectively, for Benin, Kenya, and Senegal, and less than 10 percent for the three other firm samples). More generally, these proportions are low compared to those observed in developed countries. The share of exporting firms is important in Mauritius (64 percent), Morocco (57 percent), Kenya (51 percent), and Senegal (50 percent), while it is comparatively low in Madagascar (30 percent), Benin (22 percent), and Uganda (18 percent). Mauritian firms thus are the most concerned with international competition for their product markets. Finally, there are some important differences in the sectoral distribution of firms across countries. The agro-industry sector is prevalent in Kenya, Senegal, and Uganda, while the textile sectors are significant in Morocco, as is the metal products sector in Madagascar. By contrast, firms are less concentrated sectorally in the Beninese sample.[15]

To summarize, the firm samples are different in many respects, with particularly distinct sizes, female proportions, export capacity, and sectors of activity. Thus, it is important to account for firm heterogeneity in the empirical analysis.[16] The study matched employer-employee data to control for both the characteristics of the workers and the firms. There were several ways to proceed. A first possibility would be to include in the regressions a large set of explanatory variables related to the firm in wage equations. The drawbacks of this method are that many firm characteristics are potentially collinear and this would not account for the unobserved firm heterogeneity component. Thus the preferred strategy is to control for both observed and unobserved heterogeneity at the firm level using fixed effect models, which is easy to implement with linear wage regression. This implementation is also possible in the context of quantile regressions.

How Large Are Gender Wage Differences?

To examine the wage distributions by gender in the different countries, the study measured wages based on hourly earnings (including other monetary advantages and premiums) and thus takes into account the potential heterogeneity in hours worked between men and women. Annex table 4A.1 shows higher mean wages for men in five out of seven countries. The two exceptions are Senegal and Uganda, where women's average wages slightly exceed those of men.

Figure 4.2 shows the magnitude of the gender wage gap at the mean of the sample (panel a) and along the wage distribution (panel b). In all countries, the median wage (50th percentile) is much lower than the mean wage. While in Mauritius the gap is important all along the wage distribution (the difference in log wages between men and women reaches about 50 percentage points of log), the gender gaps are insignificant at the mean point of the sample in Benin, Madagascar, and Uganda. In Kenya, the gap is about 11 percent at the mean (indicating that women earn on average 11 percent less than men), while it reaches 26 percent in Morocco, which is highly significant. In the case of Senegal, as pointed out earlier, the gap is significantly in favor of women (at the 10 percent level) and reaches about 14 percent at the mean point of the sample.

Unfortunately, the data show that calculations at the sample means can hide significant differences in the magnitude of the gaps along the wage distribution. This is particularly true for Benin, Morocco, and Uganda, where the gaps vary significantly depending on the workers' relative position in the wage distribution. In Benin, for instance, the gap is significantly in favor of men in the lower part of the wage distribution, while it favors women in the upper part (from about the median of the distribution). By contrast, the reverse is true for Uganda, where the gap changes sign and is detrimental to women in the upper part of the distribution. In Morocco, the large gap increases steadily all along the wage distribution, thereby revealing the potential existence of a glass ceiling effect against women on top of the distribution (Nordman and Wolff 2009a). These preliminary statistics then justify turning to a distributional approach for a proper view of the magnitude of the gender wage gaps in Africa.

In the selected African manufacturing firms, the profiles among workers are very different. Albeit preliminary, these findings suggest that the gender wage gaps observed in the formal sectors of these countries are quite diverse.

Figure 4.2 Descriptive Statistics of the Gender Wage Gap

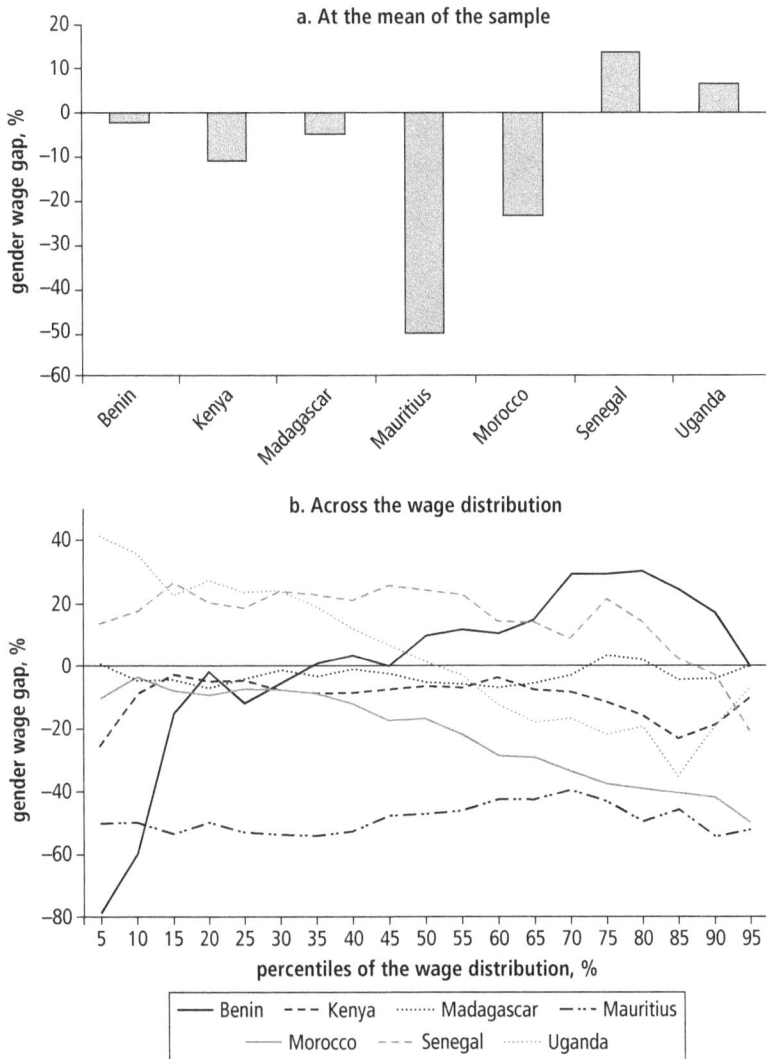

a. At the mean of the sample

b. Across the wage distribution

Legend:
— Benin   – – – Kenya   ········· Madagascar   — ·· — Mauritius
——— Morocco   – – – Senegal   ········· Uganda

Sources: Investment Climate Surveys for Benin (2004), Kenya (2003), Madagascar (2005), Mauritius (2005), Senegal (2003), and Uganda (2003); FACS for Morocco (2000); authors' calculations.

Econometric Results

To further understand the factors that influence the magnitude of this gender gap, we turn in the next section to an econometric analysis using OLS, fixed effects, and quantile regression, relying on decomposition methods to examine whether the gender wage gap stems from differences in endowments between men and women or from differences in the returns to these characteristics. Finally, the role of job segregation across firms in the magnitude of the gender wage gap is assessed.

Evidence on the Mean Gender Wage Gap

The empirical analysis begins by assessing the magnitude of the gender wage gap in the seven African countries using OLS regressions with the log hourly wage as dependent variable (see Annex 4B). For each country, the linear model is estimated on the pooled sample comprising both male and female employees. The different covariates introduced into the regressions are "marital status," "completed years of education," "years of experience in the firm," and "years of tenure in the firm" (with quadratic profile for the last three variables).[17] Actual experience in the firm was chosen instead of the years of potential experience because the measurement of potential experience may lead to gender-specific measurement errors (errors being more likely for women).[18] As women are more likely to be out of the labor market, a measure of potential experience is expected to systematically overstate the actual experience of women. Note that regional dummies are not included in the various regressions. The geographical differences will implicitly be controlled for in the fixed effects regressions.

The following focuses on the gender coefficient in the earnings equation (Annex table 4A.3, columns 1A–7A). A brief investigation suggests that a distinction must be made between two groups of countries. On one hand, there is no significant difference in male and female earnings in Benin, Kenya, Madagascar, Senegal, and Uganda. On the other hand, earnings are statistically different between men and women both in Mauritius and in Morocco. On average, women earn 12.4 percent less than men in Morocco and 35.3 percent less in Mauritius. Several explanations related to either employees' or firms' characteristics or to the functioning of the labor market may be helpful to understand these differences.

An interesting feature of the study's comparative data is the apparent correlation between the proportion of female employees within firms and the gender wage gap. In the first group of countries (no gap), the share of women in the manufacturing sectors is somewhat low. It amounts to 14.5 percent in Benin, 18.9 percent in Kenya, 17.6 percent in Senegal, and 19.0 percent in Uganda. The situation of Madagascar is different because the proportion of women in the manufacturing sectors is much higher (37 percent), which is not far from the cases of Mauritius and Morocco (43.9 percent and 40 percent, respectively). Therefore, the differences among the seven African countries are certainly a result of some selection effects, that is, the idea of different access of workers to jobs. As there are few women working in the formal manufacturing sectors in Benin, Kenya, Senegal, and Uganda, the women in these sectors are likely to have unobserved characteristics positively correlated with their productivity. This is expected to strongly reduce differences in earnings between men and women.

Another difference between the selected African countries may lie in the composition of occupations within firms, which are not controlled for in the first columns of each set of country-specific regressions. Nevertheless, a difficulty with occupations is that they may be endogenous if employers discriminate between male and female workers on the basis of the type of job they do (Albrecht, Björklund, and Vroman 2003). Despite this shortcoming, a set of occupational dummies[19] are added in columns 1B–7B. As Annex table 4A.3 shows, this has little effect on the magnitude of the gender wage gap. Again, there is no significant difference in earnings between men and women in Benin, Kenya, Senegal, and Uganda. The gender gap is now slightly higher in Mauritius (39.7 percent instead of 35.3 percent) and slightly lower in Morocco (8.6 percent instead of 12.4 percent), while it is now significant and approximately equal to 10 percent in Madagascar.

As we controlled only for individual characteristics in the previous linear models, this means that heterogeneity at the firm level is not taken into account. This is undoubtedly likely to bias the gender estimated coefficient, because some firms' characteristics may influence wages of men and women in a different way. For example, this would be the case if the gender wage gap rises as a result of gender-specific sorting of workers across firms that pay different wages. Turning to fixed effects models (see Annex 4B), we implicitly assume that the firms' heterogeneity components are correlated with the exogenous explanatory variables. This is very important in the study's context if we (plausibly) assume that there is a sorting of workers across firms, that is, workers self-select or are selected into certain types of firms. In particular, employees (either male or female) with "good" unobservable characteristics are more likely to work in firms paying higher wages.[20]

According to the fixed effect estimates (Annex table 4A.3, columns 1C–7C), the gender wage gap is now only significant in Mauritius and Morocco. Curiously, there is a slight increase in the absolute value of the gender coefficient for Morocco (13.3 percent instead of 12.4 percent), while the gender coefficient is divided by two in Mauritius. This is consistent with the idea that part of the gender gap is a result of firm sorting and that firms' characteristics influence the earnings of men and women differently. Two further comments are in order. First, the gender gap remains insignificant in Benin, Kenya, Madagascar, Senegal, and Uganda. Second, additional controls for occupations in the fixed effects regression substantially reduce the gender gap in Morocco.

Relative Importance of Gender in Wage Determination

Results from OLS regressions suggest that gender matters in understanding differences in individual wages, at least in Mauritius and Morocco, and that firms' effects are important. The following analysis attempts to assess the relative impact of the different explanatory variables introduced in the linear wage regressions. For that purpose, the analysis follows the regression-based decomposition approach proposed in Fields (2004). The idea is to decompose the explained portion of the regression into weights for each of the covariates (the methodology is described in Annex 4B).

When considering the basic specification with no controls for occupations and firm heterogeneity (Annex table 4A.4, rows 1A–7A), we find that the gender variable has very little influence in Benin, Kenya, Madagascar, Senegal, and Uganda. In these countries, the gender dummy explains, at most, 0.5 percent (in Madagascar) of the overall wage differences. The weight of the gender coefficient is much more important in Morocco (5.6 percent), and it is even three times higher in Mauritius (18.6 percent). So, among the selected African countries, the problem of gender inequality in earnings is greatest in Mauritius. The contribution of the gender variable still amounts to 17.5 percent when occupations are taken into account, and to 15.7 percent when both occupations and firm fixed effects are controlled for (rows 4A–4C).

It is interesting, then, to examine the relative contribution of the other covariates. In all countries, wages are mainly explained by years of schooling. The contribution of the education variable is greater than 70 percent in Benin, Madagascar, Morocco, and Uganda, and it exceeds 50 percent in all seven African countries. Years of experience and years of tenure come after, the contribution of seniority being substantially higher than that of experience (except in Kenya and Uganda). Significant changes are observed in the weights once occupations are taken into account (rows 1B–7B). Occupations are very important in Kenya, Madagascar, Morocco, and Uganda, where they explain about one-half of the total wage differences.[21]

A last finding concerns the inclusion of firm fixed effects (rows 1C–7C). The contribution of the firm heterogeneity is substantial, as it exceeds 20 percent in Madagascar and Morocco, up to 30 percent in Benin and Uganda. Furthermore, controlling for the firm effects significantly reduces the contribution of the schooling variable. This may be a result of the sorting of workers, the most productive workers being hired in firms offering higher wages.

Gender Wage Gap Along the Conditional Wage Distribution

According to the ICA surveys, the mean wage level of is significantly different for men and women in both Mauritius and Morocco. However, a gender wage gap not being seen for the other countries using OLS regressions does not necessarily mean that there is no gender wage gap in the manufacturing firms. In the context of a developed country, Albrecht, Björklund, and Vroman (2003) show that the gender gap is unlikely to remain constant throughout the wage distribution. We thus turn to quantile regressions, further described in Annex 4B, to investigate the magnitude of the gender wage gap along the wage distribution using the male-female pooled samples (Koenker 2005).

We first focus on two countries where men and women receive different mean wages (Annex table 4A.5). On one hand, the gender wage gap does not really vary across the wage distribution in Mauritius; for example, the difference in earnings is 35.9 percent at the 25th percentile, 34.6 percent at the median, and 38.1 percent at the 90th percentile. Thus, there is no sharp increase in the gender gap when considering the upper part of the wage distribution of that country. On the other hand, the gender gap is almost three times higher at the 90th percentile than at the 10th percentile in Morocco (16.8 percent instead of 6.1 percent, respectively).

The quantile estimates for the five other countries show that the shape of the gender wage gap is really country-specific. In Benin, differences in earnings between men and women are now significant in the lower part of the wage distribution. Women receive much lower wages than men at the 10th and 25th percentiles, respectively, 30.8 percent and 9.3 percent. The opposite pattern holds true in Uganda. Women out-earn men in the lower part of the wage distribution, with a female wage premium exceeding 20 percent. However, women receive significantly lower wages at the 90th percentile. Finally, there is no clear variation across the distribution in Kenya, Madagascar, and Senegal. Accounting for occupations also affects the magnitude of the gender gap, which is significant, in particular, at the 25th and 75th percentiles in Madagascar when controlling for occupations in the quantile regressions.[22]

Quantile Decomposition of Differences in Distributions

A very restrictive assumption in the previous regressions is the fact that the returns to individual characteristics must be the same for men and women. Unfortunately, this hypothesis of equal returns is unlikely to hold if there are strong selection effects of female employees, for example, resulting from sorting of firms and workers. It is straightforward to decompose the total difference in earnings between men and women into two components, one due to differences in labor market characteristics and one due to differences in the returns to these characteristics (see Annex 4B). For each country, figure 4.3 shows the plot of the magnitude of the gender wage gap across the earnings distribution calculated from gender-specific regressions. The relative contribution of the differences in characteristics and in coefficients are also indicated.

The analysis first focuses on Mauritius and Morocco, two countries where gender differences are large. While the gender wage gap remains fairly flat in

Figure 4.3 Quantile Decompositions of the Gender Wage Gap, by Country

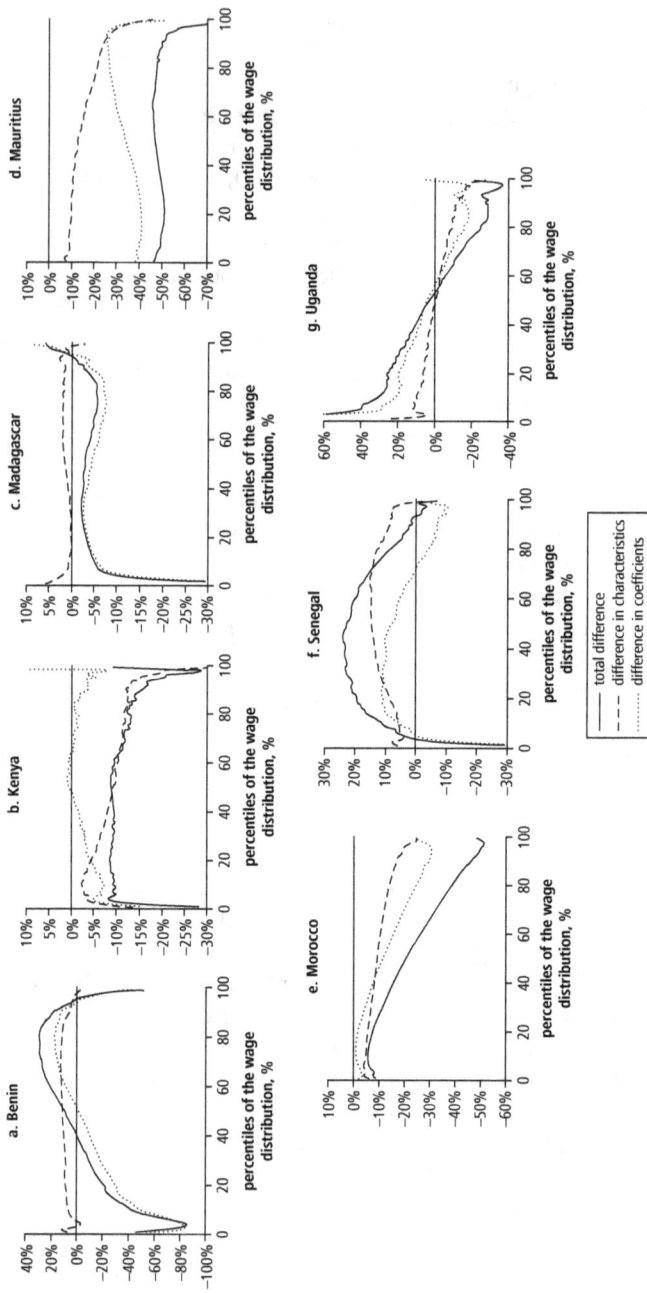

a. Benin

b. Kenya

c. Madagascar

d. Mauritius

e. Morocco

f. Senegal

g. Uganda

percentiles of the wage distribution, %

— total difference
--- difference in characteristics
······ difference in coefficients

Sources: Investment Climate Surveys for Benin (2004), Kenya (2003), Madagascar (2005), Mauritius (2005), Senegal (2003), and Uganda (2003); FACS for Morocco (2000); authors' calculations.

the former country, it is strongly increasing in absolute value in the latter. In Mauritius, the role of differences in characteristics is higher in the upper part of the distribution (above the 90th percentile), while differences of returns to these characteristics matter more in the lower part. For example, differences in coefficients are about four times higher than differences in characteristics until the median earnings. An opposite pattern holds in Morocco. The role of labor market returns is increasing along the distribution, and the weight of differences in coefficients exceeds the weight of differences in characteristics above the 40th percentile.

Regarding the other countries, the contribution of differences in coefficients, when explaining earnings inequality between men and women, strongly varies across the wage distribution. In Benin and Senegal, women would receive higher wages than men if they were paid on the same basis for their individual characteristics. In Kenya, the gender wage gap essentially results from the fact that men and women working in the manufacturing sectors have different individual characteristics, as can be seen in the curves of total difference and difference in endowments, which are almost merged, especially above the median. Conversely, in Madagascar and Uganda, the gender wage gap essentially stems from differences in returns to the disadvantage of women.

The Role of Firm Characteristics

From the previous discussion, it is clear that wage policies settled by firms are likely to influence gender earnings differentials. An interesting question, then, is to discover whether firms' characteristics tend to increase or reduce the gender earnings gap. For that purpose, the previous Oaxaca-Blinder decomposition was extended following Meng (2004) to account for the role of the firm fixed effects (see Annex 4B). The total earnings differential is given by the sum of three terms: one related to differences in individual characteristics, one related to differences in the returns to these characteristics, and one related to difference in the firm's premium paid to male and female employees. When this last term is negative, it means that the firm tends to narrow the gender wage gap, in which case the gap would have been higher without the role of the firm's wage policy.

As Meng (2004) points out, the above decomposition does not account for the possibility of gender segregation across firms. The first step to controlling for the role of gender segregation is to estimate gender-specific wage equations, including both individual and firm explanatory variables, and add into the list of covariates the proportion of female employees measured at the firm level. This allows inclusion of the effect of the gender employment ratio on earnings. In the second step, these estimates are used to compute for each employee the predicted value of earnings, which is now net of gender segregation across firms.[23] Finally, the fixed effects decomposition is performed using the adjusted wage as dependent variable.

Estimating gender-specific fixed-effect regressions implies that the sample is now restricted to firms with at least two male and two female employees. This significantly reduces the size of the selected samples, especially in countries like Benin, Kenya, Senegal, and Uganda, where the proportion of female employees is somewhat low in the formal manufacturing sectors. As a consequence, we note that the total difference in earnings between men and women is substantially higher with the new sample selection in Kenya and Uganda, for example.

As shown in Annex table 4A.6 and figure 4.4, the main conclusion from the decomposition of the fixed effects model is that firms do not really influence the magnitude of the gender earnings gap in the African labor markets, except in Senegal. In Benin, the positive sign for the component of the firm effects indicates that the firm wage policies are associated with a rise in the gender earnings gap,

Figure 4.4 Decomposition of Gender Earnings Differentials Accounting for Gender Segregation Across Firms

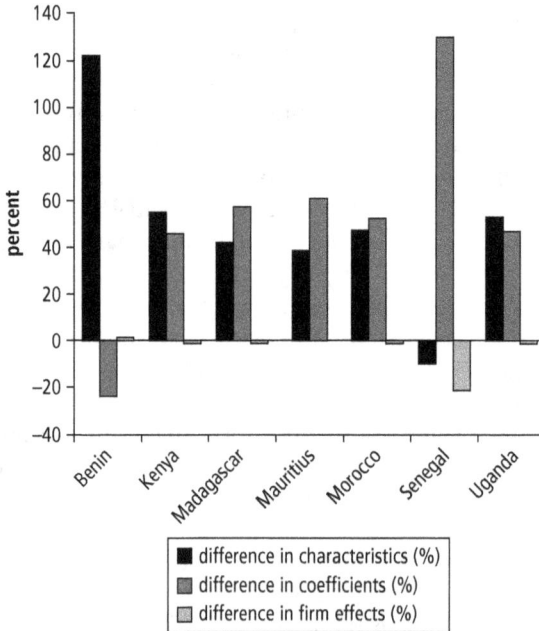

Sources: Investment Climate Surveys for Benin (2004), Kenya (2003), Madagascar (2005), Mauritius (2005), Senegal (2003), and Uganda (2003); FACS for Morocco (2000); authors' calculations.

but the corresponding impact remains very limited (1.5 percent). An opposite pattern is found in Kenya, with a decrease of 0.9 percent of the gender gap, while the variation is even smaller in Madagascar, Mauritius, Morocco, and Uganda. The negative coefficient is larger in Senegal, indicating that firms pay a higher wage premium to their female employees than to their male employees.[24] On the whole, the study findings thus suggest that African manufacturing firms do not really attempt to narrow gender differences in pay.

Conclusions

This study makes use of matched employer-employee data collected in seven African countries (Benin, Kenya, Madagascar, Mauritius, Morocco, Senegal, and Uganda) to shed light on the magnitude of the gender wage gap in the manufacturing sector. With such data, it is possible to account for the effect of the firm's wage policy on gender earnings differentials. This is crucial if firms tend to pay men and women differently. Taking into account the employer's effect on wages is also a way to reduce the bias in the gender wage gap estimates that can be present if the workers sort across firms offering different wages. Such analysis would not be feasible using only household surveys, where there is generally no information on the respondent's employer.

The various empirical analyses conducted in this study lead to the following conclusions. First, preliminary statistics justify taking a distributional approach to obtain a proper view of the magnitude of the gender wage gaps in Africa. Indeed, raw gender gaps calculated at the mean of the samples tend to hide significant differences in the magnitude of the gaps along the wage distribution. This is particularly true in the cases of Benin, Morocco, and Uganda, where the raw gaps vary significantly depending on the workers' relative position in the wage distribution. In Benin, for instance, the raw gap is significantly in favor of men in the lower part of the wage distribution, while it favors women in its upper part. By contrast, the reverse holds true for Uganda, where the gap reverses sign and is detrimental to women in the upper part of the distribution. In Morocco, the significant gap increases steadily all along the wage distribution, thereby revealing the potential existence of a glass ceiling effect against women at the top of the distribution (Nordman and Wolff 2009a).

Second, wage regressions were estimated controlling for workers' human capital and job characteristics and for heterogeneity at the firm level. This investigation suggests that a distinction should be made between two groups of countries. In the first group, Benin, Kenya, Madagascar, Senegal, and Uganda, there is no significant evidence of difference in male and female earnings once worker, job, and firm characteristics are accounted for. In the second group,

Mauritius and Morocco, earnings are found to be statistically different between men and women.

We then investigated the belief that differences among the seven African countries might be a result of the presence of selectivity effects, through gender differences in access to jobs. Indeed, since there are few women working in the formal manufacturing sectors in Benin, Kenya, Senegal, and Uganda, these women are likely to have unobserved characteristics positively correlated with their productivity. This is expected to strongly reduce differences in earnings between men and women. Unfortunately, not much can be done to correct selectivity effects with such datasets, which is a shortcoming of the present study.

The study then performed a regression-based decomposition of the explained portion of the individual wage differentials into weights for each of the considered covariates (including gender, workers' human capital, and firm effects). In Benin, Kenya, Madagascar, Senegal, and Uganda, the gender dummy explains at most 0.5 percent of the overall wage difference, while the weight of gender is much more important in Morocco (5.6 percent), and even three times higher in Mauritius (18.6 percent). Thus, among the selected African manufacturing sectors, gender inequality in earnings is of greatest concern in Mauritius. By contrast, the contribution of education in this decomposition is much more important since it exceeds 50 percent in the seven African countries. The weight of firm heterogeneity in earnings differentials is also important, with contributions of about 20 percent in Madagascar and Morocco, up to 30 percent in Benin and Uganda.

An additional step in the analysis is to investigate the pattern of the adjusted gender wage gaps along the wage distribution using quantile regressions. Indeed, not observing an adjusted gender gap using regressions at the means (OLS regressions) does not necessarily signify that there is no unfair earnings treatment in the investigated manufacturing firms. We find that the adjusted gender gap does not really vary across the wage distribution in Mauritius. By contrast, the adjusted gender gap is almost three times higher at the ninth decile than at the first decile in Morocco. The quantile estimates for the other countries show that the shape of the adjusted gender gap is country-specific. For example, in Benin, unexplained differences in earnings between men and women hold only in the lower part of the wage distribution, while the opposite pattern is found in Uganda. In addition, there is no clear variation across the distribution in Kenya, Madagascar, and Senegal.

Next, earnings decompositions at quantiles were performed, which separate the total difference in earnings between men and women into two components: one resulting from differences in individuals' labor market characteristics and the other resulting from differences in the returns to these characteristics. In Mauritius, the role of differences in characteristics is higher in the upper part of the distribution, while differences of returns to these characteristics matter more in its lower part. An opposite pattern holds in Morocco, where the role of labor market returns is increasing along the distribution and the weight of differences in coefficients exceeds the weight of differences in characteristics above the fourth decile. Results are mixed for the other countries, where the contribution of differences in returns in explaining earnings inequality between men and women was found to vary strongly along the wage distribution. For instance, in Benin and Senegal, female employees would receive higher wages than their male counterparts if they were paid on the same basis for their individual characteristics.

An interesting question is whether the firms' characteristics tend to increase or reduce the gender earnings gap. Thus, a third term was added to the preceding decompositions: the difference in the firm's premium paid to male and female employees. A negative third term would indicate that the firm tends to narrow the gender wage gap. In addition, we account for the possible firm sorting by adjusting wages using the proportion of female employees in each firm. This is a way to correct for the potential bias in the gender wage gap estimates resulting from the sorting of males and females across firms offering different wages. The main conclusion from these last decompositions is that firms do not really influence the magnitude of the gender earnings gap in the African labor markets, except in Senegal. This suggests that African manufacturing firms do not really attempt to narrow gender wage inequalities.

This last result is in contrast to findings in developed countries, where the impact of the firm effects on the magnitude of the gender wage gap appears more substantial. In Australia and France, for example, Meng (2004) and Meng and Meurs (2004) show that firm wage policies are associated with a significant narrowing of the gender earnings gaps, especially in the former. Nevertheless, it is not possible to provide comparison points with other developing countries because, to the best of our knowledge, this study of the gender wage gaps with matched data on African countries is the first of its kind. Nevertheless, it is likely that the nature of the data used in this study—that is, collected in relatively homogenous manufacturing sectors, while those used in developed countries usually include service industries (Meng and Meurs 2004)—hides the possible existence of more influential firm wage strategies in Africa, in particular in large firms.

A few caveats should be noted when interpreting these results. First, focusing on the manufacturing sectors only means the nature of the samples is highly specific. It would then be worthwhile to expand the availability of matched data for further studies in other formal sectors, not only in the study countries but also in other African countries. A second shortcoming is the impossibility of further examining the selection effect resulting from unequal access to job opportunities among men and women. As shown in our empirical analysis, the very low proportion of women employed in some countries suggests that access to jobs in the manufacturing sector may be very selective.

It would then be of interest to better understand why countries such as Mauritius and Morocco have so many more women hired than the other countries in the study. It could be a result of different sectoral composition of the economy, but might also stem from the labor markets functioning in different ways. Clearly, more information is needed to understand the factors behind access to jobs, especially for women. A complementary analysis based on cross-sectional data, with information on both working and non-working people, would allow for an analysis of the factors explaining the probability that a woman would have a job and for an estimate of selectivity-corrected wage regressions. The drawback with such household data is the lack of firm characteristics for those who have jobs, which is certainly needed as our analysis has highlighted the necessity to account for the firms' characteristics (either observed or unobserved).

While understanding the driving forces behind hiring is a task left for future research, institutional and economic policies that might be pursued to encourage equal hiring in different countries with different industrial profiles are strongly recommended to reduce the magnitude of earnings differences between men and women. To reduce the gender gap, policies aimed at promoting women's access to quality jobs in high-paying firms in the formal sector, as well as policies intended to foster equal pay for equal jobs, would be needed. As it stands, our empirical analysis sheds light on the necessity of further examining the gender wage gap in all African countries and of assessing the role of gender-specific access to jobs on this gap. For that purpose, additional quantitative findings along with qualitative analysis would be helpful.

Annex 4A Tables

Table 4A.1 Descriptive Statistics on the Workforce

	Benin			Kenya			Madagascar			Mauritius		
	Men	Women	All	Men	Women	All	Men	Women	All	Men	Women	All
Log hourly earnings	5.68	5.65	5.67	4.14	4.03	4.12	8.03	7.98	8.01	4.46	3.96	4.24
Female	0	1	0.14	0	1	0.19	0	1	0.37	0	1	0.44
Married	0.69	0.65	0.69	n.a.	n.a.	n.a.	0.79	0.65	0.74	0.70	0.70	0.70
Years of completed schooling	9.50	10.04	9.58	11.63	12.27	11.75	11.63	12.34	11.89	10.15	9.85	10.02
Years of experience off the firm	3.67	3.19	3.60	4.43	2.08	3.99	5.75	3.70	4.99	7.12	5.17	6.26
Years of tenure in the current firm	5.96	5.57	5.90	9.25	7.15	8.85	6.26	5.70	6.05	9.99	7.39	8.85
Occupations												
Owners (as managers)	0.07	0.04	0.06	0.02	0	0.02	0.01	0.01	0.01	0.02	0.01	0.01
Employed managers	0.06	0.15	0.07	0.09	0.06	0.08	0.02	0.02	0.02	0.05	0.01	0.04
Professionals (university degree)	0.10	0.12	0.10	0.06	0.06	0.06	0.07	0.09	0.08	0.07	0.06	0.06
Technicians (with diploma or other formal qualification)	0.21	0.06	0.19	0.14	0.07	0.12	0.07	0.04	0.06	0.10	0.02	0.06
Skilled foremen and supervisors	0.05	0.04	0.05	0.13	0.05	0.11	0.08	0.08	0.08	0.14	0.08	0.11
Skilled machine maintenance and repair workers	0.03	0.01	0.03	0.16	0.01	0.13	0.07	0.02	0.05	0.15	0.07	0.11
Unskilled production workers	0.20	0.16	0.20	0.23	0.20	0.22	0.47	0.40	0.44	0.24	0.29	0.26
Health workers, office and sales workers	0.07	0.35	0.11	0.11	0.46	0.17	0.06	0.22	0.12	0.12	0.33	0.21
Service workers (cleaners, guards)	0.21	0.07	0.19	0.07	0.08	0.08	0.15	0.13	0.14	0.12	0.14	0.13
Number of observations	1,346	228	1,574	1,522	354	1,876	1,093	641	1,734	764	599	1,363

continued

Table 4A.1 Descriptive Statistics on the Workforce *continued*

	Morocco			Senegal			Uganda		
	Men	Women	All	Men	Women	All	Men	Women	All
Log hourly earnings	2.68	2.45	2.59	6.57	6.71	6.60	6.75	6.82	6.76
Female	0	1.00	0.40	0	1.00	0.18	0	1.00	0.19
Married	0.64	0.33	0.51	0.68	0.59	0.67	n.a.	n.a.	n.a.
Years of completed schooling	8.81	8.51	8.69	10.05	12.82	10.53	11.56	12.07	11.66
Years of experience off the firm	1.86	1.26	1.62	4.75	2.91	4.42	4.02	2.49	3.73
Years of tenure in the current firm	8.14	6.04	7.30	8.52	6.82	8.22	5.29	4.94	5.22
Occupations									
Owners (as managers)	0.07	0.02	0.05	0.02	0	0.02	0.11	0.06	0.10
Employed managers	0.11	0.07	0.10	0.04	0.07	0.05	0.14	0.04	0.12
Professionals (university degree)				0.12	0.11	0.12	0.08	0.12	0.09
Technicians (with diploma or other formal qualification)	0.40[a]	0.39[a]	0.40[a]	0.14	0.07	0.12	0.07	0.03	0.06
Skilled foremen and supervisors				0.06	0.02	0.05	0.12	0.06	0.11
Skilled machine maintenance and repair workers				0.10	0.01	0.08	0.07	0.02	0.06
Unskilled production workers	0.27	0.33	0.29	0.35	0.14	0.32	0.29	0.24	0.28
Health workers, office and sales workers	0.15[b]	0.18[b]	0.16[b]	0.06	0.51	0.14	0.04	0.26	0.08
Service workers (cleaners, guards)	0[c]	0.01[c]	0[c]	0.11	0.06	0.10	0.07	0.16	0.09
Number of observations	4,686	3,120	7,806	1,112	237	1,349	1,058	248	1,306

Sources: Investment Climate Surveys for Benin (2004), Kenya (2003), Madagascar (2005), Mauritius (2005), Senegal (2003), and Uganda (2003); FACS for Morocco (2000).
Note: For Morocco, the occupations correspond to different regroupings: a. skilled workers and technicians; b. nonproduction employees; and c. apprentices.

176

Table 4A.2 Descriptive Statistics on the Firms

	Benin		Kenya		Madagascar		Mauritius	
	Mean	Standard deviation	Mean	Standard deviation	Mean	Standard deviation	Mean	Standard deviation
Total number of employees	38.90	74.03	227.27	443.59	191.91	446.07	174.19	424.89
Share of female employees	0.13	0.18	0.14	0.14	0.33	0.31	0.38	0.30
Principal owner is female (1 if yes)			0.03	0.18	0.20	0.40	0.10	0.30
Share of managers/executives in the permanent employees	0.17	0.14	0.16	0.17	0.06	0.05	0.10	0.17
Share of executives in the permanent employees	0.09	0.13	0.05	0.09	0.06	0.07	0.03	0.05
Exporting firm (1 if yes)	0.22	0.41	0.51	0.50	0.30	0.46	0.64	0.48
Sector dummies								
Agro industry	0.20	0.40	0.29	0.45	0.11	0.31		
Chemicals and related products	0.05	0.21	0.09	0.28	0.04	0.20		
Materials for construction	0.05	0.22	0.06	0.23	0.06	0.24		
Furniture	0.19	0.39	0.03	0.18	0.13	0.34		
Metallic products	0.11	0.32	0.15	0.36	0.29	0.46		
Industry of paper, paper products and plastics products	0.24	0.43	0.15	0.36	0.02	0.14		
Textiles and leather	0.02	0.14	0.18	0.39	0.23	0.42		
Wood	0.13	0.34	0.04	0.21	0.02	0.16		
Other	0.01	0.07	0	0	0.09	0.28		
Number of observations	194		248		281		189	

continued

177

Table 4A.2 Descriptive Statistics on the Firms *continued*

	Morocco		Senegal		Uganda	
	Mean	Standard deviation	Mean	Standard deviation	Mean	Standard deviation
Total number of employees	123.46	198.95	123.26	411.11	144.35	617.29
Share of female employees	0.56	2.13	0.11	0.14	0.17	0.18
Principal owner is female (1 if yes)	0.05	0.21	0.05	0.22	0.05	0.21
Share of managers/executives in the permanent employees	0.05	0.07	0.15	0.19	0.28	0.29
Share of executives in the permanent employees	0.04	0.06	0.07	0.09	0.08	0.14
Exporting firm (1 if yes)	0.57	0.50	0.50	0.50	0.18	0.39
Sector dummies						
Agro industry/Food for Morocco	0.10	0.30	0.36	0.48	0.40	0.49
Chemicals and related products/Chemicals only for Morocco	0.09	0.28	0.13	0.34	0.06	0.25
Materials for construction/Textile for Morocco	0.24	0.42	0.07	0.25	0.14	0.34
Furniture/Garments for Morocco	0.37	0.48	0.02	0.15	0.15	0.36
Metallic products/Electrical for Morocco	0.05	0.21	0.10	0.30	0.07	0.26
Industry of paper, paper products, and plastics products/Plastics products only for Morocco	0.09	0.28	0.19	0.40	0.10	0.30
Textiles and leather/Leather only for Morocco	0.08	0.27	0.09	0.29	0.05	0.22
Wood	0	0	0.04	0.19	0.02	0.14
Other						
Number of observations	842		249		264	

Sources: Investment Climate Surveys for Benin (2004), Kenya (2003), Madagascar (2005), Mauritius (2005), Senegal (2003), and Uganda (2003); FACS for Morocco (2000).

178

Table 4A.3 Linear Regression of the Log Hourly Wages

	Benin				Kenya				Madagascar				Mauritius			
	(1A)	(1B)	(1C)	(1D)	(2A)	(2B)	(2C)	(2D)	(3A)	(3B)	(3C)	(3D)	(4A)	(4B)	(4C)	(4D)
Female	-0.101	-0.085	-0.005	-0.036	-0.010	-0.064	-0.011	-0.036	-0.056	-0.098**	0.011	-0.047	-0.353***	-0.397***	-0.227***	-0.223***
	(0.97)	(0.82)	(0.10)	(0.72)	(0.18)	(1.29)	(0.25)	(0.87)	(1.29)	(2.19)	(0.32)	(1.33)	(7.98)	(9.26)	(6.37)	(6.25)
Married	0.188***	0.180***	0.108*	0.070					0.094**	0.118***	0.040	0.052	0.084**	0.070*	0.125***	0.107***
	(2.81)	(2.76)	(1.94)	(1.39)					(2.21)	(2.82)	(1.07)	(1.55)	(1.98)	(1.74)	(3.97)	(3.57)
Years of completed schooling	0.044	0.043	-0.030	-0.036*	0.188***	0.093***	0.149***	0.048***	0.047**	0.028*	0.041**	0.015	-0.033*	-0.054***	-0.009	-0.027
	(1.22)	(1.34)	(1.45)	(1.67)	(7.43)	(4.71)	(6.31)	(2.64)	(2.18)	(1.67)	(2.57)	(1.27)	(1.72)	(3.28)	(0.42)	(1.51)
(Years of completed schooling)²/10	0.037**	0.027*	0.056***	0.038***	-0.032***	-0.016***	-0.034***	-0.012	0.010	0.005	0.009	0.006	0.062***	0.049***	0.050***	0.036***
	(2.29)	(1.83)	(5.50)	(3.78)	(4.70)	(3.15)	(3.25)	(1.64)	(1.12)	(0.73)	(1.35)	(1.40)	(6.03)	(5.67)	(4.40)	(4.08)
Years of experience off the firm	0.014	0.013	0.055***	0.043***	0.077***	0.049***	0.079***	0.049***	0.003	0.005	0.004	0.004	0.028***	0.020**	0.017**	0.010
	(0.99)	(0.92)	(4.78)	(3.76)	(8.28)	(5.92)	(9.58)	(6.85)	(0.36)	(0.76)	(0.61)	(0.63)	(3.26)	(2.46)	(2.31)	(1.44)
(Years of experience off the firm)²/100	0.003	0.006	-0.111**	-0.118***	-0.183***	-0.118***	-0.171***	-0.108***	0.030	0.010	0.028	0.017	-0.052	-0.038	-0.005	0.002
	(0.04)	(0.11)	(2.53)	(2.72)	(4.74)	(3.65)	(5.11)	(4.12)	(0.93)	(0.34)	(0.93)	(0.58)	(1.46)	(1.10)	(0.14)	(0.05)
Years of tenure in the current firm	0.041***	0.040**	0.027**	0.008	0.057***	0.055***	0.041***	0.040***	0.034***	0.031***	0.033***	0.027***	0.056***	0.050***	0.056***	0.048***
	(2.68)	(2.57)	(2.04)	(0.74)	(5.41)	(5.89)	(3.86)	(4.65)	(3.11)	(2.87)	(3.57)	(3.00)	(7.25)	(6.90)	(8.03)	(7.38)
(Years of tenure in the current firm)²/100	-0.041	-0.054	0.003	0.007	-0.071**	-0.096***	-0.041	-0.071**	-0.064	-0.072**	-0.056**	-0.059**	-0.091***	-0.084***	-0.098***	-0.089***
	(0.77)	(1.03)	(0.07)	(0.17)	(2.14)	(3.21)	(1.10)	(2.36)	(1.62)	(1.98)	(2.01)	(2.19)	(3.72)	(3.72)	(4.75)	(4.66)
Constant	4.451***	4.648***	4.931***	5.353***	1.802***	3.993***	2.372***	4.074***	7.065***	7.925***	7.158***	8.356***	3.461***	4.563***	3.319***	4.455***
	(22.74)	(21.10)	(43.68)	(37.83)	(7.61)	(15.20)	(13.61)	(23.68)	(52.47)	(30.77)	(69.56)	(35.43)	(32.29)	(14.49)	(28.66)	(32.19)
Dummies for occupation	No	Yes	No	Yes	No	Yes	No	Yes	No	Yes	No	Yes	No	Yes	No	Yes
Firm fixed effects	No	No	Yes	Yes	No	No	Yes	Yes	No	No	Yes	Yes	No	No	Yes	Yes
Observations	1574	1574	1574	1574	1876	1876	1876	1876	1734	1734	1734	1734	1363	1363	1363	1363
R-squared	0.35	0.37	0.69	0.73	0.24	0.45	0.61	0.75	0.21	0.32	0.66	0.73	0.36	0.43	0.70	0.75

Table 4A.3 Linear Regression of the Log Hourly Wages *continued*

	Morocco				Senegal				Uganda			
	(5A)	(5B)	(5C)	(5D)	(6A)	(6B)	(6C)	(6D)	(7A)	(7B)	(7C)	(7D)
Female	-0.124*** (8.27)	-0.086*** (6.20)	-0.133*** (10.07)	-0.075*** (6.32)	0.037 (0.69)	-0.063 (1.00)	0.024 (0.49)	-0.042 (0.81)	0.075 (0.84)	0.109 (1.27)	-0.128 (1.26)	-0.005 (0.05)
Married	0.129*** (8.84)	0.081*** (6.20)	0.110*** (9.64)	0.070*** (7.04)	0.239*** (5.47)	0.196*** (4.69)	0.099** (2.13)	0.071* (1.70)	0.174*** (3.48)	0.069 (1.60)	0.094** (2.31)	0.021 (0.58)
Years of completed schooling	-0.043*** (5.26)	-0.014** (2.50)	-0.046*** (7.66)	-0.011** (2.60)	0.026** (2.22)	0.013 (1.24)	0.016 (1.49)	0.005 (0.57)	-0.025 (1.13)	-0.003 (0.16)	0.001 (0.04)	0.004 (0.26)
(Years of completed schooling)²/10	6.001*** (10.36)	2.718*** (6.38)	5.926*** (13.73)	1.892*** (6.26)	0.028*** (4.83)	0.017*** (3.41)	0.025*** (4.57)	0.013*** (2.86)				
Years of experience off the firm	0.030*** (7.99)	0.020*** (5.78)	0.030*** (9.62)	0.019*** (6.75)	0.034*** (4.13)	0.027*** (3.26)	0.032*** (4.18)	0.027*** (3.70)	0.084*** (3.55)	0.056*** (2.71)	0.066*** (3.57)	0.031** (2.22)
(Years of experience off the firm)²/100	-0.063*** (6.63)	-0.044*** (4.62)	-0.049*** (7.82)	-0.034*** (5.24)	-0.063* (1.85)	-0.060* (1.75)	-0.034 (1.07)	-0.041 (1.41)	-0.174* (1.68)	-0.121 (1.30)	-0.121 (1.54)	-0.067 (1.11)
Years of tenure in the current firm	0.022*** (6.31)	0.017*** (5.23)	0.033*** (9.44)	0.019*** (5.74)	0.054*** (5.56)	0.049*** (5.34)	0.041*** (3.85)	0.034*** (3.35)	0.056*** (3.16)	0.030 (1.51)	0.074*** (4.35)	0.026* (1.79)
(Years of tenure in the current firm)²/100	-0.886 (0.73)	0.040 (0.03)	-4.686*** (3.94)	-2.312** (2.07)	-0.066** (2.03)	-0.063** (1.98)	-0.056* (1.69)	-0.051 (1.57)	-0.134** (2.34)	-0.084 (1.29)	-0.156*** (3.10)	-0.073 (1.35)
Constant	2.120*** (78.80)	3.019*** (53.15)	2.125*** (88.24)	3.164*** (63.26)	5.276*** (61.03)	6.102*** (36.91)	5.608*** (68.17)	6.643*** (52.84)	4.656*** (14.51)	5.853*** (18.52)	5.185*** (17.32)	5.936*** (24.19)
Dummies for occupation	No	Yes	No	Yes	No	Yes	No	Yes	No	Yes	No	Yes
Firm fixed effects	No	No	Yes	Yes	No	No	Yes	Yes	No	No	Yes	Yes
Observations	7,806	7,806	7,806	7,806	1,349	1,349	1,349	1,349	1,306	1,306	1,306	1,306
R-squared	0.33	0.44	0.65	0.74	0.39	0.46	0.70	0.75	0.18	0.27	0.70	0.77

Sources: Investment Climate Surveys for Benin (2004), Kenya (2003), Madagascar (2005), Mauritius (2005), Senegal (2003), and Uganda (2003); FACS for Morocco (2000); authors' calculations.
Note: Standard errors are robust to clustering at the firm level.
*** = significant at 1%, ** = significant at 5%, * = significant at 10%.

Table 4A.4 Decomposition Using Fields of the Log Hourly Wages

Country	Gender (%)	Marital status (%)	Explanatory variables Years of schooling (%)	Years of experience (%)	Years of tenure (%)	Occupation (%)	Firm effects (%)	Total (%)
Benin								
(1A) Basic	0.09	4.66	83.78	2.40	9.07	—	—	100.00
(1B) Basic + occupations	0.05	4.15	64.09	2.26	7.25	22.19	—	100.00
(1C) Basic + occ. + fixed effects	0.00	3.77	39.92	2.22	4.65	16.52	32.92	100.00
Kenya								
(2A) Basic	0.04	n.a.	65.25	18.46	16.25	—	—	100.00
(2B) Basic + occupations	0.22	n.a.	17.35	6.25	6.94	69.24	—	100.00
(2C) Basic + occ. + fixed effects	0.14	n.a.	15.89	6.04	5.92	55.94	16.08	100.00
Madagascar								
(3A) Basic	0.52	2.32	83.98	1.33	11.85	—	—	100.00
(3B) Basic + occupations	0.59	1.93	31.50	0.62	6.06	59.30	—	100.00
(3C) Basic + occ. + fixed effects	0.56	1.30	20.58	0.41	4.70	48.78	23.68	100.00
Mauritius								
(4A) Basic	18.52	1.71	51.84	3.40	24.52	—	—	100.00
(4B) Basic + occupations	17.46	1.18	23.63	2.13	17.97	37.64	—	100.00
(4C) Basic + occ. + fixed effects	15.75	1.08	20.85	1.81	15.49	33.62	11.40	100.00
Morocco								
(5A) Basic	5.56	6.17	72.42	3.47	12.37	—	—	100.00
(5B) Basic + occupations	2.88	2.91	28.42	1.63	8.08	56.07	—	100.00
(5C) Basic + occ. + fixed effects	2.33	2.31	17.84	1.29	5.44	48.86	21.91	100.00
Senegal								
(6A) Basic	0.23	8.14	64.70	6.27	20.67	—	—	100.00
(6B) Basic + occupations	-0.33	5.71	31.95	3.81	15.52	43.34	—	100.00
(6C) Basic + occ. + fixed effects	-0.06	5.09	26.38	3.84	10.53	38.50	15.72	100.00
Uganda								
(7A) Basic	0.17	n.a.	71.60	23.12	5.12	—	—	100.00
(7B) Basic + occupations	0.18	n.a.	24.51	9.76	1.68	63.87	—	100.00
(7C) Basic + occ. + fixed effects	-0.08	n.a.	15.33	3.76	0.69	44.72	35.59	100.00

Sources: Investment Climate Surveys for Benin (2004), Kenya (2003), Madagascar (2005), Mauritius (2005), Senegal (2003), and Uganda (2003); FACS for Morocco (2000); authors' calculations.

Note: occ. = occupation.

Table 4A.5 Gender Estimates from Quantile Regressions of the Log Hourly Wages

Country	Percentile					Mean
	10th	25th	50th	75th	90th	
Benin						
Basic	-0.308***	-0.093*	-0.012	-0.015	0.049	-0.101
	(4.73)	(1.73)	(0.21)	(0.24)	(0.44)	(0.97)
Basic + occupations	-0.196**	-0.139***	-0.085	0.014	0.129	-0.085
	(2.32)	(2.86)	(1.38)	(0.18)	(1.27)	(0.82)
Basic + occupation + fixed effects	0.001	-0.001	-0.032	-0.031	-0.052	-0.036
	(0.02)	(0.02)	(0.52)	(0.61)	(0.89)	(0.72)
Kenya						
Basic	-0.005	-0.030	0.019	-0.020	-0.041	-0.010
	(0.09)	(0.85)	(0.35)	(0.25)	(0.37)	(0.18)
Basic + occupations	-0.086*	-0.068	-0.063	-0.080	-0.221*	-0.064
	(1.70)	(1.48)	(1.28)	(1.21)	(1.86)	(1.29)
Basic + occupation + fixed effects	-0.000	-0.028	-0.080*	-0.075	-0.022	-0.036
	(0.01)	(0.88)	(1.77)	(1.45)	(0.40)	(0.87)
Madagascar						
Basic	-0.048	-0.036	-0.004	-0.061	0.014	-0.056
	(1.51)	(0.93)	(0.10)	(1.20)	(0.16)	(1.29)
Basic + occupations	-0.049	-0.080***	-0.054	-0.124***	-0.130	-0.098**
	(1.19)	(2.58)	(1.44)	(2.68)	(1.59)	(2.19)
Basic + occupation + fixed effects	-0.043	-0.039	-0.036	-0.038	-0.046	-0.047
	(1.49)	(1.56)	(1.57)	(1.17)	(1.29)	(1.33)
Mauritius						
Basic	-0.320***	-0.359***	-0.346***	-0.368***	-0.381***	-0.353***
	(5.90)	(8.22)	(8.18)	(7.73)	(5.64)	(7.98)
Basic + occupations	-0.342***	-0.365***	-0.406***	-0.430***	-0.478***	-0.397***
	(4.98)	(9.09)	(9.78)	(10.20)	(7.12)	(9.26)
Basic + occupation + fixed effects	-0.195***	-0.253***	-0.237***	-0.235***	-0.275***	-0.223***
	(5.18)	(9.40)	(8.12)	(7.95)	(7.58)	(6.25)

Morocco						
Basic	-0.061***	-0.069***	-0.095***	-0.137***	-0.168***	-0.124***
	(4.89)	(7.22)	(8.65)	(10.07)	(7.33)	(8.27)
Basic + occupations	-0.053***	-0.057***	-0.066***	-0.102***	-0.135***	-0.086***
	(3.78)	(7.10)	(7.26)	(8.27)	(7.54)	(6.20)
Basic + occupation + fixed effects	-0.022**	-0.036***	-0.044***	-0.067***	-0.091***	-0.075***
	(1.99)	(28.62)	(17.59)	(6.83)	(79.57)	(6.32)
Senegal						
Basic	0.113	0.014	0.025	0.037	0.026	0.037
	(1.14)	(0.25)	(0.53)	(0.51)	(0.25)	(0.69)
Basic + occupations	0.066	-0.035	-0.060	-0.058	-0.118	-0.063
	(0.52)	(0.52)	(1.02)	(0.80)	(1.22)	(1.00)
Basic + occupation + fixed effects	0.057	-0.001	-0.074	-0.085*	-0.082	-0.042
	(1.24)	(0.03)	(1.62)	(1.95)	(1.25)	(0.81)
Uganda						
Basic	0.224*	0.243***	0.050	-0.157	-0.360**	0.075
	(1.76)	(2.61)	(0.53)	(1.26)	(2.41)	(0.84)
Basic + occupations	0.279**	0.113	0.055	-0.073	-0.191	0.109
	(2.52)	(1.15)	(0.73)	(0.57)	(1.20)	(1.27)
Basic + occupation + fixed effects	0.088	0.038	-0.015	-0.145	-0.322*	-0.067
	(0.61)	(0.43)	(0.17)	(0.98)	(1.79)	(0.78)

Sources: Investment Climate Surveys for Benin (2004), Kenya (2003), Madagascar (2005), Mauritius (2005), Senegal (2003), and Uganda (2003); FACS for Morocco (2000); authors' calculations.

*** significant at 1%, ** significant at 5%, * significant at 10%.

Table 4A.6 Decomposition of the Gender Earnings Differentials Accounting for Gender Segregation Across Firms

Country		Benin	Kenya	Madagascar	Mauritius	Morocco	Senegal	Uganda
Difference in characteristics	Value	0.1002	0.1172	0.0271	0.1629	0.1254	−0.0011	0.2516
	%	122.0	55.0	42.3	38.7	47.6	−9.5	53.2
Difference in coefficients	Value	−0.0193	0.0979	0.0369	0.2574	0.1384	0.0148	0.2208
	%	−23.5	45.9	57.4	61.2	52.6	130.0	46.7
Difference in firm effects	Value	0.0012	−0.0018	0.0002	0.0000	−0.0005	−0.0023	0.0002
	%	1.5	−0.9	0.3	0.0	−0.2	−20.5	0.1
Total difference	Value	0.0821	0.2132	0.0642	0.4203	0.2633	0.0114	0.4727
	%	100.0	100.0	100.0	100.0	100.0	100.0	100.0

Sources: Investment Climate Surveys for Benin (2004), Kenya (2003), Madagascar (2005), Mauritius (2005), Senegal (2003), and Uganda (2003); FACS for Morocco (2000); authors' calculations.

Annex 4B Methodology

Regression Analysis

OLS regressions are used to account for gender differences at the mean wage level. We control for several individual characteristics (like age, education, etc) and include in the list of controls a gender dummy variable, so that the model estimated is (with i and j as subscripts, respectively, for the employee and the firm):

$$\ln w_{ji} = \beta X_{ji} + \gamma F_{ji} + \varepsilon_{ji} \qquad (4A.1)$$

with $\ln w_{ji}$ the log hourly wage, X_{ji} the set of covariates, F_{ji} the gender dummy, β and γ parameters to be estimated, and ε_{ji} a residual supposed to be normally distributed. With completed questionnaires for several employees per firm, we calculate robust standard errors (using a clustering procedure) because the different workers within a firm will certainly have correlated characteristics. By accounting for both male and female workers when estimating (equation 4A.1), the underlying assumption is that the returns to the different explanatory variables are not gender-specific.

With repeated information for several employees per firm, we can control for observed and unobserved heterogeneity at the firm level using fixed effects models. Again, we rely on a linear specification of the form:

$$\ln w_{ji} = \beta X_{ji} + \gamma F_{ji} + \delta_j + \varepsilon_{ji} \qquad (4A.2)$$

where δ_j is a firm fixed effect. The model is estimated by adding a set of firm dummy variables in the OLS regressions. The firms' heterogeneity component δ_j is supposed to be correlated with the covariates X_{ji}. Since the workplace is the same for all the workers belonging to a given firm, all the firm characteristics are picked up by the fixed effect.

Fields Decomposition

The decomposition suggested by Fields (2004) may be implemented in the following way. Omitting the different subscripts for simplicity, we consider the linear regression $\ln w = \beta X + \gamma F + \varepsilon$ and assume that there are K exogenous regressors in X indexed by k (with $k = 1,\ldots,K$). Then, the variance of the dependent variable $\ln w$ can be expressed as:

$$\mathrm{var}(\ln w) = \sum_k \mathrm{cov}(\beta_k X_k, \ln w) + \mathrm{cov}(\gamma F, \ln w) + \mathrm{cov}(\varepsilon, \ln w) \cdot \qquad (4A.3)$$

Let us define $s(X_k) = \mathrm{cov}(\beta_k X_k, \ln w) / \mathrm{var}(\ln w)$, $s(F) = \mathrm{cov}(\gamma F, \ln w) / \mathrm{var}(\ln w)$ and $s(\varepsilon) = \mathrm{cov}(\varepsilon, \ln w) / \mathrm{var}(\ln w)$. Using Fields (2004), it follows that:

$$\sum_k s(X_k) + s(F) + s(\varepsilon) = 100\% \qquad (4A.4)$$

which indicates the relative contribution of the various covariates and the residual. The first two terms on the left-hand side of equation 4A.4 sum exactly to the R-squared, so that $s(F)$ and $s(X_k)$ provide, respectively, the weight of gender and the weight of each regressor k.

Quantile Regressions

Quantile wage regressions consider specific parts of the conditional distribution of the hourly wage and indicate the influence of the different explanatory variables on wages, respectively, at the bottom, at the median, and at the top of the log hourly wage distribution. Using our previous notation, the model that we seek to estimate is:

$$q_\theta (\ln w_{ji}) = \beta(\theta)X_{ji} + \gamma(\theta)F_{ji} \qquad (4A.5)$$

where $q_\theta (\ln w_{ji})$ is the θth conditional quantile of the log hourly wage. The set of coefficients $\beta(\theta)$ provides the estimated rates of return to the different covariates (gender being excluded) at the θth quantile of the log wage distribution, and the coefficient $\gamma(\theta)$ measures the part of the wage gap that is due to gender differences. In a quantile regression, the distribution of the error term is left unspecified. The quantile regression method provides robust estimates, particularly for misspecification errors related to non-normality and heteroskedasticity.

Mean and Quantile Decompositions

For the presentation, let $\ln w^H$ and $\ln w^F$ be the log hourly wage of men and women, respectively. From separate regressions, $\ln w^H = \beta^H X^H + \varepsilon^H$ and $\ln w^F = \beta^F X^F + \varepsilon^F$, performed on the male and female subsamples, we deduce that the gender wage gap is $\ln w^H - \ln w^F = \beta^H X^H - \beta^F X^F + \varepsilon^H - \varepsilon^F$. This gap can be decomposed as follows (Oaxaca and Ramson 1994):

$$\ln w^H - \ln w^F = \beta^H (X^H - X^F) + (\beta^H - \beta^F) X^F + (\varepsilon^H - \varepsilon^F) \qquad (4A.6)$$

In equation 4A.6, the first term on the right-hand side $\beta^H (X^H - X^F)$ is the explained part of the gender wage gap, which is a result of differences in individual characteristics between men and women (endowment effects). The second term, $(\beta^H - \beta^F) X^F$, is a result of the difference in the price the market pays to male and female workers for their personal characteristics.

As shown in Machado and Mata (2005), this decomposition may be implemented at the various quantiles of the earnings distribution. The distribution of earnings conditional on individual characteristics is first estimated using linear quantile regressions, then the conditional distribution is approximated by estimating a large number of quantile regressions, and the conditional distribution of earnings is finally integrated over the covariates to obtain the unconditional distribution.

Finally, a similar decomposition may be done in the presence of fixed effects. Using the same notation, we first estimate fixed effects regressions, respectively, for the subsamples of men and women. From $\ln w^H = \beta^H X^H + \delta^H + \varepsilon^H$ and $\ln w^F = \beta^F X^F + \delta^F + \varepsilon^F$ and recalling that δ^H and δ^F are firm fixed effects, it follows that:

$$\ln w^H - \ln w^F = \beta^H (X^H - X^F) + (\beta^H - \beta^F)X^F \\ + (\delta^H - \delta^F) + (\varepsilon^H - \varepsilon^F) \tag{4A.7}$$

According to equation 4A.7, the total earnings differential may be expressed as a sum of three terms. The first one, $\beta^H (X^H - X^F)$, is related to differences in personal characteristics between men and women. The second one, $(\beta^H - \beta^F) X^F$, is a result of differences in the returns to these individual characteristics. Finally, the term $(\delta^H - \delta^F)$ is the difference in the firm's premium, which is paid to male and female employees.

Notes

1. Studies on the gender wage gap in Africa include Glewwe (1990) for Ghana; Cohen and House (1993) for Sudan; Milne and Neitzert (1994) and Agesa (1999) for Kenya; Glick and Sahn (1997) for Guinea; Lachaud (1997) for Burkina Faso and Cameroon; Armitage and Sabot (1991) for Kenya and Tanzania; Appleton, Hoddinott, and Krishnan (1999) for Côte d'Ivoire, Ethiopia, and Uganda; Isemonger and Roberts (1999) for South Africa; Siphambe and Thokweng-Bakwena (2001) for Botswana; Kabubo-Mariara (2003) for Kenya; Temesgen (2006) for Ethiopia; Nordman, Robilliard, and Roubaud (2010) for seven West African capitals using household data; Kolev and Suárez Robles (2010) for Ethiopia; Nordman, Rakotomanana, and Robilliard (2010), and Nordman and Roubaud (2009) for Madagascar; Nordman and Wolff (2009a) for Morocco; and Nordman and Wolff (2009b) for a comparison between the formal sectors of Madagascar and Mauritius.
2. The Africa Regional Program on Enterprise Development is an ongoing research project whose overall purpose is generating business knowledge and policy advice useful to private-sector manufacturing development in Sub-Saharan Africa. For further details, see http://www.worldbank.org/rped.
3. Some studies using household data even end up relying essentially on estimates without selectivity correction to avoid this difficulty (Appleton, Hoddinott, and Krishnan 1999; Nordman, Robilliard, and Roubaud 2010; Nordman and Roubaud 2009).
4. For instance, there may be differences in the wage levels offered to female workers by female and male employers. Neglecting the sex of the managers thus will affect the various returns to individual characteristics when estimating wage regressions.
5. There is thus a trade-off between accounting for selectivity in labor market entry with the use of household data and controlling for jobs and firms' heterogeneity with matched worker-firm data. In the absence of definite theoretical argument, the question remains unsettled.

6. Unfortunately, limitations of the study made it impossible to disentangle the determinants of the within-firm wage gap across countries, as in Nordman and Wolff (2009a) in Morocco. For a within-firm analysis, one would need larger datasets, including a large number of firms with interviews of at least two male and two female employees per firm.

7. Its GDP per capita ($13,240 in 2005 at purchasing power parity) places the Mauritius Island in the category of "newly industrialized country."

8. After observations with missing values are deleted, the sizes of the worker samples are, respectively, 1,574 for Benin, 1,876 for Kenya, 1,734 for Madagascar, 1,363 for Mauritius, 7,806 for Morocco, 1,349 for Senegal, and 1,306 for Uganda.

9. For further details, see the RPED Web site, www.worldbank.org/rped.

10. In the Moroccan FACS, there are seven sectors: electronics, textiles, garments, food, pharmaceuticals, leather and shoe products, and plastics.

11. For the Malagasy case, see Nordman et al. (2010); for the other countries, see DIAL (2007).

12. Among other possible explanations, note that Madagascar has been one of the few low-income countries to recognize the early the importance of developing its educational system and has made rapid progress in the development of public primary schools. Madagascar is also one of the few African countries to have achieved equal access to schooling between boys and girls, at least at low levels of the education system (World Bank 2001).

13. Using representative household surveys from seven West African capitals (including those of Benin and Senegal), Kuepie, Nordman, and Roubaud (2009) show that the education gap is always largely in favor of men for paid-work participants.

14. Note that, even if many Beninese firms are small, they still belong to the formal sector, as defined by international standards of informal activities, because, to be included in the sampling frame, they are necessarily registered businesses.

15. In Mauritius, the data do not allow clear identification of the different sectors. This is not an important drawback as we can control for the firms' observed and unobserved characteristics thanks to the matching employer-employee nature of the data.

16. However, as we only have cross-sectional data, controlling for unobserved heterogeneity at the worker level is impossible.

17. For the purpose of comparability of the covariates, the marital status variable is approximated in the case of Morocco, where, as in Kenya and Uganda, the marital status was not collected from the workers. Instead, we use the fact of having declared children where information on children is available. In Africa, it is reasonable to assume that all individuals who have declared children are (or have been) married because of the social norms in force.

18. See the results of using potential versus actual experience in Nordman and Roubaud (2009) for the case of Madagascar. In the case of Morocco, the actual experience variable concerns experience accumulated in the preceding job only.

19. Specifically, we introduce nine occupational dummy variables related to occupations in six countries of our sample, while there are six occupations in the Moroccan data.

20. We implement statistical tests to test the relevance of our econometric specification. For the seven African countries, we find that the fixed effects specification is the most appropriate one.

21. In addition, including occupations strongly affects the relative contributions of the other covariates, in particular education. For instance, in Kenya, the weight associated with years of schooling is 65.2 percent without controls for occupations, but it amounts to 17.4 percent once occupations are included in the list of regressors.
22. We have also estimated fixed effects quantile regressions following Koenker (2005). As in the linear regression, the gender quantile coefficients are much lower with the fixed effects specifications in Mauritius and in Morocco.
23. Our empirical analysis does not account for the possibility that the effect of gender segregation across firms depends on the type of occupation within the firms.
24. However, this result has to be interpreted with caution, given the limited size of the Senegalese sample once the latter is restricted to firms comprising at least two male and two female employees.

References

Agesa, R. U. 1999. "The Urban Gender Wage Gap in an African Country: Findings from Kenya." *Canadian Journal of Development Studies* 20 (1): 59–76.

Albrecht, J., A. Björklund, and S. Vroman. 2003. "Is there a Glass Ceiling in Sweden?" *Journal of Labor Economics* 21 (1): 145–77.

Appleton, S., J. Hoddinott, and P. Krishnan. 1999. "The Gender Wage Gap in Three African Countries." *Economic Development and Cultural Change* 47 (2): 289–312.

Armitage, J., and R. Sabot. 1991. "Discrimination in East African's Urban Labor Market." In *Unfair Advantage: Labor Market Discrimination in Developing Countries*, ed. Nancy Birdsall and Richard Sabot. Washington DC: World Bank.

Barnet-Verzat, C., and F. C. Wolff. 2008. "Gender Wage Gap and the Glass Ceiling Effect: A Firm-Level Investigation." *International Journal of Manpower* 29 (6): 486–502.

Blau, F., and L. Kahn. 2000. "Gender Differences in Pay." *Journal of Economic Perspectives* 14 (4): 75–99.

Cohen, B., and W. J. House. 1993. "Women's Urban Labour Market Status in Developing Countries: How Well Do They Fare in Khartoum, Sudan?" *Journal of Development Studies* 29 (3): 461–83.

de la Rica, S., J. J. Dolado, and V. Llorens. 2008. "Ceilings or Floors? Gender Wage Gaps by Education in Spain." *Journal of Population Economics* 21 (3): 1432–75.

DIAL (Développment, Institutions and Analyses de Long Terme). 2007. "Youth and Labour Markets in Africa. A Critical Review of Literature." Working Paper 49, Département de la Recherche, Agence Française de Développement (AFD), DIAL Working Paper DT/2007-02. DIAL, Paris.

Fafchamps, M., M. Söderbom, and N. Benhassine. 2006. "Job Sorting in African Labor Markets." Center for the Study of African Economies, Working Paper WPS/2006-02, University of Oxford, United Kingdom.

Fields, G. 2004. "Regression-Based Decompositions: A New Tool for Managerial Decision-Making." Unpublished paper, Cornell University, Ithaca, NY.

Glewwe, P. 1990. "Schooling, Skills and the Return to Education: an Econometric Exploration Using Data from Ghana." Living Standards Measurement Working Paper 76, World Bank, Washington DC.

Glick, P., and D. E. Sahn. 1997. "Gender and Education Impacts on Employment and Earnings in West Africa: Evidence from Guinea." *Economic Development and Cultural Change* 45 (4): 793–823.

Hellerstein, J. K., D. Neumark, and K. R. Troske. 2002. "Market Forces and Sex Discrimination." *Journal of Human Resources* 37 (2): 353–80.

Heywood, J. S. 1988. "The Union Wage Profile of Women: Potential versus Actual Experience." *Economics Letters* 27 (2): 189–93.

Isemonger, A. G., and Neil Roberts. 1999. "Post-entry Gender Discrimination in the South African Labour Market." *Journal for Studies in Economics and Econometrics* 23 (2): 1–25.

Jellal, M., C. J. Nordman, and F. C. Wolff. 2008. "Evidence on the Glass Ceiling in France Using Matched Worker-Firm Data." *Applied Economics* 40 (24): 3233–50.

Kabubo-Mariara, J. 2003. "Wage Determination and the Gender Wage Gap in Kenya: Any Evidence of Gender Discrimination?" Research Paper 132, African Economic Research Consortium, Nairobi, Kenya.

Koenker, R. 2005. "Quantile Regression." Econometric Society Monograph Series, Cambridge University Press, United Kingdom.

Kolev, A., and P. Suárez Robles. 2010. "Exploring the Gender Pay Gap Through Different Age Cohorts: The Case of Ethiopia." In *Gender Disparities in Africa's Labor Market,* ed. Jorge Saba Arbache, Alexandre Kolev, and Ewa Filipiak, 57–86. Washington, DC: World Bank.

Kuepie, M., C. J. Nordman, and F. Roubaud. 2009. "Education and Earnings in Urban West Africa." *Journal of Comparative Economics* 37 (3): 491–515.

Lachaud, J-P. 1997. *Les Femmes et le Marché du Travail Urbain en Afrique Subsaharienne.* Paris: l'Harmattan.

Machado, J. A., and J. Mata. 2005. "Counterfactual Decomposition of Changes in Wage Distributions Using Quantile Regression." *Journal of Applied Econometrics* 20: 445–65.

Mairesse, J., and N. Greenan. 1999. "Using Employee Level Data in a Firm Level Econometric Study." Working Paper 7028, National Bureau of Economic Research, Cambridge, MA.

Meng, X. 2004. "Gender Earnings Gap: The Role of Firm Specific Effects." *Labour Economics* 11: 555–73.

Meng X., and D. Meurs. 2004. "The Gender Earnings Gap: Effects of Institutions and Firms. A Comparative Study of French and Australian Private Firms." *Oxford Economic Papers* 56: 189–208.

Milne, W., and M. Neitzert. 1994. "Kenya." In *Labor Markets in an Era of Adjustment: Issues Papers,* vol. 2, ed. Susan Horton, Ravi Kanbur, and Dipak Mazumdar, 405–57, EDI Development Studies. Washington DC: World Bank.

Nordman, C. J., F. H. Rakotomanana, and A. S. Robilliard. 2010. "Gender Disparities in the Malagasy Labor Market." In *Gender Disparities in Africa's Labor Market,* ed. Jorge Saba Arbache, Alexandre Kolev, and Ewa Filipiak, 87–154. Washington, DC: World Bank.

Nordman, C. J., A.-S. Robilliard, and F. Roubaud. 2010. "Decomposing Gender and Ethnic Earnings Gaps in Seven West African Cities." In *Labour Markets in Urban West Africa*, ed. P. De Vreyer and F. Roubaud, forthcoming.

Nordman, C. J., and F. Roubaud. 2009. "Reassessing the Gender Wage Gap in Madagascar: Does Labour Force Attachment Really Matter?" *Economic Development and Cultural Change* 57 (4): 785–808.

Nordman, C. J., and F. C. Wolff. 2009a. "Is There a Glass Ceiling in Morocco? Evidence from Matched Worker-Firm Data." *Journal of African Economies* 18 (4): 592–633.

———. 2009b. "Islands Through the Glass Ceiling? Evidence of Gender Wage Gaps in Madagascar and Mauritius." In *Labor Markets and Economic Development*, ed. Ravi Kanbur and Jan Svejnar, 521–544. Routledge Studies in Development Economics. London: Routledge.

Oaxaca, R. L., and M. R. Ramson. 1994. "Identification and the Decomposition of Wage Differentials." *Journal of Econometrics* 61: 5–21.

Siphambe, H. K., and M. Thokweng-Bakwena. 2001. "The Wage Gap Between Men and Women in Botswana's Formal Labour Market." *Journal of African Economies* 10 (2): 127–42.

Temesgen, T. 2006. "Decomposing Gender Wage Differentials in Urban Ethiopia: Evidence from Linked Employer-Employee (LEE) Manufacturing Survey Data." *Global Economic Review* 35 (1): 43–66.

Weichselbaumer, D., and R. Winter-Ebmer. 2005. "A Meta-Analysis of the International Gender Wage Gap." *Journal of Economic Surveys* 19 (3): 479–511.

World Bank. 2001. *Education and Training in Madagascar: Towards a Policy Agenda for Economic Growth and Poverty Reduction. Volume 2: Main report.* Report No. 22389–MAG. Africa Region, Human Development IV, June. Washington, DC: World Bank.

Chapter 5

Addressing Gender Inequality in Ethiopia: Trends, Impacts, and the Way Forward

Caterina Ruggeri Laderchi, Hans Lofgren, and Rahimaisa Abdula

The third United Nations Millennium Development Goal (MDG) is to promote gender equality empower women.[1] Despite the global progress achieved in the past decade, gender inequality persists and is pervasive. Global projections to 2015, for example, show no evidence the gender gap will close in education at the secondary or tertiary levels. In 27 of 118 countries, the female-to-male student ratio at the secondary education level falls below 0.90 (and in seven countries, the ratio is below 0.70). In addition, other indicators suggest that the challenge of meeting the target remains daunting: women's representation in national legislatures remains below 10 percent on average, and the share of women in non-agricultural wage employment in 2002 exceeded 50 percent in only 17 countries (UNDP 2005).

Ethiopia, one of the poorest countries in the world, offers an interesting perspective on the challenges of realizing gender equality. On one hand, its commitment to addressing gender disparities has strengthened over time, and a number of legislative measures have been adopted to ensure equality under the law. Gender considerations have also played an important part in designing major policy interventions such as a land certification program and the Productive Safety Nets Project. On the other hand, the current Poverty Reduction Strategy Paper (PASDEP, the Plan for Accelerated and Sustained Development to End Poverty) emphasizes gender within the general context of promoting broad-based development rather than focusing on specific targeted interventions.

Despite Ethiopia's government having undertaken some specific actions, such as the creation of a Ministry of Women's Affairs, the overriding assumption at the basis of the Ethiopian strategy to address gender disparities seems to be that they will gradually be addressed by fulfilling the country's overall development needs. The evolution of a number of indicators over the last 10 years suggests that this strategic direction has paid off, though progress has been more marked in some areas than in others. Yet international comparisons show that, despite recent progress, in a number of dimensions ranging from provision of health services to exposure to gender violence, Ethiopia still compares relatively poorly to the averages for Sub-Saharan Africa (SSA) and low-income countries (LICs).

But, given the scale of Ethiopia's development challenges, is it realistic to expect a deeper and more focused commitment to gender equality from that country? The question is also one of broader interest, as Ethiopia is obviously not alone in facing competing and pressing development priorities. To contribute to this policy debate, this chapter looks more closely at the Ethiopian experience and prospects by analyzing recent trends and providing estimates of the economic benefits of policies aimed at strengthening women's economic empowerment. Note that our emphasis on economic empowerment in no way detracts from the need to realize other important objectives related to gender equality, such as equality under the law and the elimination of gender violence. Similarly, the emphasis here on the economic benefits of addressing gender disparities in no way detracts from rights-based arguments that gender disparities violate human rights.

This study's findings suggest that the benefits of policies supporting women's economic empowerment could be significant, such that, "Gender equality is smart economics," to borrow the motto of World Bank Gender Action Plan (which has generously funded part of this research). The policy implications of these findings are clear: first, far from being a luxury, women's economic empowerment is a goal to which all poor countries should aspire, for its economic benefits as well as considerations of human rights and social justice. Second, while much can be achieved by pursuing broad development policies, evidence of the heterogeneity of women as a category, the difficulties of reaching those most deprived, and the fact that greater household monetary resources do not necessarily translate into lower gender disparities suggest that there is a place for carefully designed, targeted interventions to support the achievement of a women's economic empowerment agenda.

This chapter is structured as follows: the first section puts Ethiopia's progress in an international context. The next section focuses on gender trends in education, empowerment, and monetary poverty over the period 1995/96 to 2004/05, with analysis based on two comparable household surveys. The third section presents a new gender-sensitive version of the maquette for MDG simulations (MAMS) model for the Ethiopian economy and discusses results from scenarios that simulate a package of interventions aimed at strengthening women's economic empowerment. The final section offers conclusions, extracting the policy implications of the analysis.

An International Perspective on Trends in Gender Disparities

Global comparisons show that Ethiopia lags behind other countries in achieving gender equality. For example, according to the Gender Empowerment Measure (GEM), an aggregated index developed by the United Nations Development Programme (UNDP) to measure women's and men's capacities to actively participate in economic and political life,[2] in 2005, Ethiopia ranked 72nd out of 93 countries. Given the strong assumptions underlying any aggregate index, figure 5.1 panels a and b, compare Ethiopia with the rest of Sub-Saharan Africa and the average of low-income countries in two periods (2005 and the 1990s) for a number of separately considered indicators. This disaggregated analysis highlights a complex picture.

According to the latest internationally comparable data (for 2005), Ethiopia did very well according to at least one indicator: the proportion of national parliament seats held by women. Ethiopia is ahead of the SSA average in both under-five mortality and life expectancy for women. The indicators for which Ethiopia lags the most behind the other SSA and low-income countries are percentage of births attended by skilled health staff and tertiary school enrollment. Female primary completion rates and the female-male ratio in secondary enrollment are also areas in which Ethiopia falls short of the SSA average.

Comparison of figure 5.2a with data from the 1990s shows how the current mixed picture reflects significant progress in some of these dimensions (figure 5.2, panel b). For enrollment in primary education, where the gender disparity is now small, progress since the 1990s has been significant. Primary completion rates for women increased significantly, from 24 percent to 61 percent of the SSA average. Also, the gap between Ethiopia and other SSA countries in the female-male ratio in primary enrollment has significantly decreased over the past 10 years. In contrast, at higher levels of education, the gaps are greater and have been increasing over time: the disparity between Ethiopia and other SSA countries in the female-male ratio in secondary enrollment has grown, and, despite increasing more than fourfold since the 1990s, female enrollment at the tertiary level is now one-third of the SSA average (which, at 4 percent, still remains very low).

National Data on Gender Disparities over the Last Decade

Data from two sets of matched household surveys, the Household Income and Consumption Expenditure Survey (HICES) and Welfare Monitoring Survey (WMS) of 1995/96 and 2004/05 and the Demographic and Health Surveys (DHSs) of 2000 and 2005, provide a closer look at recent trends in gender

Figure 5.1 Selected Gender Indicators

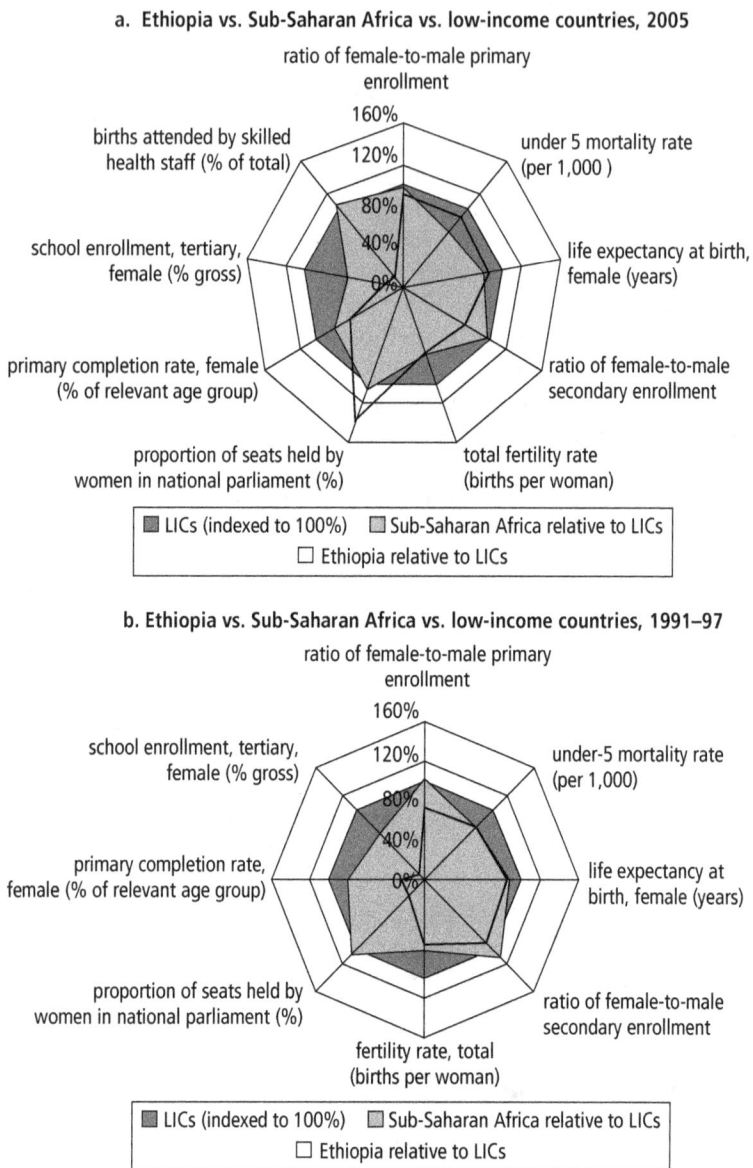

a. Ethiopia vs. Sub-Saharan Africa vs. low-income countries, 2005

b. Ethiopia vs. Sub-Saharan Africa vs. low-income countries, 1991–97

Source: World Development Indicators. For detailed data, see Annex table 5A.2.
Note: The figure for birth attended by skilled health staff refers to 2004 for Ethiopia and to 2006 for SSA and LICs. The figure for primary completion rate in Ethiopia refers to 2006. For detailed data, see Annex table 5A.1.

Figure 5.2 Profile of Educational Attainment by Age Cohort, Gender, and Rural and Urban Location

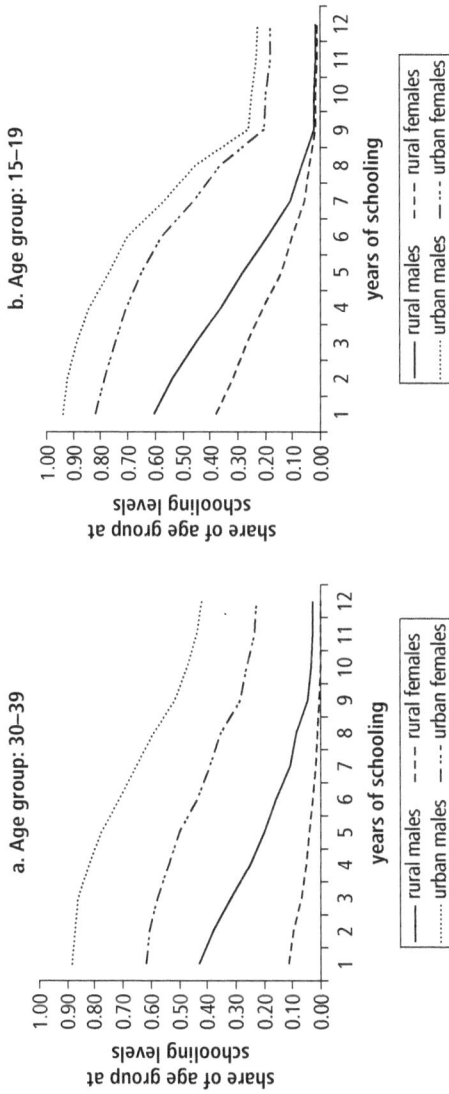

a. Age group: 30–39

b. Age group: 15–19

Source: Household Income and Consumption Expenditure Survey (HICES) 2005.

disparities. We focus in particular on indicators of education, empowerment, and monetary poverty, which are central to this study's focus on economic empowerment.[3] Key elements that emerge from this analysis are outlined as follows (see also Annex tables 5A.1 and 5A.2).[4]

Education

Significant progress has been made in school enrollment, though gender disparities persist. The greatest progress has been made in access to primary education: net primary enrollment rates for girls doubled from 1995 to 2005, from 21 percent to 42 percent. It is notable that efforts to promote higher and more equal access to primary education have benefited lower income groups. The literacy rate in the bottom expenditure quintile has grown at a faster pace than in the top quintile, increasing from 7 percent to 20 percent among women and from 24 percent to 48 percent among men.

Improving access to secondary education remains a challenge. Enrollment increased over the decade, driven mostly by improvements in rural areas. A closer look at the data reveals an interesting trend: despite improvements in rural areas and no change in urban ones, the overall gender gap actually increased. This occurred because, in 2005, rural girls represented a greater share of the relevant age group (13–18) than they did in 1995, possibly as a reflection of long-term changes in fertility patterns between rural and urban areas.

Figure 5.2 compares profiles of educational attainments of two cohorts in the 2005 survey. Each point shows the percentage of the age group which has achieved at least a given grade. Younger cohorts in 2005 (aged 15–19) were more likely to reach each level of education than the older cohort, with smaller gender gaps between rural and urban areas. Despite a certain narrowing, gaps between rural and urban areas remain significant, affecting girls more than boys.

Empowerment of Women

The broad dimensions of empowerment that can be explored with the Demographic and Health Surveys—gender violence, attitudes towards domestic violence and harmful practices, and access to information[5]—show a mixed picture.

The prevalence of and support of the population for female genital mutilation (FGM) is declining, at a rate in urban areas more than twice that in rural areas. Particularly encouraging is that while on average the decline was 4 percentage points, comparing data for mothers and daughters in the same families reveals more significant progress, declining from 52 percent to 38 percent at similar rates in urban and rural areas. Further, data on women's support for FGM reveal significant declines, particularly in urban areas. Even in rural areas, where the decline in acceptance of this practice has been more limited than in urban areas, the percentage of women who believe this practice should continue dropped by half in five years. The greater decline in support for FGM, compared to the smaller actual decline in incidence among daughters, is notable and suggests that, particularly in rural areas, women lack power to suppress the practice.

Yet data on women's acceptance of other forms of violence as a form of conflict resolution suggest women's low level of awareness of their rights.[6] Urban areas registered a decline in an indicator of women's acceptance of wife beating, although it remains very high, at more than 80 percent. No progress appears to have occurred in rural areas.

Access to information, as proxied by access to radio, shows significant gender disparities. In both 1995 and 2005, men were about twice as likely as women to listen to the radio, although overall radio penetration remained very low. The gap decreased in urban areas where access to radio was already more widespread.

Monetary Poverty

A central issue in debates on gender and economic empowerment is whether women experience poverty more than men, and whether this trend has been strengthening over time (the so-called feminization of poverty). This is an issue that cannot be easily answered by household survey data.

In the case of Ethiopia, standard poverty measures based on household-level resources do not show either a greater prevalence of monetary poverty among women or the feminization of poverty. Indeed, they support quite the opposite view. The percentage of women living in poverty (incidence) is lower than the percentage of men, and the same applies for other poverty indexes. Since these standard poverty measures are based on average household resources, all that can be concluded, then, is that women are not under-represented in poor households. It is possible that these measures underestimate poverty experienced by women because they fail to provide information on the individual's access to resources or the well-being derived from consumption. If there is any systematic bias against women in the intra-household allocation of resources, at least some women in non-poor households, by enjoying less than an equal share of resources, would be poor. Similarly, women in poor households would experience a more severe poverty than suggested by an estimate based on a household average.

The presence of systematic bias is supported by the growing qualitative and quantitative evidence that men dominate intra-household allocation of resources, with other elements, such as age and role in the family, also playing a role. Ethiopian evidence includes the work of Fafchamps and Quisumbing (2002), which found gendered patterns of control over income streams, and Dercon and Krishnan (2000), which found incomplete risk sharing, with women bearing the brunt of adverse shocks. More recently, Koohi-Kamali (2008) found a systematic bias against female children in the allocation of consumption. While there is no reason to assume that the extent of discrimination toward daughters and sons captures overall discrimination toward women in the household, the systematic nature of the bias suggests that the reality might be different from the equal sharing of resources assumed by standard monetary indicators.

This evidence, while not shedding light on whether there has been a feminization of poverty, suggests that women might be experiencing poverty at a greater rate than is captured by standard poverty measures.

A subset of people whose poverty status is similarly subject to apparently counterintuitive findings by standard measures is female-headed households (FHHs). Women in this category, according to qualitative studies, are subject to severe discrimination. This group of households is particularly prevalent in Ethiopia, especially in urban areas, where they represent 39 percent of households (compared to 23 percent in rural areas). Both quantitative and qualitative sources emphasize that FHH women adopt different livelihood strategies, reflecting the gendered division of labor prevalent in agriculture (for example, cultural norms preventing women from using the plow) and customary practices related to access to productive factors. Female-headed households, therefore, tend to rely more than male-headed households (MHHs) on non-agricultural activities (34 percent versus 28 percent in urban areas, 11 percent compared to 2 percent in rural areas), and on transfers from other households, which represent the main source of income for 12 percent of FHHs in urban areas (compared to 3 percent for MHHs) and 4 percent of FHHs in rural areas (less than 1 percent for men).[7]

These different livelihood strategies appear to be linked with greater vulnerability, possibly because of the marginal or socially sanctioned nature of many of the non-agricultural activities women heads are pushed into (Bardasi and Asfaw 2007). Also panel evidence (Bigsten and Shimeles 2006) suggests that FHHs experience greater volatility than MHHs, that is, in relatively good years they are more likely to be above the poverty line, while in downturns they appear to be more affected. FHHs' greater vulnerability also manifests itself in terms of reported food shortages (in urban areas) and food shortage duration (in rural areas).

Yet, despite these findings on FHHs, standard poverty measures suggest that this group is on average less poor than its MHH counterparts; however, it is a group characterized by great heterogeneity, with households of divorced and separated women experiencing higher poverty than their male counterparts. Self-selection is likely to play an important part in these findings, with FHHs that can afford to survive on their own, rather than joining other households, not necessarily found among the poorest households.[8]

Heterogeneity of Women's Achievements

A key finding of our trend analysis, and one that is often lost in looking at averages, is that there is significant heterogeneity in terms of achievement among women. For example, for some indicators, the disparities across individuals in different locations (rural and urban areas) are greater than those across genders.

Regional disparities, though in general less marked, persist and in some cases have increased (for example, in incidence of FGM, secondary enrollment, and acceptance of gender violence). In some cases, for example, acceptance of wife beating, disparities across regions have increased because regions with lower achievements have recorded indicators that have gotten worse, rather than other regions making significant progress. Differential access to services and cultural factors might explain both regional variation and its persistence: the percentage of women reporting health problems and seeking treatment ranges from 36 percent in Amhara to 80 percent in Afar. The case of education effectively illustrates the point about persistence: despite significant progress, gender disparities in primary education remain in those regions that in 1995 had the highest gender gaps (Oromiya, SNNP [Southern Nations, Nationalities, and People's Region], and Harari).

An interesting aspect of heterogeneity across regions is that the identification of best and worst performing regions varies across indicators, although more urbanized regions (Addis Ababa, Dire Dawa, Harari) appear more likely to score better than their more rural counterparts. This suggests that policies aimed at addressing the specific constraints to gender equality that characterize each region might be needed.

Finally, household monetary resources are associated in various ways with different indicators of gender disparities. Net female primary enrollment, for example, shows significant disparities across quintiles, from 28 percent in the bottom quintile to 45 percent in the highest quintile, while the gender bias remains constant. For other indicators, such as access to information, women in the poorest households have much less access information (only 2 percent listen to radio weekly, compared to 10 percent of men), while the gender gap is less marked for the top quintile (38 percent versus 55 percent, possibly because these women can enjoy the use of public goods like radios within the household).

The Macroeconomic Benefits of Addressing Gender Inequalities

Previous sections have shown that, despite considerable—albeit uneven—progress, Ethiopia still falls short of achieving gender-related MDGs and lags behind many other countries in terms of gender equity. Given this and the commitment of the government to strive to achieve the MDGs for gender (as well as nongender MDGs), this section examines the macroeconomic and economywide effects of measures designed to address women's lack of economic empowerment. The study then simulates the effects of a package of measures that provide broad support for education and promote the ability of women to enter the labor market and earn good wages.

The Engendered Version of MAMS

This analysis uses an engendered version of MAMS, an economywide simulation model created to analyze development strategies. The model integrates a relatively standard dynamic-recursive computable general equilibrium (CGE) model, with an additional module in which MDG outcomes are linked to MDG-related interventions and other determinants. These links are made possible by a relatively detailed treatment of government activities (disaggregated by function) and disaggregation of the labor force by educational achievement. Prior to this round of work, the model was never disaggregated by gender, either for Ethiopia or any other country.

When "engendering" MAMS, the model further disaggregates population, labor, and the student body by gender. With regard to labor and time use, instead of covering only time dedicated to market activities (the output of which is part of the GDP), the model now accounts for the full time use (excluding personal care time) of the labor-force-age population that is not in school (disaggregated by gender and educational achievement). More specifically, the time use for this population is disaggregated into work in activities that are part of the GDP, work in home services (including food preparation, cleaning, and child care) that are not part of the GDP, and leisure. This disaggregation of time use is paralleled by the introduction of production activities for home services and leisure. Given the important role of social norms, only quite limited changes in the share of its time each part of the population allocates to leisure and home service were permitted.[9]

The advantage of using a gender-sensitive, economywide model like MAMS to analyze policies promoting gender equality in education and work is that it captures the broader, dynamic economic repercussions of these policies, considering the roles of constraints in labor markets and at the macro level (represented by fiscal, foreign exchange, and savings-investment balances).

The MAMS-based analysis is of broader interest, extending beyond the Ethiopian case. Macroeconomic studies aimed at analyzing the effects of greater gender equality have been plagued by technical controversies, despite the wealth of micro-economic evidence in this area. On the basis of cross-country evidence, earlier analyses identified a puzzling negative association between female primary and secondary schooling and growth; however, it turned out that these findings were not robust to alternative model specifications. Subsequent studies suggest that gender inequality in itself lowers growth (Hill and King 1995), and that accelerating the educational access of women may have a positive impact on subsequent growth (Klasen 2002; Knowles, Lorgelly, and Orian Owen 2002), as well as on other indicators such as mortality rates and undernutrition (Abu-Ghaida and Klasen 2002).

Yet, cross-country regressions, including those that control for gender disparities, remain problematic (Sinha, Raju, and Morrison 2007), not least because they do not control for likely two-way links between growth and gender equality. Furthermore, on average, cross-country relations between macro-economic aggregates may not be useful where specific countries and policy actions are concerned. At the same time, it should be noted that the development of the required MAMS database required a considerable effort as well as the application of judgments in the face of data gaps and limited knowledge about the detailed workings of Ethiopia's economy. Therefore, the numerical results should be viewed as indicators of broad magnitudes and directions of change and complementary to insights based on other analytical approaches.

Increasing Gender Equality in Education and the Labor Market

For analysis of the impact of policies that would improve women's participation in the market economy, seven simulations were run. As summarized in table 5.1, these simulations explore the macroeconomic effects of a policy package that focuses on the following:

- Investment in increased quality of education after the first primary cycle.
- Reduced barriers facing women in search of market jobs (proxied by increased elasticity of substitution between men and women in market activities).
- Increased productivity in home service production, that is, time saving in home production, most likely brought about by improvements in technology and access to infrastructure; such changes free up time for other uses, including greater participation in market work.
- Reduction of the "wage discrimination"[10] against women, through policies aimed at generating attitudinal changes (media campaigns, changes in the curricula, and so on), and possibly the introduction and enforcement of

Table 5.1 Description of Simulations

Name	Description
BASE	Business-as-usual scenario with 6 percent annual growth in real GDP at factor cost
EDTX	Tax-financed expansion (increased quality) in education after 1st primary cycle
ED	Same as EDTX, except that financing is provided by foreign grants
ED + EL	ED + high male-female labor substitution elasticities in GDP activities
ED + EL + HP	ED + EL + increased productivity growth in home service production
ED + EL + HP + PP	ED + EL + HP + increased productivity growth in private GDP production
ED + EL + HP + PP + RD	ED + EL + HP + PP + removal of discrimination against women

Source: Authors.

laws requiring equal pay for equal work or the extension of the affirmative action measures adopted by the public sector to the private formal sector.

The results of the simulations are summarized in a set of tables and figures. Tables 5.2–5.4 provide information about the main macro indicators (table 5.2); the educational system (table 5.3); and the labor market (wages, employment, and wage incomes by education and gender) (table 5.4). Annex table 5A.4 shows time use by education and gender. Figures 5.3–5.5 (in the next section) summarize the evolution of GDP at factor cost, the secondary gross enrollment rate, and wage growth for labor with secondary education, respectively.

Base Scenario. The base scenario serves as the benchmark to which non-base scenarios are compared. It is designed to represent a plausible projection into the future, following the medium- and long-run trends of Ethiopia's economy. We impose an annual growth rate of 6 percent for real GDP at factor cost. (For non-base scenarios, GDP growth is endogenous.) It assumes the government adjusts its service provision so as to maintain unchanged educational quality (measured by real services per student) at all levels, except for the first primary level, where it gradually improves quality after the recent rapid expansion of enrollment.

Under this simulation, Ethiopia makes considerable progress overall, as well as reducing gender equalities in education and the labor market. Such progress is linked to education and labor market developments brought about by sustained growth. More specifically:

- Most macro aggregates grow at rates of 5 to 7 percent, including private consumption; in per-capita terms, private consumption grows at 3.5 percent (table 5.2).

- For the period 2005–30, enrollment growth is more rapid in higher cycles and for women relative to men in each cycle (table 5.3).

- In the labor market, female (market) employment grows more rapidly than male employment at all educational levels (table 5.4). In general, the higher the level of education, the more rapid the rate of employment growth.

- In terms of time use (for the simulation results, see Annex table 5A.4), in 2005 men at the lowest educational level spent more time in GDP activities than their female counterparts; whereas, at higher levels of education, men and women were equally involved in market work. Women spent more time in nonmarket (domestic) services than their male counterparts at all levels of education, but especially among the least educated. At all levels of education, men enjoyed more leisure. The situation projected for 2030 in this phase of the simulation is quite different: for both genders and at all levels

Table 5.2 Simulation Results: Macro Indicators

	2005	Simulations						Deviation from BASE				
	Bn. Eth. Birr	BASE	EDTX	ED	ED+EL	ED+EL+H+P	ED+EL+H+P+PP	EDTX	ED	ED+EL	ED+EL+H+P	ED+EL+H+P+PP
		% growth per year										
Absorption	1036.9	5.7	5.9	6.6	6.6	7.0	7.5	0.1	0.8	0.8	1.3	1.8
Consumption—private	666.6	5.8	5.5	6.2	6.2	6.7	7.3	-0.2	0.4	0.4	0.9	1.5
Consumption—government	121.8	4.8	6.2	6.5	6.5	7.0	7.2	1.4	1.7	1.7	2.2	2.4
Fixed investment—private	144.9	6.6	6.3	7.4	7.4	7.8	8.2	-0.4	0.8	0.8	1.2	1.6
Fixed investment—government	103.6	5.1	6.9	7.3	7.3	8.0	8.3	1.8	2.1	2.2	2.8	3.2
Exports	141.3	6.7	7.1	7.1	7.1	8.0	8.9	0.4	0.4	0.4	1.4	2.2
Imports	360.4	5.8	6.0	6.8	6.8	7.3	7.7	0.2	1.0	1.0	1.5	1.9
GDP at market prices	817.8	5.9	6.1	6.5	6.5	7.1	7.8	0.2	0.6	0.6	1.2	1.9
GDP at factor cost	753.1	6.0	6.2	6.6	6.6	7.1	7.9	0.2	0.6	0.6	1.1	1.9
Total factor employment (index)	100	3.4	3.5	3.6	3.6	4.4	4.4	0.2	0.3	0.3	1.0	1.1
Total factor productivity (index)	100	2.6	2.6	2.9	2.9	2.8	3.5	0.0	0.3	0.3	0.1	0.8
Real exchange rate (index)	100	0.3	0.4	0.2	0.2	0.4	0.5	0.2	-0.1	-0.1	0.1	0.2
	% of GDP			% of GDP in 2030								
Foreign aid (% of GDP)	8.3	7.5	7.3	15.0	15.0	13.8	12.3	-0.2	7.5	7.5	6.3	4.8
Domestic taxes (% of GDP)	7.3	11.3	20.7	11.3	11.5	12.6	13.4	9.4	0.0	0.2	1.3	2.0

Source: Authors' calculations based on gender-sensitive version of MAMS model.
Note: Bn. Eth. Birr = billion Ethiopian birr.

Table 5.3 Simulation Results: Enrollment and Gross Enrollment Rate (GER) by Cycle and Gender

Enrollment		2005	Simulations						Deviation from base				
			BASE	EDTX	ED	ED+EL	ED+EL+ H+P	ED+EL+ H+P+PP	EDTX	ED	ED+EL	ED+EL+ H+P	ED+EL+H+ P+PP
1st primary	male	4753.8	1.1	1.1	1.1	1.1	1.1	1.1	0.0	0.0	0.0	0.0	0.0
	female	4074.9	1.7	1.7	1.7	1.7	1.7	1.7	0.0	0.0	0.0	0.0	0.0
2nd primary	male	2058.4	3.9	4.1	4.1	4.1	4.1	4.2	0.2	0.3	0.3	0.3	0.3
	female	1371.0	5.8	5.9	5.9	6.0	6.0	6.0	0.1	0.1	0.1	0.1	0.2
Secondary	male	770.6	4.1	5.7	5.9	5.9	6.0	6.1	1.6	1.8	1.8	1.9	2.0
	female	419.5	6.5	8.1	8.3	8.3	8.5	8.6	1.6	1.8	1.8	2.0	2.1
Tertiary	male	105.5	5.5	9.2	9.7	9.7	9.9	10.1	3.7	4.2	4.2	4.4	4.6
	female	30.9	10.0	14.2	14.7	14.8	15.1	15.4	4.3	4.7	4.8	5.2	5.4
GER													
1st primary	male	101.7	97.2	97.1	97.3	97.3	97.3	97.4	-0.1	0.1	0.0	0.1	0.2
	female	87.9	97.3	97.2	97.3	97.4	97.4	97.5	-0.1	0.0	0.1	0.1	0.2
2nd primary	male	50.1	85.4	89.9	91.1	91.0	91.5	92.0	4.5	5.7	5.7	6.1	6.6
	female	33.6	92.1	93.8	94.7	94.8	95.4	95.7	1.6	2.5	2.6	3.2	3.6
Secondary	male	21.3	35.9	52.0	54.7	54.6	55.7	57.1	16.1	18.9	18.7	19.8	21.2
	female	11.7	34.4	49.9	52.4	52.7	54.8	56.2	15.5	18.0	18.3	20.4	21.8
Tertiary	male	3.4	7.3	17.4	19.3	19.2	20.1	21.2	10.1	12.0	11.9	12.8	13.8
	female	1.0	6.0	15.6	17.4	17.6	19.0	20.0	9.6	11.3	11.6	12.9	14.0

Source: Authors' calculations based on gender-sensitive version of MAMS model.
Note: Bn. Eth. Birr = billion Ethiopian birr.

Table 5.4 Simulation Results: Wages, Employment, and Wage Income by Education and Gender

	2005	Simulations						Deviation from base				
		BASE	EDTX	ED	ED+EL	ED+EL+H+P	ED+EL+H+P+PP	EDTX	ED	ED+EL	ED+EL+H+P	ED+EL+H+P+PP
Wage												
Male, < completed secondary (=1)	1.0	2.4	2.5	3.1	3.1	2.9	3.6	0.0	0.7	0.6	0.5	1.2
Female, < completed secondary	0.5	2.1	2.0	2.8	2.9	2.0	2.6	-0.1	0.7	0.8	-0.1	0.5
Male, completed secondary	2.6	4.2	3.5	4.1	3.9	3.5	4.1	-0.7	-0.1	-0.3	-0.7	-0.1
Female, completed secondary	2.8	3.0	2.2	2.8	3.2	2.5	3.1	-0.8	-0.3	0.1	-0.6	0.0
Male, completed tertiary	7.3	8.0	5.4	5.8	5.5	4.9	5.4	-2.5	-2.2	-2.5	-3.0	-2.5
Female, completed tertiary	6.7	6.7	3.8	4.1	4.9	4.1	4.5	-2.9	-2.6	-1.8	-2.7	-2.2
Employment												
Male, < completed secondary	27.7	2.9	2.7	2.7	2.7	3.0	3.0	-0.2	-0.2	-0.2	0.1	0.1
Female, < completed secondary	16.1	3.3	3.2	3.1	3.1	5.3	5.2	-0.1	-0.2	-0.2	2.0	2.0
Male, completed secondary	2.8	2.1	2.8	2.9	2.9	3.3	3.3	0.7	0.8	0.8	1.2	1.2
Female, completed secondary	0.9	4.3	5.2	5.3	5.4	6.9	7.0	0.9	1.0	1.1	2.6	2.7
Male, completed tertiary	0.2	4.2	7.2	7.6	7.6	8.1	8.3	3.0	3.4	3.4	3.9	4.1
Female, completed tertiary	0.1	6.4	10.3	10.8	10.9	12.7	12.9	4.0	4.4	4.5	6.3	6.5
Wage income												
Male, < completed secondary (=1)	1.0	5.4	5.3	5.9	5.9	6.1	6.8	-0.1	0.5	0.5	0.7	1.4
Female, < completed secondary	0.3	5.5	5.2	6.0	6.1	7.3	8.0	-0.2	0.5	0.7	1.9	2.6
Male, completed secondary	0.3	6.4	6.4	7.1	6.9	6.8	7.5	0.0	0.7	0.5	0.5	1.1
Female, completed secondary	0.1	7.5	7.6	8.3	8.7	9.5	10.2	0.1	0.8	1.2	2.1	2.8
Male, completed tertiary	0.1	12.5	13.0	13.8	13.4	13.5	14.2	0.5	1.3	1.0	1.0	1.7
Female, completed tertiary	0.0	13.5	14.6	15.4	16.3	17.2	18.0	1.1	1.9	2.8	3.7	4.5

Source: Authors' calculations.

of education, the time shares for market activities increase at the expense of home services. The reduction is larger the higher the level of education, and larger for women than men.

- In terms of indicators used to monitor MDG 3, the female-male enrollment ratio increases significantly for all three cycles, as an unweighted average from 55 percent to 93 percent (table 5.3). However, the higher the educational cycle, the weaker the female performance relative to male performance.[11]

Expansion of Higher Education. Two simulations introduce a government policy shift toward improved quality of education (measured by total services per student) for all cycles except first primary. This change is motivated by current low levels of spending per student. In the first simulation (EDTX), the required expansion in government spending is financed by scaling up domestic direct and indirect tax rates. As shown in tables 5.2–5.4, under this simulation:

- The macro effects include a dramatic increase in the GDP share of domestic taxes (by approximately 8 percentage points, reaching 20 percent in 2030). Private consumption and investment decline slightly, while government expenditure rises.

- The fact that GDP growth increases despite lower private investment points to the positive growth effects of a drastic increase in enrollment growth at the secondary and tertiary levels.

- The secondary and tertiary gross enrollment rates (GERs) increase by 11 and 8 percentage points, respectively, with very similar gains for both men and women. Accordingly, employment declines slightly for men and women at the lowest educational level while it grows more rapidly for those with more education.

- In terms of wages, the more positive the changes in employment growth, the more negative the changes in wage growth. This does not reverse, however, the fact that the higher the level of education, the stronger the growth in wages. Incomes increase or are unchanged for each labor segment.

- The changes in the MDG indicators are small, with some improvement for the different indicators of MDG 3.

The following simulation (ED) is identical to EDTX, except that marginal government financing needs are covered by foreign grants instead of domestic taxes, leaving the GDP share of domestic taxes in 2030 at the same level as in the base scenario, while the foreign aid GDP share increases by 7.5 percentage points. Compared to EDTX, the following changes are observed:

- Growth gains from increased private savings and investment are added to the gains from a more educated labor force, resulting in a 0.4 percentage point increase in growth per year.

- Slight gains are registered in secondary and tertiary GERs and enrollment figures. In the labor market, wage, employment, and income gains follow for all labor types, with the exception of a slight wage decline for female labor with completed tertiary education.

- In response to higher private income growth and more government investment in public infrastructure, marginal gains are realized for virtually all MDG indicators.

Reduced Gender Bias in Employment Decisions. Under the preceding simulations, expansion in the supply of educated female labor has been particularly rapid, leading to a widened wage gap between men and women. At least in part, the growing wage gap reflects gender biases in employment decisions, which are driven by a host of social and cultural factors, making the absorption in the job market of the rapidly growing number of women more difficult; in addition, it may reflect differences in experience or skills or in the specific nature of the skills that men and women pursue.

Under the next simulation (ED + EL), the elasticities of substitution between male and female labor at each educational level in market activities (excluding agriculture) are gradually tripled (during the period up to 2015), reflecting a switch to more gender-blind employment decisions. For this and all following simulations, the grant aid received under the ED simulation is kept unchanged in foreign currency. For this simulation, the following changes relative to the preceding simulation (ED) are observed:

- The macroeconomic repercussions are very limited, but there is a significant impact on relative wages. For the two more educated labor categories, the male-female gap in wage growth shrinks from 1.3–1.7 percentage points to 0.6–0.7 percentage points.

- According to other indicators, the simulated differences are positive but negligible, as wage income from men and women are added to a common pool of resources without capturing differences between male and female spending patterns.

Future work on MAMS will expand the model to incorporate the key channels through which reduced wage discrimination influences male vs. female income control, among other things, leading to changes in consumption patterns, including spending on health and education and MDG outcomes.

Increased Productivity Growth. In the next two simulations, increased productivity growth in selected parts of the economy is introduced. In the first simulation (ED + EL + HP), this increase benefits home services. Relative to the preceding simulation (ED + EL), we add two percentage points of growth in annual total (and labor) productivity in home services. As noted, such changes may follow from improvements in technology and access to infrastructure.[12] Compared to ED + EL, note the following differences in outcomes:

- The macro impact of this change is positive. For GDP and most components of domestic final demand, growth increases by 0.3–0.7 percentage points. For private consumption, growth increases by 1.1 percent with respect to the base.

- The supply of labor to the market increases as a result of this productivity increase, especially for women with the least education. This puts downward pressure on their wages while wages for other labor types grow more rapidly as a result of the acceleration of overall growth.

- All MDG indicators register marginal improvement.

In the second simulation (ED + EL + HP + PP), increased productivity growth in private GDP production is added. Such improvements may be associated with simulated improvements in education and related labor market developments. More specifically, this simulation adds increases in annual TFP (total factor productivity) growth in agriculture, industry, and private services of 1.0, 0.5, and 0.1 percentage points, respectively. In sum, the results indicate the following (compared to ED + EL + HP):

- The effect of these productivity increases is positive. Annual real GDP growth reaches 7.9 percent, an increase of 0.7 percentage points relative to the preceding scenario. For most components of domestic final demand, growth accelerations are in the range of 0.2–0.6 percentage points.

- The gains in education and the changes in the labor market are qualitatively similar to those of the preceding scenario, except in this case the least educated women also enjoy more rapid wage growth.

- This also applies to the MDG indicators. One exception is that, given that this simulation favors the agricultural sector, the share of non-agriculture in female employment declines slightly.

In a final simulation (not reported in the tables), wage discrimination against women was removed. It is identical to the previous one in all respects except for the removal of a 15 percent wage discrimination against women (so that now women are paid the marginal value of what they produce). Given the current way MAMS has been rendered gender sensitive, this simulation only influences the distribution of wages between men and women. (As mentioned, the model could be extended to capture likely repercussions of changes in wage distribution between men and women, for example, by affecting fertility decisions, investment in female children, and so on).

Insights from the MAMS Modeling

Overall, the scenarios indicate that broad-based education expansion reaching (but not limited to) women, combined with selective labor market interventions, may lead to a major reduction in gender disparities in education and the labor market, as well as to improved overall macroeconomic performance. This general-equilibrium perspective complements the analysis of micro-evidence and is needed in contexts like Ethiopia where any significant steps toward gender equality have strong economywide repercussions via their impact on growth, the labor market, and the educational system.

Note, first, that in the base scenario, economic growth and the expansion of education already bring about significant improvements in the MDG 3 indicators. This reflects the basic insight that, by continuing current efforts of scaling up education, more and more women (who are more likely to be the marginal child not yet enrolled) will benefit. Furthermore, the results indicate that the economywide effects of simulated educational policy changes are significant. Rapid growth in the number of women with higher education holds the promise of accelerating GDP growth and improving overall welfare as well as a wide range of MDG indicators.

Similarly, lowering the constraints that prevent women from allocating more time to market work can amplify the effects of a better educated labor force. More generally, the broader repercussions of improvements in female education depend on developments in the economy as a whole. Rapid female wage growth is contingent upon rapid overall growth in the demand for educated labor, as well as addressing the broad set of social and cultural factors that contribute to reduced labor market opportunities for women. Explicit discrimination, which the government of Ethiopia is currently tackling through affirmative action in the civil service, is only one of the mechanisms that constrain the opportunities of women. Creating equal opportunities for women and men in the labor market will require focusing on a much broader set of measures, including public information campaigns, changes in school curricula, and possibly targeted incentives for households with school-age girls.

Figures 5.3 through 5.5 focus on changes in GDP growth, educational outcomes, and the labor market across the seven scenarios. The key results related to education and the labor market (outcomes related to the secondary education segment are highlighted, though the overall picture is similar for tertiary education, albeit at lower rates of gross enrollment) are as follows:

• Expanded spending on education is expected, especially if aid-financed, and more rapid productivity growth in home services and/or the private sector, all of which have a positive impact on GDP growth (figure 5.3). Note that,

Figure 5.3 Simulation Results: GDP Growth at Factor Cost

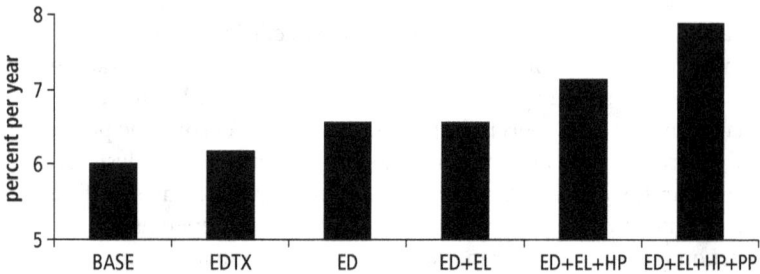

Source: Authors.

Figure 5.4 Simulation Results: Gross Enrollment Rate, Secondary

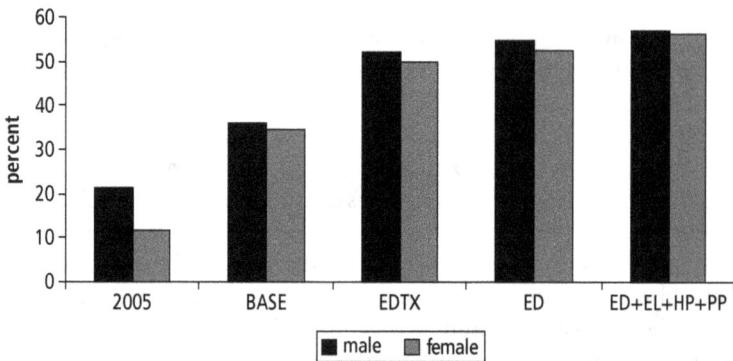

Source: Authors.

with one exception, the differences across scenarios in terms of private consumption growth follow the same pattern. (The exception, for EDTX, was noted in the above discussion of this scenario.)

- The stronger the rate of growth in GDP (and private consumption), the better the educational outcomes for a given level of government resources devoted to education (figure 5.4; compare the scenarios EDTX and ED).

- Under all scenarios except the last, the male-female wage gap grows as wages grow more rapidly for men than women (figure 5.5 shows this for secondary labor); this reflects that the female labor supply grows more rapidly than male labor and that men and women are imperfect substitutes as factors of production.

Figure 5.5 Simulation Results: Wage Growth for Labor with Secondary Education

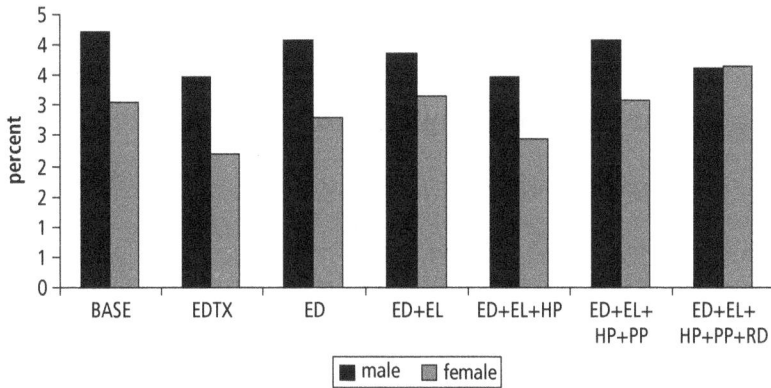

Source: Authors.

- In addition, the outcomes in terms of wage growth for men and women with secondary education, shown in Figure 5.5, suggest that, other things being equal, the following results hold true:

  o The wage repercussion of a rapid increase in growth in the supply of educated labor to the market depends on GDP growth (compare the scenario with education expansion with extra foreign aid, ED, to its preceding scenario, EDTX; also compare the scenario with increased factor-neutral private productivity growth, ED + EL + HP + PP, to its preceding scenario).

  o Addressing gender bias and its broad set of determinants may significantly reduce gender gaps in wage growth (cf. ED + EL to ED).

  o If the increase in productivity growth is limited to labor (not affecting capital and land), despite increased GDP growth, the wage gender gap might increase (cf. ED + EL + HP to its preceding scenario).

  o A gradual removal of "wage discrimination" could mitigate or overcome market pressures toward slower wage growth for women, given the rapid growth in the number of women entering the labor market (see the last scenario).

These insights are preliminary; further analysis of the effects of reduced gender disparities is needed. In particular, drawing on existing microeconomic evidence, the incorporation of links between incomes under female control and the allocation of spending across different types of consumption and savings is a priority. Another priority is to add female education indicators to the determinants of health and education outcomes. Such an extension should permit the investigation of additional channels through which improved female education may contribute positively to long-run human development.

Conclusions and Policy Implications

This chapter has examined recent trends in gender disparities in Ethiopia and the potential economic benefits of implementing a package of policies aimed at strengthening women's economic empowerment by increasing their education and ability to benefit from labor market participation. Using an innovative modeling approach provides evidence that, over a 25-year horizon, the impact of such policies on average growth rate and welfare could be significant. Pursuing gender equality is therefore not only a luxury to which richer countries can aspire, but a sound investment in a poor country's future, even based on a relatively simple modeling framework not considering a number of positive spillover effects of women's economic empowerment.

This study focused on Ethiopia as an interesting example of a low-income country committed to greater gender equality, albeit aiming to pursue it first and foremost through a broad-based development strategy rather than targeted interventions. Because in Ethiopia both women and men often have poor well-being indicators and the residence location is often a better predictor of deprivation than is gender, a broad-based strategy has ample scope to improve women's outcomes.

Indeed, our analysis of the trends over the decade 1995–2005 shows significant progress in some indicators despite the lack of a targeted strategy. This progress was very visible in primary education, where efforts to promote higher and more equal access have benefited the poorest citizens. This trend is also confirmed by our simulations that find that broad-based education expansion tends to benefit girls in particular, as they are over-represented among those currently out of school.

While our findings suggest that the overall policy direction embedded in Ethiopia's Poverty Reduction Strategy (MoFED 2005) is working, there are still significant challenges to overcome, as shown by international comparisons, and regional and social inequalities to be corrected. Even the significant progress in primary enrollment has not yet brought Ethiopia on par with SSA averages.

Given this situation, the Ethiopian government should consider some adjustments in its policies, while continuing on its strategic path, to include the introduction of targeted measures to address the challenges faced by specific groups, particularly the most vulnerable. Note that the simulations (which are at an aggregate, national level) do not address whether the groups that so far have been excluded (whether boys or girls) can be reached more effectively with the help of complementary and targeted measures that address the specific constraints of different groups. Children in rural areas and broader groups in lagging regions are examples of groups that may require such measures, which often may need a gender component.

Nevertheless, the results from the MAMS simulations and the microeconomic findings that underpin them imply that key policy areas, where payoffs are likely to be high, include policies where targeted interventions are needed. Those include policies aimed at improving women's human capital, freeing their ability to participate in labor market activities, and reducing discrimination.[13]

Annex 5A Tables

Table 5A.1 Selected Gender Indicators: Ethiopia vs. Sub-Saharan Africa vs. Low-Income Countries, 2005

Gender indicator	Ethiopia	SSA	LIC
Adolescent fertility rate (births per 1,000 women ages 15–19)	100.3	133.2	88.2
Ratio of female to male primary enrollment	82.6	88.7	91.0
Under-5 mortality rate (per 1,000)	127.0	159.1	113.9
Life expectancy at birth, female (years)	53.4	50.0	61.0
Ratio of female to male secondary enrollment	58.6	79.9	81.8
Total fertility rate (births per woman)	5.4	5.3	3.6
Proportion of seats held by women in national parliament (%)	21.2	16.2	15.4
Primary completion rate, female (% of relevant age group)	42.4	54.7	69.3
School enrollment, tertiary, female (% gross)	1.3	3.9	6.9
Births attended by skilled health staff (% of total)	5.7	45.1	43.1

Source: World Development Indicators.
Note: LIC = low-income country, SSA = Sub-Saharan Africa. The figure for birth attended by skilled health staff refers to 2004 for Ethiopia and 2006 for SSA and LICs. The figure for primary completion rate in Ethiopia refers to 2006.

Table 5A.2 Selected Gender Indicators: Ethiopia vs. Sub-Saharan Africa vs. Low-Income Countries, 1991–97

Gender indicator	Ethiopia	SSA	LICs	Year
Adolescent fertility rate (births per 1,000 women ages 15–19)	120.2	141.4	108.8	1997
Ratio of female to male primary enrollment	60.6	85.6	83.2	1999
Under-5 mortality rate (per 1,000)	178.5	179.1	133.8	1995
Life expectancy at birth, female (years)	50.5	51.5	58.8	1995
Ratio of female to male secondary enrollment	67.6	82.0	74.4	1999
Total fertility rate (births per woman)	6.5	5.9	4.3	1995
Proportion of seats held by women in national parliament (%)	2.0	9.7	8.9	1997
Primary completion rate, female (% of relevant age group)	13.6	45.7	56.9	1999
School enrollment, tertiary, female (% gross)	0.3	3.1	4.7	1999

Source: World Development Indicators.
Note: LIC = low-income country, SSA = Sub-Saharan Africa.

Table 5A.3 Ethiopia: Selected Aggregate and Disaggregated Indicators of Gender Disparities, 1995

	Total		Rural		Urban		Bottom quintile		Top quintile		Best performing region		Worst performing region	
	Women	Men	Women	Men	Women	Men	Women	Men	Women	Men	Women	Men	Women	Men
Share of population[a]	50.4	49.6	49.5	50.5	55.1	44.9	48.7	51.3	53.5	46.5	—	—	—	—
Poverty incidence[a]	46.1	48.4	49.9	51.3	29.4	29.3	—	—	—	—	17.0[f]	17.3[f]	57.7[k]	59.3[k]
Poverty severity index[a]	5.2	5.5	5.7	5.9	2.8	3.3	—	—	—	—	0.7[f]	0.8[f]	8.2[g]	8.6[g]
Poverty gap index[a]	13.1	13.9	14.3	14.7	7.1	8.3	—	—	—	—	2.9[f]	3.0[f]	18.8[g]	19.5[g]
Literacy rate (aged 15+)[a]	16.4	36.5	8.1	29.8	52.6	76.6	7.6	24.2	30.5	52.4	72.4[e]	90.6[e]	7.3[h]	10.8[h]
Primary net enrollment rate[a,b]	18.2	23.9	9.9	17.1	70.6	68.0	11.8	18.7	32.8	38.2	73.4[e]	78.4[e]	9.4[h]	5.1[h]
Secondary net enrollment rate[a,c]	9.1	9.0	0.9	1.8	39.2	49.0	1.9	3.7	19.0	21.7	57.3[e]	56.6[e]	1.3[i]	2.3[i]
FGM Prevalence among women (aged 15–49)[c]	79.9	—	79.9	—	79.8	*	n.a.	—	n.a.	—	35.7[f]	—	99.7[h]	—
Percentage of women with at least one daughter circumcised[d]	51.9	—	53.2	—	43.8	—	n.a.	—	n.a.	—	37.0[g]	—	78.5[k]	—
Percentage of women (aged 15–49) who support FMG	59.7	—	66.1	—	31.0	—	n.a.	—	n.a.	—	16.2[e]	—	77.3[h]	—
Percentage of women (aged 15–49) who agree that a husband is justified in hitting or beating his wife for at least one specified reason[d]	84.5	—	87.9	—	69.0	—	n.a.	—	n.a.	—	54.4[e]	—	88.4[k]	—
Listening to radio at least once a week[d]	11.2	23.8	5.7	17.0	36.0	63.5	n.a.	n.a.	n.a.	n.a.	46.7[e]	67.2[e]	7.7[h]	10.8[h]

Source: Authors.

Note: a. Data from 1995 WMS; b. Ratio of children aged 7–12 and attending grades 1–6 to total number of children aged 7–12 years; c. Ratio of children aged 7–12 to total number of children aged 13–18 and attending grades 7–12 to total number of children aged 13–18; d. Data from DHS 2000; e. Addis Ababa; f. Harari; g. SNNP; h. Somali; i. Tigray; j. Benshangul-Gumuz; k. Amhara.

217

Table 5A.4 Ethiopia: Selected Aggregate and Disaggregated Indicators of Gender Disparities, 1995

	Total		Rural		Urban		Bottom quintile		Top quintile		Best performing region		Worst performing region	
	Women	Men	Women	Men	Women	Men	Women	Men	Women	Men	Women	Men	Women	Men
Share of population[a]	50.7	49.3	50.2	49.8	53.9	46.1	49.0	51.0	53.1	46.9	—	—	—	—
Poverty incidence	37.5	40.1	38.1	40.1	33.9	36.5	—	—	—	—	26.1[f]	28.6[f]	46.7[i]	50.0[i]
Poverty severity index	2.6	2.8	2.6	2.8	2.4	2.6	—	—	—	—	1.3[f]	1.6[f]	3.4[i]	3.7[i]
Poverty depth (poverty gap index)[a]	8.0	8.7	8.2	8.8	7.4	8.0	—	—	—	—	5.0[f]	5.9[f]	9.9[i]	10.8[i]
Literacy rate[a] (aged 15 +)	22.3	50.0	14.0	43.4	60.2	85.6	20.4	47.7	31.2	60.4	71.9[e]	91.4[e]	13.0[h]	37.3[h]
Primary net enrollment rate[a,b]	35.9	39.2	30.3	34.6	75.6	78.6	28.5	34.8	45.4	53.3	75.8[e]	85.5[e]	22.6[h]	26.7[h]
Secondary net enrollment rate[a,c]	12.9	17.3	6.5	11.4	40.1	50.3	12.3	15.1	16.8	24.6	38.8[e]	53.2[e]	6.7[h]	12.0[h]
FGM Prevalence among women (aged 15–49)[d]	74.3		75.5		68.5		73.0		70.6		29.3[i]		97.3[h]	
Percentage of women with at least one daughter circumcised[d]	37.7		38.7		30.0		38.2		33.7		23.5[g]		85.1[i]	
Percentage of women (aged 15–49) who support FGM	31.4		36.3		10.4		48.3		14.1		5.6[e]		74.3[h]	
Percentage of women (aged 15–49) who agree that a husband is justified in hitting or beating his wife for at least one specified reason[d]	81.0		85.8		59.0		87.0		65.6		41.7[e]		91.3[h]	
Listening to radio at least once a week[d]	16.0	31.3	10.7	25.7	40.4	62.8	2.2	10.4	37.9	58.1	45.9[e]	55.7[e]	5[b]	22.0[e]

Sources: Welfare Monitoring Survey 2004–05; Demographic and Health Surveys 2005.
Notes: a. Data from 2004–05 WMS; b. Ratio of children aged 7–12 and attending grades 1–6 to total number of children aged 7–12 years; c. Ratio of children aged 13–18 and attending grades 7–12 to total number of children aged 13–18; d. Data from DHS 2005; e. Addis Ababa; f. Harari; g. SNNP; h. Somali; i. Tigray; j. Amhara.

Table 5A.5 Simulation Results: Time Use by Education and Gender—Selected Scenarios
(percent)

	Simulations						Deviation from 2005				
	Agr	Ind	Sergdp	Sernongdp	Leisure	Total	Agr	Ind	Sergdp	Sernongdp	Leisure
BASE											
2005											
Male, < completed secondary (=1)	27.4	1.5	5.8	10.1	55.2	100.0					
Female, < completed secondary	8.9	2.8	6.7	43.5	38.1	100.0					
Male, completed secondary	19.8	1.5	13.3	10.1	55.2	100.0					
Female, completed secondary	4.1	1.9	20.9	35.1	38.1	100.0					
Male, completed tertiary	11.6	1.2	21.8	10.1	55.2	100.0					
Female, completed tertiary	4.0	0.4	22.3	35.1	38.1	100.0					
BASE											
2030											
Male, < completed secondary (=1)	25.9	2.0	6.9	9.2	56.1	100.0	-1.5	0.5	1.1	-0.9	0.8
Female, < completed secondary	9.7	4.3	7.3	39.8	38.9	100.0	0.8	1.5	0.6	-3.7	0.8
Male, completed secondary	14.9	2.5	17.7	9.2	55.7	100.0	-4.9	1.0	4.3	-0.9	0.5
Female, completed secondary	2.8	2.8	24.3	32.1	38.0	100.0	-1.3	0.9	3.4	-3.0	-0.1
Male, completed tertiary	11.5	2.8	22.6	9.2	53.9	100.0	-0.1	1.6	0.8	-0.9	-1.4
Female, completed tertiary	4.1	1.0	25.8	32.1	37.1	100.0	0.0	0.6	3.5	-3.1	-1.0
EDTX											
2030											
Male, < completed secondary (=1)	25.6	1.8	7.4	9.2	56.0	100.0	-1.8	0.3	1.6	-0.9	0.7
Female, < completed secondary	9.8	4.1	7.5	39.8	38.9	100.0	0.9	1.3	0.8	-3.7	0.8
Male, completed secondary	15.0	2.3	17.9	9.2	55.6	100.0	-4.8	0.9	4.5	-0.9	0.3
Female, completed secondary	2.8	2.7	24.5	32.1	37.9	100.0	-1.3	0.8	3.7	-3.0	-0.2
Male, completed tertiary	12.1	2.8	22.1	9.2	53.8	100.0	0.5	1.5	0.3	-0.9	-1.5
Female, completed tertiary	4.3	1.0	25.7	32.1	37.0	100.0	0.2	0.5	3.4	-3.1	-1.1

continued

Table 5A.5 Simulation Results: Time Use by Education and Gender—Selected Scenarios *continued*
(percent)

		Simulations						Deviation from 2005				
		Agr	Ind	Sergdp	Sernongdp	Leisure	Total	Agr	Ind	Sergdp	Sernongdp	Leisure
ED												
2030	Male, < completed secondary (=1)	24.8	2.2	7.7	9.2	56.1	100.0	-2.5	0.7	1.8	-0.9	0.9
	Female, < completed secondary	9.3	4.7	7.3	39.8	38.9	100.0	0.4	1.9	0.6	-3.7	0.8
	Male, completed secondary	14.4	2.7	18.0	9.2	55.6	100.0	-5.4	1.2	4.6	-0.9	0.4
	Female, completed secondary	2.6	3.1	24.3	32.1	38.0	100.0	-1.4	1.2	3.4	-3.0	-0.1
	Male, completed tertiary	11.7	3.3	22.0	9.2	53.8	100.0	0.2	2.0	0.1	-0.9	-1.5
	Female, completed tertiary	4.2	1.2	25.6	32.1	37.0	100.0	0.1	0.7	3.3	-3.1	-1.1
ED + EL												
2030	Male, < completed secondary (=1)	25.1	2.0	7.5	9.2	56.1	100.0	-2.3	0.6	1.7	-0.9	0.9
	Female, < completed secondary	9.0	4.8	7.6	39.8	38.9	100.0	0.1	2.0	0.9	-3.7	0.8
	Male, completed secondary	15.2	2.6	17.2	9.2	55.7	100.0	-4.6	1.1	3.9	-0.9	0.5
	Female, completed secondary	2.2	3.1	24.7	32.1	37.9	100.0	-1.9	1.3	3.9	-3.0	-0.2
	Male, completed tertiary	12.9	3.3	20.7	9.2	53.8	100.0	1.3	2.1	-1.1	-0.9	-1.4
	Female, completed tertiary	2.9	1.3	26.7	32.1	36.9	100.0	-1.1	0.9	4.4	-3.1	-1.2

ED + EL + HP

2030											
Male, < completed secondary (=1)	28.4	1.8	7.6	5.7	56.6	100.0	1.0	0.3	1.8	-4.5	1.3
Female, < completed secondary	13.8	8.0	14.0	24.3	39.9	100.0	4.9	5.2	7.3	-19.2	1.8
Male, completed secondary	18.4	2.7	17.0	5.7	56.3	100.0	-1.4	1.2	3.6	-4.5	1.0
Female, completed secondary	3.1	4.5	34.6	19.6	38.2	100.0	-1.0	2.7	13.7	-15.5	0.1
Male, completed tertiary	15.4	3.6	21.4	5.6	53.9	100.0	3.8	2.4	-0.4	-4.5	-1.3
Female, completed tertiary	4.0	2.0	37.5	19.6	37.0	100.0	0.0	1.5	15.2	-15.5	-1.1

ED + EL + HP + PP

2030											
Male, < completed secondary (=1)	28.6	1.6	7.6	5.7	56.5	100.0	1.2	0.2	1.8	-4.5	1.3
Female, < completed secondary	14.1	7.7	14.0	24.3	39.9	100.0	5.2	4.9	7.4	-19.2	1.8
Male, completed secondary	18.8	2.5	16.8	5.7	56.2	100.0	-1.0	1.0	3.5	-4.5	1.0
Female, completed secondary	3.2	4.3	34.7	19.6	38.2	100.0	-0.9	2.5	13.9	-15.5	0.1
Male, completed tertiary	16.0	3.4	21.0	5.6	53.9	100.0	4.4	2.2	-0.8	-4.5	-1.3
Female, completed tertiary	4.1	1.9	37.4	19.6	37.0	100.0	0.1	1.5	15.1	-15.5	-1.1

Source: Authors.

Notes: agr = agriculture; ind = industry; sergdp = services in GDP; sernongdp = services not in GDP (nonmarketed home-produced services). Units: % of full time excluding time for personal care.

Annex 5B A Brief Description of the Engendered Ethiopia MAMS Application

The maquette for MDG (Millennium Development Goals) Simulations (MAMS) is an economywide simulation model created to analyze development strategies. The model integrates a relatively standard, dynamic-recursive, open-economy, computable general equilibrium (CGE) model, with an additional module that links specific MDG or poverty-related interventions to poverty and other MDG achievements. The relatively detailed treatment of government activities in MAMS makes this linking possible.

The core CGE model is disaggregated into 24 sectors, each comprising an activity that produces a commodity. The government is split into eight sectors, disaggregated by function: four types of education (two primary, secondary, and tertiary cycles); health; water-sanitation; (other) infrastructure; and other government services. Like other production activities, these government sectors use production factors and intermediate inputs to produce an activity-specific output; in the case of the government, this means different types of services. The private GDP sectors are divided into agriculture, industry, health services, and other private services. Private provision of education and health services contributes to MDGs, complementing government services. Private non-GDP services (home services) are split into six sectors, defined by the gender and the level of education of the labor that provides the service. Similarly, on the basis of the population (labor) type involved, the model includes six leisure sectors.

The factors of production in the model include six types of labor, disaggregated by gender and education: less than completed secondary education, completed secondary education but incomplete tertiary, and completed tertiary. The growth for each type of labor depends on initial stocks, inflows from the education system, and attrition (retirement). The non-labor factors of production include public capital stocks (one per government activity), private capital stock, and agricultural land.

The inputs of each government activity are labor (of different types), one type of government capital, and intermediates. Government investment in each capital stock is driven by the need to make sure that over time it grows at the same rate as the relevant type of services. Private GDP activities use labor (of different types), private capital (which is mobile across activities), land (for agriculture), and intermediates. Home services and leisure activities only use one input: the relevant type of labor. Private factor demand and production is driven by profit maximization; government producers adjust the composition of their labor demand with the same objective.

The government finances its activities from domestic taxes, domestic borrowing, and foreign aid (borrowing and grants). The provision of education, health, and water-sanitation services contributes directly to the MDGs. Growth in the stock of public infrastructure capital contributes to overall growth by adding to the productivity of other production activities.

These different MDGs are covered in an additional set of functions that link the level of each MDG indicator to a set of determinants. The determinants include the delivery of relevant services (in education, health, and water-sanitation) and other indicators, also allowing for the presence of synergies between MDGs, that is, the fact that achievements in terms of one MDG can have an impact on other MDGs. Aside from education, service delivery for other MDGs is expressed relative to the size of the population. In education, students are identified by the cycle of schooling they attend (primary, secondary, tertiary) and gender. The model tracks base-year stocks of students and new entrants through the four cycles. In each year, students will successfully complete their grade, repeat it, or drop out of their cycle. Student performance (disaggregated by gender) depends on educational quality (quantity of services per student); household welfare (measured by per capita household consumption); the level of public infrastructure; wage incentives (expressed as the ratio between the wages for labor at the next higher and current levels of education for the student in question; an indicator of payoff from continued education); and health status (proxied by MDG 4).

Compared to the standard version of MAMS, the engendered version (summarized above) incorporates the following changes:

- Instead of covering only labor time dedicated to market activities (defined as part of GDP), the model now accounts for the full-time use (excluding personal care time) of the population of labor-force age (15–64), including time spent on home services and leisure.

- The population of labor-force age is disaggregated not only by educational achievement but also by gender.

- In the educational system (disaggregated into four cycles or levels in this application), the students and their performance are disaggregated by gender. Students exiting the school system or becoming of labor-force age while not in school enter the labor force at the relevant educational level.

- Demand for labor is nested. Aside from home services and leisure, an aggregate labor input is "produced" by labor types disaggregated by education, each of which is produced by labor further disaggregated by gender.

- For leisure and home services, the outputs are demanded only by the household. The outputs are disaggregated by gender and education, with each output using only one kind of labor as input. Substitutability between leisure and home service work from different parts of the population is captured from the demand side, not from substitutability in the production function. Given the important roles of social norms, we permit only limited changes in the share of its time each part of the population allocates to leisure and home service. This is accomplished by designing a demand side that has low income and price elasticities and links minimum per-capita quantities of leisure and home services to the growth of the different population categories. For home services, productivity growth may change this picture by scaling down the time required from each population category to meet demand.

• Across all market activities, wage discrimination against women is captured in the form of the payment of a wage to female labor that is below its marginal value product (MVP). The surplus (the gap between the MVP and the wage paid to female labor) is paid to male labor at the same educational level. This formulation considers the fact that the economic benefits of increasing female emp loyment exceed the financial benefits reaped by female workers.

Notes

1. This goal encompasses one target—"Eliminate gender disparity in primary and secondary education, preferably by 2005, and in all levels of education no later than 2015"—and four groups of indicators (ratio of girls to boys in primary, secondary, and tertiary education; ratio of literate women to men ages 15–24; share of women in wage employment in the nonagricultural sector; and proportion of seats held by women in national parliament).
2. GEM is a composite index based on gender-disaggregated data on shares of parliamentary seats; shares of positions as legislators, senior officials, and managers; shares of professional and technical positions; and estimated earned income.
3. Note that other recent studies have focused on other aspects of gender disparities, such as the analysis of gender disparities in the labor market (Kolev and Suárez Robles 2010 [Chapter 2 in this volume]; Suárez Robles 2010 [Chapter 8 in this volume], and differences in female and male entrepreneurship.
4. The tables provide a snapshot of gender gaps in 1995/96 and 2004/05, according to indicators related to poverty, education (primary and secondary enrollment, literacy), and women empowerment (female genital mutilation, gender violence, and access to media).
5. These indicators are not intended to give a comprehensive picture, as many forms of violence against women, including domestic violence, rape, marriage by abduction, and early marriage, are still quite widespread (UNFPA 2008).
6. This evidence is collected by the Demographic and Health Survey using a well-established and internationally reputable methodology. The data do not refer to actual wife beating, but to women's view of when wife beating is acceptable.
7. Remittances from abroad represent a very minor income source overall, with private transfers from abroad as the main income source for 0.83 percent of FHH and 0.15 percent of MHH.
8. Similarly, note the finding that widower status is also associated with higher poverty rates, which may reflect the circumstance that better-off men can afford to remarry (Pankhurst and Bevan 2007).

9. For a brief description of MAMS and more details on the gender-related modifications, see Annex 5B. For more details on MAMS, see Bourguignon, Diaz-Bonilla, and Lofgren (2008); and Lofgren and Diaz-Bonilla (2010).

10. This chapter refers to "wage discrimination" as shorthand for the broad set of factors responsible for the difference in earnings between women and men, even conditional on controlling for several worker or job characteristics. While there is at least anecdotal evidence of explicit wage discrimination in Ethiopia (see World Bank 2009a for the example of daily laborers in the construction sector), here we aim to capture mostly factors such as culture and gendered preferences affecting the type of education that women and men pursue and, more generally, the gender segmentation of the labor markets, differences in the sharing of household tasks (which affect women's ability to enter into certain sectors less compatible with their household duties), and so on, which drive the disparity in returns to labor of women and men. "Wage discrimination," as we see it, therefore, is not primarily generated in the labor market, but by a complex set of factors that shape the environment in which women and men live. It is in this light that we consider a policy package that, for example, through public information campaigns, aims to address all the factors that result in women and men receiving different earnings.

11. In addition, in terms of sectoral employment, both the share of women in non-agricultural wage employment and the share of female employment in non-agricultural activities increase by around 3 percentage points.

12. During the period up to 2030, the time needed to produce a given bundle of home services is likely to decline gradually as GDP and per capita private incomes grow and families get better access to water, roads, and electricity, the latter making it possible to start using basic home appliances (washing machines, refrigerators). Improved electricity access is likely, given ongoing large government investments, and will also be facilitated by rural-urban migration. Note that improved electricity access is possible, even "off grid"; see the specific examples discussed in World Bank (2009b).

13. Note that, despite an emphasis on broad-based development as opposed to targeted interventions, the National Action Plan on Gender Equality (MoWA 2006) includes policies in line with these objectives, such as promoting gender equality in access to productive resources broadly defined and promoting women's earning potential, reducing the costs to women of their household roles, and strengthening women's voice and representation.

References

Abu-Ghaida, Dina, and Stephan Klasen. 2002. "The Cost of Missing the Millennium Development Goal on Gender Equity." *World Development* 32 (7): 1075–107.

Bardasi, Elena, and Abay Asfaw. 2007. "Gender and Non-Farm Activities in Rural Ethiopia: An Analysis for the Amhara Region." Background paper for the *Rural Investment Climate Report*, World Bank, Washington, DC.

Bigsten, Arne, and Abebe Shimeles. 2006. "Chronic Poverty, Vulnerability, and the Persistence of Poverty in Ethiopia: 1994–2004." Background paper for the Ethiopia Poverty and Gender Update, World Bank, Washington, DC.

Bourguignon, François, Carolina Diaz-Bonilla, and Hans Lofgren. 2008. "Aid, Service Delivery and the Millennium Development Goals in an Economywide Framework" In *The Impact of Macroeconomic Policies on Poverty and Income Distribution: Macro-Micro Evaluation Techniques and Tools*, ed. François Bourguignon, Maurizio Bussolo, and Luiz A. Pereira da Silva, 283–315. Washington, DC: World Bank.

Dercon, Stefan, and Pramila Krishnan. 2000. "In Sickness and in Health: Risk Sharing within Households in Rural Ethiopia." *Journal of Political Economy* 108 (4): 688–727.

Fafchamps, Marcel, and Agnes Quisumbing. 2002. "Control and Ownership of Assets Within Rural Ethiopian Households." *The Journal of Development Studies* 38 (6): 47–82.

Hill, M. Anne, and Elizabeth King. 1995. "Women's Education and Economic Well-Being." *Feminist Economics* 1 (2): 21–46.

Klasen, Stephan. 2002. "Low Schooling for Girls, Slower Growth for All? Cross-Country Evidence on the Effect of Gender Inequality in Education on Economic Development." *World Bank Economic Review* 16 (3): 345–73.

Knowles, Stephen, A. K. Lorgelly, and Dorian Orian Owen. 2002. "Are Educational Gender Gaps a Brake on Economic Development? Some Cross-Country Empirical Evidence." *Oxford Economic Papers* 54 (1): 118–49.

Kolev, Alexandre, and Pablo Suárez Robles. 2010. "Exploring the Gender Pay Gap Through Different Age Cohorts: The Case of Ethiopia." In *Gender Disparities in Africa's Labor Market*, ed. Jorge Saba Arbache, Alexandre Kolev, and Ewa Filipiak, 57–86. Washington, DC: World Bank.

Koohi-Kamali, Feridoon. 2008. "Dimensions of Child Gender Bias Effects in Ethiopian Consumption Patterns." Background paper for the Ethiopia Poverty and Gender Update, World Bank, Washington, DC.

Lofgren, Hans, and Carolina Diaz-Bonilla. 2010. "MAMS: An Economy-wide Model for Development Strategy Analysis." Draft, World Bank, Washington, DC. www .worldbank.org/mams (permanent URL: go.worldbank.org/EIZYZXV4N0).

MoFED (Ministry of Finance and Economic Development). 2005. *Ethiopia: Building on Progress. A Plan for Accelerated and Sustained Development to End Poverty (PASDEP)*. Addis Ababa, Ethiopia: MoFED.

MoWA (Ministry of Women's Affairs). 2006. *National Action Plan for Gender Equality (NAP-GE) 2006–2010*. Addis Ababa, Ethiopia: MoWA.

Pankhurst, Alula, and Philippa Bevan. 2007. "Unequal Structures, Unbuffered Shocks, and Undesirable Coping Strategies. Qualitatively-Informed Qualitative Investigations into the Causes of Extreme Poverty in Rural Ethiopia in 2004." Paper prepared for the research study, "Strategies to Address Extreme Poverty in Low-Income Countries: Balancing Prevention and Protection." World Bank, Washington, DC.

Sinha, Nistha, Dhushyanth Raju, and Andrew Robert Morrison. 2007. "Gender Equality, Poverty and Economic Growth." Policy Research Working Paper 4349, World Bank, Washington, DC.

Suárez Robles, P. 2010. "Gender Disparities in Time Allocation, Time Poverty, and Labor Allocation Across Employment sector in Ethiopia." In *Gender Disparities in*

Africa's Labor Market, ed. Jorge Saba Arbache, Alexandre Kolev, and Ewa Filipiak, 299–332. Washington, DC: World Bank.

UNDP (United Nations Development Programme). 2005. *Taking Action: Achieving Gender Equality and Empowering Women.* Task Force on Gender Equality, UN Millennium Project. New York: UNDP.

UNFPA (United Nations Population Fund). 2008. *Inequality and Women's Empowerment: In-depth Analysis of the Ethiopian Demographic and Health Survey 2005.* Addis Ababa, Ethiopia: Ethiopian Society of Population Studies.

World Bank. 2009a. *The Employment Creation Effects of the Addis Ababa Integrated Housing Programme.* Washington, DC: World Bank.

———. 2009b. *Unleashing the Potential of Ethiopian Women: Trends and Options for Economic Empowerment.* Washington, DC: World Bank.

Part 3

Disparities in Labor Income: Macro–Micro Simulations

Chapter **6**

Gender, Time Use, and Labor Income in Guinea: Micro and Macro Analyses

Juan Carlos Parra Osorio and Quentin Wodon

Introduction

Gender disparities in labor markets have important economic implications in sub-Saharan Africa. At least three different aspects of poverty and income generation can be related to the decisions made by various household members in terms of their allocation of time and their prospects for labor income. First, traditional consumption-based poverty is directly related to the earnings of household members as well as to household size. Increasing the earnings of women, either by closing the gender gap in earnings with men or by facilitating the entry of women into labor markets, thus can be directly beneficial for household incomes and poverty reduction.

Second, relative power within households (including whether the household head or the spouse makes key decisions, either separately or jointly) also depends on the earnings of various household members and can have long-term effects on children. Typically, the less women are engaged in income-generating activities, the less influence they have on household decision making and the less the household will invest in the human capital of children, which may reduce the likelihood that the children will be able to avoid poverty in the future as well as reduce prospects for income growth (Hoddinott and Haddad 1995).

The authors gratefully acknowledge review by Jorge Arbache and Mayra Buvinic and the work of Prospere Backiny-Yetna, who cooperated on constructing the income aggregate and the wage regressions using the Guinea household survey. The views expressed in this chapter are those of the authors and need not reflect those of the World Bank, its executive directors, or the countries they represent.

Third, time poverty (working a larger number of hours than desirable) is also an important welfare measure, and it is the direct result of the decisions made within the household regarding the allocation of both domestic and productive work. For example, women tend to work much less in the labor market, but this is more than compensated for by long hours of domestic work, so that they tend to be more time-poor (that is, a higher share of women than men work extra long hours; see Blackden and Wodon 2006).

In a microeconomic setting, standard regression analysis techniques can be used with household survey data to measure the likelihood of labor force participation, as well as the time spent on various household activities by different household members. The same techniques can be used to see how expected levels of earnings for women compare to those for men. Differences between men and women can then be analyzed using alternative decomposition methods to assess the factors that drive differences in earnings and find out what remains unexplained.[1] Access to basic infrastructure services, such as electricity and water, is important here, because such access has a direct effect on the time allocation of household members, especially in Africa, as well as an impact on the productivity of labor. The first contribution of this chapter is to summarize recent results from the analysis of household survey data in Guinea, with a focus on the differential in earnings between men and women who are already working, as well as the differences in time use by gender.

However, while standard microeconomic techniques can shed light on gender disparities, they typically do not provide insights into how broad structural shifts in the economy differently affect work opportunities for men and women. As noted by Nganou, Parra Osorio, and Wodon (2009), for any economic analysis that supposes the existence of general equilibrium feedback effects, a multisectoral approach is typically preferable to a partial, household survey–based framework, because links among different parts of the economy are too complex to be considered in partial equilibrium models. In principle, applied general equilibrium analysis can be performed using econometric methods (Jorgenson 1984, 1998) on a system of simultaneous linear or nonlinear equations describing technology and consumption behavior of the various sectors and institutions considered. But such an approach requires a considerable amount of data, which are not readily available for many countries, even in industrial economies. Especially in African countries, the data required for the econometric approach to general equilibrium analysis are often missing, and the capacity to understand in-depth and apply such techniques among local researchers is often weak.

To circumvent these data and capacity requirement limitations, researchers have used static input-output and SAM-based (Social Accounting Matrix) general equilibrium models in much empirical work on developing economies, and especially in Africa. These models require only a single year of data (the base year).

Input-output or SAM databases are transformed into models to evaluate the impact of exogenous shocks on endogenous accounts (outputs, factor payments, and institutional incomes), yielding comparative static analysis with respect to base-year values. The use of input-output models can be traced back to seminal work by Leontief (1951, 1953), who gave impetus to the development of applied general equilibrium models. Since then, an extensive body of literature on both input-output tables and SAMs has been produced, some of which is reviewed in the next section. As discussed in the brief literature review provided here, the models have rather strong limitations. But they are still useful for conducting simple stylized simulations from an analysis of the structure of economies.

In the second part of this chapter, our objective is to use a recent SAM for Guinea to assess how demand shocks in various sectors of the economy are likely to differently affect the incomes of both women and men, with a focus on comparing domestic and export-oriented sectors. In so doing, we can analyze both direct and indirect effects of sectoral growth on labor income shares between men and women.

This chapter is structured as follows. The next section reviews results from the analysis of recent household survey data from Guinea regarding earnings and time use differentials by gender. Next is a brief review of the literature on SAMs, a description of the structure of a standard SAM, and details on the 2005 Guinea SAM used for the analysis, including its disaggregation of labor income shares from different sectors by gender. Then presented are the results of simulations using the Guinea SAM of the potential impact of sectoral growth patterns on labor income shares, following similar work done on Senegal (Fofana, Parra Osorio, and Wodon 2009). A brief conclusion follows.

Gender, Labor Income, and Time Use from Household Survey Analysis

This section reviews existing information on labor income and time-use patterns in Guinea, focusing on gender and building on a poverty assessment conducted by the World Bank (2005) and work by Bardasi and Wodon (2006a, 2006b). The analysis in both cases relies on the 2002/03 nationally representative EIBEP survey (Enquête Intégrée de Base pour l'Evaluation de la Pauvreté or Basic Integrated Poverty Evaluation Survey), which was also used to construct the 2005 Guinea SAM used here. First discussed are the results on labor income and continue with analysis of the relationship between gender and time use and the implications of this relationship for household income and consumption. These results suggest that the income, wage, and time use data in the survey are reliable; that women stand at a disadvantage, both in terms of labor income and time use patterns; and that higher participation by women in labor markets could increase labor income and reduce poverty.

Labor Income

There is a strong correlation between household consumption per capita and household income per capita in Guinea. Two alternative definitions of income are constructed from the data. A first definition (income 1) takes into account all sources of income identified in the survey. According to the data, most non-agricultural household enterprises would appear to operate at a loss, a finding that is unrealistic but may result from the fact that income from small firms and household enterprises is much harder to measure accurately, given the need to take into account both sales and costs. This is why a second definition (income 2) excludes income obtained from non-agricultural activities. The explanation for the construction of these income sources is provided in Annex 6.A. The key finding is that, irrespective of the approach used, there is a rather strong correlation between income and consumption with, as expected, consumption and income being noticeably higher in the top (fifth) quintile than in the rest of the distribution (see figure 6.1). However, in each quintile of consumption, average income is lower than average consumption, a result that is not unusual in the African context, given the difficulty of measuring income accurately. The differences between income and consumption are actually not large by Sub-Saharan African standards, which in turn suggests that an income-based analysis is likely to be reliable in capturing key factors affecting the standards of living of households in Guinea.

Figure 6.1 Average Household Income and Consumption by Consumption Quintile in Guinea

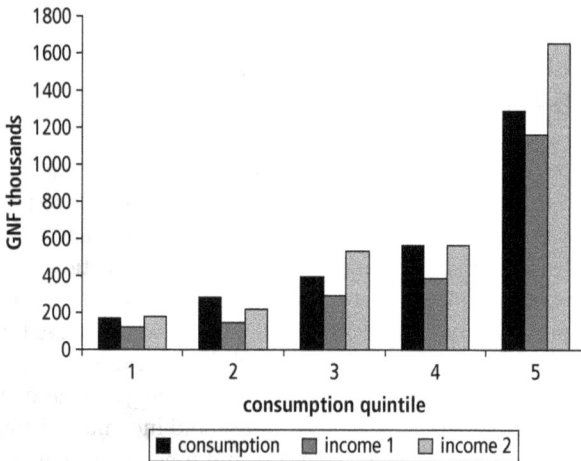

Source: World Bank (2005).

The World Bank poverty assessment does not provide a detailed analysis of the various income sources by gender, but it does show that wages and earnings represent by far the largest source of household income and that there are large differences in earnings between men and women. The wage gaps between men and women are large, as shown when described in statistical terms (without regressions). In urban areas, women earn 41 percent less than men (25 percent less in rural areas). In geographic terms, rural men earn 64 percent less than those in towns, whereas rural women earn 55 percent less than urban women. These gaps in gender and geographic terms remain in the econometric analyis presented in table 6.1 (standard log wage regressions are used, but without Heckman selection in order to focus on individuals who are already in the labor market). In the regressions, after controlling for other variables, the gender gap remains at 43 percent in urban areas and 35 percent in rural areas. Similarly, the geographic gaps in wages remain large, with rural men earning 34 percent less than urban men, and rural women earning 20 percent less than urban women. Furthermore, in relation to unmarried people, married persons apparently enjoy a wage bonus. Polygamous men earn 36 percent more than unmarried men in urban areas and 33 percent more in rural areas; married women earn 21 percent more than single women, but only in urban areas.

The gains associated with education in table 6.1 are statistically significant and large, especially in urban areas, where up to the second cycle of secondary education the gains are greater for men than women (24 percent increase for primary education in relation to a total lack of education, 32 percent for the first cycle of secondary education, and 38 percent for the second cycle of secondary education). However, the gains from technical and university education are greater for women than men (62 percent increase for technical education and 93 percent for university education), but relatively few women have achieved these education levels.

With regard to the sector of activity, agricultural workers earn considerably less than workers in the manufacturing sector, while positive differentials exist for men employed in trade and transport (in urban areas). Moreover, a negative differential is estimated for women in urban areas working in public administration, health, and education, possibly because women in public services tend to be clustered in lower-paying jobs. Employees in the informal sector earn 38 percent to 43 percent less than those in the formal sector in urban areas. Finally, the more or less permanent nature of employment also influences wages. Seasonal workers (for men in urban areas) earn much less than permanent workers (47 percent less), while rural women performing piecework appear to earn 47 percent more than permanent workers, a somewhat surprising result that may be related to the fact that most rural women with permanent work are involved in low-skill agricultural production that typically pay low wages.

Table 6.1 Analysis of the Correlates or Determinants of Individual (Log) Wage Incomes in Guinea, 2002–03

	All	Men	Women	Urban	Rural	Urban		Rural	
						Men	Women	Men	Women
Age	0.030***	0.039***	0.037***	0.043***	0.016	0.058***	0.052***	0.012	0.010
Age squared	-0.000***	-0.000***	-0.000***	-0.000***	-0.000	-0.001***	-0.001***	-0.000	-0.000
Female *(base: male)*	-0.407***			-0.431***	-0.345***				
Handicapped *(base: not handicapped)*	-0.031	0.045	-0.180	-0.002	-0.249	0.030	-0.084	-0.074	-0.486
Marital status (base: single)									
Monogamous	0.200***	0.157**	0.183**	0.230***	0.047	0.153*	0.208**	0.073	0.050
Polygamous	0.279***	0.373***	0.135	0.317***	0.146	0.364***	0.188*	0.331**	0.012
Divorced	0.207**	-0.111	0.216*	0.184*	0.162	-0.206	0.183	-0.047	0.188
Widower/widow	0.071	0.252	0.057	0.094	-0.048	0.227	0.145	0.079	-0.176
Education completed (base: no education)									
Primary	0.199***	0.211***	0.189**	0.207***	0.188	0.242***	0.175**	0.175	0.359
1st cycle secondary	0.320***	0.333***	0.288**	0.295***	0.434**	0.320***	0.248**	0.379*	2.147*
2nd cycle secondary	0.338**	0.354**	0.268	0.316*	0.266	0.383**	0.087	0.102	1.522
Technical	0.634***	0.615***	0.656***	0.618***	0.439	0.583***	0.616***	0.521*	0.707
University	0.761***	0.742***	0.994***	0.737***	0.996***	0.734***	0.927***	1.080***	0.707

Industrial sector (base: manufacturing sector)

Agriculture	-0.919***	-0.801***	-1.112***	-0.506***	-1.106***	-0.309**	-0.815***	-1.136***	-0.986***
Mining	0.530***	0.727***	-0.039	0.684***	-0.387	0.851***	0.141	-0.618	-0.065
Energy	0.073	0.266	-1.742	0.106		0.335	-1.704		
Construction	0.087	0.174	-0.415	0.067	0.146	0.176	-0.430	0.167	
Trade	0.155***	0.301***	-0.014	0.136**	0.265*	0.312***	-0.088	0.347*	0.331
Transport	0.163*	0.266***	-0.011	0.187**	0.614	0.306***	0.010	0.641	2.487
Finance, IT	-0.173	-0.089	-0.286	-0.136	-0.399	-0.050	-0.270	-0.378	
Public administration, education, health	-0.158**	-0.067	-0.399***	-0.089	-0.030	0.011	-0.374***	-0.054	-0.160
Employment status (base: employee in formal private sector)									
Employee in the public sector	0.332***	0.338***	0.219	0.269***	1.070***	0.228**	0.221	1.120***	1.955
Employee in the informal private sector	-0.346***	-0.361***	-0.423**	-0.381***	0.212	-0.382***	-0.433**	0.137	1.678
Self-employment	0.141*	0.218**	-0.082	0.224***	0.533	0.280***	-0.017	0.608	1.900
Type of contract (base: permanent)									
Seasonal	-0.227***	-0.309***	-0.165***	-0.182**	-0.095	-0.466***	0.015	-0.128	-0.054
Daily work/piecework	-0.060	-0.048	-0.066	-0.136**	0.322***	-0.102	-0.169**	0.190	0.472***
Rural (base: urban)	-0.275***	-0.344***	-0.198***						

Source: World Bank (2005) based on EIBEP 2002/03 (Basic Integrated Poverty Evaluation Survey).
Notes: The dependent variable is the logarithm of the hourly wage spatially adjusted (using poverty lines) for regional differences in purchasing power; * significant at 10% level, ** significant at 5% level, *** significant at 1% level.

Time Use

The previous section suggested that men and women who are working have very different wage expectations, even after controlling for a wide range of individual characteristics. In addition, the likelihood of being engaged in labor market work and the number of hours worked differ substantially between men and women. Indeed, Bardasi and Wodon (2006a, 2006b) show that major differences exist in time use by gender.

Table 6.2 presents estimations of hours worked by individuals in income-generating and domestic activities. The survey did not collect information on the time used to care for children and ill or handicapped persons. Thus, it is assumed that these activities are usually performed as "secondary activities," that is, in parallel with other "productive" activities recorded in the survey. The time used to help other households or perform community services is taken into account, however. Two definitions of "work time" are used. According to the first definition, work time includes the time devoted to domestic chores (collecting wood, fetching water) and income-generating activites (work on the labor market). According to definition 2, work time is total time worked as calculated using definition 1, plus the time used to help other households and perform community activities.

Table 6.2 Work Time (hours/week) of Individuals Over Age 15 in Guinea, 2002–03

	Average	Median	25th percentile	75th percentile
Not including time spent helping other households and performing community activities				
All	44.6	47.0	19.0	64.0
Urban	36.2	31.0	5.0	61.0
Rural	48.7	49.0	32.0	65.0
Regional gap (%)	+34.5	+58.1	+540.0	+6.6
Men	38.8	44.0	8.0	57.0
Women	49.3	51.0	25.0	70.0
Gender gap (%)	+27.1	+15.9	+212.5	+22.8
Including time spent helping other households and performing community activities				
All	46.1	48.0	20.0	66.0
Urban	36.7	32.0	5.0	62.0
Rural	50.6	51.0	34.0	68.0
Regional gap (%)	+37.9	+59.4	+580.0	+9.7
Men	40.5	46.0	9.0	60.0
Women	50.6	52.0	26.0	72.0
Gender gap (%)	+24.9	+13.0	+188.9	+20.0

Source: Bardasi and Wodon (2006a).

Table 6.2 shows that time worked in hours per week is higher on average in rural areas than in urban centers. The distribution of time worked in urban areas shows a large proportion of low values, as the considerable difference between the average and the median would suggest. Total individual median time worked in rural areas is 1.5 times higher than the corresponding value in urban areas. The gap between the total individual time worked in urban and rural areas, according to definition 2, is even greater than the gap as calculated according to definition 1. This is because individuals living in rural areas devote more time to helping other households and performing community activities than do urban individuals, despite the fact that they already record a higher total time working.

The data reveal considerable differences in time worked between men and women, the latter working longer hours (including domestic chores). Table 6.3 presents estimates of the use of time per activity, broken down for children and adults by gender and region. Using the second definition of work time (which also includes the time spent helping other households and performing community activities), the gap between men and women decreases somewhat because men spend more time performing community services; however, the qualitative results remain unchanged. Adult women spend much more time than men performing domestic chores (cooking, cleaning, washing, ironing, shopping), in particular in rural areas (18.3 hours/week compared to 2.6 hours/week for men). In urban areas, the differential, although lower, remains considerable at 15.5 hours/week for women and only 4.0 hours/week for men. Moreover, women must also provide the household with water and wood for cooking, especially in rural areas. Men, however, spend more time than women in the labor market, in particular in income-generating activities. Women record a high total work time in rural areas (55 hours/week), that is, 25 percent more than the time spent working by men, while in urban areas women work less, at about 39 hours/week, but still more than men. Gender differences also exist for the younger members of the population. In rural areas, children spend a substantial part of their time performing income-generating activities, almost exclusively in the agricultural sector (11 hours/week for boys and girls).

Some 18 percent of adults can be considered "time-poor" in that they devote abnormally long hours to various domestic and productive activities compared to the rest of the population. This assessment of time poverty is based on considering as time-poor those individuals who work above a threshold equivalent to 1.5 times the median for the individual time distribution. Table 6.4 provides data on the rate of time poverty. The rate of time poverty is higher for women (24.2 percent) than for men (9.5 percent) and higher in rural areas (18.8 percent) than in urban centres (15.1 percent). More women living in rural areas are time-poor (26.5 percent) than in urban areas (18.6 percent). Conversely, urban men are more likely to be time-poor than rural men (11.7 percent compared to 8.3 percent).

Table 6.3 Time (hours/week) Devoted to Different Work Activities by Sex, Age, and Region, 2002–03

		Age 6–14			Age 15+		
		Men	Women	All	Men	Women	All
	Urban						
1	Cooking	0.1	1.2	0.6	0.2	6.8	3.4
2	Cleaning	0.4	1.4	0.9	0.5	2.3	1.4
3	Washing	8.0	1.3	1.0	0.8	2.4	1.6
4	Ironing	0.2	0.2	0.2	0.7	1.1	0.0
5	Market/shopping	0.2	0.5	0.4	0.2	3.0	1.6
6	**Domestic chores (total 1 to 5)**	**1.7**	**4.6**	**3.2**	**4.0**	**15.5**	**8.9**
7	Collecting wood	0.3	0.1	0.2	0.2	0.2	0.2
8	Fetching water	0.6	0.9	0.8	0.4	1.2	0.8
9	Helping other households	0.0	0.1	0.1	0.2	0.4	3.0
10	Performing community activities	0.1	0.1	1.0	0.3	0.2	0.3
11	Working for a wage	0.4	5.0	0.5	25.9	18.	22.3
12	Working on a family farm	1.0	0.9	0.9	4.0	3.2	4.0
13	**Work on the labor market (11+12)**	**1.3**	**1.4**	**4.0**	**30.7**	**21.9**	**26.3**
14	**Total time (definition 1)**	**3.9**	**7.1**	**5.5**	**33.6**	**8.0**	**36.2**
15	**Total time (definition 2)**	**4.0**	**7.2**	**5.6**	**34.1**	**39.4**	**36.7**
	Rural						
1	Cooking	0.2	2.7	1.4	0.3	9.2	5.0
2	Cleaning	0.4	1.7	1.0	0.4	2.8	1.8
3	Washing	0.9	8.0	1.3	0.7	3.1	2.1
4	Ironing	0.1	0.2	0.2	0.3	0.5	0.4
5	Market/shopping	0.3	0.8	0.6	0.0	2.8	2.0
6	**Domestic chores (total 1 to 5)**	**1.9**	**7.0**	**5.0**	**2.6**	**18.3**	**11.7**
7	Collecting wood	2.5	1.5	2.0	1.6	2.4	2.1
8	Fetching water	1.5	2.6	2.0	0.7	3.3	2.2
9	Helping other households	0.2	0.3	0.3	1.1	1.0	1.1
10	Performing community activities	0.2	0.1	0.2	1.2	6.0	0.9
11	Working for a wage	0.4	0.5	0.5	13.1	8.6	10.5
12	Working on a family farm	10.6	10.6	10.6	23.0	21.0	2.0
13	**Work on the labor market (11+12)**	**11.0**	**11.0**	**11.0**	**37.0**	**29.**	**32.7**
14	**Total time (definition 1)**	**16.9**	**22.4**	**19.6**	**41.8**	**53.7**	**48.7**
15	**Total time (definition 2)**	**17.3**	**22.9**	**20.0**	**44.2**	**55.2**	**50.6**

Source: Bardasi and Wodon (2006a).
Notes: Observations with a value of zero are included in the computation of averages. Total time (definition 1) is the sum of categories 6 (all domestic chores), 7 (collecting wood), 8 (fetching water), and 13 (work on the labor market). Total time (definition 2) is the sum of total time according to definition 1 plus categories 9 (helping other households) and 10 (performing community activities).

Table 6.4 Rate of Time Poverty of Individuals Over Age 15 in Guinea, 2002–03
(percent)

	Time poverty line 70.5 hours/week			Time poverty line 94 hours/week		
	Urban	Rural	All	Urban	Rural	All
Men	11.7	8.3	9.5	2.7	1.8	2.1
Women	18.6	26.5	24.2	4.7	7.9	7.0
All	15.1	18.8	17.6	3.7	5.3	4.8

Source: Bardasi and Wodon (2006a).
Notes: The time poverty line of 70.5 hours/week corresponds to 1.5 times the median number of hours for all adults over age 15 (47 hours/week). The time poverty line of 94 hours/week corresponds to 2 times the median.

If we adopt a time poverty threshold of twice the median for the individual time distribution, the rates of time poverty are naturally lower (the overall rate of time poverty falls to 4.8 percent), but proportional differences between men and women increase.

In order to understand the correlates or determinants of time poverty, Bardasi and Wodon (2006a) also estimate a probit model. The results confirm that women are more likely to be time-poor than men, after controlling for a range of individual characteristics, but other factors independent of sex also play a role in determining time poverty. For example, level of education is a powerful predictive variable for time poverty, both for men and women, and particularly in urban areas. An increase in the level of education is associated with a lower probability of time poverty. In rural areas, where an education above the primary level is rare, particularly among women, the fact of having completed primary education also greatly reduces the probability of being time-poor in comparison to individuals with no education (–4 percentage points for men and –14 percentage points for women).

Well-being per quintile of consumption is only slightly associated with time poverty when other factors are taken into account as controls. A statistically significant effect can be observed for men living in rural areas—those in the fourth and fifth quintiles of consumption per capita have a 6 percent higher probability of being time-poor than those in the first quintile. For men living in urban areas, a similar result is obtained, although only for those in the fifth quintile (an increase of 4 percentage points compared to men in the first quintile). However, there is no significant effect for women (except for those living in rural areas and situated in the third quintile, who are 4 percentage points more likely to be time-poor than other women).

Household size and composition also could matter, but the relationships are not straightforward. The coefficients for number of children do not provide clear indications. Young children may need more time spent on them by adult members of the household, but time devoted exclusively to children was not explicitly collected in the survey. Moreover, slightly older children can help their parents, thereby enabling adults to save time. A positive coefficient is only estimated for men in rural areas, indicating for this group that each additional child increases the probability of being time-poor (one percentage point per additional child). A negative coefficient for the number of older children is estimated for men living in urban areas, meaning that, for this group, each additional child aged 6 to 14 reduces the probability of being time-poor at a decreasing rate. Time poverty for women, however, does not seem to be affected by the number of children in the household, whereas a greater number of adults in the household reduces the probability of being time-poor, indicating that the workload is more equally distributed between household members. This effect is more marked for women living in rural areas. The presence of handi- capped persons in the household increases the probability of being time-poor for women living in rural areas (by approximately three percentage points), whereas it reduces the probability of being time-poor for men living in urban areas by about two percentage points, but the reasons for this are unclear.

Other factors, including geographic location, matter as well. Unlike women, men living in rural areas are *less* time-poor than men living in urban areas. Being handicapped substantially and significantly reduces the probability of being time-poor, given that these individuals are often less able to work. Marital status is also associated with variations in the probability of being time-poor, but this effect is only significant (and substantial) for women. Married women (monog- amous or polygamous) are more time-poor than single women (a difference of about 10–11 percentage points in urban areas and 13 percentage points in rural areas). A similar effect is estimated for divorced women. Christian or non- Muslim women living in rural areas are more time-poor (difference of 18–19 percentage points compared to Muslim women in rural areas). Geographical differences can also be observed.

Benefits of Full Employment for Poverty Reduction

In general, poorer households have more members who are time-poor. While the regressions indicate the existence of a weak correlation between time pov- erty and well-being as measured by consumption, the most vulnerable catego- ries (women and individuals with a lower level of education) are still more time-poor. This result suggests that time poverty could be associated with pov- erty as measured by income or consumption. The main reason for this is that, in poor households, long hours are devoted to low-productivity work, resulting in weak output (in terms of income or consumption). In addition, because of long hours worked, there is limited time left to increase labor income and thus household consumption.

Still, at the same time, many households, including poor households, do have members who are working well below the time poverty line. These house- hold members have time available that could be used in productive activities to increase income and thereby reduce poverty. Bardasi and Wodon (2006b) performed simulations to measure the potential additional earnings of households that would be obtained from full employment of those who want to work (thus, all workers would work up to the time poverty line). For workers not currently working, or for those working without pay, two techniques are used to assess potential earnings. The first is to impute a wage level based on log wage regressions. The second technique divides total household consumption by total number of hours worked in the household and uses this as the value of time for all individuals in the household. We use the first technique for our results and the second technique to check their robustness.

The simulations are performed with and without a redistribution of work time among household members from individuals who are time-poor to those who are not. The results, shown in table 6.5, suggest that richer individuals and households would gain the most from working additional hours, but the gains for the poor are important as well. The disparity in potential household income gains is particularly large when additional work time is valued using the household productivity measure instead of the expected wage rate of each adult. When work time is reallocated within the household, the average increase in per capita income, and thereby consumption, is lower (several productive members would work less if they were time-poor), with a larger reduction in the bottom quintile than the top quintile in comparison with simulations without redistribution of work in the households. Nevertheless, there is still a substantial potential to increase income among the poor and others alike.

Even if poor individuals tend to be more time-poor and less productive than richer ones, an increase in work time would contribute to a substantial reduction in poverty. The simulations in table 6.6 suggest that the increase in weekly consumption per capita following an increase in the work time of individuals

Table 6.5 Effects of Work Time Increases by Individuals Over Age 15 on Household Income or Consumption in Guinea, 2002–03

| Quintile of consumption | Without redistribution | | With redistribution | |
	Time evaluated at individual hourly wage (1)	Time evaluated at level of household consumption (2)	Time evaluated at individual hourly wage (3)	Time evaluated at level of household consumption (4)
1	2,532	2,195	1,995	1,856
2	3,555	4,076	2,980	3,546
3	5,618	6,742	4,956	6,124
4	6,717	11,045	6,043	10,261
5	8,855	30,910	8,005	29,268

Source: Bardasi and Wodon (2006b).

Table 6.6 Effect of Increase and Reallocation of Work Time on Monetary Poverty and Inequality in Guinea, 2002–03

Quintile	Average routine consumption	Without redistribution/reallocation				With redistribution/reallocation			
		Time evaluated at wage rate		Time evaluated at household consumption productivity		Time evaluated at wage rate		Time evaluated at household consumption productivity	
		Simulated average consumption	Percentage increase	Simulated average consumption	Percentage increase	Simulated average consumption	Percentage increase	Simulated average consumption	Percentage increase
1	171,536	303,183	76.7	285,675	66.5	275,279	60.5	268,063	56.3
2	284,974	469,817	64.9	496,913	74.4	439,953	54.4	469,354	64.7
3	396,760	688,876	73.6	747,329	88.4	654,472	65.0	715,232	80.3
4	562,227	911,512	62.1	1,136,551	102.2	876,451	55.9	1,095,813	94.9
5	1,288,049	1,748,514	35.7	2,895,367	124.8	1,704,293	32.3	2,809,980	118.2
Rate of poverty	49.1	29.2		26.2		33.0		30.3	
Gini index	40.7	41.2		52.8		42.7		54.0	

Source: Bardasi and Wodon (2006b).

(below the time poverty line) is weaker in the lower part of the distribution. Nevertheless, this smaller increase in absolute terms still represents a substantial increase in percentage of consumption of poor households, in particular when the additional work time is evaluated using the hourly wage. Table 6.6 presents annual average per capita consumption simulated per quintile of consumption, together with the corresponding average increase. The increase in per capita consumption at the bottom of the distribution is large when the additional work time is evaluated at the hourly wage, while it is smaller when this time is evaluated according to household productivity. The estimated rates of poverty would fall from 49.1 percent to 29.2 percent and 26.2 percent, respectively; inequality, however, would increase because richer individuals would reap larger gains from additional work. This said, the largest portion of time still available among poor households to increase earnings comes from individuals who are now unable to find proper employment, rather than from the additional hours that could be worked by those already gainfully employed. Consequently, job creation policies would be needed to contribute to reducing poverty through higher time worked. Furthermore, although not discussed here, it is also necessary (and probably more beneficial) to implement actions that would increase labor productivity among the poor, in particular in rural areas. Higher productivity could have a larger impact on total earnings than would more working hours.

Macroeconomic Analysis of Sectoral Growth and Labor Income Shares

The previous section provided stylized facts based on household survey data about earnings and time use in Guinea. One obvious yet important conclusion is that, for both men and women, better job opportunities would help increase household income and reduce poverty. But where would jobs come from? In the household surveys used to conduct the analyses presented so far, the identification of individuals participating in the labor force in terms of their sector of activity is often limited to a few aggregate categories, which makes it difficult to identify more precisely which sectors are more in need of efforts to increase women's participation in the labor market. In addition, the type of analysis presented thus far, while useful to assess the determinants of wages and time use, does not provide insights into the multiplier effects that policies aimed at boosting production, and thereby employment in specific sectors, could yield. For a look at both a more detailed picture of the potential employment for women of specific sectors, and the potential multiplier effects that sectoral policies might generate for the economy as a whole, an analysis based on general equilibrium models is more appropriate.

The simplest such general equilibrium model is the SAM, which is illustrated within this chapter. Specifically, the next two sections provide a SAM-based macroeconomic analysis of the Guinean job market. A 2005 SAM for Guinea is used to assess how growth in various sectors of the economy might affect the labor incomes of women and men, both directly and indirectly, through multiplier effects. This section starts with a brief literature review on the use of SAMs in applied economic analysis, a presentation of the main characteristics of a SAM and of the SAM model, and a description of some of the features of the Guinea SAM. Then in the next section, simulation results are presented on the potential impact of sectoral growth patterns on labor income shares by gender.

Brief Literature Review of SAMs[2]

Early work on developing countries includes that by Adelman and Taylor (1990), who use a SAM of Mexico to explore the intersectoral impacts of alternative adjustment strategies, and Dorosh (1994), who develops a semi-input-output model based on a 1987 SAM to analyze how changes in economic policies and external shocks affected poor households in Lesotho. Taylor and Adelman (1996) develop the concept of village SAMs, which they apply to India, Indonesia, Kenya, Mexico, and Senegal. Thorbecke and Jung (1996) develop a decomposition method of the fixed multiplier matrix to analyze poverty alleviation. They study the impact of sectoral growth on poverty alleviation in Indonesia, concluding that agriculture and service sectoral growth could contribute more to overall poverty reduction than industrial growth.

In a study of South Africa, Khan (1999) explores the link between sectoral growth and poverty alleviation along the same lines as Thorbecke and Jung (1996). Other lines of research by the International Food Policy Research Institute include Arndt, Jenson, and Tarp (2000), who adopt the SAM multiplier approach to argue the relative importance of sectors of activity in Mozambique; and Bautista, Robinson, and El-Said (2001), who use SAM and computable general equilibrium (CGE) frameworks to analyze alternative industrial development paths for Indonesia. Although Bautista, Robinson, and El-Said (2001) recognize the limitations of the SAM multiplier analysis (which is linear and, in some cases, ignores supply constraints), they conduct simulations under the two frameworks and obtain the same result: agricultural demand–led industrialization yields higher increases in real GDP than two other industrial-led development paths (food processing–based and light manufacturing–based industry). Good reviews of the SAM model can be found in Defourny and Thorbecke (1984) and in Thorbecke (2000), which provides a comprehensive presentation of the SAM as both database and model, including the concept of structural path analysis.

Input-output, SAM, and CGE models all belong to the same family of economywide, or general equilibrium, models. There is, however, a key difference between input-output and SAM models and CGE models. Assume that we need to assess the impact of a demand quantity shock. A SAM will typically yield only the direct income effect from this shock in the economy, assuming no change in behavior among economic agents. But there could also be indirect (general equilibrium) effects of the exogenous shock through changes in prices. Taylor et al. (2002) argue that indirect effects may be ignored if all prices are given for a local economy by outside markets, that is, if the tradability of all goods and factors is assumed, or if a perfect elasticity of supply of all goods and services is assumed. But often this assumption is not valid. Input-output and SAM-based models are Keynesian demand-based systems based on the assumption of unconstrained resources (excess capacity in all sectors) and perfectly elastic supplies (for example, unemployment/underemployment of factors of production).

Thus, implicitly underlying many input-output and SAM multiplier models is the assumption that the economy is operating below its efficiency level. Exogenous changes in demand are also assumed not to influence local prices. The excess capacity assumption was relaxed in the literature in two steps. First, Lewis and Thorbecke (1992) allowed sectors with zero excess capacity in their analysis of economic links in the town of Kutus, Kenya. Later, Parikh and Thorbecke (1996) relaxed the assumption a bit further by including sectors with small excess capacity, while studying the impact of decentralization of industries on rural development. As to the price assumption, and the lack of behavioral response to shocks more generally, it cannot be dealt with easily, which is why some authors prefer to use CGE models.

Other assumptions in input-output and SAM models include the linearity of so-called technological coefficients, as well as linearity on the consumption side caused by assuming unitary income elastic demand (that is, the activities in SAM models assume Leontief production functions and there is no substitution between imports and domestic production in the commodity columns [Arndt, Jensen, and Tarp 2000; Thorbecke and Jung 1996]).

Another important limitation of the "traditional" SAM model is the assumption that the average expenditure propensities (technical coefficients) hold for exogenous demand shocks, implying income elasticities equal to one. A more realistic alternative, noted in Lewis and Thorbecke (1992), is to use marginal expenditure propensities.

Beyond the estimation of the impact of a shock, additional insights can be gained by looking at the main factors behind specific impacts. This can be done using a decomposition analysis of the multiplier model along the lines of Pyatt and Round (1979) and Thorbecke (2000). (The derivation of the decomposition is provided in Annex 6B.) Essentially, three separate effects are distinguished under this approach: transfer effects, spillover effects, and feedback effects. Transfer (or within-account) effects capture the interindustry (input-output) interactions among production activities or any interdependencies emanating from the patterns of transfers of income between households. Spillover (or open-loop/cross) effects show the impacts transmitted to other categories of endogenous accounts (for example, factor payments and household accounts) when a set of accounts (say, activities) is affected by an exogenous shock, with no reverse effects. Feedback (also called between-account or closed-loop) effects capture the full impact of a shock caused by the full circular flow (Round 1985). They capture how a shock to a sector travels outward to other sectors or endogenous accounts and then back to the point of original shock. Closed-loop effects ensure that the circular flow is completed among endogenous accounts by capturing injections that enter through one subgroup but do not return after a tour through other subgroups (Pyatt and Round 1979).

Basic Structure of a SAM

In technical terms, SAMs are numerical arrays representing the circular flow of income in an economy between sectors or activities, as well as between sectors, the government, households, and the rest of the world.[3] Each cell in a SAM, denoted by SAM_{ij}, reflects payments from an account j to another account i. When using a SAM for simulations, some accounts have to be set as endogenous (which means that they can react to a shock in the economy), and the rest of the accounts are set as exogenous (no change in the account following a shock). It is customary to set the government, capital, and rest of the world accounts as exogenous, but this choice depends on the nature of the analysis. Mathematically, the structure of simulations can be presented using a simple representation of a SAM (table 6.7).

The core of the SAM analysis is the multiplier model. Assume there are n endogenous accounts. Let A_{nxn} denote the matrix of technical coefficients, that is, the matrix resulting from dividing every cell T_{ij} in T_{nxn} by the respective column sum Y_j. Let Y_{nx1}, N_{nx1}, and X_{nx1} denote column vectors with the sums of total expenditures for the endogenous accounts, the endogenous component of those expenditures, and the exogenous component, respectively. Then by construction, the following two equations hold: $Y = N + X$ and $N = AY$. Combining these equations yields $Y = AY + X$, which can be rewritten as $Y = (I-A)^{-1}X = MX$ where I is the $n \times n$ identity matrix. The matrix $M = (I-A)^{-1}$ is known as the accounting multiplier matrix, the Leontief inverse matrix, or simply the inverse

Table 6.7 Schematic Social Accounting Matrix

Income/Expenditure	Endogenous accounts	Exogenous accounts	Total
Endogenous accounts	T	X	Y
Exogenous accounts	L	W	Y_x
Total	Y	Y_x	

Source: Adapted from Defourny and Thorbecke (1984).

matrix. Each cell m_{ij} of M quantifies the change in total income of account i as a result of a unitary increase in the exogenous component of account j. This change takes into account all the interactions in the economy that follow from an initial shock, so that SAMs are general equilibrium models.

When using SAMs for simulations of standard demand shocks (for example, an increase in the demand of tourism from the rest of the world), it is important to understand that a number of assumptions are implicit in the framework. The two main assumptions are that all prices remain fixed, as do all expenditure propensities, whether one considers productive activities or commodities purchased by households. Thus, a SAM is essentially a picture at one point in time of the economy and of the relations between different sectors, as well as between institutions or groups of agents. When using the SAM for simulations, we assume that the structural relations observed in the economy do not change, which is to say that there are no behavioral adjustments by agents following a shock. This is a strong assumption, which implies that the analysis obtained from a SAM is often tentative and indicative only and may lead to an overestimation of the impact of a shock.

Description of the Guinea SAM

The Guinea SAM, constructed by Fofana, Doumbouya, and Gassama (2007), includes 21 activities and commodities, 18 categories of labor, 9 types of capital as a production factor, 1 account for enterprises, 8 types of households, 6 accounts for government, 2 accounts for investment, and 1 account for the rest of the world. The labor income accounts are disaggregated according to gender, area of residence (urban versus rural), education (skilled versus unskilled workers in urban areas), wage earners (permanent versus occasional), and independent workers. The accounts for capital and households are based on occupation. Table 6.8 provides basic data on the sectors included in the SAM. The table shows that Modern Commerce, Agriculture and Other Nontradable Services are by far the largest contributors to value-added, with shares of 17.3, 15.2, and 15.2 percent, respectively. These sectors are followed by Informal Transport and Communications, Aluminum, and Other Tradable Services, with shares between 6.5 and 9.0 percent.

In terms of international trade, Guinea imports mainly manufactured goods and oil. These two groups accounted for 62 percent of total imports in CIF (cost, insurance, and freight) value for 2005. The country imports 50 percent more manufactured goods than are produced domestically, and almost 40 percent of the production of Transport and Communications. Aluminum represents 52 percent of total exports in FOB value, while Gold accounts for 23 percent. In terms of export propensity, more than 90 percent of the production of Aluminum, Gold, and Diamonds is exported.

Table 6.8 Sectoral Analysis for the Guinea SAM, 2005 (in GNF billions)

	Production (Q)		Value-added at factor costs		Imports (M)		Exports (X)		M/Q	X/XS
	Value	Share (%)	Value	Share (%)	Value	Share (%)	Value	Share (%)		
Agriculture	1,052.7	12.8	887.5	15.2	100.4	9.5	33.7	2.2	9.5	3.2
Logging and Forestry	122.4	1.5	113.1	1.9	0.1	0	1.0	0.1	0.1	0.8
Fishery	155.9	1.9	127.0	2.2	15.5	0.9	67.6	4.4	3.3	43.4
Livestock	464.9	5.6	323.3	5.5	0	0	0.0	0.0	0	0.0
Aluminum	849.5	10.3	421.4	7.2	0	0	796.2	51.8	0	93.7
Modern Diamond Mining	13.2	0.2	6.5	0.1	0	0	11.5	0.7	0	87.2
Informal Diamond Mining	92.1	1.1	74.4	1.3	0	0	92.1	6.0	0	100.0
Modern Gold Mining	275.5	3.3	131.2	2.2	0	0	275.5	17.9	0	100.0
Informal Gold Mining	98.9	1.2	96.8	1.7	0	0	80.6	5.2	0	81.5
Other Minerals	155.2	1.9	150.3	2.6	0	0	0	0	0	0
Oil, Kerosene, and Gas			152.4	2.6	330.2	20.1	0	0	0	0
Modern Manufacturing	407.3	4.9	154.5	2.6	620.8	37.8	20.0	1.3	152.4	4.9
Informal Manufacturing	244.9	3.0	46.7	0.8	67.1	4.1	10.0	0.7	27.4	4.1
Electricity, Gas, and Water	87.8	1.1	265.2	4.5	0	0	0	0	0	0
Modern Construction	354.7	4.3	375.3	6.4	0	0	0	0	0	0
Informal Construction	438.0	5.3	257.9	4.4	0	0	0	0	0	0
Modern Commerce	416.5	5.1	1,013.6	17.3	0	0	0	0	0	0
Informal Commerce	1,099.4	13.3	226.5	3.9	0	0	0	0	0	0
Modern Transport and Communications	332.8	4.0	129.6	2.2	124.7	7.6	13.4	0.9	37.5	4.0
Informal Transport And Communications	184.0	2.2	508.4	8.7	0	0	0	0	0	0
Other Tradable Services	621.9	7.5	381.8	6.5	188.1	11.4	56.9	3.7	30.2	9.2
Other Nontradable Services	776.3	9.4	887.5	15.2	197.2	12.0	78.2	5.1	25.4	10.1
All	8,243.9	100.0	5,843.4	100.0	1,644.1	100.0	1,536.8	100.0	19.9	18.6

Source: Authors.
Notes: M/Q = Import share within sector production; X/XS = Export share of production; M = Imports.

Gender Disaggregation for Labor Income in the Guinea SAM

In order to analyze the impact of exogenous shocks on labor income shares by gender, we need to have gender-disaggregated SAM accounts. Some descriptive statistics are displayed in table 6.9. Overall, Livestock is the most female-intensive labor activity, with 46.3 percent of total payments to labor going to female workers. Informal Manufacturing and Agriculture follow, with shares of labor income for women of 37.1 and 36.7 percent, respectively. Both Modern and Informal Commerce, and Modern Manufacturing have female labor shares exceeding or very close to one third. These female-labor-intensive sectors differ widely in labor intensity (share of labor in value-added). While labor income represents more than 80 percent of the value-added in Agriculture, it represents between 10 and 15 percent in the cases of Livestock and Commerce.

Table 6.9 Summary Data on Labor Income Shares in the Guinea SAM

	Female labor income share (percent)	Labor intensity (percent)
Livestock	46.3	10.3
Informal Manufacturing	37.1	51.5
Agriculture	36.7	81.4
Modern Manufacturing	34.1	55.8
Modern Commerce	32.3	16.6
Informal Commerce	31.6	15.6
Other Tradable Services	24.5	18.0
Other Nontradable Services	14.1	92.0
Informal Gold Mining	13.8	1.8
Modern Gold Mining	13.6	2.3
Informal Diamond Mining	13.1	20.0
Aluminum	13.1	20.2
Modern Diamond Mining	13.1	48.7
Other Minerals	3.5	1.6
Logging and Forestry	1.6	13.8
Modern Transport and Communications	1.0	34.2
Informal Transport and Communications	0.6	26.0
Modern Construction	0.5	10.3
Electricity, Gas, and Water	0.5	36.2
Informal Construction	0.4	9.3
Fishery	0.4	7.0

Source: Authors.

In the analysis of labor income shares, the disaggregation of labor income in the SAM is interesting because it provides additional insights into gender issues, as well as into poverty issues, at least in urban areas, because households with less well-educated workers tend to be much poorer.

To conclude, when implementing SAM-based simulations, we are able to provide data on expected changes in labor income shares not only by gender, but also according to location (urban and rural areas) and education (skilled and unskilled workers). The next section turns to the empirical simulation results.

Sectoral Demand Shocks and Impact on Labor Income Shares by Gender

All the computations in this section were performed using SimSIP SAM, a powerful and easy-to-use Microsoft® Excel based application, with MATLAB® running in the background, which can be used to conduct policy analysis under a SAM framework. The tool was developed by Parra and Wodon (2009) and is distributed free of charge,[4] together with the necessary MATLAB components. The accompanying user's manual describes the theory behind the computations. The application can be used to perform various types of analysis and decompositions, as well as to obtain detailed and graphical results for experiments.

Table 6.10 starts by showing the effect on labor income of an exogenous demand shock equal to 1 percent of aggregate exports, by gender as well as for different subgroups, for several sectors in Guinea. The first three sectors—Livestock, Agriculture, and Informal Manufacturing—have high female labor intensities and are mostly nontradable, while the other three sectors—Modern Construction, Aluminum, and Fishery—have low female labor intensities, and in the case of Aluminum and Fishery, have high export propensities (see tables 6.8 and 6.9). Because of the much higher value of payments to male workers, the impacts are larger for men than women. For example, an additional 1 percent of aggregate exports in Livestock generates an increase in male labor income of GNF 5,598.3 million after multiplier effects are taken into account, while the corresponding increase in female labor income is only GNF 2,901.7 million.

An exogenous demand shock in Agriculture has the highest impact on labor income among the six sectors. Even though men seem to benefit more from these demand shocks, the percentage changes show a different picture. Female labor income is growing faster than male labor income for Livestock, Agriculture, Informal Manufacturing, and Fishery, thus the gender gap would be smaller as a consequence of a shock in these sectors. A demand shock on Modern Construction or Aluminum would widen the gender gap in terms of labor income shares. There are also differences by location, as well as according

Table 6.10 Effect on Labor of an Exogenous Demand Shock of 1 Percent of Aggregate Exports, 2005

(GNF 15,368 million—percentage change in parentheses)

Destination/Origin	Livestock	Agriculture	Informal Manufacturing	Modern Construction	Aluminum	Fishery
Male workers						
Urban skilled permanent wages	205.1 (0.07)	202.1 (0.07)	255.9 (0.09)	181.7 (0.06)	1035.3 (0.37)	214.7 (0.08)
Urban skilled occasional wages	20.1 (0.07)	22.0 (0.08)	24.3 (0.09)	80.4 (0.30)	16.2 (0.06)	23.1 (0.09)
Urban skilled independent	564.7 (0.34)	669.4 (0.40)	1402.6 (0.84)	539.7 (0.32)	269.6 (0.16)	638.1 (0.38)
Urban unskilled permanent wages	147.8 (0.15)	136.9 (0.14)	210.9 (0.21)	118.6 (0.12)	310.4 (0.31)	366.7 (0.36)
Urban unskilled occasional wages	49.4 (0.26)	59.9 (0.32)	57.6 (0.31)	74.0 (0.40)	89.0 (0.48)	90.3 (0.48)
Urban unskilled independent	816.3 (0.36)	1186.0 (0.52)	2341.0 (1.03)	776.3 (0.34)	360.0 (0.16)	899.7 (0.39)
Rural permanent wages	196.4 (0.19)	360.6 (0.35)	194.5 (0.19)	107.3 (0.10)	72.5 (0.07)	204.8 (0.20)
Rural occasional wages	187.1 (0.55)	538.4 (1.58)	133.1 (0.39)	118.1 (0.35)	47.0 (0.14)	142.5 (0.42)
Rural independent	3411.5 (0.78)	8709.2 (1.99)	2365.8 (0.54)	899.4 (0.21)	578.5 (0.13)	2393.3 (0.55)
Female workers						
Urban skilled permanent wages	16.7 (0.03)	18.1 (0.03)	31.8 (0.06)	11.6 (0.02)	181.2 (0.32)	21.1 (0.04)
Urban skilled occasional wages	2.3 (0.13)	3.0 (0.17)	6.7 (0.39)	1.1 (0.06)	1.2 (0.07)	2.7 (0.15)
Urban skilled independent	143.9 (0.31)	166.9 (0.36)	801.4 (1.72)	75.5 (0.16)	88.2 (0.19)	174.7 (0.38)

continued

Table 6.10 Effect on Labor of an Exogenous Demand Shock of 1 Percent of Aggregate Exports, 2005

(GNF 15,368 million—percentage change in parentheses) continued

Destination/Origin	Livestock	Agriculture	Informal Manufacturing	Modern Construction	Aluminum	Fishery
Urban unskilled permanent wages	11.7 (0.18)	13.4 (0.20)	20.1 (0.30)	6.6 (0.10)	11.7 (0.18)	18.1 (0.27)
Urban unskilled occasional wages	214.8 (3.03)	31.3 (0.44)	32.1 (0.45)	12.7 (0.18)	9.3 (0.13)	33.4 (0.47)
Urban unskilled independent	326.9 (0.34)	535.4 (0.56)	1404.3 (1.48)	148.3 (0.16)	148.3 (0.16)	375.3 (0.39)
Rural permanent wages	390.6 (1.74)	130.4 (0.58)	69.3 (0.31)	27.1 (0.12)	21.5 (0.10)	75.8 (0.34)
Rural occasional wages	67.4 (0.65)	204.4 (1.98)	46.2 (0.45)	18.2 (0.18)	23.2 (0.22)	46.9 (0.45)
Rural independent	1727.5 (0.71)	5342.3 (2.19)	1185.0 (0.48)	460.8 (0.19)	312.1 (0.13)	1201.2 (0.49)
Aggregation						
Male	5598.3 (0.40)	11884.5 (0.85)	6985.8 (0.50)	2892.6 (0.21)	2778.5 (0.20)	4973.1 (0.36)
Female	2901.7 (0.59)	6445.2 (1.31)	3596.9 (0.73)	761.9 (0.16)	796.7 (0.16)	1949.2 (0.40)
Urban	2519.6 (0.24)	3044.4 (0.29)	6588.7 (0.64)	2023.7 (0.20)	2520.3 (0.24)	2857.9 (0.28)
Rural	5980.5 (0.70)	15285.3 (1.79)	3994.0 (0.47)	1630.8 (0.19)	1054.8 (0.12)	4064.5 (0.48)
Urban skilled	727.6 (0.13)	857.4 (0.15)	2242.5 (0.39)	627.8 (0.11)	540.1 (0.09)	836.7 (0.14)
Urban unskilled	1566.8 (0.34)	1962.9 (0.43)	4065.9 (0.89)	1133.8 (0.25)	928.7 (0.20)	1783.4 (0.39)

Source: Authors using SimSIP SAM.

to gender and worker education. Table 6.10 shows that the shocks in Livestock, Agriculture, and Fishery would benefit more rural workers than urban workers. The opposite is true for the other three sectors. All sectors benefit more unskilled workers in urban areas than skilled urban workers; not only is the monetary value of the effect higher, but it is also higher in percentage terms, which corrects for size bias.

However, while the increase in labor income is higher for male workers than for female workers in all six sectors, the proportion of total labor income that goes to female workers increases after an exogenous shock in Livestock, Agriculture, Informal Manufacturing, and Fishery. This means that expressing the changes in labor income in percentage terms rather than values paints a different picture.

The fact that the final effects of an exogenous demand shock in the six sectors studied here are much higher for male workers than for female workers can be explained by the higher initial values for male labor (more male workers earning more, on average, than female workers). The first three sectors in table 6.10 (the ones with highest female labor intensities) exhibit fairly similar importance for indirect effects for male and female workers (indirect effects are defined here as closed loop effects divided by total effects; see Annex 6B on multiplier decompositions for details). For the other three sectors, indirect effects are much more important for female workers (this is just a consequence of very low female labor intensities). Furthermore, indirect effects for rural workers are much higher than for urban workers for all sectors in table 6.11 but Agriculture.

In order to compare the percentage increases in labor income by gender in the six sectors in tables 6.10 and 6.11 with other sectors, we simulate an increase in demand for each of the sectors in the SAM equal to 1 percent of aggregate exports (GNF 15,368 million) and estimate the resulting increase in labor income in percentage terms. The size of the shock is arbitrary and was chosen as a percentage of aggregate exports to give an idea of importance relative to a macroeconomic aggregate. Figures 6.2 and 6.3 show the percentage increase in labor income for male and female workers, respectively, that results from the same increase in demand in each sector, as well as the elasticity of labor income to demand shocks for the various sectors.

Agriculture is the sector that generates the highest growth in male labor income (figure 6.2) with an increase in total male income of 0.85 percent, followed by Other Nontradable Services and Modern Manufacturing. Gold Mining and Other Minerals generate, on average, the lowest percentage growth in male labor income (partially explained by their very low labor intensity). The effect on labor income is related in part to the labor intensity of different activities, as well as the gender shares of labor income in the various sectors, but the multiplier effects of the various sectors also play a role. In terms of elasticities,

Table 6.11 Percentage of Total Multiplier Effect Resulting from Indirect Effects in Guinea, 2005

	Livestock	Agriculture	Informal Manufacturing	Modern Construction	Aluminum	Fishery
Male workers						
Urban skilled permanent wages	67.9	78.8	54.8	66.7	3.9	78.6
Urban skilled occasional wages	64.0	68.6	51.6	22.3	22.2	66.7
Urban skilled independent	59.8	67.0	27.7	54.3	40.2	63.6
Urban unskilled permanent wages	62.8	77.7	44.4	66.4	8.5	33.2
Urban unskilled occasional wages	78.8	74.3	66.1	52.3	12.2	54.5
Urban unskilled independent	63.4	57.9	24.2	52.5	42.5	63.6
Rural permanent wages	79.8	48.7	66.1	80.9	48.4	75.2
Rural occasional wages	94.4	37.1	90.8	74.2	71.7	96.8
Rural independent	83.1	36.1	79.9	94.7	89.7	87.9
Female workers						
Urban skilled permanent wages	56.7	79.3	37.7	80.7	2.2	61.7
Urban skilled occasional wages	74.2	76.3	30.1	93.8	47.9	76.3
Urban skilled independent	72.0	83.7	17.0	92.1	40.2	75.3
Urban unskilled permanent wages	51.5	74.9	38.2	88.4	23.7	49.9

Urban unskilled occasional wages	15.4	92.0	81.5	97.6	84.3	96.1
Urban unskilled independent	69.4	62.0	20.2	94.5	51.2	70.7
Rural permanent wages	21.2	59.0	85.3	99.4	82.4	94.5
Rural occasional wages	94.4	35.3	90.6	99.5	50.4	99.0
Rural independent	95.3	35.0	90.8	99.8	96.3	99.2
Aggregation						
Male	79.3	41.5	46.4	48.7	33.5	76.9
Female	78.1	39.1	44.2	90.6	57.3	94.7
Urban	73.3	67.9	24.3	34.9	18.6	69.6
Rural	81.2	35.3	80.8	85.5	87.0	90.5
Urban skilled	76.7	75.7	26.0	32.6	12.1	76.8
Urban unskilled	71.3	63.6	23.3	36.7	29.8	65.2

Source: Authors using SimSIP SAM.

Figure 6.2 Sectoral Impact on Male Labor and Male Labor Elasticity (Shock of 1% of Aggregate Exports)

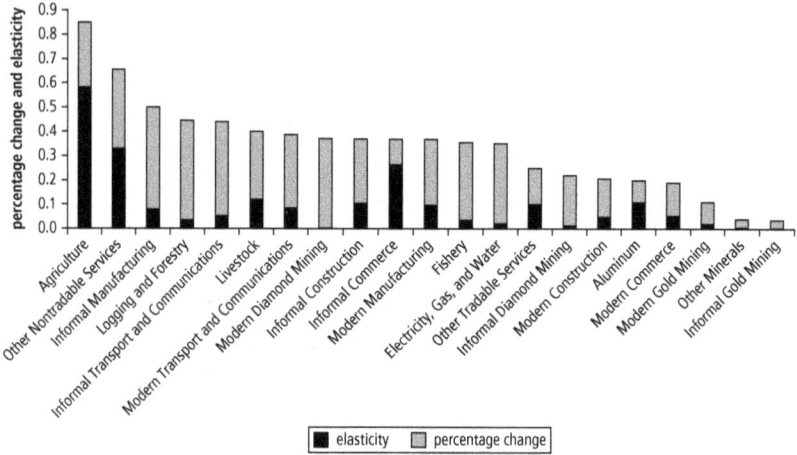

Source: Authors using SimSIP SAM.

Figure 6.3 Sectoral Impact on Female Labor and Female Labor Elasticity (Shock of 1% of Aggregate Exports)

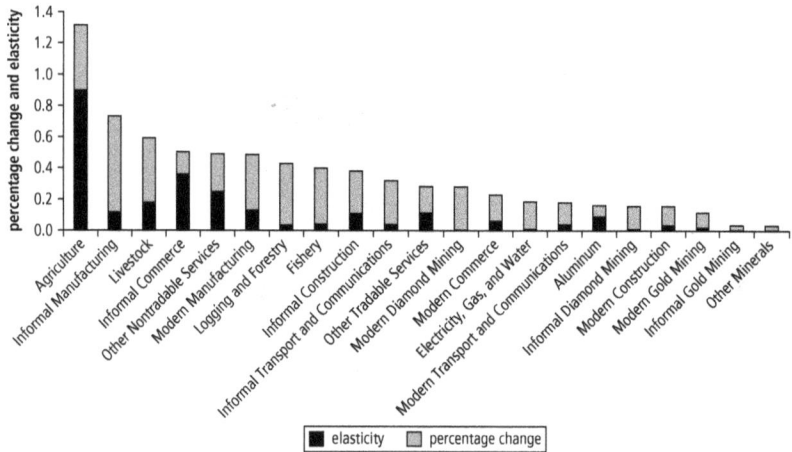

Source: Authors using SimSIP SAM.

Agriculture, Other Nontradable Services, and Informal Commerce exhibit the highest elasticity in labor income, at values of 0.58, 0.33, and 0.26, respectively.

The same procedure is used to examine the impact of shocks on female labor income, with the results shown in figure 6.3. Agriculture, Informal Manufacturing, and Livestock are the sectors with the highest growth in female labor income, with increases of 1.31, 0.73, and 0.59 percent, respectively, when all sectors receive the same demand shock of 1 percent of aggregate exports. As was the case for male labor income, Agriculture has, by far, the highest elasticity in female labor income at 0.90.

In figure 6.4, using the same demand shock for each sector of 1 percent of aggregate exports, we compute the differences in the percentage increases in labor income for male and female workers, as well as the impact on aggregate GDP that the shock might have when applied to each sector, one sector at a time. Agriculture, Informal Manufacturing, and Livestock not only benefit both male and female workers more than other sectors do, but also benefit female workers much more than male workers. Again, remember that many different factors contribute to these rankings, as well as the overall impact on labor income. One factor is the labor intensity of the various sectors. Another factor is the initial labor income shares by gender for each sector. The third factor is the multiplier effects at work, which depend in large part on the backward and forward links of the various sectors with the rest of the economy.

But clearly, even if indirect effects matter, in terms of the differentiated impacts by gender, the original labor income shares in each sector (direct effect) apparently play an important role, since the sectors that have the most pro-female labor impacts tend to be those with the highest proportion of labor income going to women (primary sector activities and Informal Manufacturing and Commerce). Another important finding is the direct relationship between how much more a sector benefits female than male workers, and the impact

Figure 6.4 Difference in Sectoral Impact on Female and Male Labor Income and Impact on Aggregate GDP (Shock of 1% of Aggregate Exports)

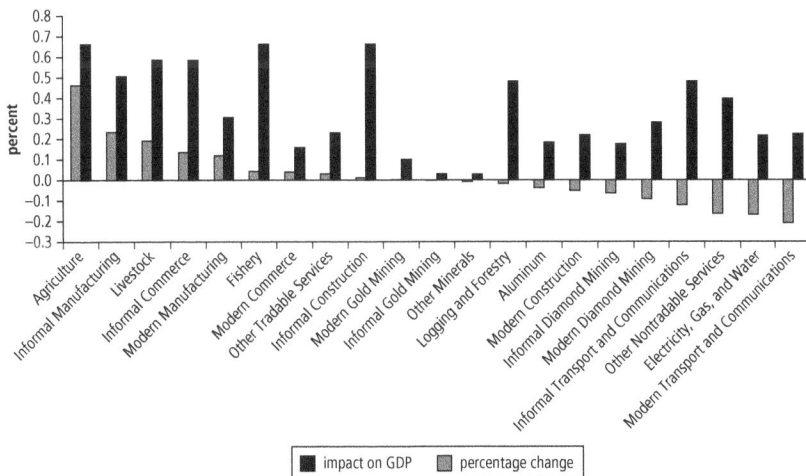

impact on GDP   percentage change

Source: Authors using SimSIP SAM.

it has on aggregate GDP. The average impact on GDP of a shock of 1 percent of aggregate exports among the sectors that benefit female workers more than male workers is 0.44, compared to 0.26 among the sectors that benefit male workers more than female workers. On top of that, five of the six sectors with the highest impact on GDP favor female workers more than male workers. This result suggests, in a stylized way, that promoting growth may be compatible with closing the gap between female and male labor income, but obviously this statement is based on a very limited analysis.

Let us be clear about what the results mean: Even if agricultural growth is conducive to overall growth, this obviously does not mean that one job created in agriculture generates the same value-added elsewhere. As shown in the discussion of household survey–based results, the lowest paying jobs are in agriculture. What is simulated is an identical value-added demand shock in various sectors; achieving a given increase in value-added in Agriculture requires the creation of many more jobs than in other sectors. Beyond the simple simulations provided here, a strategy for growth in Guinea should clearly also focus on creating jobs in the higher-productivity sectors.

In figure 6.5, we repeat the exercise presented in figure 6.3, but now comparing the percentage increases in labor income for rural and urban workers. Agriculture, Livestock, and Logging and Forestry benefit rural workers more, as expected.

Figure 6.5 Difference in Sectoral Impact on Rural and Urban Labor Income (Shock of 1% of Aggregate Exports)

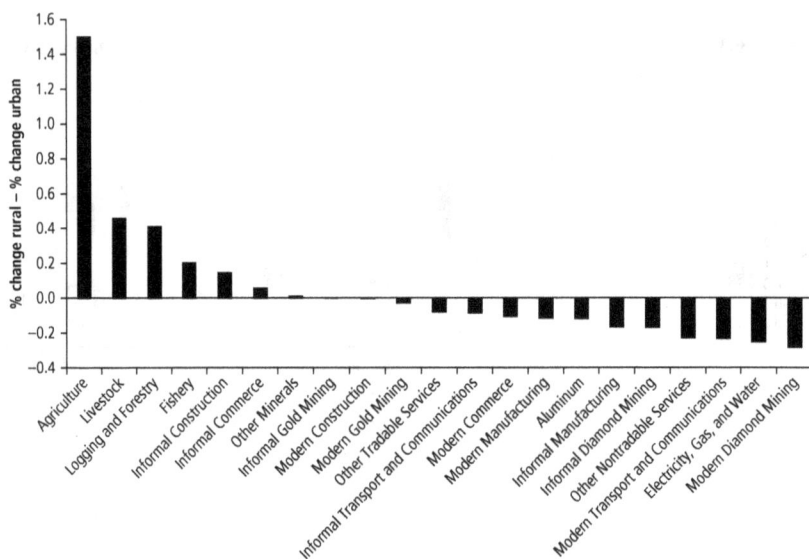

Source: Authors using SimSIP SAM.

Figure 6.6 Difference in Sectoral Impact on Urban Unskilled and Urban Skilled Labor Income (Shock of 1% of Aggregate Exports)

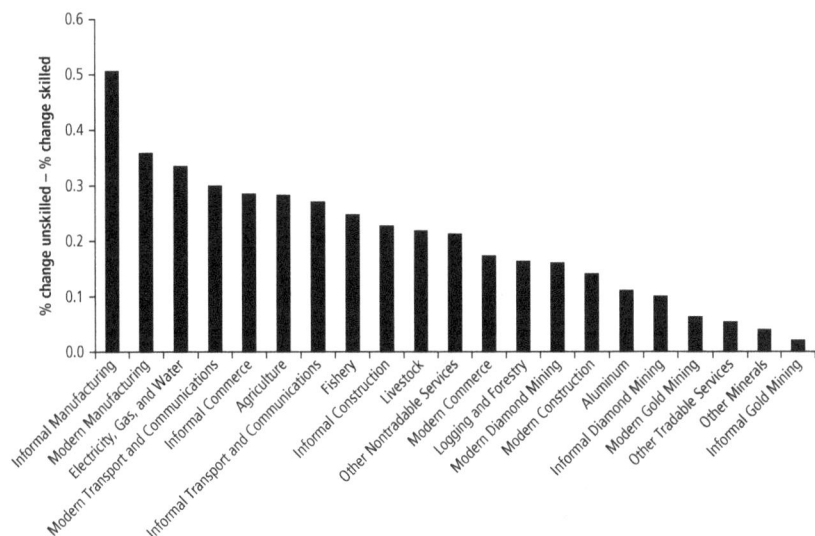

Source: Authors using SimSIP SAM.

Finally in figure 6.6, we compare the percentage increases in labor income for unskilled and skilled workers in urban areas resulting from the same aggregate shock (1 percent of total exports) applied one at a time to all sectors, one sector at a time. The fact that every sector in the Guinean economy benefits unskilled labor more than skilled labor in urban areas is striking. Informal and modern manufacturing are the sectors where the gap between the change in unskilled and skilled urban labor is highest. Mining and services sectors have relatively small differences between the changes in labor income for the different skill levels.

Conclusion

Increasing labor income for women and reducing gender disparities in labor income can have beneficial impacts on growth and poverty reduction. In addition to higher household income having a direct effect on poverty, research shows that a higher labor income share for women tends to shift household consumption choices toward more investment in human capital, including for the benefit of children.

This chapter started by reviewing some of the evidence on gender differentials in earnings and time use patterns in Guinea using household survey data. It also provided a simulation of the potential impact on poverty of an increase in the hours worked by individuals within households. But increasing hours worked presupposes that jobs are available. Using a recent SAM for Guinea, we then produced simple simulations of the potential impact on labor income shares by gender of growth in various sectors.

The results obtained from the microeconomic analysis of the Guinea survey are intuitive enough, and they are in line with what has been observed in other chapters in this book. These results suggest that, even after controlling for a wide range of explanatory variables, the differential in wages between men and women is very large, at about 40 percent. Women tend to work lower hours than men, but earn much less, because they are often confined to low-productivity jobs as well as domestic work. Unlocking the productive potential of female employment could help improve living conditions in Guinea.

The second part of the chapter was devoted to assessing whether some sectors of the economy would be especially well suited for improving the place of women in Guinea's labor markets. The empirical results were obtained with a recent Guinea SAM. We found that an expansion in agriculture especially would lead to a higher income share for women over time. This is not surprising, given the fact that many Guinean women work in agriculture. From the point of view of the implementation of Guinea's poverty reduction strategy, which places an emphasis on gender issues, the message is that investments in Agriculture, as well as other sectors such as Manufacturing, Livestock, Commerce, and Hunting, probably would help not only in reducing poverty, but also in reducing gender disparities in earnings in labor markets. Another result was that closing the gap between female and male labor incomes may also help growth in the specific sense that the sectors that comparatively favor female labor income are, on average, also the sectors that have a higher overall impact on economic growth through their multiplier effects. This is an interesting result that warrants further, more detailed analysis.

However, we advise being careful in interpreting or using the results for policy, because of the simplicity of the analysis, and, especially in the case of the SAM model, because of the strong implicit assumptions in the model. For example, the fact that agricultural growth is conducive to overall growth and a higher labor income share clearly does not mean that creating one job in agriculture has the same impact on value-added as creating one job in another sector. What was simulated is an identical value-added demand shock in different sectors. An original increase in demand of 1 percent of total value-added in agriculture implies the creation of many more jobs than an equivalent injection of 1 percent of value-added in other sectors.

The findings from this study do not imply that an actual growth strategy for Guinea should rely on sectors that favor workers with no education or sectors that favor women simply because the SAM analysis suggests that these sectors yield higher multiplier effects on overall GDP for a given shock. Such a policy would be dangerous. In the medium to long run, promoting unskilled, labor-intensive sectors, or those that traditionally employ women, would be problematic. For medium-term growth, it might be better to generate higher-quality jobs, rather than lower-paid jobs in lower productivity sectors, even if it is also necessary, of course, to provide conditions that enable individuals, especially the poor, to make a living. Because the Guinea SAM does not have data on employment by sector, we have not carried out here any analysis of the potential trade-offs between job creation, as opposed to value-added creation, and these trade-offs would need to be assessed for specific policies, none of which have been discussed here.

Even from a gender point of view, there may be trade-offs between creating many low-paid jobs versus creating better jobs for women. Better jobs for women may help not only to reduce the gender gap in pay, but also to provide incentives in order to encourage girls to pursue their education further because their prospects may then improve. Again, none of these dynamic considerations, which matter for policy, is discussed here.

There are also limits to the SAM simulations themselves. Since our goal was mostly to illustrate the type of simple analysis that can be conducted with a SAM, we chose to simulate demand shocks of an arbitrary size that, for comparison purposes, were set identically in value-added terms for all sectors of the economy. For small sectors, the magnitude of the shocks may simply not be realistic. Since the SAM model is linear, one could of course reduce the size of the shock in the simulations, and the relative findings would remain. But the point is that, before recommending any policy, a detailed analysis of the potential for value-added and job creation in various sectors would need to be conducted. Thus, when it was stated that promoting growth in Guinea may be compatible with closing the gap between female and male labor income shares, this statement may be true as a stylized fact from the SAM analysis, but it should not be taken as a policy fact.

The above comments are not meant to imply that the analysis in this chapter is useless—we do not believe it is, and we would not have carried it out if such was our belief. SAM-based analysis, as well as microeconomic analysis, provides valuable insights into the workings of the economy and the place of women in the labor market. These insights are precious, especially in poor countries where data and more sophisticated models are often not available for detailed analysis, or are not well understood locally because of limited capacity to carry out analytical work based, for example, on more complex computable general equilibrium models. But, in conclusion, we do want to emphasize that there is a difference between trying to better understand the basic structure of an economy through the type of simulations implemented here and claiming that the results should orient actual policy making.

The simplicity of the SAM model is both its main weakness and its strength. This simplicity is a weakness because it comes from serious limitations of the model, including the fact that no behavioral responses are taken into account, and that the model cannot be used to simulate at the same time price and quantity shocks (when a price shock is simulated, quantities are held constant, and when a quantity shock is simulated using a SAM, prices are held constant). A SAM also has limitations in examining sectoral labor movements in response to demand and other exogenous shocks. Simplicity is also a strength because the SAM-based model is relatively easy to understand and use, and its results can be easily replicated. More complex models, such as CGE models, can take into account behavioral responses, but their results depend on many assumptions made by the user that are not always easy to assess for the external reader. Of course the SAM model also makes some strong assumptions, but they are fewer and usually easier to understand. Thus, while SAM-based analysis can help us to better understand the structure of an economy, it does not mean that the results from simulations should be taken literally in order to inform policy.

While we have focused on some of the limits of the SAM model in the conclusions of this chapter, similar caution, of course, is also warranted in the use of microeconomic survey-based empirical results such as the ones presented in the first part of this chapter. But these tend to be well understood, as the community of practitioners for such work is much larger than the community of practitioners for SAM and other general equilibrium models.

Annex 6A Construction of Total Income in the EBEIP Household Survey

To obtain total annual household income, modules for employment, agricultural and non-agricultural activities, transfers, and other activities in the EIBEP survey (Enquête Intégrée de Base pour l'Evaluation de la Pauvreté or Basic Integrated Poverty Evaluation Survey) were used. Auto-consumption was derived from the consumption module. Aggregate annual income is defined as the sum of the incomes of household members obtained from main and secondary jobs surveis (including benefits), income obtained from the sale of agricultural products (net of costs), profits from sales of agricultural equipment and tools, other incomes from agricultural and breeding activities, profits from non-agricultural activities, auto-consumption, payments received, transfers, and other incomes. Some of those costs and incomes are based on data collected over a short period (the last 15 days or the last period of payment). When this is the case, the amounts are adjusted to correspond to an annual activity. Incomes are collected separately for each household member and aggregated at the household level in order to obtain the total annual household income. Annex table 6A.1 shows how the main components of aggregate income have been derived. The second definition of household income used in this paper is given in the last line of the table.

Table 6A.1 Definition of Aggregate Household Income

Detailed components		Aggregated income components (equal to the sum of detailed components by row)
+ Cash wages from the main job + Allowances and bonuses + Payments in kind (food, animals, etc.) + Value of housing assigned by the company + Reimbursement of transport costs	=	+ Income from main job
+ Cash wages from the second job + Payments in kind (food, animals, etc.) + Other payments in kind (housing, transport, goods and services)	=	+ Income from secondary job
+ Profits from the sale of agricultural products − Costs from activities linked to agriculture and breeding	=	+ Profits from the sale of agricultural production
		+ Incomes from the sales of agricultural tools
		+ Other income from agriculture and breeding
+ Turnover from non-agricultural firms − Costs from non-agricultural firms − Value of depreciation	=	+ Profits from non-agricultural activities
		+ Auto-consumption
		+ Payments received
		+ Transfers and other income
		= Total Annual Household Income
Total Annual Household Income − Profits from non-agricultural activities = Income 2		

Annex 6B Block Decomposition of the SAM Multiplier Matrix

As mentioned in the chapter text, the core of the SAM analysis is the multiplier model. With n endogenous accounts, let A_{nxn} denote the matrix of technical coefficients, i.e., the matrix resulting from dividing every cell T_{ij} in T_{nxn} by the respective column sum Y_j. Let Y_{nx1}, N_{nx1}, and X_{nx1} denote column vectors with the sums of total expenditures for the endogenous accounts, the endogenous component of those expenditures, and the exogenous component, respectively. Then by construction, the following two equations hold: $Y = N+X$, and $N = AY$. Combining these equations gives

$$Y = AY + X \qquad (6.1)$$

which can be rewritten as:

$$Y = (I - A)^{-1} X = MX \qquad (6.2)$$

where I is the nxn identity matrix. The matrix $M = (I - A)^{-1} X$ is known as the accounting multiplier matrix.

Cell m_{ji} of the multiplier matrix M quantifies the change in total income of account i as a result of a unitary increase in the exogenous component of sector j. In order to decompose the matrix M^5, for any nxn nonsingular matrix, we can rewrite equation (6.2) as:

$$Y = (A - \tilde{A})Y + \tilde{A}Y + X \qquad (6.3)$$

$$Y = A^* Y + (I - \tilde{A})^{-1} X \qquad (6.4)$$

where

$$A^* = (I - \tilde{A})^{-1} (A - \tilde{A}) \qquad (6.5)$$

Multiplying through by A^* yields:

$$A^* Y = A^{*2} Y + A^* (I - \tilde{A})^{-1} X \qquad (6.6)$$

From equation (6.2) we have an expression for $A^* Y$. Replacing it on the left-hand side yields:

$$Y = A^{*2} Y + (I + A^*) (I - \tilde{A})^{-1} X \qquad (6.7)$$

Multiplying equation (6.2) through by A^{*2} and replacing the expression for $A^{*2} Y$ from equation (6.6) yields:

$$Y = (I - A^{*3})^{-1} (I + A^* + A^{*2}) (I - \tilde{A})^{-1} X \qquad (6.8)$$

Notice that we just decomposed multiplicatively the multiplier matrix M from equation (6.2) into three different matrices. Define:

$$M_1 = (I - \tilde{A})^{-1}, \; M_2 = (I + A^* + A^{*2}), \text{ and } M_3 = (I - A^{*3})^{-1} \tag{6.9}$$

Then $M = M_3 M_2 M_1$. It is also possible to present the decomposition in an additive way:

$$M = I + \frac{(M_1 - I)}{TR} + \frac{(M_2 - I)M_1}{OL} + \frac{(M_3 - I)M_2 M_1}{CL} \tag{6.10}$$

where the first term (the identity matrix) is the initial unitary injection, matrix M_1 captures the net effect of a group of accounts on itself through direct transfers, matrix M_2 captures all net effects between partitions, and matrix M_3 captures the net effect of circular income multipliers among endogenous accounts. The terms in the additive decomposition (labeled TR for transfer effects, OL for open-loop effects, and CL for closed-loop effects), have broadly the same interpretation as the corresponding multiplicative effects (the matrices M_i).

The $n \times n$ matrix $\tilde{A}$ (partition of A) was chosen as follows, considering that the first row (and column) corresponds to the activities/commodities group, the second to the production factors, and the third to enterprises/households:

$$\tilde{A} = \begin{pmatrix} A_{11} & 0 & 0 \\ 0 & 0 & 0 \\ 0 & 0 & A_{33} \end{pmatrix}$$

Using the definition of A^* from equation (6.5) yields

$$A^* = (I - \tilde{A})^{-1}(I - \tilde{A}) = \begin{pmatrix} (I - A_{11})^{-1} & 0 & 0 \\ 0 & I & 0 \\ 0 & 0 & (I - A_{33})^{-1} \end{pmatrix} \begin{pmatrix} 0 & 0 & A_{13} \\ A_{21} & 0 & 0 \\ 0 & A_{32} & 0 \end{pmatrix}$$

$$= \begin{pmatrix} 0 & 0 & A_{13}^* \\ A_{21}^* & 0 & 0 \\ 0 & A_{32}^* & 0 \end{pmatrix}, \begin{cases} A_{13}^* = (I - A_{11})^{-1} A_{13} \\ A_{21}^* = A_{21} \\ A_{32}^* = (I - A_{33})^{-1} A_{32} \end{cases} \tag{6.11}$$

Using the expression for A^* and the definitions in equation (6.9) yields

$$M_1 = \begin{pmatrix} (I - A_{11})^{-1} & 0 & 0 \\ 0 & I & 0 \\ 0 & 0 & (I - A_{33})^{-1} \end{pmatrix} \tag{6.12}$$

$$M_2 = \begin{pmatrix} I & A_{13}^* A_{32}^* & A_{13}^* \\ A_{21}^* & I & A_{21}^* A_{13}^* \\ A_{32}^* A_{21}^* & A_{32}^* & I \end{pmatrix} \tag{6.13}$$

$$M_3 = \begin{pmatrix} \left(I - A_{13}^* A_{32}^* A_{21}^*\right)^{-1} & 0 & 0 \\ 0 & \left(I - A_{21}^* A_{13}^* A_{32}^*\right)^{-1} & 0 \\ 0 & 0 & \left(I - A_{32}^* A_{21}^* A_{13}^*\right)^{-1} \end{pmatrix} \tag{6.14}$$

We can provide expressions for the matrices TR, OL, and CL defined in equation (6.10):

$$TR = \begin{pmatrix} \left(I - A_{11}\right)^{-1} - I & 0 & 0 \\ 0 & 0 & 0 \\ 0 & 0 & \left(I - A_{33}\right)^{-1} - I \end{pmatrix} \tag{6.15}$$

$$OL = \begin{pmatrix} 0 & A_{13}^* A_{32}^* & A_{13}^* (I - A_{33})^{-1} \\ A_{21}^* (I - A_{11}^*)^{-1} & 0 & A_{21}^* A_{13}^* (I - A_{33})^{-1} \\ A_{32}^* A_{21}^* (I - A_{11}^*)^{-1} & A_{32}^* & 0 \end{pmatrix} \tag{6.16}$$

$$CL = \begin{pmatrix} C_{132}(I - A_{11})^{-1} & C_{132} A_{13}^* A_{32}^* & C_{132} A_{13}^* (I - A_{33})^{-1} \\ C_{132} A_{21}^* (I - A_{11})^{-1} & C_{213} & C_{213} A_{21}^* A_{13}^* (I - A_{33})^{-1} \\ C_{321} A_{32}^* A_{21}^* (I - A_{11})^{-1} & C_{321} A_{32}^* & C_{321} (I - A_{33})^{-1} \end{pmatrix} \tag{6.17}$$

where $C_{132} = (I - A_{13}^* A_{32}^* A_{21}^*)^{-1} - I$, $C_{213} = (I - A_{21}^* A_{13}^* A_{32}^*)^{-1} - I$ and $C_{321} = (I - A_{32}^* A_{21}^* A_{13}^*)^{-1} - I$

We now interpret and describe some features of the matrices TR, OL, and CL defined in equation (6.10). TR, which quantifies the net effect (net with respect to the initial unitary effect of a shock to an account on itself) of groups of accounts into themselves (intra), is a block diagonal matrix with a zero block in the second block on the diagonal, a consequence of the absence of transfers among production factors. OL, which captures the net direct effect (net with respect to the matrix M_1) between (inter) accounts, has zeros along the diagonal. CL, the matrix that captures the net closed-loop effects (net with respect to the product $M_2 M_1$), has no special structure.

Notes

1. While there is a consensus on the existence of gender disparities in African labor markets, assessing their nature and extent remains a challenge. Available databases provide incomplete and limited information on the relative situations of men and women, use very diverse methodologies and definitions of employment and earnings, and focus mostly on urban areas (see, for example, Appleton, Hoddinott, and Krishnan 1999; Brilleau, Roubaud, and Torelli 2004). Drawing on a recent meta-analysis of studies on the gender pay gap, Weichselbaumer, Winter-Ebmer, and Zweimüller (2007) find that only about 3 percent of these studies stem from African data out of all the empirical literature on the topic since the 1960s.
2. This discussion is adapted with minor changes from Nganou, Parra Osorio, and Wodon (2009); see also Nganou (2005).
3. This discussion follows closely Fofana, Parra Osorio, and Wodon (2009).
4. The latest version can be obtained from www.simsip.org.
5. For more details about computation, see Pyatt and Round (1979).

References

Adelman, I., and J. Edward Taylor. 1990. "A Structural Adjustment with a Human Face Possible? The Case of Mexico." *Journal of Development Studies* 26 (3): 387–407.

Arndt, C., H. Jensen, and F. Tarp. 2000. "Structural Characteristics of the Economy of Mozambique: A SAM–Based Analysis." *Review of Development Economics* 4 (3): 292–306.

Bardasi, E., and Q. Wodon. 2006a. "Measuring Time Poverty and Analyzing its Determinants: Concepts and Application to Guinea." In *Gender, Time Use and Poverty in Sub-Saharan Africa*, ed. C. M. Blackden and Q. Wodon, World Bank Working Paper 73. Washington, DC: World Bank.

———. 2006b. "Poverty Reduction from Full Employment: A Time Use Approach." In *Gender, Time Use and Poverty in Sub-Saharan Africa*, ed. C. M. Blackden and Q. Wodon, World Bank Working Paper 73. Washington, DC: World Bank.

Bautista, R., S. Robinson, and M. El-Said. 2001. "Alternative Industrial Development Paths for Indonesia: SAM and CGE Analyses." In *Restructuring Asian Economics for the New Millennium*, vol. 9B, ed. J. Behrman, M. Dutta, S. L. Husted, P. Sumalee, C. Suthiphand, and P. Wiboonchutikula, 773–90. Amsterdam: Elsevier Science/North Holland.

Blackden C. M., and Q. Wodon. 2006. *Gender, Time Use and Poverty in Sub-Saharan Africa*, World Bank Working Paper 73. Washington, DC: World Bank.

Defourny, J., and E. Thorbecke. 1984. "Structural Path Analysis and Multiplier Decomposition within a Social Accounting Matrix Framework." *Economic Journal* 94 (373): 111–36.

Dorosh, Paul A. 1994. "Adjustment, External Shocks, and Poverty in Lesotho: A Multiplier Analysis." Working Paper 71, Cornell Food and Nutrition Program, Ithaca, NY.

Fofana, I., S. F. Doumbouya, and I. S. Gassama. 2007. "La matrice de comptabilité sociale finale de la Guinée pour l'année 2005," unpublished manuscript, University of Laval Quebec, Canada.

Fofana, I., J. C. Parra Osorio, and Q. Wodon. 2009. "Exports and Labor Income by Gender: A Social Accounting Matrix Analysis for Senegal." In *Gender Aspects of the Trade and Poverty Nexus: A Macro-Micro Approach*, ed. M. Bussolo and R. E. De Hoyos. Washington, DC: World Bank and Palgrave MacMillan.

Hoddinott, J., and L. Haddad. 1995. "Does Female Income Share Influence Household Expenditures? Evidence from the Côte d'Ivoire." *Oxford Bulletin of Economics and Statistics* 57 (1): 77–96.

Jorgenson, D. 1984. "Econometric Methods for Applied General Equilibrium Analysis." In *Applied General Equilibrium Analysis*, ed. H. E. Scarf and J. B. Shoven, 139–203. New York: Cambridge University Press.

Jorgenson, D., ed. 1998. *Growth Volume 2: Energy, the Environment, and Economic Growth*. Cambridge, MA: MIT Press.

Khan, H. A. 1999. "Sectoral Growth and Poverty: A Multiplier Decomposition Analysis for South Africa." *World Development* 27 (3): 521–30.

Leontief, W. 1951. *The Structure of the American Economy 1919–1939*, 2nd ed. New York: Oxford University Press.

Leontief, W. 1953. *Studies in the Structure of the American Economy*. New York: Oxford University Press.

Lewis, B., and E. Thorbecke. 1992. "District-Level Economic Linkages in Kenya: Evidence Based on a Small Regional Social Accounting Matrix." *World Development* 20 (6): 881–97.

Nganou, Jean-Pascal Nguessa. 2005. "A Multisectoral Analysis of Growth Prospects for Lesotho: SAM-Multiplier Decomposition and Computable General Equilibrium Perspectives." Ph.D. thesis, American University, Washington, DC.

Nganou, J.-P., J. C. Parra Osorio, and Q. Wodon. 2009. "Oil Price Shocks, Poverty and Gender: A Social Accounting Matrix Analysis for Kenya." In *Gender Aspects of the Trade and Poverty Nexus: A Macro-Micro Approach*, ed. M. Bussolo and R. E. De Hoyos. Washington, DC: World Bank and Palgrave MacMillan.

Parikh, A., and E. Thorbecke. 1996. "Impact of Rural Industrialization on Village Life and Economy: A Social Accounting Matrix Approach." *Economic Development and Cultural Change* 44 (2): 351–77.

Parra, J. C., and Q. Wodon. 2009. "SimSIP SAM: Policy Analysis under a SAM Framework." World Bank, Washington, DC.

Pyatt, G., and J. Round. 1979. "Accounting and Fixed Price Multipliers in a Social Accounting Matrix Framework." *Economic Journal* 89 (356): 850–73.

Round, J. I. 1985. "Decomposing Multipliers for Economic Systems Involving Regional and World Trade." *Economic Journal* 95 (378): 383–99.

———. 1989. "Decomposition of Input-Output and Economy-Wide Multipliers in a Regional Setting." In *Frontiers of Input-Output Analysis*, ed. Ronald E. Miller, Karen R. Polenske, and Adam Z. Rose, 103–118. Oxford: Oxford University Press.

Taylor, J. Edward, and I. Adelman. 1996. *Village Economies*. New York: Cambridge University Press.

Taylor, J. Edward, Antonio Yunez-Naude, George A. Dyer, Micki Stewart, and Sergio Ardila. 2002. "The Economics of 'Eco-Tourism': A Galapagos Island Economywide Perspective." *Economic Development and Cultural Change* 51 (4): 977–97.

Thorbecke, Erik. 2000. "The Use of Social Accounting Matrices in Modeling." Paper prepared for the 26th General Conference of the International Association for Research in Income and Wealth, Cracow, Poland, August 27–September 2.

Thorbecke, Erik, and Hong-Sang Jung. 1996. "A Multiplier Decomposition Method to Analyze Poverty Alleviation." *Journal of Development Economics* 48 (2): 279–300.

Weichselbaumer, D., R. Winter-Ebmer, and M. Zweimüller. 2007. "Market Orientation and Gender Wage Gaps: An International Study." Economics working papers 2007–12, Department of Economics, Johannes Kepler University, Linz, Austria.

World Bank. 2005. *Guinée: Diagnostique de la Pauvreté*, Report No. 32822-GN, World Bank, Washington, DC.

Chapter **7**

How Does Growth Affect Labor Income by Gender? A Structural Path Analysis for Tanzania

Juan Carlos Parra Osorio and Quentin Wodon

Introduction

Social accounting matrices (SAMs) have been used fairly extensively to model the effects of shocks on a nation's economy. A brief literature review on SAMs and examples of their use for simple simulations were provided by Parra and Wodon (2009b) in chapter 6 of this volume. That chapter highlighted the strengths and weaknesses of SAMs and emphasized the need to be careful before using SAM-based simulation results in order to inform policy. It is worthwhile to start here by summarizing briefly some of the key features of SAMs from that chapter.

A social accounting matrix is a database with information on cross-purchases between different agents and sectors in the economy. But it can also be used as a simple, static yet comprehensive model of an economy. As such model, the SAM assumes that all agents and accounts behave according to their expenditure propensities, which represent what one agent or account in the economy buys from other agents or accounts. It is also assumed that these propensities are unaffected by the shocks simulated in the model; that is, there are no behavioral responses or changes following a shock. This means, among other things, that when a SAM is used for quantity shocks, prices are held constant, and when it is used for simulating price shocks, quantities used or consumed are also held constant.

The authors gratefully acknowledge review by Jorge Arbache and Mayra Buvinic. The views expressed in this chapter are those of the authors and need not reflect those of the World Bank, its executive directors, or the countries they represent.

The general equilibrium nature of the SAM model comes from the fact that the model takes into account multiplier effects. If production in one account or sector is increased, that sector by assumption must buy inputs from other accounts, which in turn must purchase additional inputs, and so on. All these spillover effects from an initial shock are taken into account in the SAM model, which gives us the overall impact of a shock on the economy or on households after the economy has reached a new equilibrium following the shock.

The core of the SAM model is the technical coefficients matrix containing the expenditure propensities for every account in the matrix. The equilibrium character of the model is given by the fact that, at a solution, there are no forces suggesting additional changes. In the simplest form of the model, no resource constraint is specified because it is assumed that any additional production required is feasible, so that all resources (factors) required to undertake additional production are available (this assumption can be relaxed).

SAMs have been used to measure the impact, or multiplier effects, of a wide variety of shocks in an economy, such as those discussed in Chapter 6, to assess how sectoral growth patterns may affect household labor income by gender. This type of analysis is feasible when the labor income accounts in the SAM are disaggregated by gender.

Beyond measurement of multipliers, SAMs can also be used to better understand exactly how an initial shock affects the economy and ends up in an overall final impact that is larger than the initial shock. These shock effects are what this chapter focuses on; specifically, structural path analysis (SPA) is used to examine the transmission channels through which an initial shock travels through the economy to affect all the other accounts of the SAM, with a focus here on the impact of shocks on labor income by gender. This analysis is used to characterize what we call the concentration, strength, and speed of various transmission channels. Concentration refers to the share of the total impact of a shock that travels through one or more paths linking various accounts in the SAM. Strength, by contrast, depends on the size of the contribution of a path to the total multiplier effect estimated through the SAM. Finally, speed relates to the share of the contribution of the path that travels directly from the origin to the destination, without going through any account more than once, with paths of higher lengths typically taking more time to materialize because a higher number of transactions need to take place.

This chapter builds on several previous papers that have relied on SPA in the literature on SAMs. The SPA methodology was initially proposed by Lantner (1974) who applied it to an input-output table (Lantner 1972). Defourny and Thorbecke (1984) applied SPA to a SAM for the first time using a 1968 SAM for the Republic of Korea. Their analysis concentrated on the effects of production activities on other production activities, on factors of production, on households, and finally the influence of households on production activities. Xie (2000) illustrates the use of SPA to an environmentally extended SAM in China.

Using economic links, fields of influence, and SPA on a 1995 SAM for Australia, Lanzen (2003) concludes that considerable environmental and resource pressure is exerted along paths that lead to exports. Beef cattle for exported meat products, exports of non-ferrous metal products, and exported sheep and wool were found to be the sectors exerting most of the pressure. The environmental effects are measured through emission of greenhouse gases, and measures of energy consumption, water use, and land disturbance are also used.

Ferri and Uriel (2002) use SPA on a 2000 SAM for Spain to study the distributive effects of exogenous shocks to public spending and exports. They conclude that Other Services is the key sector to increase labor income of qualified workers. More than 80 percent of the total effect of Other Services on labor income of qualified workers is explained by direct payments, with no other account as intermediary.

Roberts (2005) uses SPA to analyze the role of different types of households in the rural Western Isles region of Scotland in 1997. Quantifying the importance of all paths that include household accounts, she concludes that households with children, compared to households without children and retired households, play a key role in connecting production and consumption, accounting for more than half of the total household-related multiplier effects for every economic sector. The study was motivated by the observation that, because of limited inter-industry links in rural areas, households have a high influence on multiplier effects.

Khan and Thorbecke (1989) analyze the gradual substitution of traditional technologies using a highly disaggregated 1975 SAM for Indonesia. In particular, the authors compare the structures of hand-pounded rice with that of rice milling, and the structures of brown and refined sugars. They conclude that the higher multiplier effect of hand-pounded rice on agricultural employees is explained by higher backward links between hand-pounded rice and farm food crops, as compared to milled rice and farm food crops. In the case of sugar, the links to the factors of production in the rural areas are much larger for brown than for refined sugar.

This chapter uses a recent SAM for Tanzania to show how SPA can be used to better understand the transmission channels through which sectoral growth patterns are likely to have different effects on the incomes of women and men. To our knowledge, this is the first time that structural path analysis has been used to study gender issues. As mentioned, one must be careful in using results from SAM simulations for policy direction. Our goal here is not to inform policy in Tanzania, but simply to illustrate the type of gender and labor analysis that can be performed with a SAM, especially using SPA.

The next section provides a brief description of the Tanzania SAM with a focus on the gender disaggregation (for a more generic description of the basic structure of a standard SAM, see Chapter 6 on Guinea). The third and fourth sections present the results of basic simulations and the structural path analysis, respectively, followed by a brief conclusion.

Main Features of the 2001 Tanzania SAM

This section presents a description of the structure of the SAM used for our analysis, as well as some descriptive statistics on indicators like production, value-added, exports, and imports. A more detailed description is provided for the labor disaggregation in the SAM (by gender and education level), including the labor intensity, and female labor intensity and share for every sector in the SAM.

Description of the Accounts in the Tanzania SAM

The 2001 Tanzania SAM was constructed by Thurlow and Wobst (2003) at the International Food Policy Research Institute.[1] It includes 43 activities and commodities, 10 categories of labor, 2 types of capital as a production factor, 1 account for land, 1 for enterprises, 12 types of households, 7 accounts for government, 1 account for investment, and 1 account for the rest of the world. The labor income accounts are disaggregated according to gender and education (with the following categories: individuals with no formal education, individuals not having completed primary school, individuals with primary school but not having completed secondary school, and individuals with secondary or higher education). Child labor is also included as a separate account. Capital is divided into agricultural and non-agricultural capital accounts. Household accounts are based on the area of residence, poverty status, and education of the head of household.

Table 7.1 provides basic data on the sectors included in the SAM. The table shows that Real Estate, Public Administration, Trade, and Maize are the largest contributors to value-added, with shares of total value-added of, respectively, 14.4 percent, 11.3 percent, 7.2 percent, and 6.1 percent.

In terms of international trade, imports are mainly for Transport and Communications, Equipment, and Petroleum Refineries sectors, which together account for 60 percent of total imports in CIF (cost, insurance, and freight) value. For the following goods, the imports exceed domestic production (the imports as a share of domestic production is provided in parenthesis): Wheat (72 percent), Chemicals (170 percent), Fertilizers and Pesticides (110 percent), Petroleum Refineries (880 percent), Rubber and Plastic (112 percent), Metal Products (94 percent), Equipment (484 percent), and Transport and Communications (57 percent). The Transport and Communications sector represents 44 percent of total exports in FOB value, while the Cashew Nuts and Coffee sectors account for 7 percent each of total exports. In terms of export propensity, almost the entire domestic production of coffee and cashew nuts is exported.

Gender Disaggregation for Labor Income

The impact of exogenous shocks on labor income shares by gender can be analyzed in this chapter because those accounts are disaggregated by gender in the SAM. Basic descriptive statistics are displayed in table 7.2. Overall, the Beans sector

Table 7.1 Sectoral Analysis for Tanzania SAM, 2001 (T Sh million)

	Production (Q)		Value added at factor cost		Imports (M)		Exports (X)		M/Q	X/XS
	Value	Share (%)	Value	Share (%)	Value	Share (%)	Value	Share (%)		
Maize	851.9	6.1	750.0	9.9	16.2	0.8	1.0	0.1	1.9	0.1
Paddy	406.3	2.9	283.0	3.7	21.7	1.1	2.6	0.2	5.3	0.6
Sorghum	126.1	0.9	100.1	1.3	0	0	0.1	0	0	0.1
Wheat	26.3	0.2	17.5	0.2	19.0	0.9	0.1	0	72.4	0.2
Beans	211.3	1.5	178.2	2.3	0	0	1.1	0.1	0	0.5
Cassava	155.8	1.1	152.0	2.0	0	0	0	0	0	0
Other Cereals	34.4	0.2	25.7	0.3	0	0	0.1	0	0	0.4
Oil Seeds	125.0	0.9	113.1	1.5	0.2	0	4.5	0.3	0.2	3.6
Other Roots and Tubers	131.0	0.9	122.7	1.6	0	0	0	0	0	0
Cotton	96.1	0.7	47.7	0.6	0	0	41.5	3.2	0	43.2
Coffee	87.3	0.6	57.6	0.8	0	0	94.9	7.3	0	108.8
Tobacco	74.7	0.5	40.8	0.5	0.2	0	48.1	3.7	0.2	64.4
Tea	38.8	0.3	20.9	0.3	0.2	0	26.4	2.0	0.5	68.1
Cashew Nuts	87.2	0.6	78.2	1.0	0	0	93.6	7.2	0	107.3
Sisal Fiber	16.5	0.1	7.1	0.1	0	0	0	0	0	0
Sugar	160.6	1.1	120.3	1.6	50.3	2.5	12.8	1.0	31.3	7.9
Fruits and Vegetables	527.7	3.8	499.0	6.6	7.9	0.4	27.5	2.1	1.5	5.2
Other Crops	67.1	0.5	60.5	0.8	0.1	0	4.5	0.3	0.2	6.7
Poultry and Livestock	294.9	2.1	248.8	3.3	2.8	0.1	6.4	0.5	1.0	2.2
Fishing	334.2	2.4	302.2	4.0	0.1	0	65.1	5.0	0	19.5
Hunting and Forestry	302.0	2.1	278.7	3.7	0.5	0	5.5	0.4	0.2	1.8
Mining	128.2	0.9	110.4	1.5	13.3	0.7	19.9	1.5	10.4	15.5

continued

Table 7.1 Sectoral Analysis for Tanzania SAM, 2001 (T Sh million) *continued*

	Production (Q) Value	Share (%)	Value added at factor cost Value	Share (%)	Imports (M) Value	Share (%)	Exports (X) Value	Share (%)	M/Q	X/XS
Meat and Dairy	327.9	2.3	176.2	2.3	3.9	0.2	0.6	0	1.2	0.2
Grain Milling	647.6	4.6	50.5	0.7	15.5	0.8	6.8	0.5	2.4	1.0
Processed Food	421.9	3.0	150.4	2.0	73.6	3.7	7.0	0.5	17.4	1.7
Beverages and Tobacco Products	173.1	1.2	65.6	0.9	16.5	0.8	1.2	0.1	9.5	0.7
Textiles and Leather Products	412.3	2.9	229.3	3.0	76.3	3.8	16.9	1.3	18.5	4.1
Wood, Paper, Printing	147.3	1.0	71.8	0.9	67.9	3.4	5.6	0.4	46.1	3.8
Chemicals	65.8	0.5	16.2	0.2	111.7	5.6	3.2	0.2	169.9	4.8
Fertilizers and Pesticides	11.2	0.1	3.0	0	12.4	0.6	0.1	0	110.4	0.5
Petroleum Refineries	27.5	0.2	13.6	0.2	241.8	12.0	0.1	0	880.0	0.4
Rubber, Plastic	54.4	0.4	17.5	0.2	60.9	3.0	1.3	0.1	111.9	2.4
Glass and Cement	89.2	0.6	30.0	0.4	6.4	0.3	6.7	0.5	7.2	7.5
Metal Products	133.1	0.9	41.7	0.6	125.3	6.2	1.1	0.1	94.1	0.8
Equipment	115.0	0.8	47.1	0.6	557.1	27.7	7.8	0.6	484.2	6.8
Utilities	216.4	1.5	132.2	1.7	0	0	0	0	0	0
Construction	769.6	5.5	342.3	4.5	2.4	0.1	0	0	0.3	0
Trade	1,013.4	7.2	792.9	10.5	0	0	0	0	0	0
Hotels and Restaurants	453.8	3.2	198.5	2.6	0	0	00	0	0	0
Transport and Communications	684.6	4.9	438.4	5.8	392.6	19.5	578.6	44.3	57.4	84.5
Real Estate	2,032.6	14.4	452.8	6.0	0	0	0	0	0	0
Public Administration	1,585.1	11.3	470.3	6.2	17.4	0.9	71.3	5.5	1.1	4.5
Business and Other Services	401.9	2.9	227.9	3.0	94.5	4.7	142.1	10.9	23.5	35.4
All	**14,066.9**	**100.0**	**7,582.4**	**100.0**	**2,009.0**	**100.0**	**1,306.0**	**100.0**	**2,160.3**	**615.2**

Source: Authors.
Note: M/Q = Import share within sector production; X/XS = Export share of production; M = Imports.

Table 7.2 Summary Data on Labor Income Shares in Tanzania SAM

Activity	Labor intensity (percent)	Female labor income intensity (percent)	Female labor income share (percent)	Activity	Labor intensity (percent)	Female labor income intensity (percent)	Female labor income share (percent)
Maize	16.7	66.1	9.8	Grain Milling	76.7	38.6	1.8
Paddy	39.6	57.9	7.7	Processed Food	14.0	36.5	0.9
Sorghum	16.9	58.3	1.1	Beverages and Tobacco Products	17.6	3.0	0
Wheat	47.4			Textiles and Leather Products	52.5	39.9	5.7
Beans	35.3	75.6	5.7	Wood, Paper, Printing	23.3	3.8	0.1
Cassava	9.5	54.1	0.9	Chemicals	81.5	0	0
Other Cereals	44.0	62.5	0.8	Fertilizers and Pesticides	70.7	0	0
Oil Seeds	36.7	60.7	3.0	Petroleum Refineries	27.5	0	0
Other Roots and Tubers	23.6	64.7	2.2	Rubber, Plastic	21.8	29.2	0.1
Cotton	50.3	36.5	0.9	Glass and Cement	22.9	0.8	0
Coffee	46.1	40.7	1.3	Metal Products	23.3	2.0	0
Tobacco	50.2	40.2	1.0	Equipment	9.1	8.2	0
Tea	49.2	0	0	Utilities	20.3	4.3	0.1
Cashew Nuts	50.2	28.9	1.3	Construction	67.9	1.6	0.4
Sisal Fiber	50.0	10.8	0.0	Trade	7.9	25.9	1.9
Sugar	50.2	54.6	3.9	Hotels and Restaurants	23.5	54.4	3.0
Fruits and Vegetables	30.8	62.9	11.3	Transport and Communications	12.7	14.0	0.9
Other Crops	27.9	49.0	0.9	Real Estate	5.7	53.8	3.7
Poultry and Livestock	41.5	58.4	6.5	Public Administration	95.9	33.8	18.2
Fishing	47.3	11.3	1.9	Business and Other Services	32.1	24.5	2.1
Hunting and Forestry	20.6	53.8	3.7				
Mining	1.8	13.1	0.0				
Meat and Dairy	1.0	30.0	0.1				

Source: Authors.

279

is the most female-intensive labor activity, with 75.6 percent of total payments to labor going to female workers. The Maize sector, Fruits and Vegetables sector, as well as the Other Cereals sector, follow with shares of labor income allocated to women of, respectively, 66.1 percent, 62.9 percent, and 62.5 percent. Other sectors with high female labor intensities (exceeding 50 percent) are Paddy, Sorghum, Cassava, Oil Seeds, Other Roots and Tubers, Sugar, Poultry and Livestock, Hunting and Forestry, and Hotels and Restaurants.

However, these female-labor-intensive sectors (as defined by the share of total income allocated to female workers) differ widely in terms of their labor intensity (as measured through the share of labor income in the total value-added of the sector). While labor income represents 50 percent of the value-added in the Sugar sector, it represents only between 10 and 20 percent of value-added in the Cassava, Maize, and Sorghum sectors.

Sectoral Growth and Impact on Labor Income Shares by Gender

All the computations in this section were performed using SimSIP SAM, a powerful and easy-to-use Microsoft® Excel based application, with MATLAB® running in the background, which can be used to conduct policy analysis under a SAM framework. The tool was developed by Parra and Wodon (2009a) and is distributed free of charge,[2] together with the necessary MATLAB components. The accompanying user's manual describes the theory behind the computations. The application can be used to perform various types of analysis and decompositions, as well as to obtain detailed and graphical results for experiments.

In table 7.3, using an approach similar to that of Parra and Wodon (2009b) in chapter 6, we start by showing the effect of an exogenous demand shock equal to 100 million Tanzanian shillings (T Sh) (1.3 percent of GDP) on labor income by gender, as well as on the labor incomes obtained by different subgroups defined according to the education level of the workers. This is done for six sectors: Maize, Beans, Sorghum, Trade, Transport and Communications, and Real Estate. The size of the shock is arbitrary—it was picked to make the results of our simulations easier to interpret as a proportion of the initial shock. However, because the SAM model is linear, the results obtained with larger or smaller shocks would be proportionately identical (a shock twice as large would have an impact twice as large).

Simulations were conducted on sectors with both high and low female labor intensities. The first three of the six sectors considered (Maize, Beans, and Sorghum) have high female labor intensities (66.1 percent, 75.6 percent, and 58.3 percent, respectively), while the last three (Trade, Transport and Communications, and Real Estate) have relatively low female labor intensities (25.9 percent,

Table 7.3 Effect on Labor of Exogenous Demand Shock of T Sh 100 million
(percentage changes in parentheses)

Destination/Origin	Maize	Beans	Sorghum	Trade	Transport and Communications	Real Estate
Female workers						
No formal education	4.4 (6.3)	6.4 (9.1)	5.7 (8.2)	2.3 (3.3)	2.2 (3.1)	2.4 (3.4)
Unfinished primary school	4.2 (5.1)	5.4 (6.7)	3.4 (4.2)	2.8 (3.5)	2.6 (3.2)	2.7 (3.4)
Unfinished secondary school	26.6 (5.0)	38.7 (7.3)	22.6 (4.3)	17.5 (3.3)	16.4 (3.1)	17.6 (3.3)
Secondary or higher education	2.2 (1.4)	2.3 (1.5)	2.2 (1.4)	2.7 (1.7)	3.3 (2.1)	3.6 (2.3)
Male workers						
No formal education	3.5 (4.3)	3.7 (4.5)	4.1 (5.0)	2.5 (3.0)	2.3 (2.8)	2.6 (3.1)
Unfinished primary school	10.5 (3.9)	12.3 (4.6)	9.8 (3.7)	7.7 (2.9)	7.2 (2.7)	8.2 (3.1)
Unfinished secondary school	19.4 (2.9)	20.2 (3.0)	19.3 (2.9)	18.1 (2.7)	18.4 (2.7)	21.0 (2.1)
Secondary or higher education	6.8 (1.6)	6.7 (1.6)	6.7 (1.6)	8.8 (2.1)	11.5 (2.7)	12.2 (2.9)

continued

Table 7.3 Effect on Labor of Exogenous Demand Shock of T Sh 100 million
(percentage changes in parentheses) continued

Destination/Origin	Maize	Beans	Sorghum	Trade	Transport and Communications	Real Estate
Gender						
Female	37.4 (4.5)	52.7 (6.3)	33.9 (4.1)	25.4 (3.0)	24.4 (2.9)	26.3 (3.1)
Male	40.2 (2.8)	43.0 (3.0)	39.8 (2.8)	37.1 (2.6)	39.4 (2.7)	44.0 (3.0)
Education						
No formal education	7.9 (5.2)	10.1 (6.6)	9.8 (6.4)	4.8 (3.2)	4.5 (2.9)	5.0 (3.3)
Unfinished primary school	14.7 (4.2)	17.7 (5.1)	13.1 (3.8)	10.6 (3.0)	9.8 (2.8)	11.0 (3.2)
Unfinished secondary school	46.1 (3.8)	58.9 (4.9)	42.0 (3.5)	35.6 (2.9)	34.8 (2.9)	38.6 (3.2)
Secondary or higher education	9.0 (1.6)	9.0 (1.6)	8.9 (1.5)	11.5 (2.0)	14.7 (2.6)	15.8 (2.7)

Source: Authors using SimSIP SAM.

14.0 percent, and 10.7 percent, respectively). In conducting the analysis, it is best to express many of the changes in percentage terms to correct for the size effect that is present when reporting changes in levels (that is, large accounts tend to have bigger changes as results of exogenous shocks, but not necessarily bigger percentage changes.) After the initial shock, it turns out that, in percentage terms, payments to female workers increase more than payments to male workers for all six sectors; the same is true for workers without formal education compared to workers with higher levels of education. This means that an exogenous increase in the demand for any of the six sectors would help (at the margin) to close the gap between total pay for male and female workers, and between total pay for educated and non-educated workers. The exogenous demand shock in the Beans sector has the highest impact on female labor income (in percentage terms) among the six sectors, as well as on total labor income in levels, and on the labor income of workers with less than finished secondary education.

For comparison of the percentage increases in labor income by gender in the six sectors with other sectors, a demand shock of T Sh100 million was applied to each sector in the economy, one at a time, and compared with the resulting percentage changes in labor income. Figure 7.1 presents two computations that result from applying this demand shock. On the left vertical axis are the differences in the percentage increases in labor income for male and female workers, and on the right vertical axis is the impact on aggregate GDP caused by the shock. For example, the first shaded bar on the left indicates that a demand shock of T Sh100 million to the Beans sector would result in a percentage increase for female labor income 3.2 percent higher than the percentage change for male labor income (thereby closing at the margin the gap between female and male labor income); the hollow bar indicates that the same shock would generate a percentage change in GDP of about 4.5 percent (as measured on the right vertical axis). Beans, Other Cereals, Oil Seeds, and Fruits and Vegetables are the sectors with the largest difference between the percentage increase in female labor income and the increase in male labor income, and they all lead to larger proportional gains for female workers. Only 12 of the 43 sectors favor male over female workers, with Chemicals, Tea, Wheat, and Construction being the most favorable to male workers.

Another finding regards the direct relationship between how much a sector benefits female more than male workers, and the impact it has on aggregate GDP. The thick horizontal lines in figure 7.1 represent the average impact on GDP. For sectors that favor female workers, the average impact on GDP is a 3.96 percent increase, while this figure is only an increase of 3.42 percent for sector that favor male workers. Nine of the 10 sectors with the highest impact on GDP favor female workers over male workers. These two results would suggest that promoting value added growth in Tanzania could help close the gap between female and male labor income.

Figure 7.1 Difference Between Sectoral Impact on Female and Male Labor Income, and Impact on Aggregate GDP (Shock of T Sh 100 million)

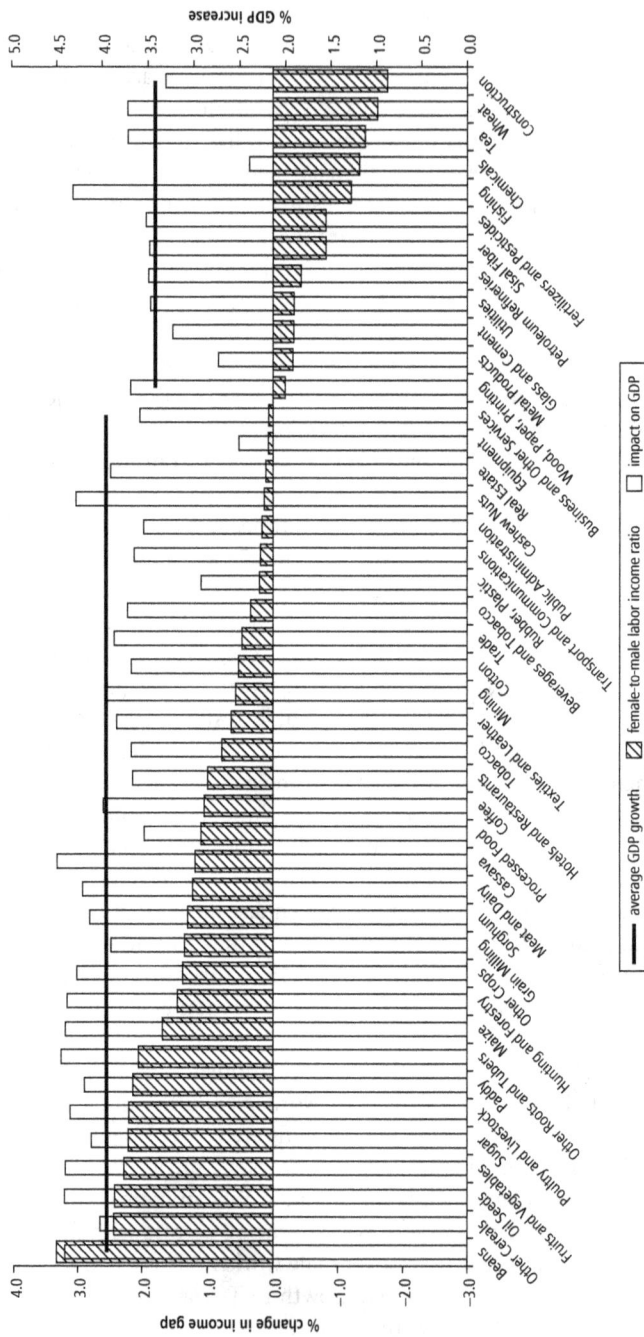

Source: Authors using SimSIP SAM.

At the same time, care must be taken about what is actually measured here. We are simulating shocks of the same magnitude to different sectors, but because women tend to work in lower-productivity sectors, achieving an initial shock of T Sh 100 million in sectors with a higher female intensity of labor would normally require the creation of more jobs than achieving the same initial shock in sectors with a higher male intensity of labor. Also, while governments are under pressure to help create jobs, if only to cope with demographic pressure, they also aim to create higher-quality jobs that on a per-job basis contribute more to growth than low-skilled jobs. Thus, the simple analysis presented here should not be used to argue that Tanzania's growth strategy should be oriented to the sectors with a high female intensity of labor. Designing appropriate policies for job creation is much more complex than that and requires more detailed analysis of the growth and employment potential of various sectors of the economy.

Figure 7.2 shows estimates of the differences in the percentage increases in labor income for workers with no formal education and workers with unfinished secondary, resulting from the same aggregate shock (T Sh 100 million) applied to all sectors, one at a time. The results are very similar to the ones shown in figure 7.1, with 26 of the 31 sectors that favor female workers favoring workers with no formal education. As was the case in figure 7.1, the sectors that favor workers with no formal education exhibit a higher average impact on GDP (3.93 percent) than the sectors favoring workers with unfinished secondary (3.45 percent). But the same caveats mentioned earlier for the proper interpretation of the results apply.

Structural Path Analysis

In many cases, knowing the total potential impact of an exogenous shock on GDP growth and labor income is not sufficient to discuss options for policy. The multiplier analysis provided in the SAM model is useful to get an order of magnitude for the potential of shocks, but if no further analysis is conducted, this functions essentially as a black box that does not help in understanding how the economy functions. One of the key advantages of SAMs, versus more complex Computable General Equilibrium (CGE) models, may be the fact that because the SAM model relies on much simpler assumptions, it is possible to trace how a shock propagates itself through the economy, and thereby to better understand the mechanism at work in the multiplier effect.

With structural path analysis (SPA), it is possible to decompose the final effect of the shock along the different paths through which it unfolds as it travels in the economy, starting from the account that receives the initial shock. To put it another way, the SPA decomposition provides information about the economic structure of a country by fully describing the (most important) paths used by a shock to travel from an origin account (the one that receives the initial shock) to any account labeled as "final destination." A full description of SPA consists of a

Figure 7.2 Difference Between Sectoral Impact on Workers with No Formal Education and Unfinished Secondary (Shock of T Sh 100 million)

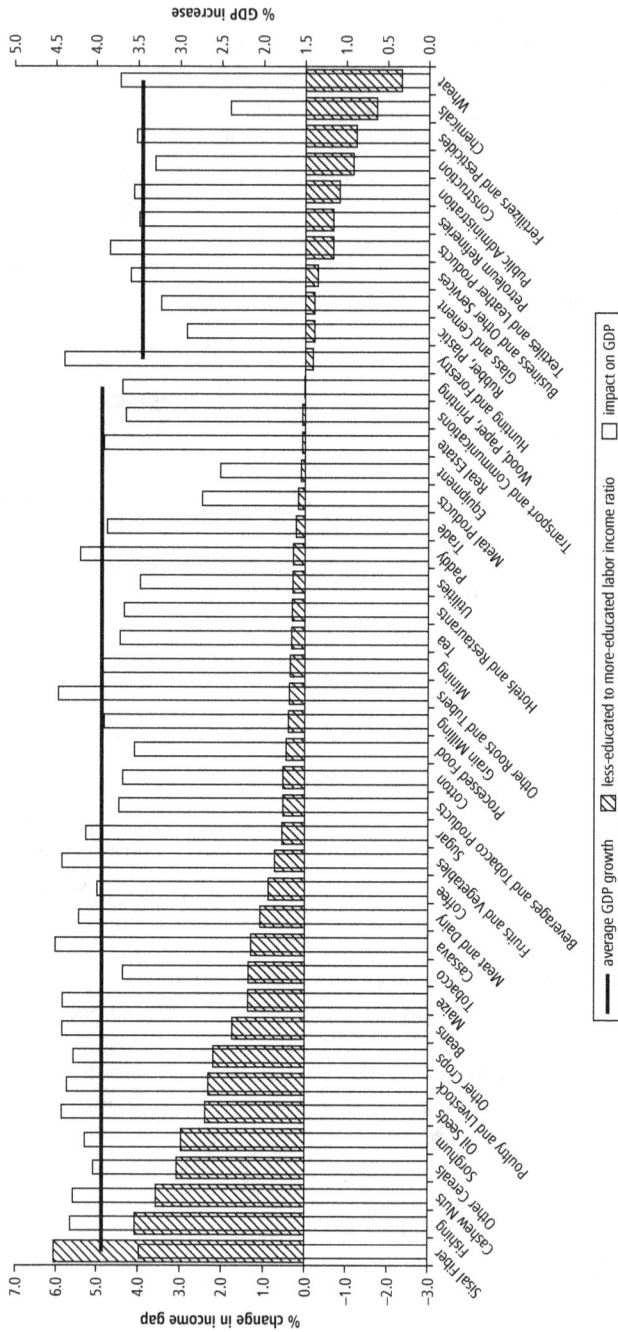

Source: Authors using SimSIP SAM.

list of the accounts involved along a given path, together with different measures of the influence traveling along that path.

A description of the SPA principles is provided in the annex. If account i and account j are directly connected along a path, in that order, it means that account j makes payments to account i, or in other words, account j uses what account i produces. The intensity of the connection is measured by the respective element a_{ij} of the technical coefficients matrix. (The matrix of technical coefficients is the result of dividing every cell T_{ij} in a SAM by the respective column sum T_{j}.) Note that if account i is connected with account j (again, the order is important), meaning that account j makes payments to account i, then it is not necessarily the case that account i is connected with account j. In most cases presented in Annex table 7.A (which provides examples of results obtained from the SPA), a sector is directly connected to a labor account. This means that the sector pays for the use of the corresponding type of labor.

Suppose that we want to analyze how, in structural terms, an exogenous demand shock of T Sh 100 million[3] on the Maize sector affects female workers with nonformal education (Fem Nonformal—see the first row of table 7.4). The size of the final effect is given by the cell $m_{FemNonformal, Maize}$ of the inverse matrix M times the size of the shock (100 in this case), and is equal to T Sh 4.4 million. The most important elementary path (a path that does not go through any account on the path more than once) connecting these two accounts is the one that connects the accounts without using any other intermediate account, and it carries a total influence of T Sh 2.3 million, or 53.3 percent of the final effect. Out of the T Sh 2.3 million that travel along this path, 1.6 million (68.4 percent, according to the last column in table 7.4) would travel in a single step; this is known as "direct influence."

For a longer path, consider the second row for Transport and Communications (Trans-A) in table 7.4. The path connects Transport and Communications and female workers with nonformal education. The full path reads "Trans-A → Non Agr Capital → Firms → Rural Non Poor Unf Secondary → Maize-A → Fem Nonformal," which means that Transport and Communications (Trans-A) pays for using non-agricultural capital (Non Agr Capital); these funds are then

Table 7.4 Example of Structural Path Results

Origin	Destination	Global influence	Elementary paths	Direct influence	Total influence	Total/ Global (%)
Maize-A	Fem Nonformal	4.4	Maize-A → Fem Nonformal	1.6	2.3	53.3
Trans-A	Fem Nonformal	2.2	Trans-A → Non Agr Capital → Firms → Rural Non Poor Unf Secondary → Maize-A → Fem Nonformal	0.0	0.1	2.6

Source: Authors using SimSIP SAM.

transferred to the firms (Firms) that own the capital in this SAM, and then Firms pay dividends to some of their owners, in this case rural non-poor households with unfinished secondary education (Rural Non Poor Unf Secondary), who auto-consume Maize (Maize-A) produced in the household, and who finally hire female workers with nonformal education (Fem Nonformal) for their home production. Hence, even though the initial shock was applied to Transport and Communications, it was through Maize production that the shock finally reached female workers with nonformal education. Only T Sh 2.2 million would reach the female workers with nonformal education as a result of the initial demand shock of T Sh 100 million to Transport and Communications (third column of table 7.5), once all multiplier effects are taken into account. Of those T Sh 2.2 million, merely 0.1 million would travel along the path described in this paragraph (2.6 percent).

Detailed results for the path analysis for the same six sectors studied above as origin accounts (each of these accounts would receive an exogenous demand shock of T Sh 100 million) and the six categories of labor as destination accounts can be found in Annex table 7.A1. Only the most important path connecting any pair of accounts is shown. More detailed results can be obtained from the authors upon request.

We now highlight what we consider the three main results of the path analysis. First, the strength of a path can simply be associated with its contribution to the total multiplier effect of a shock. Second, the percentage of the multiplier carried along the most important path, or what we refer to as the concentration of transmission channels, is higher for female workers and workers with nonformal education in the three agricultural sectors, and higher for male workers and workers with completed secondary education or higher in the three services sectors. Figure 7.3 compares the most important paths for the Transport and Communications and Beans sectors.

Third, Transport and Communications, and especially Real Estate, display a structure with longer (more indirect) paths that are more important than in the other four sectors. For all categories of labor, except highly educated males, it takes at least three steps (transactions) for a shock in Real Estate to reach the workers, while it takes only one step for most labor categories in Maize, Beans, Sorghum, and Trade. Construction serves as the sector linking Real Estate and male workers, with Public Administration linking the sector and female workers of medium qualification. Figure 7.4 presents the paths connecting both Maize and Real Estate to female workers with unfinished primary. Sorghum would be the sector where the effects of a demand shock would be transmitted "the soonest," while Real Estate would be the "slowest" in transmitting the full effects of the shock.

References to length of time are in quotations because the SAM model is a comparative statics exercise and therefore lacks a temporal dimension. The time concept alluded to here is based on the distinction between the direct and

Figure 7.3 Concentration of Selected Transmission Channels from Growth to Labor Income

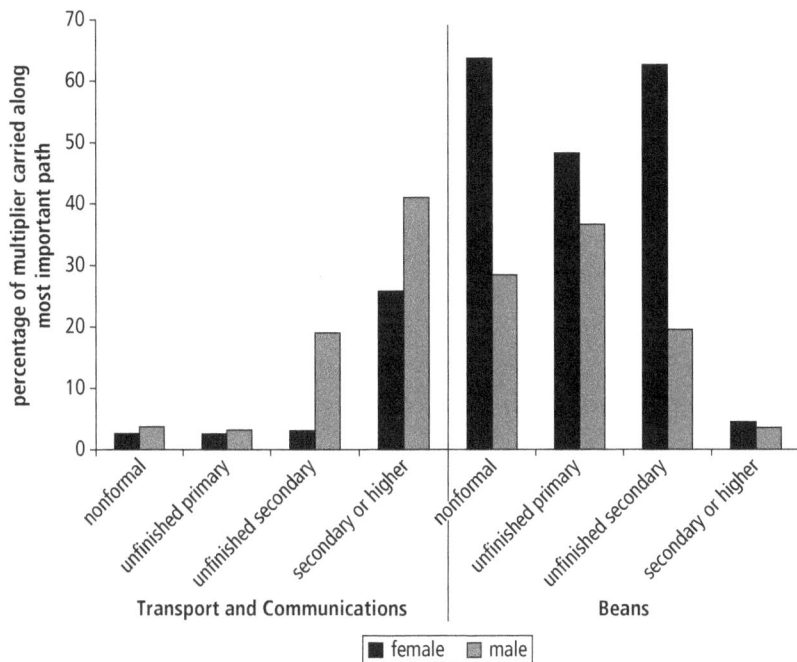

Source: Authors using SimSIP SAM.

Figure 7.4 Example of Paths to a Category of Labor

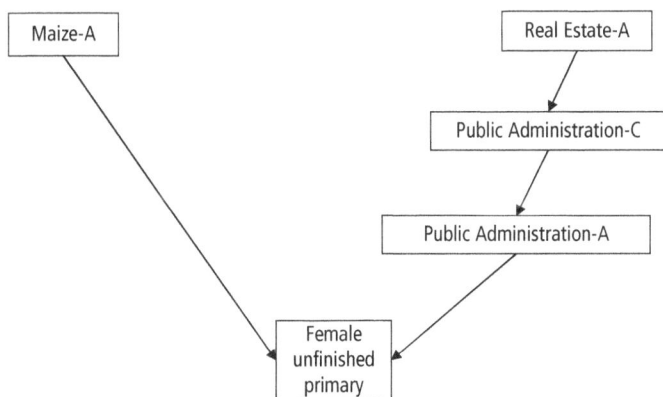

Source: Authors using SimSIP SAM.

indirect components of the influence. As its name indicates, the direct influence is made up of direct connections between accounts; on the other hand, the indirect influence is the set of circuits and all possible indirect paths connecting two accounts. Intuitively, the circuits and indirect connections take more time than a direct connection. Hence, if most of the total influence is direct, we could say that it might take less time to unfold. Along these lines, the last column in annex table 7.A1 contains the fraction of the total influence traveling along a path that is accounted for by direct links between accounts on that path.

The first three sectors—Maize, Beans, and Sorghum—with high female labor intensities, and Trade, with a low female labor intensity, have a relatively high percentage of the total influence being explained by direct connections, with percentages ranging from 60 to 90 percent. Real Estate has, by far, the lowest importance of direct connections, with no direct to total ratio exceeding 30 percent. This implies that for Maize, Beans, Sorghum, and Trade, the effects on labor income would probably unfold more quickly than effects initiated at Transport and Communications or at Real Estate. Figure 7.5 presents the "transmission speeds" for male workers in Sorghum (fastest) and Real Estate (slowest).

Figure 7.5 Speed of Selected Transmission Channels of Shocks from Growth to Labor Income

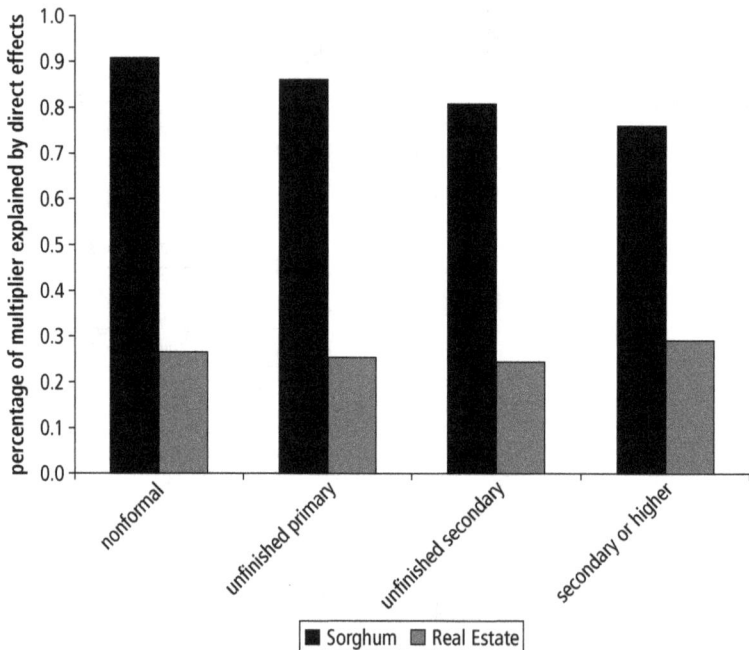

Source: Authors using SimSIP SAM.

Conclusions

As discussed by Parra and Wodon (2009b) in Chapter 6, SAMs have both strengths and weaknesses. The simplicity of the SAM model is an advantage, first, because it relies on less data than a typical CGE. And in some sub-Saharan countries, good data are not easy to get, for example, to estimate the parameters of a CGE. A second strength of the SAM-based model is that it is relatively straightforward, and thus easier to understand as well as to manipulate to conduct simulations. This is again an advantage for use in countries where capacity is limited. But at the same time, the SAM model also has weaknesses. It cannot easily be adapted to factor in behavioral effects, and it has other very strong assumptions embedded in it.

However, there are some useful analyses that can be conducted with SAMs and cannot be conducted (or at least not as easily) with more complex models such as CGEs. One such unique feature of the SAM model is structural path analysis, which is made feasible by the linear structure of the SAM. This type of analysis helps the analyst understand the transmission channels through which an initial shock travels through an economy. The analysis can be used to characterize the concentration, strength, and "speed" of various transmission channels; those concepts were illustrated in this chapter using a SAM for Tanzania.

Concentration relates to the share of the total impact of a shock that travels through one or more specific paths linking accounts in the SAM. Strength simply relates to the contribution of a path to the total effect at play, in absolute value as opposed to percentage terms. Speed relates to the share of the contribution to the multiplier that travels directly from the origin to the destination account, without going through any account more than once, with paths of higher lengths typically taking more time to materialize because of the higher number of transactions that need to take place. By providing detailed analysis of the ways through which shocks affect an economy, structural path analysis thus can enable analysts to better understand the economy itself, which in turn can be useful in the design of development policies.

Annex 7A Structural Path Analysis[4]

The SAM multiplier framework can be used to quantify the effect of an increase in the exogenous component of an endogenous account into another endogenous account. But this framework is unable to show how this effect is conducted through the economic system. That is exactly what the structural path analysis does. Some basic definitions are as follows.

We associate the notion of expenditure with that of influence. Take the matrix of technical coefficients A_{nxn}. Any endogenous account can be considered a *pole*. Any two poles, i, j, are connected by an arc starting from i and ending at $j - arc(i, j) -$. The cell, a_{ji} of A, is the *intensity* of $arc(i, j)$. A sequence of consecutive arcs defines a *path*. The *length* of a path is equal to its number of arcs. An *elementary path* is one that does not visit any pole more than once. A *circuit* is a path that starts and ends in the same pole.

Three kinds of influence between accounts can be distinguished: direct influence, total influence, and global influence. Let $(i \rightarrow j)_p$ denote the path p from i to j. See figure 7A.1 below from Shantong, Ying, and Jianwu (2004).

Direct Influence
The direct influence of i on j, through an elementary path, is the change in the income of j caused by a unitary injection in i, where the only incomes that are allowed to change are those of the poles in the elementary path. The direct influence from i to j through the elementary path p is given by the product of the intensities of all arcs constituting the path. For example, the direct influence caused by the elementary path is given by $I^D_{(i \rightarrow j)} = a_{ki}a_{mk}a_{jm}$.

Total Influence
Given an elementary path from i to j, the total influence of i on j is the influence transmitted along the elementary path, including all indirect effects imputable to that path. This definition can be better understood through an example.

Figure 7A.1 Sketch Map for Calculation of Total Influence

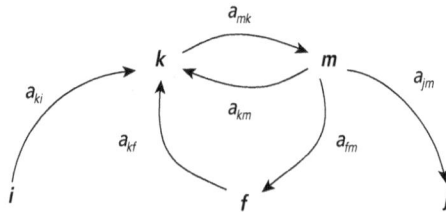

Consider the structure described in figure 7A.1. In order to compute the total influence, we need to include all possible ways of going from i to j in the structure. First, influence from i to k, and from m to j is given by the respective direct influences. The total influence from k to m requires further explanation. One way to go from k to m is to travel along the elementary path; the influence attributed to that path is the direct influence a_{mk}. Another way to go involves the circuit between k and m and the circuit that connects k and m through f. After one round of feedback, the influence from k to m is given by $a^2_{mk}a_{km} + a_{fm}a_{kf}a^2_{mk}(a_{km}+a_{fm}a_{kf})$. After t rounds of feedback, the influence is given by $a_{mk}[a_{mk}(a_{km}+a_{fm}a_{kf})]^t a_{mk}[a_{mk}+ a_{fm}a_{kf}]^t$. Finally, any influence has to be transmitted from m to j with an influence of . Using a geometric series argument, we finally get that the total influence is given by:

$$I^T(i \rightarrow j)_p = a_{ki}a_{mk}a_{jm}[1-a_{mk}(a_{km}+a_{fm}a_{kf})]^{-1} \tag{7.1}$$

Note that the first product is just the direct influence along the path p, and the second term is called the *path multiplier M_p*. Then equation (7.1) can be rewritten as: $I^T(i \rightarrow j)_p = I^D_{(i \rightarrow j)p} M_p$

Global Influence

The global influence from i to j is simply given by the accounting multiplier m_{ji} from the inverse matrix. Annex table 7A.1 presents the structural path analysis for all types of labor in each of the six sectors studied in this chapter. The global influence is just the multiplier for the accounts in the first two columns. For each row, the next column describes the nodes of the elementary path connecting the two accounts. The next four columns present the direct and total influence (see definitions above) in levels and as percentages of the global influence, for the elementary path described on that row.

Table 7A.1 Structural Path Analysis for Tanzania, 2001

Origin	Destination	Elementary paths	Global influence	Direct influence	Total influence	Total/Global (%)	Direct/Total (%)
Maize-A	Fem Nonformal	Maize-A → Fem Nonformal	4.4	1.6	2.3	53.3	68.4
	Fem Unf Primary	Maize-A → Fem Unf Primary	4.2	1.1	1.6	37.4	68.1
	Fem Unf Secondary	Maize-A → Fem Unf Secondary	26.6	7.0	11.2	42.1	62.2
	Fem Sec or Higher	Maize-A → Subsistence → Rural Non Poor Unf Sec → Cloth-C → Cloth-A → Fem Sec or Higher	2.2	0.0	0.1	2.4	36.5
	Male Nonformal	Maize-A → Male Nonformal	3.5	0.7	1.0	29.0	68.1
	Male Unf Primary	Maize-A → Male Unf Primary	10.5	1.9	2.9	28.0	65.6
	Male Unf Secondary	Maize-A → Male Unf Secondary	19.4	2.2	3.5	17.9	62.3
	Male Sec or Higher	Maize-A → Male Sec or Higher	6.8	0.2	0.2	3.5	66.3
Beans-A	Fem Nonformal	Beans-A → Fem Nonformal	6.4	3.2	4.0	63.7	79.7
	Fem Unf Primary	Beans-A → Fem Unf Primary	5.4	2.1	2.6	48.3	79.5
	Fem Unf Secondary	Beans-A → Fem Unf Secondary	38.7	17.1	24.3	62.7	70.7
	Fem Sec or Higher	Beans-A → Fem Sec or Higher	2.3	0.1	0.1	4.5	80.0
	Male Nonformal	Beans-A → Male Nonformal	3.7	0.8	1.1	28.4	79.5
	Male Unf Primary	Beans-A → Male Unf Primary	12.3	3.4	4.5	36.6	75.7
	Male Unf Secondary	Beans-A → Male Unf Secondary	20.2	2.8	4.0	19.5	71.0
	Male Sec or Higher	Beans-A → Male Sec or Higher	6.7	0.2	0.2	3.6	77.3
Sorghum-A	Fem Nonformal	Sorghum-A → Fem Nonformal	5.7	3.1	3.4	59.7	91.0
	Fem Unf Primary	Sorghum-A → Fem Unf Primary	3.4	0.5	0.5	15.7	90.6
	Fem Unf Secondary	Sorghum-A → Fem Unf Secondary	22.6	4.1	5.1	22.6	79.6
	Fem Sec or Higher	Sorghum-A → Cloth-C → Cloth-A → Fem Sec or Higher	2.2	0.1	0.2	6.8	78.3
	Male Nonformal	Sorghum-A → Male Nonformal	4.1	1.4	1.6	38.5	90.8
	Male Unf Primary	Sorghum-A → Male Unf Primary	9.7	1.6	1.9	19.2	86.1
	Male Unf Secondary	Sorghum-A → Male Unf Secondary	19.3	2.3	2.9	14.9	80.7
	Male Sec or Higher	Sorghum-A → Cloth-C → Cloth-A → Male Sec or Higher	6.7	0.1	0.2	2.6	76.0
Trade-A	Fem Nonformal	Trade-A → Fem Nonformal	2.3	0.1	0.1	5.0	79.0
	Fem Unf Primary	Trade-A → Fem Unf Primary	2.8	0.2	0.2	8.4	78.9

	Fem Unf Secondary	17.5	Trade-A → Fem Unf Secondary	1.0	1.4	8.2	70.5
	Fem Sec or Higher	2.7	Trade-A → Fem Sec or Higher	0.3	0.4	14.2	79.6
	Male Nonformal	2.5	Trade-A → Male Nonformal	0.1	0.2	6.7	79.0
	Male Unf Primary	7.7	Trade-A → Male Unf Primary	0.4	0.5	6.8	75.5
	Male Unf Secondary	18.1	Trade-A → Male Unf Secondary	2.3	3.2	17.8	71.7
	Male Sec or Higher	8.8	Trade-A → Male Sec or Higher	1.7	2.3	25.6	77.5
Trans-A	Fem Nonformal	2.2	Trans-A → Non Agr Capital → Firms → Rural Non Poor Unf Secondary → Maize-A → Fem Nonformal	0.0	0.1	2.6	39.5
	Fem Unf Primary	2.6	Trans-A → Hotel-C → Hotel-A → Fem Unf Primary	0.1	0.1	2.6	77.3
	Fem Unf Secondary	16.4	Trans-A → Fem Unf Secondary	0.4	0.5	3.1	76.9
	Fem Sec or Higher	3.3	Trans-A → Fem Sec or Higher	0.7	0.8	25.8	88.3
	Male Nonformal	2.3	Trans-A → Non Agric Capital → Firms → Rural Non Poor Unf Secondary → Fish-C → Fish-A → Male Nonformal	0.0	0.1	3.8	45.1
	Male Unf Primary	7.2	Trans-A → Male Unf Primary	0.2	0.2	3.2	83.1
	Male Unf Secondary	18.4	Trans-A → Male Unf Secondary	2.7	3.5	19.0	78.2
	Male Sec or Higher	11.5	Trans-A → Male Sec or Higher	4.0	4.7	41.1	85.6
Estate-A	Fem Nonformal	2.4	Estate-A → Subsistence → Rural Non Poor Unf Secondary → Maize-A → Fem Nonformal	0.0	0.0	1.6	14.4
	Fem Unf Primary	17.6	Estate-A → Pub Admin-C → Pub Admin-A → Fem Unf Primary	0.1	0.6	3.3	12.0
	Fem Unf Secondary	3.6	Estate-A → Pub Admin-C → Pub Admin-A → Fem Unf Secondary	0.2	1.4	37.7	13.6
	Male Nonformal	2.6	Estate-A → Const-C → Const-A → Male Nonformal	0.0	0.1	5.5	26.5
	Male Unf Primary	8.2	Estate-A → Const-C → Const-A → Male Unf Primary	0.2	0.8	10.0	25.4
	Male Unf Secondary	21.0	Estate-A → Const-C → Const-A → Male Unf Secondary	1.3	5.4	25.6	24.4
	Male Sec or Higher	12.2	Estate-A → Male Sec or Higher	1.0	3.4	27.6	29.1

Source: Authors, using SimSIP SAM.

Notes

1. Tanzania Social Accounting Matrix, 1998–2001; 2003 datasets. Washington, D.C.: International Food Policy Research Institute (IFPRI) http://www.ifpri.org/data/Tanzania02.htm
2. The latest version can be obtained from www.simsip.org.
3. The size of the shock is arbitrary and was chosen to make results easier to interpret.
4. This section is based on Defourny and Thorbecke (1984) and Shantong, Ying, and Jianwu (2004).

References

Defourny, J., and Erik Thorbecke. 1984. "Structural Path Analysis and Multiplier Decomposition Within a Social Accounting Matrix Framework." *Economic Journal* 94 (373): 111–36.

Ferri, J., and Ezequiel Uriel. 2002. "Multiplicadores Contables y Análisis Estructural en la Matriz de Contabilidad Social: Una Aplicación al Caso Español." *Investigaciones Económicas* 24 (2): 419–53.

Khan, H. A., and Erik Thorbecke. 1989. "Macroeconomic Effects of Technology Choice: Multiplier and Structural Path Analysis Within a SAM Framework." *Journal of Policy Modeling* 11 (1): 131–56.

Lantner, Roland. 1972. "Recherche sur l'Interprétation du Déterminant d'une Matrice Input-Output." *Revue d'Économie Politique* 82 (2): 435–42.

———. 1974. *Théorie de la Dominance Économique.* Paris: Dunod.

Lanzen, Manfred. 2003. "Environmentally Important Paths, Linkages and Key Sectors in the Australian Economy." *Structural Change and Economic Dynamics* 14: 1–34.

Parra J. C., and Q. Wodon. 2009a. "SimSIP SAM: A Tool to Analyze Social Accounting Matrices." Unpublished manuscript, World Bank, Washington, DC.

Parra J. C., and Q. Wodon. 2009b. "Gender, Time Use and Labor Income in Guinea: Micro and Macro Analysis." In *Gender Disparities in Africa's Labor Market*, ed. J. S. Arbache, A. Kolev, and E. Filipiak, 225–66. Washington, DC: World Bank.

Roberts, Deborah. 2005. "The Role of Households in Sustaining Rural Economies: A Structural Path Analysis." *European Review of Agricultural Economics* 32 (3): 393–420.

Shantong, L., G. Ying, and H. Jianwu. 2004. "SAM-based Multiplier Analysis for China's Economy." Paper prepared for the XIIINFORUM World Conference, Marina di Ascea-Velia, Italy, September 5–11.

Thurlow, J., and P. Wobst. 2003. "Poverty-focused Social Accounting Matrices for Tanzania." TMD Discussion Paper No. 112, International Food Policy Research Institute, Washington, D.C.

Xie, Jian. 2000. "An Environmentally Extended Social Accounting Matrix." *Environmental and Resource Economics* 16: 391–406.

Part 4

Disparities in Time Use

Chapter **8**

Gender Disparities in Time Allocation, Time Poverty, and Labor Allocation Across Employment Sectors in Ethiopia

Pablo Suárez Robles

Gender equality and empowerment of women has become a great challenge for many developing economies, especially for Sub-Saharan African countries that face high levels of poverty and where the prevailing traditional societies remain male-dominated. With the aim of reaching the goals of human development and poverty eradication, many of these countries adopt, among other development strategies, the overall objective of reaching the United Nations Millennium Development Goals (MDGs), particularly the third MDG goal of gender equality and empowerment of women. This goal is related to others, such as the achievement of universal primary education and the reduction of child and maternal mortality.

With regard to the third MDG goal, the government of Ethiopia has made remarkable efforts toward universal primary education and gender equality. While large gender disparities in education still exist, Ethiopia has seen an enormous increase in primary education enrollment that has contributed to reducing the gender imbalance (MoFED 2005). The elimination of gender disparities in school is all the more important because it increases women's employment opportunities. But this positive effect will be limited if other obstacles prevent women from participating in the labor market and obtaining better jobs.

Thus, it is crucial to focus on gender disparities in the labor market. It is well-recognized that when regular, full-time jobs that provide clear career prospects exist and are accessible to women, they usually contribute to their empowerment and offer alternative interests and achievements to domestic work or motherhood (Lim 2002). In addition, it is also generally recognized that women's earnings can influence their status and decision making power within the family and in society, and are especially important for children because women tend to spend their earnings directly on children's needs (see Chapter 10 in this volume and UNICEF 1999).

Despite the fact that in Ethiopia the Civil Code and Constitution, adopted in 1994, provide women with the same rights and protections as men, previous works on Ethiopia's labor market reveal the striking disadvantages Ethiopian women face. For instance, a recent report on Ethiopia's urban labor market (World Bank 2007) found as a major result that women typically face worse outcomes than men in the labor market, with higher levels of unemployment, lower wages, and a greater concentration in the informal sector. In brief, empirical evidence shows that women are less likely to participate in the labor market; when employed, they are disproportionately concentrated in unpaid or flexible jobs that offer low earnings and low protection, a result of their low skills, burden of household responsibilities, and labor market discrimination. For instance, recent studies found that, even when they have the same human capital and job characteristics as men, women earn on average much less (Appleton, Hoddinott, and Krishnan 1999; Temesgen 2006; Kolev and Suárez Robles 2007).

Using the Ethiopia Labor Force Survey 2005, this chapter sheds light on three dimensions of gender disparities in Ethiopia's labor market: time allocation between market and household work, time poverty, and labor allocation across employment sectors.

The issue of gender inequalities in allocating time to market work (productive activities) and housework (reproductive activities) has been insufficiently treated in the literature on developing countries in general, and regarding Ethiopia in particular, because data on time use is scarce and because most gender studies focusing on labor supply ignore the tradeoffs between these two types of work and neglect the dimension of housework. Besides contributing to a better understanding of the labor supply, extending the analysis to this dimension of work is important because household tasks, which are for the most part low-productive, time- and labor-intensive, are essential for family survival. Empirical evidence shows that these tasks are primarily carried out by women. As pointed out by Blackden and Morris-Hughes (1993), the housework burden on women limits their time available to market work and allows them to engage only in productive activities compatible with their household duties. According to Blackden and Wodon (2006), the gender-based division of labor, which is characterized by the fact that men are engaged in productive activities while women bear the brunt of domestic tasks, is especially significant in Africa.

However, some studies show that there is no perfect substitution between market and household work. For instance, Medeiros, Guerreiro Osorio, and Costa (2007), using data from urban Bolivia, argue that such a tradeoff is only partial. Women tend to accumulate both types of work; therefore, they are double burdened and have a higher total workload than men. Because women suffer from time deprivation as a result of their multiple roles, they enjoy less leisure and time for rest, and thereby are more likely to be "time poor."

What is the situation regarding these factors in Ethiopia? The first goal of this study is to examine the differences in how Ethiopian men and women allocate their time between market and household work, identify a possible gender-based division of labor, analyze the determinants of market and household work time across gender, and explore the gender disparities in total workload and time poverty. The second goal is to show new evidence on gender disparities in the labor force and in employment status in Ethiopia, and to identify the determinants of labor allocation across employment sectors and sexes.

The structure of this chapter is as follows. The next section presents the dataset, concepts, and the methodology used to analyze gender disparities in time allocation between market and household work, time poverty, and labor allocation across employment sectors in Ethiopia. Then the results of this study are presented, followed by conclusions.

Data, Concepts, and Methodology

Before presenting the dataset, concepts, and methodology employed for the analysis of labor allocation across employment sectors, this section first deals with those used for the analysis of time allocation between market and household work, and time poverty.

Market and Household Work, and Time Poverty

To analyze gender inequalities in allocating time to market and household work and to address the issue of time poverty, we draw upon the Labor Force Survey (LFS) collected in Ethiopia by the Central Statistical Agency (CSA) in 2005. The sample survey covered 51,946 households in all rural and urban parts of the country, except all zones of Gambela region (excluding Gambela town), and the non-sedentary population of three zones of the Afar and six zones of the Somali regions. Out of the total 230,680 individuals interviewed, about 50 percent were located in urban areas; women account for 52 percent of the sample.

For household members aged 5 and older, the survey records the number of hours spent, during the seven days prior to the date of interview, in collecting firewood and fetching water for own consumption and in domestic activities. In addition, for those who were engaged in any kind of productive activities during the reference period, the survey records, excluding lunch and journey time and including overtime, the total number of hours spent in all jobs.

This information gathered in the LFS 2005 on how surveyed individuals allocate their time is not as detailed as that in surveys using time-diary methods.

Indeed, the time-diary approach can provide information on individuals' allocation of time among large numbers of activities, as well as the sequence of these
activities and the context in which they are performed. Moreover, as time-diary
methods ask respondents to fill in activities and time used in the present or the
past day in slots of a diary, the diary-based estimates contain, to a lesser extent,
recall biases related to the difficulty for a respondent to remember and report
exactly the amount of time used, and they do not produce total time used greater
than the total time available in the reference period. Stylized (questionnaire-
based) estimates, like those derived from the LFS 2005, are, therefore, less accu-
rate than diary-based estimates. In addition, the data used in this study do not
include information on some time-intensive household activities (such as care of
family members), and thus housework is most probably underestimated, especially for women, who bear the brunt of domestic tasks. However, given that the
survey questionnaire does not provide a list of domestic activities, it is impossible
to know exactly what activities were taken into account by respondents. According to Fenstermaker Berk and Shih (1980), Press and Townsley (1998), and Warner (1986), women likely report their time spent in housework more accurately
than men, since they undertake the bulk of housework and therefore should be
more familiar with how much time each chore has cost them. Furthermore, stylized estimates of housework tend to be higher than diary-based estimates, which
is in part attributable to the double counting of multiple activities performed
simultaneously (Juster and Stafford 1991; Marini and Shelton 1993). This bias
is expected to affect women more than men because women perform various
domestic activities simultaneously more often (Lee and Waite 2005).[1]

Time-diary as well as nationally representative time-use surveys have not
been carried out in Ethiopia. However, despite its shortcomings, the LFS 2005
offers great opportunities to analyze gender-differentiated time-use patterns
and to address the issue of time poverty.

In this study, time-use estimates are measured in hours per week. Individuals
allocate the "total time available" (168 hours a week) between tertiary activities, leisure, and work, which includes market and household work. The "time
devoted to tertiary activities" is the time needed to maintain a person's biological
functioning (time spent for rest, personal hygiene, and nourishment).[2] The LFS
2005 does not provide information on tertiary activities. According to Ting and
Malhotra (2005), on average an adult needs to sleep eight hours per day. Therefore, the time devoted to tertiary activities should be higher in order to take
into account other self-care activities. However, following Medeiros, Guerreiro
Osorio, and Costa (2007), the time devoted to tertiary activities is set at 8 hours
per day (56 hours a week) for all individuals to deal with extreme workloads.

Subtracting the time spent for tertiary activities from the total time available, we obtain the "total time available for work" (112 hours a week), which is
allocated between market and household work, and leisure.

The "time devoted to market work" corresponds to the number of hours worked at all jobs, excluding lunch and journey time and including overtime, and the "time devoted to housework" equals the total number of hours worked in fetching water and collecting firewood for own consumption, and in domestic activities. We assume that such activities are not market oriented, since market work includes all productive activities. All individuals who did not report the number of hours worked at all jobs, or at least in one of the household activities, or who have a total workload that exceeds 112 hours a week, are dropped from the sample.

Finally, "leisure" is defined as all dispensable activities that we cannot pay somebody else to do for us, and corresponds by default to total time available for work minus "total work time" (leisure is thus treated as a residual).

When total work time exceeds a certain threshold, individuals do not have enough time for rest and leisure, and therefore are considered "time poor."

The survey divided the population aged 10 years and older into economically active and inactive categories. This low age limit was fixed to allow comparisons with other countries and to incorporate information about these children, who often start taking part in many types of economic activities at young ages (CSA 2006). However, in line with other recent studies of Ethiopia's labor market, this study focuses on individuals aged 15 and older.[3]

Out of the total 134,714 surveyed individuals aged 15 and older, two-thirds did not completely report their time spent in activities. The response rate is thus very low. In fact, while the survey provides estimates of time spent in market work and domestic activities for almost all individuals aged 15 and older, it does not provide estimates of time spent fetching water or collecting firewood for the vast majority. Excluding all individuals who did not report their time spent in market work or at least in one of the household activities, as well as all individuals who reported a total workload that exceeds 112 hours a week, reduces the sample to 44,195 individuals.

It is noteworthy that women, people living in rural areas, and illiterates are overrepresented among individuals who completely reported their time spent in activities. Unemployed workers and inactive people, as well as individuals living in Addis Ababa, are in turn underrepresented. Furthermore, high- and low-skilled white-collar workers, permanent employees, wage earners, and workers engaged in tertiary sector activities are also underrepresented. Finally, looking at the mean and the distribution of monthly earnings in the main job, it appears that earnings of wage-employed workers excluded from the sample were higher. In the final sample, 68 percent of individuals are women and less than 20 percent were located in urban areas. As a matter of fact, these results should be taken with caution, since they are computed from a subsample that is certainly biased as a result of the large number of dropped observations and consequent underrepresentation of certain segments of respondents. Notwithstanding this problem, our results lead to the same conclusions as those generally found in the literature on time use in Sub-Saharan Africa.

Decomposition of Total Work Time. The average total work time corresponds to the sum of the averages of time devoted to market work and housework and is equivalent to the sum of the products of the incidence and the duration of each type of work. The incidence of a given activity is defined as the share of the population engaged (who spent at least one hour) in this activity, and the duration is the average amount of hours devoted to the activity by those who perform it. The average of time devoted to housework is calculated as the sum of the averages of time spent fetching water, collecting firewood, and domestic activities, and is also decomposed in terms of the incidence and duration of each type of housework.

The results of this decomposition obtained for men are compared to those obtained for women to identify the gender inequalities in allocating time to market and household activities. Gender differences in the average total work time are explored as well. This simple decomposition is interesting because it enables an assessment of gender disparities in both incidence and duration of each activity. Therefore, a comprehensive picture of the gender-based division of labor, which is characterized not only by the fact that some activities are primarily carried out by women while others are male-dominated, but also by the fact that the amount of time spent in each activity significantly varies across gender, can be provided.

Time Poverty. According to Bardasi and Wodon (2006), there is no trace in the literature of formal discussion and measurement of the concept of time poverty alongside the techniques used for measuring consumption poverty. Following these authors, we simply apply the traditional concepts and techniques used for the analysis of income or consumption poverty to time poverty. We use the first two poverty measures of the so-called FGT class after Foster, Greer, and Thorbecke (1984).

The first measure is the headcount index of time poverty, or the "time poverty rate," which represents the share of the population that is time poor. The second measure is the "time poverty gap," which represents the mean distance separating the population from the time poverty line, with those who are not time poor being given a distance of zero. In other words, the time poverty gap represents the time that would be necessary on average, expressed as a percentage of the time poverty line, for all time-poor individuals to escape time poverty. To analyze gender disparities in time poverty, these two measures are computed separately for men and women in order to make comparisons.

The time poverty line represents a certain threshold work time above which individuals do not have enough time for rest and leisure, and thereby are considered time poor. This threshold is arbitrarily chosen because of the impossibility of determining the correct level of rest and leisure time that individuals need. Following Bardasi and Wodon (2006), we use two "relative" time poverty lines, a lower threshold equal to 1.5 times the median number of total individual working hours distribution and a higher threshold equal to 2 times the median. These time poverty lines are calculated accounting for all individuals in the sample population. The lower and higher thresholds are 70.5 and 94 hours per week, respectively.

Determinants of Market and Household Work Time. Finally, we investigate the determinants of market and household work time across gender. The hours spent in each type of work are estimated separately for men and women using Tobit models, econometric models in which the dependent variable is not always observed because it is truncated or censored. In our sample, there are many men and women who do not participate in market or household work, and thus the dependent variables are censored at value zero. The Tobit specification is then preferable to the OLS (ordinary least squares) because the latter yields inconsistent parameter estimates with censored data.

Labor Allocation Across Employment Sectors

To analyze gender disparities in the labor market, and to estimate the determinants of labor allocation across employment sectors by gender, we also draw upon the LFS 2005, a good source for this study because it includes a broad range of information about individual, household, and job characteristics.

Individuals aged 15 and older are divided into economically active and inactive categories. The economically active population or the labor force includes all persons either engaged in, or available to undertake, productive activities. Employed workers are defined as all those who were engaged in productive activities for at least four hours in the reference period (the last seven days in the LFS 2005). Also included among them are all those who were working less than four hours or were not working during the reference period, and who were paid for duration of absence or had an assurance or an agreement for returning to work.

Employed workers are classified in two main components: "wage employment" and "non-wage employment." Wage employment is further decomposed into three segments: "public wage employment" (government and parastatal employees), "private formal wage employment" (employees in formal private organizations and nongovernmental organizations [NGOs]), and "private informal wage employment" (employees in informal private organizations and domestic employees). Public and NGO employees, as well as all those working in private organizations that have at least 10 employees or that have a license or a book account, are considered to be part of formal wage employment. On the other hand, informal wage employment includes domestic employees and all those working in a private organization that has fewer than 10 employees, is not licensed, and does not have a book account. It also includes employees in private organizations for which this information is missing and who are paid only in kind or are doing casual work.

Non-wage employment, in turn, is decomposed into "self-employment" and "unpaid family work." The LFS 2005 provides a more detailed decomposition of non-wage employment, including categories for member of a cooperative, employer, and apprentice. These additional categories, which represent less than 3 percent of non-wage employees, are included by default in self-employment.

Descriptive Statistics. Gender disparities in the labor market are first analyzed by presenting some basic descriptive statistics. Measures of labor force participation, unemployment, and labor supply are computed separately for men and women. Further comment is made on the distributions of male and female workers by employment sectors, sectors of activity, occupations, and terms of employment.

Determinants of Labor Allocation. Finally, we estimate the determinants of labor allocation across employment sectors by gender. Marginal impacts of covariates on male and female segment employment choices, computed at the means of the independent variables, are derived after multinomial logit estimations are made. The marginal effect is defined as the change in the probability of the dependent variable for an infinitesimal change in each independent, continuous variable and, by default, the discrete change in the probability for binary variables. The five employment sectors described above are considered. The reference category is non-participation in employment (inactive and unemployed workers).

Results

How do men and women allocate their time between market and household work? Do they perform the same amount of total work and are they equally affected by time poverty? What are the determinants of market and household work time across gender? Using the LFS 2005, the first part of this section attempts to answer these questions. The second part focuses on gender disparities in labor allocation across employment sectors. Using the same data, we first present some descriptive statistics broken down by gender and then we analyze the determinants of labor allocation across sectors and sexes.

Market and Household Work, and Time Poverty

First presented are the results of the investigation of the gender disparities in time allocation between market and household work, and time poverty. We first begin with the interpretation of the decomposition results of the average total work time, then comment on the time poverty measures, and finally analyze the determinants of market and household work time across sexes.

Total Work Time. Table 8.1 shows the decomposition results of the average total work time for the overall sample population, as well as separately for men and women. Individuals aged 15 and older work 47 hours per week on average, which represents almost 30 percent of the total time available (168 hours [hr] a week) and more than 40 percent of the total time available for work (112 hr a week). They spend on average much more time on household activities (27 hr) than on market work (20 hr). Both incidence and duration of market work are lower, which means that there are more individuals working in the household (80 percent), where they experience longer average work shifts (34 hr), than in the market (71 percent), where the average duration of work is lower (28 hr). Almost 30 percent of individuals aged 15 and older are not engaged at all in domestic activities. Given this finding, and the fact that most of these activities are time-intensive, it is not surprising that the average hours dedicated to domestic activity by those who perform it rises to 27 hours per week, which, for

Table 8.1 Decomposition of Average Total Work Hours Per Week by Gender in Ethiopia, 2005

	Men	Women	Total
Total work time	35.9	52.0	46.9
Market work			
Incidence (%)	82	67	71
Duration	35.5	23.8	28.0
Incidence × duration	29.1	15.9	19.9
Household work			
Incidence (%)	50	93	80
Duration	13.6	38.8	33.8
Incidence × duration	6.8	36.1	27.0
Fetching of water			
Incidence (%)	29	71	58
Duration	5.8	7.3	7.1
Incidence × duration	1.7	5.2	4.1
Collecting of firewood			
Incidence (%)	28	54	46
Duration	6.5	7.3	7.1
Incidence × duration	1.8	3.9	3.3
Domestic activities			
Incidence (%)	27	92	72
Duration	12.4	29.4	27.4
Incidence × duration	3.3	27.0	19.7

Source: LFS 2005.
Note: Individuals aged 15 and older.

example, is as high as the average duration of market work. Less than half of the sample population collect firewood, and almost 60 percent fetch water for own consumption. The average duration of both activities is about 7 hours per week.

As shown in table 8.1, on average women work much more than men. Interestingly, gender inequality in total work time observed in Ethiopia, as in many developing countries, contrasts with the iso-work phenomenon observed in developed countries.[4] The average total work time per week rises to 52 hours for women, while it is only about 36 hours for men. Accordingly, women spend almost one-third of their time working, which is 10 percent higher than men. Expressed as a percentage of the total time available for work, the share of hours spent working is 46 percent for women, while for men it only represents 32 percent. On average, women allocate 16 hours and men 29 hours to market work. With regard to housework, the average time allocated is 36 hours for women and 7 hours for men. The incidence of market work is higher among men (82 percent) than among women (67 percent). In contrast, almost all women do housework, while half of men are not involved in any of the household activities. Moreover, the average duration of housework is nearly three times higher for women (39 hr), while the average duration of market work is more than 10 hours longer for men (36 hr). These results show a clear gender-based division of labor which is characterized by both women (men) participating more and spending longer hours in household (market) work. However, the incidence and the average duration of market work for women are important and much higher than those of housework for men. Thus, compared to men, who generally focus only on market work, women tend to accumulate both types of work, and thereby are double-burdened.

The gender average total work time differential is attributable mainly to gender inequalities in housework time and participation. If the average duration of housework for women were the same as for men, women would work on average more than 23 hours per week less, and the work burden on men would exceed that on women by more than 7 hours. Conversely, the average total work time for men would increase by almost 13 hours, and the gender differential would be reduced to nearly 3 hours, if the average duration of housework for men was as lengthy as for women. Performing these simulations again, but now switching incidences of housework, it turns out that, in the first case, women would work on average 17 hours less, which would be enough to eliminate the gender differential in average total work time, and in the second case, this differential would be reduced to 10 hours, as men would work on average 6 hours more.

Finally, it is noteworthy that in Ethiopia all household activities are predominantly considered "feminine." The proportions of women fetching water and collecting firewood (71 percent and 54 percent, respectively) are twice men's (29 percent and 28 percent, respectively). In addition, the average durations of these activities are higher for women (7.3 hours for both) than for men (5.8 hr and 6.5 hr, respectively). Gender inequalities are more apparent in domestic activities. In fact, 92 percent of women do domestic activities, while only 27 percent of men do. Furthermore, the average duration of domestic activities for women (29 hr) is more than two times higher than for men (12 hr).

Table 8.2 displays the results of the decomposition of the average total work time by place of residence and gender. On average, individuals work much more in rural (48 hr) than in urban areas (41 hr). The average time per week dedicated to work by women is 46 hours in urban areas and 54 hours in rural areas. Similarly, men spend on average more time working in rural areas (37 hr) than in urban areas (32 hr). It is noteworthy that the gender gap in average total work time, which is already impressive in urban areas (14 hr), widens in rural parts (17 hr).

The other striking picture that emerges from table 8.2 is the gender-based division of labor, which is much more acute in rural areas. Indeed, gender gaps

Table 8.2 Decomposition of Average Total Work Hours Per Week by Place of Residence and Gender in Ethiopia, 2005

	Urban			Rural		
	Men	Women	Total	Men	Women	Total
Total work time	32.2	45.9	41.3	36.9	53.6	48.3
Market work						
Incidence (%)	60	52	54	87	70	75
Duration	39.0	32.3	34.6	35.0	22.4	27.0
Incidence × duration	23.4	16.8	18.7	30.5	15.7	20.3
Household work						
Incidence (%)	57	91	80	49	94	80
Duration	15.5	32.0	28.3	13.1	40.3	35.0
Incidence × duration	8.8	29.1	22.6	6.4	37.9	28.0
Fetching of water						
Incidence (%)	36	58	51	28	74	59
Duration	5.8	6.4	6.3	5.8	7.5	7.2
Incidence × duration	2.1	3.7	3.2	1.6	5.6	4.2
Collecting of firewood						
Incidence (%)	24	40	35	29	58	48
Duration	7.0	7.5	7.4	6.4	7.3	7.1
Incidence × duration	1.7	3.0	2.6	1.9	4.2	3.4
Domestic activities						
Incidence (%)	40	89	74	24	93	71
Duration	12.4	25.1	22.9	12.5	30.3	28.4
Incidence × duration	5.0	22.3	16.9	3.0	28.2	20.2

Source: LFS 2005.
Note: Individuals aged 15 and older.

in the incidence, as well as in the average duration, of both market and house-hold work are greater in rural areas. In urban parts men's incidences of market and household work are, respectively, 8 percent higher and 34 percent lower than women's, while in rural parts, these are, respectively, 17 percent higher and 45 percent lower. Moreover, in urban areas, men's average durations of mar-ket and household work are, respectively, 7 hours longer and 17 hours shorter than women's, while in rural areas, these are, respectively, 13 hours longer and 27 hours shorter. According to these results, the sexual division of labor is greater in rural areas, where housework is even more feminine, and market work even more masculine, than in urban areas.

Compared to their urban counterparts, on average rural men devote much more time to market work (the lower average duration is largely offset by the higher incidence), and spend much less time on housework (both incidence and average duration are lower). In contrast, on average, rural women devote much more time to housework (both incidence and average duration are higher), and spend barely less time in market work (the lower average duration is almost offset by the higher incidence), than their urban counterparts. The double work burden on women, then, is more pronounced in rural areas, where more men focus only on market work, while more women tend to accumulate both types of work.

Unsurprisingly, the incidence and average duration of fetching water are higher in rural parts, where people have limited access to basic infrastructure. Similarly, the incidence of collecting firewood is higher in rural areas, but not the average duration, which is almost the same in both areas. Furthermore, the incidence of domestic activities is slightly higher in urban areas, while the average duration is much longer in rural ones. In both areas, women are more involved than men and for longer hours in every household activity. For instance, within the household, women are responsible for water collection (UN-Habitat 2004), and have to walk long distances to perform this task (World Bank 2006a). Finally, note that in rural areas all gender gaps in household activities are larger.

To summarize, there is a strong gender-based division of labor in Ethiopia, which is much more acute in rural areas. Women work more and for longer hours than men in the household, while the reverse is true in the labor market. However, despite the fact that market work is predominantly masculine, the proportion of women working in the labor market and the time they spend in it are important and much higher than the incidence and duration of housework for men. It appears then that women experience a double work burden, as they tend to accumulate both types of work, unlike men, who generally focus only on market work. Consequently, women spend more time at work than men, this phenomenon being observed to a greater extent in rural areas. These findings are in line with the literature on time use in Sub-Saharan Africa (see Blackden and Wodon 2006).

Beyond the sexual division of labor, what is indeed striking is the work bur-den on women, which exceeds by far that on men. However, this finding is based on the averages of the total time devoted to work by men and women. The higher average for women could be the result of a small group of women who are more heavily burdened in total. To test this hypothesis, we constructed the Generalized Lorenz Curves for the total work time by gender. The results are depicted in figures 8.1 and 8.2, respectively, for urban and rural areas. The Generalized Lorenz Curves—graphical representations of inequality that gather information about the shape and level of men's and women's workload distributions—plot on the horizontal axis the cumulative proportion of the population, ranked according to the amount of time people work, and on the vertical axis the cumulative average work time (that is, the average work time is calculated by taking the cumulative work time of a given share of the population divided by the total population).

Figures 8.1 and 8.2 show that, in both urban and rural areas, whatever the share of the population selected, the average cumulative work time of women is always higher than that of men. For instance, in urban areas, half the women who spend less time working devote on average 25 hours to work, while the equivalent half of the men devote on average 10 hours to work. The gender gap in the average cumulative work time increases continuously along the distribution of the population until the seventh decile. At this point, it rises to slightly more than 15 hours. The gender gap tends to decrease as higher points of the distribution are reached. In rural areas, the gender gap increases all along the

Figure 8.1 Generalized Lorenz Curves for Total Work Time by Gender in Urban Areas in Ethiopia, 2005

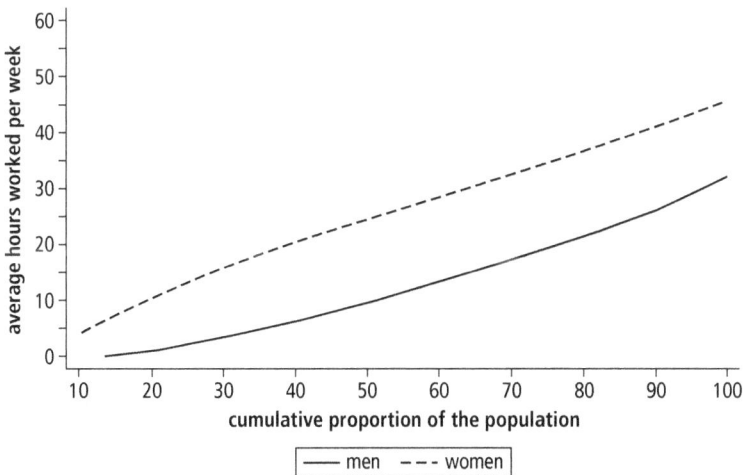

Source: LFS 2005.
Note: Individuals aged 15 and above.

Figure 8.2 Generalized Lorenz Curves for Total Work Time by Gender in Rural Areas in Ethiopia, 2005

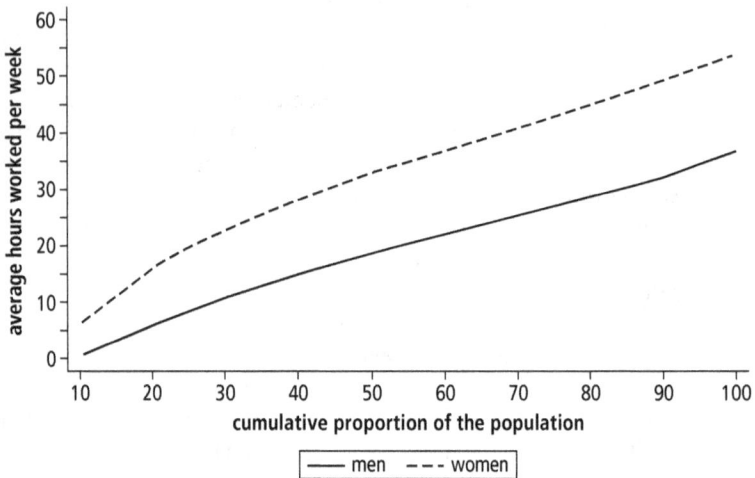

Source: LFS 2005.
Note: Individuals aged 15 and above.

distribution. Half the women that spend less time working devote on average 33 hours to work, while the equivalent half of men devote on average 19 hours. In fact, in rural areas, the gender gap at the median of the distribution, which rises to 14 hours, is slightly lower than in urban areas. This occurs also at the fourth decile, but at all the other deciles of the distribution, the gender gap is larger in rural areas.

The Generalized Lorenz Curves of women always lie above those of men. The hypothesis previously formulated is rejected. Women spend more time working than men, on average and at all points of the distribution of the population. In addition, the Generalized Lorenz Curves show strong evidence of the higher gender inequality in total work time in rural areas.

Generalized Lorenz Curves by gender have also been constructed separately for market and household work time.[5] They show that no matter the share of the population chosen, women systematically work more than men in the household, while the reverse is observed in the labor market. Finally, it appears that gender inequalities in both market and household work time are greater in rural areas, regardless of the point of the distribution chosen.

Time Poverty. Time is a limited resource. The more time an individual spends working, the more her time for rest and leisure will be reduced. When the total work time exceeds a certain threshold, the so-called time poverty line, individuals do not have enough time for rest and leisure, and thereby are considered time poor.

Table 8.3 shows the time poverty rates and the time poverty gaps by place of residence and gender. Two *relative* time poverty lines are used in what follows. These are arbitrarily set at 70.5 hours per week for the lower threshold, and at 94 hours per week for the higher threshold. According to the lower time poverty line, 19.5 percent of all individuals are time poor. People living in rural areas are 5 percent more affected by this dimension of poverty than those located in urban parts. As expected, the time poverty rate of women is high and exceeds that of men by far. Indeed, the share of time-poor women is almost four times as much as men, and rises to 25 percent. Unsurprisingly as well, the gender gap in time poverty rates is much larger in rural (20.1 percent) than in urban areas (7.6 percent). Women living in rural areas are more likely to be time poor (26.7 percent) than women living in urban areas (17.8 percent). In contrast, more men living in urban areas are time poor (10.2 percent) than men living in rural areas (6.6 percent). Using the higher time poverty line leads to the same conclusions. Note that, moving from lower to higher time poverty line, the relative gap between women's and men's time poverty rates in urban areas decreases significantly (it is almost equal to 1 using the higher threshold). In addition, the relative gap between urban and rural time poverty rates for men increases almost twofold.

The same picture emerges with measures of time poverty gaps. In summary, both incidence and average duration of extra work (hours worked above the time poverty line) are higher for women, so they are more affected by time poverty. The gender disparities in time poverty are larger in rural areas. Men are more affected by time poverty in urban than in rural areas, while the

Table 8.3 Time Poverty Rates and Gaps by Place of Residence and Gender in Ethiopia, 2005

	Time poverty line 70.5 hours per week		Time poverty line 94 hours per week	
	Time poverty rate (%)	Time poverty gap (%)	Time poverty rate (%)	Time poverty gap (%)
Men	7.3	1.4	1.5	0.1
Women	25.1	4.9	4.4	0.4
All	19.5	3.8	3.5	0.3
Urban areas				
Men	10.2	2.3	3.0	0.2
Women	17.8	3.4	3.2	0.3
All	15.4	3.1	3.2	0.2
Rural areas				
Men	6.6	1.2	1.1	0.1
Women	26.7	5.3	4.6	0.4
All	20.4	4.0	3.5	0.3

Source: LFS 2005.
Note: Individuals aged 15 and older.

reverse is true for women. The same findings are observed for Guinea by Bardasi and Wodon (2006). For example, these authors found that in that country, 24.2 percent of women are time poor compared to 9.5 percent of men.

Determinants of Market and Household Work Time. The next investigation looks at the determinants of market and household work time across gender and place of residence. Annex table 8A.1-1 reports estimates of hours worked in the labor market obtained with the Tobit method, separately for men and women in urban and in rural areas. Estimates of hours worked in the household are reported in Annex table 8A.1-2. Included as explanatory variables are human capital and other individual characteristics (levels of education, age, and dummies for marital and household head status), and other characteristics that reflect household composition (number of infants, children, senior people, male and female adults for various age cohorts, and a dummy variable for the presence of disabled people). Region dummies are also included in the regressions.

Lack of some crucial information in the LFS 2005 makes it difficult to investigate the determinants of market and household work time. Factors other than individual characteristics and household composition may also influence the number of hours spent in each type of work. For instance, information on access to basic infrastructure resources is missing, which is undoubtedly an important determinant of the time allocated by individuals to market and household work.

Looking at Annex tables 8A.1-1 and 8A.1-2, it first appears that the pseudo R-squared, which supposedly measures the goodness of fit of the models, are extremely low. We tested several specifications accounting for individual and household characteristics in order to reach higher pseudo R-squared values, but without success. On this point it is worth recalling that Tobit regression does not have an equivalent to R-squared in OLS regression, which measures the proportion of variance of the response variable explained by the predictors. Like McFadden (1973), many people have tried to come up with one, leading to a wide variety of pseudo R-squared regressions available today that have no real meaning in Tobit models, as in many others. Nevertheless, a small pseudo R-squared should make us humble about the model's explanatory ability. The following interpretations of the results should then be interpreted with caution.

First, education is often associated with lower hours of market and household work. In the labor market, men and women who have acquired a primary or general education tend to work fewer hours. In contrast, the impact of attainment beyond general education on market work hours is not significant, except for women living in rural areas for whom it is highly positive. Interestingly, a higher education level also strongly affects the time spent by rural women in housework, but in the opposite way. Then, being highly educated leads rural women to be more engaged in productive activities and less in household chores. No matter the level attained, education has a negative effect on women's housework time. For men, in turn, coefficients do not provide a clear story because they are often weakly significant or not significant. Looking at the coefficient of age and its square, we find inverted U-shaped relationships between age and time spent in both market and household work.

Actually, this finding is not observed for men in housework. Indeed, the effect of age on men's housework time has a U-shaped profile in urban areas, while it is not significant in rural ones. Being head of household is clearly associated with higher hours of work in the labor market. However, this is no longer the case in the household, where this status does not significantly affect housework time. Coefficients of marital status shed light on labor division across spouses: They show clearly that married women tend to work fewer hours in the labor market and more in the household, while the reverse is true for married men.

Looking at the coefficients on household composition, it first appears that the impact of the number of adult women, no matter the age cohort they belong to, on housework hours is strongly significant and negative for men and women alike. Because household activities are primarily carried out by women, it is not surprising then that the time spent on housework by men significantly decreases as the number of adult women in the household increases. In turn, the presence of other adult women in the household relieves individual women of part of their housework burden.

The effect of the number of adult men on women's housework time is strongly significant and positive for all age cohorts in rural areas, and only for adult men 15–24 years old in urban areas. Interestingly, in rural areas, the presence of other adult men ages 15–24 negatively affects the time spent by men in housework, while the presence of other adult men ages 35 to 64 has a positive effect, suggesting that within rural households, younger adult men tend to be more involved in housework than older adult men. However, these results are weakly significant. Age and gender composition of adult household members do not have strongly significant effects on men's hours worked in the labor market. This is also the case for women in urban areas. In turn, the presence of adult men, no matter their age, is associated with lower hours of work performed by rural women in the labor market.

The impacts of the number of infants and children on market work time are weakly significant or not significant. In contrast, the impact of the number of children on men's housework hours is strongly significant and negative, and the effect of the number of infants on women's housework time is strongly significant and positive. Within households with infants, women are more heavily burdened because they have to take care of them. As infants grow up, they start taking part in many types of household activities, allowing men to be less involved in such activities.

Finally, for both men and women, the number of senior people in the household is generally associated with higher hours of market work, and the presence of disabled individuals, with lower hours of market work.

Labor Allocation Across Employment Sectors

Before turning to the determinants of labor allocation across employment sectors by gender, we first present descriptive statistics that shed light on the gender disparities in Ethiopia's labor market.

Descriptive Statistics. Beginning with a descriptive analysis of gender disparities in Ethiopia's labor market, table 8.4 provides key indicators of the labor market broken down by gender and place of residence.

Some studies use the standard definition of unemployment developed by the International Labour Organization (ILO), while others prefer to use partially relaxed (including discouraged workers) or completely relaxed (accounting for all those without work and currently available for work) definitions. According to CSA (2006), the standard definition of unemployment, with its emphasis

Table 8.4 Labor Force Participation and Unemployment in Ethiopia, 2005

| | Women | | | Men | | | |
	Urban (%)	Rural (%)	All (%)	Urban (%)	Rural (%)	All (%)	All (%)
Standard definitions (ILO)							
Activity rate	56	77	65	73	93	82	73
Unemployment rate	20	1	10	12	1	6	8
Share of long-term unemployed	67	35	65	63	34	62	63
Partially relaxed definitions							
Activity rate	58	78	66	74	93	82	74
Unemployment rate	23	2	12	13	1	7	9
Share of long-term unemployed	64	36	62	63	33	61	62
Completely relaxed definitions							
Activity rate	66	81	72	76	94	84	78
Unemployment rate	32	6	19	16	1	8	14
Share of long-term unemployed	59	39	56	60	29	58	57

Source: LFS 2005.
Note: Individuals aged 15 and older. According to ILO conventions, an individual is considered unemployed if, during the reference period (last 7 days in the LFS 2005), he or she was without work, currently available for work, and seeking work. International Standards (13th International Conference of Labor Statisticians in 1982) introduced two types of provisions that allow for the partial or complete relaxation of the "seeking work" criterion in certain situations. Under partial relaxation, the definition of unemployment includes discouraged workers (all those who were without work, currently available for work, and not seeking work because they believed no work was available) in addition to persons satisfying the standard definition. Under complete relaxation, unemployment includes all those who were without work and currently available for work, no matter whether they were seeking work or not.

on the "seeking work" criterion, might be overly restrictive and might not fully capture the prevailing employment situations in many developing countries, including Ethiopia. This study opts for reporting results using the three definitions to establish a range within which values of activity rate, unemployment rate, and share of long-term unemployed lay.

The standard definition of long-term unemployment is that an unemployed worker has been continuously unemployed for at least 12 months. According to a recent guide for assessing labor market conditions in developing countries (World Bank 2006b), the 12-month threshold for establishing long-term unemployment, conceived with developed countries in mind, where public income support for the unemployed are offered to workers, may be too high when applied to developing countries where unemployment is often a luxury. We follow this guide and choose to use six months as the threshold for establishing long-term unemployment.

From the results in table 8.4, it appears that women face worse outcomes than men. Activity rates are clearly higher for men while unemployment rates are almost two times higher for women. Approximately 60 percent of unemployed workers have been continuously unemployed for at least six months. The share of long-term unemployed is higher for women when using standard and partially relaxed definitions, and it is higher for men when using completely relaxed definitions. While activity and unemployment rates logically increase when using relaxed definitions, the share of long-term unemployed surprisingly decreases (except for women in rural areas). This means that the shares of long-term unemployed among unemployed workers not seeking work because they are discouraged, or among all unemployed workers not seeking work, are lower than the share of long-term unemployed among those seeking work. Since it is difficult to believe that the unemployed not seeking work spend less time in unemployment than those seeking work because they better manage to get a job, concern arises over possible deterioration of the labor market, with increasing numbers of new entrants in unemployment who are not seeking work, for example, because they are discouraged. Unsurprisingly, activity rates are strongly higher, unemployment rates and shares of long-term unemployed workers are strongly lower, for both women and men in rural areas.

The next analysis is of different measures of labor supply. Previous works often offer a limited insight into what is called "the labor supply." Indeed, they usually refer to it as participation in the labor market, or in its different segments, and do not discuss the amount of labor that is supplied. Following Killingsworth and Heckman's (1986) recommendations, we consider three different measures of the labor supply: employment-to-population ratio, weekly hours of work, and weeks of work per year. These three measures, broken down by gender and place of residence, are reported in table 8.5, which also displays the annual hours worked (calculated as the product of weekly hours worked times weeks of work

Table 8.5 Measures of Labor Supply in Ethiopia, 2005

	Women			Men			All
	Urban	Rural	All	Urban	Rural	All	
Employment-to-population ratio (%)	45	76	58	64	93	77	67
Annual hours of work	1,720	909	1,271	2,054	1,546	1,780	1,545
Labor input per capita	774	691	737	1315	1438	1371	1035
Weekly hours of work	40.6	21.1	29.8	46.1	33.5	39.3	34.9
Weeks worked per year	41.1	41.2	41.2	43.3	45	44.2	42.8

Source: LFS 2005.
Note: Individuals aged 15 and older. Weekly hours of work and weeks worked per year are computed at the mean of the samples of employed workers. Weekly hours of work is defined as the total number of hours worked at all jobs in the last seven days, and weeks worked per year is defined as the number of weeks worked during the last 12 months.

per year) and a variant of the Owen's (1985) constructed measure of "labor input per capita," which is computed on an annual instead of weekly basis. More precisely, this constructed measure of "labor input per capita" is calculated as the product of employment-to-population ratio and annual hours worked.

Male labor input per capita is almost two times higher than that of females. This result is explained by the fact that both employment-to-population ratio and annual hours of work are much higher for men. The latter, in turn, is explained by the fact that both weekly hours of work and, to a lesser extent, weeks worked per year are much higher for men. All these findings are observed in urban as well as in rural areas, where such gender disparities are more pronounced. Intra-gender inequalities in both urban and rural areas are also important. For both men and women, employment-to-population ratio is much lower, and annual hours of work much higher, in urban areas. For women, the difference in employment-to-population ratio is not enough to offset the difference in annual hours of work between urban and rural areas, while for men it is. Thus, female labor input per capita is higher in urban areas, whereas male labor input per capita is higher in rural areas.

Finally, note that urban women work in a week almost twice as much as rural women, while the number of weeks worked per year by women is almost the same in both areas. For men, the difference in hours worked per week between urban and rural areas is impressive but not as important as for women. In addition, men work more weeks per year in rural areas.

Table 8.6 shows the distribution of workers by employment sector, separately for men and women. Although wage employment represents a significant share of total employment (about 25 percent), the vast bulk of workers are in nonwage employment. Almost half of workers are self-employed and nearly a third are unpaid family workers. Among wage earners, less than half are in the public

Table 8.6 Distribution of Workers by Employment Sectors in Ethiopia, 2005

	Women (%)	Men (%)	All (%)
Wage employment	22	28	25
Public	8	13	11
Private formal	6	11	9
Private informal	8	4	5
Non-wage employent	78	72	75
Self-employment	35	56	46
Unpaid family work	43	16	29

Source: LFS 2005.
Note: Individuals aged 15 and older.

sector, which is in fact the segment of the labor market that offers the highest earnings. Among the remainder of the wage earners, more than a third are in the informal private sector, which is the segment of the wage employment that offers the lowest earnings.

Women are clearly disadvantaged in terms of job allocation. The share of wage earners is higher among working men. More than half of non-wage-employed women are unpaid family workers, whereas the vast bulk of non-wage-employed men are self-employed. The public sector, as well as the private informal sector, includes slightly more than a third of wage-employed women. Among wage-employed men, nearly half are in the public sector and less than 15 percent are in the informal private sector.

Finally, table 8.7 presents the distribution of workers by sector of activity and by occupation, and the distribution of wage earners by terms of employment, separately for men and women. Half the workers are engaged in primary sector activities, 40 percent in tertiary sector activities, and 10 percent in the manufacturing sector. Male and female workers are more or less equally distributed across these sectors of activity.

More than three-fourths of workers are blue-collar and almost a third are blue-collar, low-skilled. White-collar workers thus represent less than a quarter of workers, among whom three-fourths are low-skilled. The incidence of low-skilled occupations is nearly two times higher among employed women than among employed men. Female workers are predominantly blue-collar, low-skilled, while the majority of male workers are blue-collar, high-skilled.

Permanent employees account for the biggest share of wage earners. Together with temporary employees, they represent the vast bulk of wage earners. Female wage earners are predominantly temporary employees, while male wage earners are predominantly permanent employees, suggesting that the conditions of work among wage-employed women may be less favorable than for men.

Table 8.7 Distribution of Workers by Sector of Activity, Occupation, and Terms of Employment in Ethiopia, 2005

	Women (%)	Men (%)	All (%)
Overall employment			
Sector of activity			
Primary	47	54	51
Secondary	12	7	9
Tertiary	41	39	40
Occupation-based skill class			
White-collar, high-skill	4	8	6
White-collar, low-skill	22	13	17
Blue-collar, high-skill	34	53	44
Blue-collar, low-skill	40	26	33
Wage employment			
Terms of employment			
Permanent employee	37	49	44
Temporary employee	48	34	40
Contract employee	8	10	9
Casual or other employee	7	7	7

Source: LFS 2005.
Note: Individuals aged 15 and older. White-collar, high-skill includes legislators, senior officials and managers, professionals, technicians, and associate professionals. White-collar, low-skill includes clerks, service workers, shop and sales workers, and armed forces. Blue-collar, low-skill includes skilled agricultural and fishery workers and craft and related trade workers. And blue-collar, low-skill includes plant and machine operators and assemblers and elementary occupations.

Determinants of Labor Allocation. What are the determinants of labor allocation across employment sectors and sexes? To answer this question, we ran multinomial logit regressions separately for men and women to explain their probability of participating in the different employment sectors as a function of human capital and other individual characteristics, household characteristics, and location variables. Regressors included are dummies for three levels of education attainment (primary, general, and beyond) and training (technical or vocational education and training); potential experience, which is defined by age minus years of schooling minus 6, and its square to take into account its possible decreasing returns; dummies for marital and household head status; and continuous variables for the number of infants and children in the household. We also included urban and region dummies. Multinomial logit regressions are performed using five categories: (1) public formal wage employed, (2) formal private wage employed, (3) informal private wage employed, (4) self-employed, and (5) unpaid family workers. The reference category is non-participation in employment (inactive and unemployed workers).

Annex tables 8A.2-1 and 8A.2-2 report results for men and women, respectively. These tables give the marginal effects estimated at the mean of the independent variables instead of the coefficients.

For men and women alike, education is associated with lower probabilities of participating in non-wage employment (self-employment and unpaid family work) and in informal private jobs, as well as with higher probabilities of entering the public sector. These findings suggest that public employment is the most attractive for educated people and that they would rather remain unemployed (the incidence of unemployment is higher among the most educated) than enter informal private-sector employment or self-employment in order to queue for public-sector jobs. Highly educated men are also less likely to be formal private-wage-employed, while the reverse is observed for highly educated women. In fact, in private formal wage employment, there are more highly educated women than men, indicating that access to private formal jobs may be more competitive for women.

The impacts of education on the participation in unpaid family work and private wage employment are rather low, while in self-employment and public-wage employment, they are important. Women (men) who have acquired a general education are 20 percent (17 percent) more likely to be public–wage-employed. This figure increases to 50 percent (37 percent) for women (men) with beyond-general education. In contrast, attaining general education makes men and women, respectively, 22 percent and 7 percent less likely to be self-employed. Moreover, highly educated men and women are, respectively, 37 percent and 17 percent less likely to participate in self-employment. According to these results, education has substantial effects on job allocation. As men and women become educated and reach higher education levels, they strongly increase their chances of working in the public sector, which is the most rewarding wage employment sector because it offers the highest earnings and protection.

Technical or vocational education and training are also associated with higher probability of participating in the public sector. In addition, men and women with these qualifications are also more likely to work in the formal private-wage-employment sector, suggesting that, in this sector, there is more labor demand for these skills. Note that, for women, such educational qualifications have the strongest positive impact on the probability of accessing the self-employment sector, while for men they have an adverse impact on entering this sector. These findings suggest that women who have acquired these qualifications prefer self-employment or face greater difficulties than men to get into paid jobs, and thus they fall back on less rewarding jobs in self-employment, for example, because they can only engage in activities that are compatible with their obligations in the domestic realm.

The effect of potential experience on the probability of participating in the different employment sectors has a concave profile (except for men in unpaid family work). Unsurprisingly, married men are less likely to work in the household, while the reverse is observed for married women. Household heads, who generally have the role of household breadwinner, are strongly less likely to be unpaid family workers and more likely to work in the labor market, particularly in self-employment. The number of infants is associated with a higher probability for men to engage in self-employment, and to a lower probability for women to work in the public sector or in formal private-wage employment. Besides its negative impact on participation in public and formal private-wage employment, the number of children positively affects women's probability of participating in self-employment and unpaid family work. Two effects may come into play. On one hand, women are more likely to work at home because they have to take care of their children. On the other hand, children at young ages start taking part in household activities, relieving women of part of their household duties and enabling them to engage in flexible productive activities. Finally, men and women living in urban areas are more likely to participate in wage employment and less likely to engage in self-employment or in unpaid family work.

Conclusions

Using the Labor Force Survey 2005, this study has sought to contribute to a better understanding of gender disparities in Ethiopia in three main areas: time allocation between market and household work, time poverty, and labor allocation across employment sectors. How do men and women allocate their time between market and household work? Do they perform the same amount of total work and are they equally affected by time poverty? What are the determinants of market and household work time across gender? The first part of this chapter attempted to answer these questions, while the second part commented on some basic labor market descriptive statistics broken down by gender and analyzed the determinants of labor allocation across employment sectors and sexes. The main findings can be summarized as follows.

There is a strong gender-based division of labor in Ethiopia, which is much more acute in rural areas. Women work more and for longer hours than men in the household, while the reverse is true in the labor market. However, despite the fact that market work is predominantly masculine, the proportion of women working in the labor market and the time they spend in it are important and much higher than the incidence and duration of housework for men. It appears, then, that women experience a double work burden, as they tend to accumulate both types of work, unlike men, who generally focus only on market work. Consequently, women spend more time at work than men, this phenomenon being observed to a greater extent in rural areas.

Both incidence and duration of extra work (hours worked above the time poverty line) are higher for women, so they are more affected by time poverty.

The gender disparities in time poverty are larger in rural areas. Men are more affected by time poverty in urban than in rural areas, while the reverse is observed for women.

The study estimated the determinants of market and household work time across genders using the Tobit method, accounting for individual and household characteristics. Measures of goodness of fit of the models were extremely low, meaning that these characteristics failed in explaining most of the variance of market and household work time across individuals, bringing to light the fact that some crucial information was omitted as, for instance, access to basic infrastructure resources, which is unfortunately missing in the LFS 2005, while it is undoubtedly an important determinant of the time allocated by individuals to market and household work.

However, commenting on the most robust results, it appears that education is generally associated with lower hours of market and household work. There is a gender-based division of labor across spouses: married women tend to work fewer hours in the labor market and longer hours in the household, while the reverse is true for married men. Upon further investigating intra-household labor allocation across gender, it appears that the presence of adult women in the household negatively affects men's housework time, while the presence of adult men is associated with lower hours of market work and longer hours of housework performed by women. Finally, the presence of other adult women in the household relieves women of part of their housework burden.

Women are clearly disadvantaged in terms of job allocation. Unpaid family workers account for the highest share of female workers, while the majority of male workers are self-employed. The share of wage earners is lower among female workers. For men, public-wage employment and formal private-wage employment constitute altogether the biggest share of the wage-employed. In contrast, for women, informal private jobs represent the second most frequent form of wage employment after public-wage employment. Moreover, female workers are more likely to work as low-skilled blue-collar workers and, in wage employment, as temporary employees.

Finally, marginal impacts of covariates on male and female segment employment choices were derived after multinomial logit estimations to analyze the determinants of labor allocation across employment sectors and sexes. Results show that education has substantial effects on job allocation. For men and women alike, education is associated with lower probabilities of participating in non-wage employment (self-employment and unpaid family work) and in informal private jobs, and with higher probabilities of entering the public sector. As they become educated and reach higher levels of education, men and, to a greater extent, women, strongly increase their chances of working in the public sector, which is the most rewarding wage-employment sector because it offers the highest earnings and protection.

Annex 8A.1

Table 8A.1-1 Determinants of Hours Per Week Worked in the Labor Market by Gender and Place of Residence in Ethiopia, 2005 (Tobit models)

	Men		Women	
	Urban	Rural	Urban	Rural
Individual characteristics				
Illiterate (reference category)	—	—	—	—
Primary education	−3.979**	−7.056***	−8.358***	−3.726***
	(−2.02)	(−15.38)	(−6.62)	(−8.44)
General education	−15.582***	−8.141***	−14.569***	−4.379**
	(−6.39)	(−5.18)	(−7.12)	(−2.19)
Beyond general education	−5.918	−0.036	1.215	11.321***
	(−1.48)	(−0.01)	(0.32)	(3.17)
Age	3.941***	1.060***	2.618***	1.067***
	(11.75)	(11.07)	(11.43)	(17.20)
(Age squared)/100	−4.772***	−1.487***	−3.379***	−1.537***
	(−12.40)	(−14.36)	(−12.54)	(−20.63)
Married	6.359***	1.001	−11.424***	−0.739*
	(2.70)	(1.31)	(−7.75)	(−1.79)
Head of household	10.318***	2.591***	5.564***	3.882***
	(4.50)	(2.77)	(3.39)	(7.83)
Household characteristics				
Number of Infants (under 6 years old)	0.551	0.365*	−0.128	−0.265*
	(0.60)	(1.67)	(−0.22)	(−1.90)
Number of Children (6–14 years old)	1.478**	−0.307*	0.126	−0.050
	(2.19)	(−1.66)	(0.28)	(−0.42)
Number of men (15–24 years old)	−1.010	−0.076	−0.579	−0.778***
	(−1.30)	(−0.24)	(−0.83)	(−3.76)
Number of women (15–24 years old)	1.979*	0.389	0.602	0.229
	(1.93)	(1.10)	(0.84)	(0.99)
Number of men (25–34 years old)	−0.552	−0.090	0.927	−1.161***
	(−0.45)	(−0.20)	(0.83)	(−3.58)
Number of women (25–34 years old)	2.279	0.038	0.133	0.196
	(1.30)	(0.07)	(0.12)	(0.59)
Number of men (35–64 years old)	−1.238	−0.181	2.583**	−0.714**
	(−0.73)	(−0.35)	(2.13)	(−2.07)
Number of women (35–64 years old)	1.429	0.241	−2.130*	0.685*
	(0.88)	(0.46)	(−1.81)	(1.93)
Number of seniors (65 years and older)	3.945*	2.056***	0.221	0.903**
	(1.81)	(3.50)	(0.15)	(2.35)
Presence of disabled people	−5.952**	−3.069***	−2.760	−1.389***
	(−2.42)	(−4.44)	(−1.61)	(−3.08)
Constant	−44.785***	21.497***	−30.254***	−0.070
	(−6.57)	(9.45)	(−6.62)	(−0.05)

continued

Table 8A.1-1 *continued*

	Men		Women	
	Urban	Rural	Urban	Rural
Region dummies	Yes	Yes	Yes	Yes
Observations	2490	11410	5359	24872
Pseudo R-squared	0.0427	0.0099	0.0140	0.0070

Source: LFS 2005.
Notes: — = not applicable. Individuals aged 15 and older. Primary education includes primary education in the new system (grades 1–4, basic education cycle; grades 5–8, general primary cycle), nonformal education, and literacy campaign. General education includes grades 9–12 in the new system (general secondary education, grades 9–10; preparatory secondary education, grades 11–12); and grades 9–12 in the old system. Beyond general education includes new vocational education (grades 11–12), certificate, diploma (grades 11–13), degree completed or not, and older degree.
T statistics are in parentheses. * significant at 10%, ** significant at 5%, *** significant at 1%.

Table 8A.1-2 Determinants of Hours Per Week Worked in the Household by Gender and Place of Residence in Ethiopia, 2005 (Tobit models)

	Men (age 15+)		Women (age 15+)	
	Urban	Rural	Urban	Rural
Individual characteristics				
Illiterate (reference category)	—	—	—	—
Primary education	−2.283*	0.228	−1.095*	−2.590***
	(−1.65)	(0.52)	(−1.68)	(−6.18)
General education	−1.986	−4.443***	−2.692***	−5.694***
	(−1.21)	(−2.88)	(−2.66)	(−3.04)
Beyond general education	−6.628**	4.774	−5.573***	−17.597***
	(−2.26)	(1.51)	(−2.81)	(−5.02)
Age	−1.196***	−0.082	0.648***	0.721***
	(−5.65)	(−0.90)	(6.11)	(12.86)
(Age squared)/100	1.089***	−0.071	−0.955***	−1.171***
	(4.63)	(−0.72)	(−7.95)	(−17.73)
Married	−5.012***	−5.082***	8.536***	5.740***
	(−3.12)	(−7.08)	(11.46)	(14.69)
Head of household	2.028	−0.288	0.546	0.743
	(1.39)	(−0.32)	(0.65)	(1.57)
Household characteristics				
Number of Infants (under 6 years old)	0.344	0.309	0.956***	0.445***
	(0.54)	(1.46)	(3.12)	(3.35)
Number of Children (6–14 years old)	−1.805***	−1.130***	0.065	−0.153
	(−3.86)	(−6.19)	(0.28)	(−1.36)
Number of men (15–24 years old)	−0.377	−0.568*	1.043***	1.464***
	(−0.75)	(−1.84)	(2.93)	(7.43)
Number of women (15–24 years old)	−2.161***	−3.420***	−3.021***	−3.379***
	(−3.08)	(−9.59)	(−8.21)	(−15.31)

continued

Table 8A.1-2 Determinants of Hours Per Week Worked in the Household by Gender and Place of Residence in Ethiopia, 2005 (Tobit models) *continued*

	Men (age 15+)		Women (age 15+)	
	Urban	Rural	Urban	Rural
Number of men (25–34 years old)	−0.477	0.491	0.423	1.579***
	(−0.57)	(1.14)	(0.74)	(5.12)
Number of women (25–34 years old)	−2.769**	−4.549***	−3.254***	−3.389***
	(−2.30)	(−8.76)	(−5.65)	(−10.64)
Number of men (35–64 years old)	1.958*	1.231**	−0.391	1.126***
	(1.74)	(2.45)	(−0.63)	(3.42)
Number of women (35–64 years old)	−3.792***	−5.246***	−1.524**	−2.969***
	(−3.50)	(−10.43)	(−2.56)	(−8.83)
Number of seniors (65 years and older)	−0.424	−0.035	−1.233*	1.185***
	(−0.29)	(−0.06)	(−1.68)	(3.26)
Presence of disabled people	−0.186	0.820	−0.499	−1.624***
	(−0.11)	(1.23)	(−0.57)	(−3.80)
Constant	28.111***	18.187***	19.794***	34.647***
	(6.28)	(8.39)	(8.98)	(25.98)
Region dummies	Yes	Yes	Yes	Yes
Observations	2490	11410	5359	24872
Pseudo R-squared	0.0200	0.0142	0.0170	0.0137

Source: LFS 2005.
Notes: — = not applicable. Individuals aged 15 and older. *T* statistics are in parentheses. * significant at 10%, ** significant at 5%, *** significant at 1%.

Annex 8A.2

Table 8A.2-1 Marginal Impacts of Covariates on Male Segment Employment Choices after Multinomial Logit Estimation

	Public-wage employment	Formal private-wage employment	Informal private-wage employment	Self-employment	Unpaid family work
Human capital characteristics					
Illiterate (reference category)	—	—	—	—	—
Primary education	0.0415*** (9.25)	−0.0099** (−2.09)	−0.0198*** (−9.51)	−0.1075*** (−13.24)	−0.0125*** (−9.83)
General education	0.1708*** (16.43)	−0.0123** (−2.29)	−0.0298*** (−18.01)	−0.2223*** (−21.21)	−0.0211*** (−14.19)
Beyond general education	0.3718*** (18.75)	−0.0399*** (−7.16)	−0.0361*** (−26.19)	−0.3735*** (−30.93)	−0.0261*** (−15.42)
Potential experience	0.0065*** (19.56)	0.0057*** (12.45)	0.0014*** (6.06)	0.0085*** (10.52)	−0.0015*** (−8.79)
(Potential experience squared)/100	−0.0110*** (−19.07)	−0.0116*** (−14.91)	−0.0027*** (−7.45)	−0.0123*** (−11.06)	0.0010*** (3.74)
Training	0.1058*** (19.04)	0.1084*** (15.68)	0.0236*** (6.18)	−0.1318*** (−12.36)	−0.0045 (−1.61)
Other individual characteristics					
Married	0.0193*** (6.20)	−0.0143*** (−3.03)	−0.0038 (−1.54)	0.1447*** (16.96)	−0.0141*** (−6.63)
Head of Household	0.0341*** (12.89)	−0.0023 (−0.57)	−0.0152*** (−6.73)	0.4167*** (54.81)	−0.2182*** (−28.38)

continued

Table 8A.2-1 Marginal Impacts of Covariates on Male Segment Employment Choices after Multinomial Logit Estimation *continued*

	Public-wage employment	Formal private-wage employment	Informal private-wage employment	Self-employment	Unpaid family work
Household characteristics					
Number of infants (under 6 years old)	−0.0011 (−0.84)	0.0005 (0.27)	0.0011 (1.07)	0.0198*** (6.12)	−0.0006 (−1.12)
Number of children (6–14 years old)	0.0021** (2.40)	−0.0055*** (−4.01)	−0.0022*** (−2.80)	−0.0088*** (−3.76)	0.0018*** (4.71)
Location variables					
Urban	0.0506*** (16.38)	0.0941*** (22.91)	0.0440*** (18.85)	−0.2914*** (−43.92)	−0.0729*** (−21.51)
Region dummies	Yes	Yes	Yes	Yes	Yes
Observations	59987	59987	59987	59987	59987
Pseudo R-squared	0.3815	0.3815	0.3815	0.3815	0.3815

Source: LFS 2005.

Note: — = Individuals aged 15 and older. The marginal effects are calculated at the means of the independent variables. The reference category is nonparticipation in employment (inactive and unemployed).

Z statistics are in parentheses. * significant at 10%, ** significant at 5%, *** significant at 1%.

Table 8A.2-2 Marginal Impacts of Covariates on Female Segment Employment Choices after Multinomial Logit Estimation

	Public-wage employment	Formal private-wage employment	Informal private-wage employment	Self-employment	Unpaid family work
Human capital characteristics					
Illiterate (reference category)	—	—	—	—	—
Primary education	0.0375*** (12.18)	0.0017 (1.09)	−0.0085*** (−12.59)	−0.0157*** (−2.70)	−0.0315*** (−9.32)
General education	0.2017*** (16.50)	0.0081*** (3.63)	−0.0125*** (−15.43)	−0.0753*** (−9.95)	−0.0570*** (−12.16)
Beyond general education	0.5085*** (20.88)	0.0116*** (3.16)	−0.0114*** (−15.10)	−0.1673*** (−20.44)	−0.0932*** (−16.00)
Potential experience	0.0045*** (27.56)	0.0026*** (17.32)	0.0016*** (15.80)	0.0168*** (29.31)	0.0020*** (5.02)
(Potential experience squared)/100	−0.0076*** (−26.12)	−0.0065*** (−21.92)	−0.0035*** (−17.31)	−0.0246*** (−29.42)	−0.0051*** (−8.77)
Training	0.0458*** (11.63)	0.0277*** (8.09)	−0.0016 (−1.11)	0.0623*** (4.26)	−0.0267*** (−2.65)
Other individual characteristics					
Married	0.0038*** (3.47)	−0.0180*** (−11.90)	−0.0420*** (−18.90)	0.0075 (1.53)	0.0344*** (9.88)
Head of Household	0.0184*** (12.51)	0.0077*** (5.69)	−0.0088*** (−13.34)	0.3892*** (64.85)	−0.2206*** (−71.13)

continued

Table 8A.2-2 Marginal Impacts of Covariates on Female Segment Employment Choices after Multinomial Logit Estimation *continued*

	Public-wage employment	Formal private-wage employment	Informal private-wage employment	Self-employment	Unpaid family work
Household characteristics					
Number of infants (under 6 years old)	−0.0017***	−0.0045***	0.0005*	−0.0009	−0.0011
	(−2.68)	(−6.26)	(1.76)	(−0.42)	(−0.92)
Number of children (6–14 years old)	−0.0008**	−0.0021***	−0.0003	0.0036**	0.0051***
	(−2.11)	(−4.50)	(−1.33)	(2.23)	(5.43)
Location variables					
Urban	0.0066***	0.0221***	0.0248***	−0.0199***	−0.3015***
	(5.07)	(14.32)	(18.79)	(−4.44)	(−56.89)
Region dummies	Yes	Yes	Yes	Yes	Yes
Observations	70198	70198	70198	70198	70198
Pseudo R-squared	0.3118	0.3118	0.3118	0.3118	0.3118

Source: LFS 2005.
Note: — = Individuals aged 15 and older. The marginal effects are calculated at the means of the independent variables. The reference category is nonparticipation in employment (inactive and unemployed).
Z statistics are in parentheses. * significant at 10%, ** significant at 5%, *** significant at 1%.

Notes

1. For a detailed discussion about differences between stylized (questionnaire-based) estimates and diary-based estimates of housework time collected from the same respondents, see Kan (2006).
2. Following Burda, Hamermesh, and Weil (2007), those activities that we cannot pay other people to do for us, but that we must do at least some of, are defined as tertiary activities.
3. According to World Bank (2007), including the age-group 10–15 in the working-age population creates an implicit conflict between employment and education policy objectives.
4. Burda, Hamermesh, and Weil (2007) found, contrary to the general belief, that in rich northern countries on four continents, men and women do the same amount of total work.
5. Graphs of these curves are not displayed in this chapter, but are available upon request from the authors.

References

Source of data: Labor Force Survey 2005, dataset version 1.0–May 2006, provided by the Central Statistical Authority of Ethiopia.

Appleton, S., J. Hoddinott, and P. Krishnan. 1999. "The Gender Wage Gap in Three African Countries." *Economic Development and Cultural Change* 47 (2): 289–312.

Bardasi, E., and Q. Wodon. 2006. "Measuring Time Poverty and Analyzing Its Determinants: Concepts and Application to Guinea." *Economics Bulletin* 10 (10): 1–7.

Blackden, C. M., and E. Morris-Hugues. 1993. "Paradigm Postponed: Gender and Economic Adjustment in Sub-Saharan Africa." Technical Note 13, Poverty and Human Resources Division, Technical Department, Africa Region, World Bank, Washington, DC.

Blackden, C. M., and Q. Wodon. 2006. "Gender, Time Use, and Poverty in Sub-Saharan Africa." Working Paper 73, World Bank, Washington, DC.

Burda, M., D. S. Hamermesh, and P. Weil. 2007. "Total Work, Gender and Social Norms." Working Paper 13000, National Bureau of Economic Research, Washington, DC.

CSA (Central Statistical Agency). 2006. "Report on the 2005 National Labor Force Survey." Statistical Bulletin 365, CSA, Addis Ababa, Ethiopia.

Fenstermaker Berk, S., and A. Shih. 1980. "Contributions to Household Labor: Comparing Wives' and Husbands' Reports." In *Women and Household Labor*, ed. S. Fenstermaker Berk. Beverly Hills, CA: Sage.

Foster, J. E., J. Greer, and E. Thorbecke. 1984. "A Class of Decomposable Poverty Indices." *Econometrica* 52 (3): 761–66.

Juster, F. T., and F. P. Stafford. 1991. "The Allocation of Time: Empirical Findings, Behavioral Models, and Problems of Measurement." *Journal of Economic Literature* 29 (June): 471–522.

Kan, M. Y. 2006. "Measuring Housework Participation: The Gap Between 'Stylized' Questionnaire Estimates and Diary-based Estimates." GeNet Working Paper 20, Institute for Social and Economic Research, University of Essex, Essex, United Kingdom.

Killingsworth, M. R., and J. J. Heckman. 1986. "Female Labor Supply: A Survey." In *Handbook of Labor Economics*, vol. 1, ed. O. Ashenfelter and R. Layard, 102–204. Amsterdam: North-Holland.

Kolev, A., and P. Suárez Robles. 2007. "Addressing the Gender Pay Gap in Ethiopia: How Crucial Is the Quest for Education Parity?" Unpublished paper, joint Agence Française de Développment–World Bank research project, Paris.

Lee, Y. S., and L. J. Waite. 2005. "Husbands' and Wives' Time Spent on Housework: A Comparison of Measures." *Journal of Marriage and Family* 67 (2): 328–36.

Lim, L. L. 2002. "Female Labor Force Participation." Background paper for the United Nations Population Division, Expert Group Meeting on Completing the Fertility Transition, 11–14 March 2002, New York.

Marini, M. M., and B. A. Shelton. 1993. "Measuring Household Work: Recent Experience in the United States." *Social Science Research* 22 (4): 361–82.

McFadden, D. 1973. "Conditional Logit Analysis of Qualitative Choice Behavior." In *Frontiers of Econometrics*, ed. P. Zarembka, 105–42. New York: Academic Press.

Medeiros, M., R. Guerreiro Osorio, and J. Costa. 2007. "Gender Inequalities in Allocating Time to Paid and Unpaid Work: Evidence from Bolivia." Working Paper 34, International Poverty Centre, Brasilia, Brazil.

MoFED (Ministry of Finance and Economic Development). 2005. "Ethiopia: The Millennium Development Goals (MDGs) Needs Assessment." Synthesis Report, Development Planning and Research Department, MoFED, Addis Ababa, Ethiopia.

Owen, J. 1985. *Working Lives: The American Work Force Since 1920*. Lexington, MA: D.C. Heath and Co.

Press, J. E., and E. Townsley. 1998. "Wives' and Husbands' Housework Reporting: Gender, Class and Social Desirability." *Gender and Society* 12 (2): 188–218.

Temesgen, T. 2006. "Decomposing Gender Wage Differentials in Urban Ethiopia: Evidence from Linked Employer-Employee (LEE) Manufacturing Survey Data." *Global Economic Review* 35 (1): 43–66.

Ting, L., and A. Malhotra. 2005. "Disorders of Sleep: An Overview." *Primary Care: Clinics in Office Practice* 32 (2): 305–18.

UN-Habitat. 2004. "Addis Ababa, Ethiopia: Urban Inequities Report." Global Urban Observatory, Monitoring System Branch, Nairobi, Kenya.

UNICEF (United Nations Children's Fund). 1999. "Women in Transition." The MONEE Project Regional Monitoring Report 6, UNICEF, Florence, Italy.

Warner, R. L. 1986. "Alternative Strategies for Measuring Household Division of Labor: A Comparison." *Journal of Family Issues* 7 (2): 179–95.

World Bank. 2006a. "Gender and Transport Resource Guide." Module IV: Gender and Rural Transport Initiative, World Bank, Washington, DC.

———. 2006b. "A Guide for Assessing Labor Markets Conditions in Developing Countries." Draft, World Bank, Washington, DC.

———. 2007. *Urban Labor Markets in Ethiopia: Challenges and Prospects* (2 vols.). Poverty Reduction and Economic Management Unit. Washington, DC: World Bank.

Chapter **9**

Domestic Work Time in Sierra Leone

Quentin Wodon and Yvonne Ying

Introduction

There is ample evidence that women allocate substantial time to domestic chores in Sub-Saharan Africa, and that this burden limits their economic opportunities. The constraints on time use imposed on women, not only by domestic work but also by work in the fields, were already recognized in the 1960s. Data from that period from two villages in the Central African Republic showed that men worked 5.5 hours/day, versus 8 hours/day for women (Berio 1983). Studies based on data from the 1980s and 1990s confirm large differences in time burdens according to gender (Blackden and Bhanu 1999; Ilahi 2000). For example, women have been shown to spend about three times more time in transport activities than men in Ghana, Tanzania, and Zambia (Malmberg-Calvo 1994). In Uganda, time savings from better access to water and wood were estimated at 900 hours/year, mostly to the benefit of women (Barwell 1996). More recent work using new data on Benin, Ghana, Madagascar, Mauritius, and South Africa (Charmes 2006), as well as on Guinea (Bardasi and Wodon 2006a, 2009, 2010) and Malawi (Wodon and Beegle 2006), have provided additional evidence that women have to work more than men in Sub-Saharan Africa (see also Ilahi and Grimard 2000 for Pakistan, and World Bank 2001 for a broader discussion of related gender issues).

As discussed by Blackden and Wodon (2006), existing patterns of time use have potentially important consequences for households. One key issue is that the "household time overhead" (a concept introduced by Harvey and Taylor 2000) or the number of hours that household members, especially women, must allocate to basic chores, is high. Taking care of children and possibly the elderly,

This work was prepared with funding from the Gender Action Plan at the World Bank for work on gender, time use, and infrastructure in Africa. The authors thank Jorge Arbache and Mayra Buvinic for comments. The views expressed here are those of the authors and need not reflect those of the World Bank, its executive directors, or the countries they represent.

preparing meals, washing clothes, cleaning the dwelling, and fetching water and wood may together represent a full-time occupation for several household members. When households do not have access to basic infrastructure services, such as electricity, piped water, and sanitation facilities, the time necessary for performing domestic chores is typically much higher than when such access is available. In turn, because the time spent on domestic chores is not easily dispensable, and because domestic chores are performed mainly by women, many women have limited opportunity to engage in productive activities. This may limit their income and decision power within the household. Scarcity of time also means that women have limited opportunities to further their education and training. It could thus be argued that "time poverty," especially among women, is one of the determinants of consumption poverty.

To make the argument clearer, assume that one estimated the labor market value of the time available to various household members or the value of the time savings that could be obtained from policies such as those facilitating access to infrastructure services. The value of these time savings could then be taken into account to assess how additional labor market earnings generated through additional time allocated to work in the labor market could help in reducing monetary or consumption-based poverty. This has been done, for example, by Bardasi and Wodon (2006b) using Guinea data, with the authors finding that, if all household members were indeed to work a certain given amount of time, monetary poverty could be reduced substantially. From a policy point of view, this implies that investments aiming to reduce household time overhead, especially through access to better infrastructure services, would be critical for poverty reduction.

The numerous steps and implicit assumptions needed for full proof of the above argument—that changes in time use resulting from better access to infrastructure might have a positive impact on income generation and poverty reduction—will not be fully explicated in this chapter. Because of limitations in data on time use in the Sierra Leone survey (the time spent working in the labor market by household members cannot be measured properly), we will not make here an explicit and quantified link between so-called time poverty and consumption-based poverty. The objective of this study, more limited in scope, is to provide a descriptive analysis of domestic work time in Sierra Leone. The results should still be interesting because such analysis has not been done before in Sierra Leone, simply because this is the first survey in the country for which time use information is available. The 2003–04 Sierra Leone Integrated Household Survey is used in the next section to provide basic statistics on the time allocated to domestic work according to gender, age, urban/rural location status, household consumption status, access to infrastructure, employment, and migration. Following that is a regression analysis examining the determinants or correlates of domestic time use.

Many empirical results obtained in this study confirm conventional wisdom: Women are found to work more than men on domestic tasks and the domestic workload of children is also high. Access to water and electricity is associated with a reduction in domestic work time by about 10 hours per week.[1] At the same time, it is also found that those who already work in the labor market also spend quite some time on domestic work. Said differently, the hypothesis of a clean division of labor between those who work in the labor market and those who work at home is not necessarily warranted. This means that when assessing the potential monetary benefits from basic infrastructure services in reducing the household time overhead, it should not be assumed too quickly that new household members will be able to enter the labor market thanks to the reduction in domestic work time. Also, if those who are already working in the labor market are performing a non-negligible share of the domestic work, and if there are limited opportunities for those individuals to earn more in the labor market by working more hours there, then the potential for higher earnings for the household thanks to domestic work time savings may be limited. Still, even if a substantial share of the time savings generated by access to basic infrastructure were not to be transformed into additional earnings for the beneficiary households through an increase in their labor supply and related earnings, there should be no doubt that household members would be better off from a time use point of view if they had access to better infrastructure services, simply because they would be able to allocate part of their time to alternative and rewarding endeavors.

Basic Statistics

The Sierra Leone Integrated Household Survey questionnaire distinguishes between a range of domestic chores or time use patterns, for cooking, washing motor vehicles, sweeping, disposing of garbage, ironing clothes, shopping, taking care of children, running errands, fetching wood, and fetching water. Table 9.1 provides estimates of the average number of hours per week allocated to domestic activities, as well as the shares of total domestic work accounted for by these activities. This is shown separately for urban and rural areas by gender and by age group, as well as for the overall population in both urban and rural areas.

A first expected, yet important, result is that women spend significantly more time on domestic work than men, with the total amount of time allocated to domestic work being very high for women. Female adults spend a total of 46.40 hours per week on domestic work in rural areas, and 34.64 hours in urban areas. This compares to 23.36 and 12.26 hours, respectively, for adult males. Thus, urban women aged 15 and older spend about 2.8 times more time than

Table 9.1 Domestic Work According to Gender and Age Group in Sierra Leone, 2003–04

	Age 6–14 (hours)			Age 15+ (hours)			Age 6–14 (share of total, %)			Age 15+ (share of total, %)		
	Men	Women	Total	Men	Women	Total	Men	Women	Total	Men	Women	Total
Urban												
Cooking	0.63	1.55	1.08	0.47	6.88	3.84	5.12	10.43	7.99	3.84	19.86	15.99
Washing car	0.08	0.05	0.06	0.09	0.14	0.12	0.64	0.33	0.47	0.77	0.41	0.50
Sweeping	2.04	2.50	2.27	0.91	1.92	1.44	16.64	16.83	16.74	7.39	5.54	5.99
Disposing of garbage	1.81	2.25	2.03	0.72	1.33	1.04	14.78	15.13	14.97	5.89	3.84	4.33
Ironing clothes	1.29	1.18	1.23	1.94	1.68	1.80	10.49	7.92	9.10	15.81	4.84	7.49
Shopping	0.37	0.45	0.41	1.51	3.48	2.54	3.05	3.03	3.04	12.30	10.04	10.58
Taking care of children	0.50	1.07	0.78	1.85	12.82	7.62	4.04	7.18	5.73	15.09	37.01	31.72
Running errands	1.33	1.30	1.32	2.90	3.35	3.13	10.86	8.77	9.73	23.61	9.66	13.03
Fetching wood	1.80	1.70	1.75	0.75	1.20	0.99	14.66	11.47	12.93	6.12	3.48	4.12
Fetching water	2.42	2.81	2.61	1.12	1.84	1.50	19.73	18.91	19.29	9.17	5.32	6.25
Total domestic work	12.27	14.87	13.55	12.26	34.64	24.04	100	100	100	100	100	100
Rural												
Cooking	1.01	1.92	1.45	0.81	8.99	5.29	5.76	9.18	7.55	3.45	19.37	14.71
Washing car	0.03	0.08	0.05	0.05	0.13	0.10	0.16	0.36	0.26	0.22	0.28	0.27
Sweeping	2.73	3.20	2.96	1.46	3.25	2.44	15.55	15.31	15.43	6.27	7.00	6.78
Disposing of garbage	2.46	2.89	2.66	1.53	2.71	2.18	13.96	13.85	13.90	6.53	5.85	6.05
Ironing clothes	0.77	0.71	0.74	1.55	0.96	1.22	4.37	3.42	3.87	6.63	2.06	3.40
Shopping	0.55	0.78	0.66	3.23	4.35	3.84	3.13	3.72	3.44	13.81	9.38	10.68
Taking care of children	1.05	1.49	1.26	3.55	12.72	8.58	5.94	7.13	6.57	15.21	27.42	23.84
Running errands	1.90	2.07	1.98	6.67	5.97	6.29	10.79	9.90	10.32	28.54	12.87	17.46
Fetching wood	3.64	3.81	3.72	2.59	3.71	3.21	20.68	18.27	19.42	11.10	8.00	8.91
Fetching water	3.46	3.93	3.69	1.93	3.60	2.85	19.68	18.86	19.25	8.25	7.77	7.91
Total domestic work	17.59	20.86	19.16	23.36	46.40	36.00	100	100	100	100	100	100

Source: Authors' estimation based on 2003–04 Sierra Leone Integrated Household Survey (IHS).

urban men on domestic work, while for rural areas the adult female-to-male domestic work ratio is around two. In other words, for women, the burden of domestic work essentially represents a full-time occupation, especially in rural areas. These high levels of domestic work are in part a result of taking child care into account (this is often not the case in time-use data for other countries; see, for example, the empirical papers gathered in Blackden and Wodon 2006).

Large differences are also observed in terms of the composition of domestic work. Female individuals aged 15 and older spend most of their domestic work time taking care of children and cooking. On average, in both urban and rural areas, women spend about 13 hours per week (37 percent of urban women's total domestic work time and 27 percent of rural women's) on childcare, and 7 to 9 hours per week (around 20 percent of the total domestic work time) on cooking. For adult male individuals, by contrast, running errands is the most time-consuming domestic task, at about 3 hours per week (24 percent of the total domestic work time) in urban areas, and 7 hours per week (29 percent of the total domestic work time) in rural areas. Taking care of children is another largest domestic task for men in terms of number of hours spent on the task, with both urban and rural men using up to 15 percent of their domestic work time (2 hours in urban areas and 4 hours in rural areas) on childcare.

For rural children (individuals aged 6–14), the heaviest time burden is for fetching wood and water. In rural areas, boys and girls spend 7 to 8 hours per week on average for these tasks. This work is also a heavy burden for urban children, who use more than 4 hours for fetching wood and water. As is the case for adults, total domestic work time for children is higher in rural than urban areas. The total time allocated by children to domestic work reaches about 19 hours in rural areas and 14 hours in urban areas, and in both urban and rural areas there is a slightly larger burden for girls than for boys (the difference is between 2 and 3 hours of extra work for girls). It is likely that the relatively high burden of domestic work for children takes away time from leisure and education, especially when children must spend long hours fetching wood and water. Disposal of garbage is another task to which children must allocate substantial time (about 2 to 3 hours in both urban and rural areas).

In tables 9.2 to 9.7, data on domestic work time are presented according to access to basic infrastructure (specifically, access to water and electricity), consumption level, employment, migration, and household structure. Table 9.2 gives the average number of hours per week spent on domestic work according to whether households have access to water (a household is said not to have access to water if the main source of drinking water is a well without pump, a river, a lake, a spring, a pond, or rainwater) and electricity (households are considered as having access to electric power if their main source of lighting is electric). One could consider the distance to access water as another way to measure access (instead of considering a dichotomic variable here), but we do not have

Table 9.2 Domestic Work According to Access to Water and Electricity in Sierra Leone, 2003–04

	Men				Women			
	No water & electricity	Have water or electricity	Have water & electricity	Total	No water & electricity	Have water or electricity	Have water & electricity	Total
Urban, age 6–14								
Cooking	0.89	0.69	0.34	0.63	2.75	1.31	0.55	1.55
Washing car	0.07	0.11	0.05	0.08	0.06	0.06	0.02	0.05
Sweeping	3.15	2.03	1.11	2.04	4.10	2.19	1.15	2.50
Disposing of garbage	2.67	1.83	1.06	1.81	3.73	1.81	1.18	2.25
Ironing clothes	2.14	0.97	0.90	1.29	2.12	0.86	0.54	1.18
Shopping	0.35	0.18	0.60	0.37	0.52	0.44	0.40	0.45
Taking care of children	0.96	0.46	0.14	0.50	2.06	0.63	0.51	1.07
Running errands	1.74	0.96	1.38	1.33	2.24	0.81	0.90	1.30
Fetching wood	3.05	1.97	0.55	1.80	3.16	1.65	0.21	1.70
Fetching water	4.04	2.50	0.97	2.42	4.84	2.55	0.95	2.81
Total domestic work	19.07	11.70	7.10	12.27	25.57	12.32	6.40	14.87
Urban, age 15+								
Cooking	0.70	0.51	0.31	0.47	7.86	7.18	5.95	6.88
Washing car	0.15	0.04	0.10	0.09	0.20	0.25	0.01	0.14
Sweeping	1.81	1.01	0.30	0.91	3.24	2.06	0.89	1.92
Disposing of garbage	1.48	0.83	0.19	0.72	2.83	1.31	0.32	1.33
Ironing clothes	3.22	1.73	1.35	1.94	2.86	1.64	0.90	1.68
Shopping	3.39	1.24	0.62	1.51	5.22	2.72	2.96	3.48
Taking care of children	3.03	2.11	0.96	1.85	9.94	14.85	13.01	12.82
Running errands	6.24	2.39	1.34	2.90	6.62	2.68	1.69	3.35
Fetching wood	1.54	0.96	0.12	0.75	2.57	1.37	0.12	1.20

Fetching water	2.08	1.26	0.46	1.12	3.55	2.04	0.50	1.84
Total domestic work	23.64	12.09	5.74	12.26	44.87	36.10	26.34	34.64
Rural, age 6–14								
Cooking	1.11	0.84	0.06	1.01	2.13	1.48	0.09	1.92
Washing car	0.02	0.04	0.00	0.03	0.06	0.11	0.00	0.08
Sweeping	2.81	2.72	0.47	2.73	3.28	3.09	1.14	3.19
Disposing of garbage	2.50	2.50	0.31	2.46	3.02	2.65	0.86	2.88
Ironing clothes	0.70	0.99	0.28	0.77	0.74	0.61	0.28	0.70
Shopping	0.57	0.54	0.00	0.55	0.79	0.77	0.31	0.78
Taking care of children	1.11	0.97	0.00	1.05	1.70	0.99	0.56	1.49
Running errands	2.11	1.36	1.80	1.90	2.37	1.28	1.51	2.07
Fetching wood	3.56	4.13	0.20	3.64	3.94	3.73	0.02	3.80
Fetching water	3.61	3.33	0.17	3.46	4.11	3.71	0.10	3.93
Total domestic work	18.10	17.40	3.30	17.59	22.15	18.43	4.89	20.82
Rural, age 15+								
Cooking	0.79	0.92	0.45	0.81	9.23	8.67	6.87	9.02
Washing car	0.04	0.05	0.41	0.05	0.11	0.09	1.30	0.13
Sweeping	1.64	1.18	0.33	1.47	3.45	3.01	0.64	3.26
Disposing of garbage	1.71	1.22	0.25	1.53	2.96	2.32	0.41	2.72
Ironing clothes	1.49	1.79	0.58	1.54	0.89	1.15	0.59	0.95
Shopping	3.63	2.55	0.74	3.24	4.29	4.54	4.71	4.37
Taking care of children	4.03	2.76	0.41	3.57	13.88	10.28	8.81	12.77
Running errands	7.56	5.18	0.89	6.69	6.64	4.70	1.93	5.99
Fetching wood	2.68	2.62	0.49	2.59	3.83	3.68	0.53	3.70
Fetching water	2.14	1.56	0.27	1.92	3.93	3.02	0.70	3.60
Total domestic work	25.71	19.81	4.81	23.41	49.20	41.46	26.50	46.50

Source: Authors' estimation based on 2003–04 Sierra Leone IHS.

Table 9.3 Domestic Work According to Per Capita Consumption Status in Sierra Leone, 2003–04

	Men				Women			
	Low 1/3 p.c. cons.	Middle 1/3 p.c. cons.	High 1/3 p.c. cons.	Total	Low 1/3 p.c. cons.	Middle 1/3 p.c. cons.	High 1/3 p.c. cons.	Total
Urban, age 6–14								
Cooking	0.61	0.66	0.60	0.63	1.72	2.10	0.65	1.55
Washing car	0.07	0.02	0.16	0.08	0.05	0.05	0.05	0.05
Sweeping	2.58	1.53	1.96	2.04	3.12	2.16	2.12	2.50
Disposing of garbage	2.28	1.45	1.64	1.81	2.83	1.93	1.89	2.25
Ironing clothes	1.70	0.84	1.29	1.29	1.88	0.73	0.82	1.18
Shopping	0.27	0.14	0.81	0.37	0.53	0.34	0.48	0.45
Taking care of children	0.68	0.39	0.38	0.50	1.64	0.83	0.61	1.07
Running errands	1.18	1.21	1.69	1.33	1.65	1.11	1.10	1.30
Fetching wood	2.42	1.16	1.76	1.80	2.53	1.01	1.48	1.70
Fetching water	3.24	2.06	1.76	2.42	4.01	2.32	1.85	2.81
Total domestic work	15.05	9.46	12.06	12.27	19.96	12.58	11.03	14.87
Urban, age 15+								
Cooking	0.48	0.51	0.43	0.47	6.76	7.56	6.38	6.88
Washing car	0.05	0.06	0.15	0.09	0.27	0.10	0.06	0.14
Sweeping	1.20	0.98	0.63	0.91	2.47	1.89	1.44	1.92
Disposing of garbage	0.99	0.78	0.48	0.72	1.93	1.21	0.88	1.33
Ironing clothes	1.82	1.89	2.06	1.94	1.95	1.53	1.56	1.68
Shopping	1.92	1.86	0.90	1.51	3.44	3.59	3.41	3.48
Taking care of children	2.05	2.30	1.31	1.85	10.91	15.47	12.18	12.82
Running errands	3.64	3.04	2.24	2.90	3.99	3.74	2.40	3.35
Fetching wood	1.23	0.81	0.35	0.75	2.09	1.02	0.56	1.20

Fetching water	1.58	1.19	0.74	1.12	2.55	1.97	1.08	1.84
Total domestic work	14.96	13.41	9.30	12.26	36.37	38.07	29.95	34.64
Rural, age 6–14								
Cooking	1.18	0.52	1.35	1.01	2.25	1.81	1.70	1.92
Washing car	0.00	0.06	0.02	0.03	0.03	0.07	0.12	0.08
Sweeping	2.77	2.40	3.04	2.73	2.87	3.08	3.60	3.20
Disposing of garbage	2.68	2.12	2.57	2.46	2.64	2.85	3.15	2.89
Ironing clothes	0.91	0.66	0.72	0.77	0.80	0.79	0.56	0.71
Shopping	0.94	0.42	0.27	0.55	1.21	0.65	0.49	0.78
Taking care of children	1.58	0.82	0.70	1.05	1.88	1.64	0.98	1.49
Running errands	2.63	1.45	1.58	1.90	2.97	1.61	1.64	2.07
Fetching wood	3.49	3.47	3.97	3.64	3.54	3.47	4.37	3.81
Fetching water	3.64	3.19	3.55	3.46	3.93	3.71	4.14	3.93
Total domestic work	19.82	15.13	17.79	17.59	22.14	19.70	20.75	20.86
Rural, age 15+								
Cooking	0.83	0.89	0.72	0.81	8.85	8.15	9.98	8.99
Washing car	0.04	0.03	0.08	0.05	0.05	0.20	0.15	0.13
Sweeping	1.62	1.32	1.46	1.46	3.28	3.24	3.23	3.25
Disposing of garbage	1.78	1.36	1.46	1.53	2.87	2.55	2.73	2.71
Ironing clothes	1.44	1.62	1.58	1.55	0.85	0.88	1.13	0.96
Shopping	3.46	3.46	2.82	3.23	3.97	4.19	4.90	4.35
Taking care of children	4.02	3.77	2.97	3.55	13.00	13.11	12.06	12.72
Running errands	7.26	6.89	5.97	6.67	6.09	5.93	5.90	5.97
Fetching wood	2.76	2.61	2.44	2.59	3.79	3.50	3.85	3.71
Fetching water	2.28	1.82	1.72	1.93	3.88	3.34	3.60	3.60
Total domestic work	25.51	23.78	21.21	23.36	46.63	45.09	47.52	46.40

Source: Authors' estimation based on 2003–04 Sierra Leone IHS.
p.c. cons. = per capita consumption.

Table 9.4 Domestic Work According to Employment Status in Sierra Leone, 2003–04

	Men				Women			
	Inactive	Not worked in past 12 months	Worked in past 12 months	Total	Inactive	Not worked in past 12 months	Worked in past 12 months	Total
Urban, age 6–14								
Cooking	0.70	0.00	1.17	0.63	1.49	0.00	6.54	1.55
Washing car	0.09	0.00	0.00	0.08	0.06	0.00	0.00	0.05
Sweeping	2.29	0.02	3.14	2.04	2.64	0.04	5.16	2.50
Disposing of garbage	2.06	0.01	1.45	1.81	2.36	0.02	4.96	2.25
Ironing clothes	1.44	0.00	2.08	1.29	1.32	0.00	0.72	1.18
Shopping	0.43	0.00	0.24	0.37	0.47	0.00	1.06	0.45
Taking care of children	0.56	0.00	0.61	0.50	1.18	0.00	1.11	1.07
Running errands	1.50	0.01	1.58	1.33	1.34	0.00	3.48	1.30
Fetching wood	2.00	0.00	3.95	1.80	1.85	0.03	2.52	1.70
Fetching water	2.71	0.01	4.07	2.42	3.05	0.06	4.08	2.81
Total domestic work	13.80	0.06	18.28	12.27	15.76	0.15	29.63	14.87
Urban, age 15+								
Cooking	0.48	1.50	0.45	0.47	4.91	10.05	8.81	6.88
Washing car	0.07	0.00	0.12	0.09	0.05	0.00	0.23	0.14
Sweeping	1.29	1.81	0.49	0.91	1.76	3.26	2.08	1.92
Disposing of garbage	0.98	1.15	0.45	0.72	1.04	2.54	1.61	1.33
Ironing clothes	2.21	4.65	1.63	1.94	1.48	1.33	1.87	1.68
Shopping	0.61	1.67	2.44	1.51	2.18	4.63	4.75	3.48
Taking care of children	1.11	0.97	2.63	1.85	10.49	12.92	15.14	12.82
Running errands	1.79	3.65	4.04	2.90	1.94	6.39	4.72	3.35
Fetching wood	0.91	1.74	0.57	0.75	0.87	2.87	1.53	1.20

Fetching water	1.54	2.39	0.68	1.12	1.49	3.53	2.19	1.84
Total domestic work	11.00	19.53	13.50	12.26	26.21	47.52	42.92	34.64

Rural, age 6–14

Cooking	1.13	0.02	1.36	1.01	2.01	0.04	3.48	1.92
Washing car	0.04	0.00	0.00	0.03	0.08	0.02	0.09	0.08
Sweeping	3.03	0.07	3.81	2.73	3.50	0.05	5.09	3.20
Disposing of garbage	2.70	0.07	3.52	2.46	3.16	0.07	4.58	2.89
Ironing clothes	0.91	0.02	0.74	0.77	0.81	0.00	0.99	0.71
Shopping	0.57	0.02	0.98	0.55	0.78	0.02	1.63	0.78
Taking care of children	0.99	0.00	2.45	1.05	1.53	0.01	2.89	1.49
Running errands	2.19	0.02	2.17	1.90	2.35	0.04	2.77	2.07
Fetching wood	4.03	0.11	5.05	3.64	4.22	0.10	5.72	3.81
Fetching water	3.86	0.11	4.68	3.46	4.37	0.09	5.88	3.93
Total domestic work	19.45	0.45	24.76	17.59	22.82	0.43	33.11	20.86

Rural, age 15+

Cooking	0.91	1.26	0.77	0.81	3.86	9.60	10.14	8.99
Washing car	0.12	0.11	0.03	0.05	0.13	0.00	0.13	0.13
Sweeping	2.22	2.69	1.19	1.46	2.37	5.37	3.43	3.25
Disposing of garbage	2.05	2.79	1.33	1.53	1.90	5.68	2.87	2.71
Ironing clothes	2.02	0.90	1.39	1.55	1.14	1.38	0.91	0.96
Shopping	0.95	1.16	4.04	3.23	1.60	3.49	4.98	4.35
Taking care of children	1.90	1.02	4.16	3.55	7.92	11.01	13.82	12.72
Running errands	2.24	4.01	8.24	6.67	2.26	3.71	6.83	5.97
Fetching wood	3.58	2.70	2.25	2.59	2.45	6.65	3.97	3.71
Fetching water	3.03	2.94	1.53	1.93	2.57	6.78	3.81	3.60
Total domestic work	19.03	19.55	24.92	23.36	26.20	53.67	50.90	46.40

Source: Authors' estimation based on 2003–04 Sierra Leone IHS.

Table 9.5 Domestic Work According to Migration Status in Sierra Leone, 2003–04

	Men				Women			
	Never migrated, migrated before 1991 & missing	Migrated between 1991 and 1999	Migrated after 1999	Total	Never migrated, migrated before 1991 & missing	Migrated between 1991 and 1999	Migrated after 1999	Total
Urban, age 15+								
Cooking	0.47	0.57	0.45	0.47	6.76	6.07	8.02	6.88
Washing car	0.08	0.05	0.20	0.09	0.15	0.03	0.15	0.14
Sweeping	0.87	0.30	1.33	0.91	1.80	0.95	3.09	1.92
Disposing of garbage	0.72	0.15	0.97	0.72	1.17	0.50	2.77	1.33
Ironing clothes	1.85	0.70	2.95	1.94	1.59	0.44	2.79	1.68
Shopping	1.29	1.14	3.05	1.51	3.36	1.83	4.89	3.48
Taking care of children	1.84	0.78	2.33	1.85	13.36	7.03	11.46	12.82
Running errands	2.52	2.86	5.32	2.90	2.88	3.63	6.42	3.35
Fetching wood	0.72	0.45	1.07	0.75	1.07	0.60	2.35	1.20
Fetching water	1.08	0.54	1.61	1.12	1.65	1.13	3.46	1.84
Total domestic work	11.44	7.55	19.28	12.26	33.78	22.21	45.38	34.64

Rural, age 15+

Cooking	0.88	0.20	0.77	0.81	8.66	8.83	10.14	8.99
Washing car	0.06	0.01	0.05	0.05	0.13	0.00	0.17	0.13
Sweeping	1.41	0.77	1.83	1.46	3.27	1.96	3.65	3.25
Disposing of garbage	1.39	0.79	2.16	1.53	2.62	1.58	3.44	2.71
Ironing clothes	1.42	0.62	2.22	1.55	0.82	0.70	1.52	0.96
Shopping	3.06	2.51	3.95	3.23	4.16	2.26	5.77	4.35
Taking care of children	3.55	2.99	3.74	3.55	12.46	13.14	13.46	12.72
Running errands	6.44	6.79	7.30	6.67	6.26	3.53	5.89	5.97
Fetching wood	2.45	1.45	3.36	2.59	3.77	2.27	4.04	3.71
Fetching water	1.91	0.89	2.30	1.93	3.57	2.46	4.14	3.60
Total domestic work	22.58	17.02	27.67	23.36	45.73	36.73	52.22	46.40

Source: Authors' estimation.

345

Table 9.6 Domestic Work According to Household Composition in Sierra Leone, 2003–04

	Urban men		Urban women		Rural men		Rural women	
	Mixed household	All-male household	Mixed household	All-female household	Mixed household	All-male household	Mixed household	All-female household
Cooking	0.43	1.68	6.94	4.28	0.80	2.54	8.99	8.72
Washing car	0.09	0.17	0.15	0.00	0.05	0.27	0.13	0.00
Sweeping	0.90	1.00	1.92	2.02	1.46	1.31	3.25	3.16
Disposing of garbage	0.72	0.75	1.32	1.63	1.53	1.27	2.72	2.39
Ironing clothes	1.97	0.98	1.67	2.05	1.55	0.88	0.96	0.32
Shopping	1.48	2.19	3.49	2.82	3.23	1.69	4.37	2.76
Taking care of children	1.85	2.00	12.95	7.45	3.57	0.00	12.71	13.86
Running errands	2.90	2.66	3.35	2.96	6.68	3.29	5.98	5.11
Fetching wood	0.78	0.03	1.21	0.76	2.60	0.90	3.72	2.66
Fetching water	1.14	0.75	1.84	1.95	1.93	1.60	3.60	3.61
Total domestic work	12.26	12.21	34.84	25.94	23.41	13.76	46.45	42.58

Source: Authors' estimation based on 2003–04 Sierra Leone IHS.

Table 9.7 Determinants of the Number of Hours Spent on Domestic Work per Week in Sierra Leone, 2003–04

	Urban men		Urban women		Rural men		Rural women	
	Coefficient	Standard error	Coefficient	Standard error	Coefficient	Standard error	Coefficient	Standard error
Per capita expenditure	0.223	0.485	0.865	0.787	−2.240***	0.590	−0.818	0.678
Household with water	−7.168***	0.645	−5.992***	0.945	−3.709***	0.640	−5.978***	0.740
Household with electricity	−5.822***	0.719	−5.580***	1.086	−7.454***	1.931	−4.272*	2.377
Worked in last 12 months	0.732	1.002	1.514	1.212	6.016***	1.036	10.597***	1.221
Did not work in last 12 months	−13.06***	1.279	−13.746***	1.888	−18.489***	1.133	−18.663***	1.321
Migrated in 1999 or later	2.534**	1.084	1.527	1.651	5.042***	0.947	6.009***	1.085
Migrated between 1991 & 1999	−6.224***	1.671	−14.315***	2.402	−7.361***	1.540	−11.207***	1.641
All-male household	2.055	1.966			−10.080*	5.671		
All-female household			−3.871	2.626			0.285	3.248
Age of the individual	0.190**	0.093	1.314***	0.143	0.274***	0.096	0.921***	0.115
Age squared	−0.003***	0.001	−0.017***	0.002	−0.004***	0.001	−0.014***	0.001
Primary education	1.056	0.882	−0.859	1.212	1.811**	0.843	1.783*	1.065
Secondary education	−0.801	0.928	−1.358	1.294	−2.378*	1.264	0.310	2.104
Vocational education	0.686	2.208	1.985	3.452	−0.357	3.679	14.718***	5.366
Tertiary education	−1.366	2.484	1.439	5.893	−4.549	4.410		
Koranic education	0.678	13.936	−16.565	28.653	−7.314	9.553	−15.875	34.784
Monogamous household	−0.116	1.332	19.224***	1.638	−3.419**	1.430	15.506***	1.533
Polygamous household	−0.190	1.939	15.737***	2.124	1.001	1.691	13.952***	1.566

continued

Table 9.7 Determinants of the Number of Hours Spent on Domestic Work per Week in Sierra Leone, 2003–04 *continued*

	Urban men		Urban women		Rural men		Rural women	
	Coefficient	Standard error	Coefficient	Standard error	Coefficient	Standard error	Coefficient	Standard error
Divorced individual	-3.419	2.656	11.533***	2.501	-4.379	2.846	2.801	2.469
Widowed individual	-4.463	3.693	12.418***	2.545	-1.368	3.454	6.810***	2.219
Individual in informal union	-6.427**	2.751	34.086***	4.031	-5.596	7.711	46.865***	7.604
Christian individual	0.883	2.596	3.692	3.843	7.875***	2.180	10.485***	2.325
Muslim individual	0.017	2.585	2.688	3.814	7.945***	2.107	8.494***	2.230
Number of infants (age 0–5)	2.139***	0.720	5.631***	1.069	-0.220	0.523	1.734***	0.632
Number of infants squared	-0.543**	0.234	-1.014***	0.341	0.168	0.112	-0.081	0.138
Number of children (age 6–14)	0.231	0.534	0.677	0.783	-0.878**	0.427	-1.884***	0.499
Number of children squared	0.000	0.093	-0.085	0.133	0.044	0.058	0.233***	0.069
Number of adults (age 15–60)	-0.177	0.343	-0.692	0.515	-1.004**	0.467	-2.015***	0.556
Number of adults squared	-0.014	0.024	-0.010	0.036	0.083**	0.041	0.121**	0.049
Number of seniors (age 60+)	1.133**	0.552	-1.872**	0.764	-1.871***	0.479	-0.542	0.567
Constant	17.240***	3.152	8.334*	4.619	15.963***	2.727	14.510***	3.058
Adj. R-square	0.1673		0.3314		0.1699		0.3677	

Source: Authors' estimation based on 2003–04 Sierra Leone IHS.
Notes: The time poverty line is a relative time poverty line, i.e., two times the median of total domestic work hours (20 hours per week). *** at 1% significant level; ** at 5% significant level; * at 10% significant level.

good data on the distance in time separating households from an improved water source when they do not have access to water, and the simple fact of not having access, apart from the distance, is also a key determinant of time use.

As expected, the average number hours spent on domestic work is lower for households with access to water or electricity or both, because, in such cases, the time necessary to fetch wood or water is reduced substantially or even eliminated altogether. For example, urban boys (girls) aged 6 to 14 living in households with no water and electricity have to spend 19 hours (26 hours) on domestic work per week, as opposed to 12 hours for boys and girls in households with access to either water or electricity, and only 7 hours (6 hours) for boys (girls) in households with access to both water and electricity. Urban adult males show a similar pattern: they must spend 24 hours on domestic work if they have no access to water and electricity, 12 hours if they have access to water or electricity, and 6 hours if they have access to both. For female adults as well, the gains are largest when the household has access to both water and electricity (reduction in domestic working time of 19 hours in urban areas and 23 hours in rural areas), but access to only one of the two services already is beneficial.

Table 9.3 presents the average number of hours per week spent on domestic work, according to per capita household total consumption. Rural and urban areas are considered separately for defining the category of the household as belonging to low, middle, or high consumption groups; this means that a household in the top group in rural areas may well have a level of consumption comparable to a household in the middle group in urban areas. The patterns of domestic work according to consumption levels appear to be different in urban versus rural areas. In urban areas, the average number of hours allocated to domestic work decreases with the consumption level among girls and male adults, that is, the higher the consumption of the household, the lower the number of hours spent by its members on domestic work. For example, urban girls in the low consumption group spend 20 hours per week on domestic work, while in the middle consumption group, they spend 13 hours, and in the high consumption group, they spend only 11 hours on domestic work. Urban men in the low consumption group allocate 15 hours per week to domestic work, and this decreases to 13 hours and 9 hours, respectively, in the middle and high consumption groups. However, this decrease is not obvious among urban boys and female adults. For urban boys, those in middle consumption group spend less time on domestic work than those in both low and high consumption groups. For urban women, those in the middle consumption group have the highest number of hours of domestic work.

In rural areas, the patterns for domestic work according to consumption levels look different in two respects. First, the differences in number of hours allocated to domestic work are smaller between the various consumption groups. Second, except for adult men, individuals (that is, women, girls, and boys) in the middle consumption group spend less time on domestic work than individuals in the high consumption group, although again the differences are relatively small. The fact that differences by consumption group are larger in urban areas than in rural areas could be because of the correlation between consumption and housing infrastructure. In urban areas, the correlation is stronger than in rural areas simply because access rates are much lower in rural areas. Another potential explanation could be that, in urban areas, hiring domestic workers is easier and more common than in rural areas, hence richer households can more easily reduce their domestic work time by employing servants at home.

In table 9.4, domestic work time statistics are presented according to the employment status of the individual, by distinguishing individuals who are inactive from those who are in the labor force but have not worked in the past 12 months and those who have worked in the past 12 months. The results show that, among several gender-age groups, those who worked in the labor market over the past 12 months spend *more* time on domestic work than those who did not work. For rural men, the domestic work time is 25 hours for those engaged in the labor market, verses 20 hours for those not engaged in the labor market. As for those who are inactive (not in the labor force), the amount of domestic work is also below that observed for those who did work over the past 12 months. It is also noteworthy that children who declared themselves not working over the past 12 months are also protected from domestic work. While there may be data issues in all these results, and while a close investigation of the relationship between domestic and labor market work is warranted, the results do suggest that rural male adults who are most dynamic and find work in the labor market also tend to shoulder a large share of the domestic work burden.

In table 9.5, domestic work time data are presented according to the migration status of the household. The specific social context of Sierra Leone during and after the civil war (1991–99) provides an opportunity to use the migration status of the household as a proxy for its dynamism, in a similar way to what was done for employment. The civil war, which started in 1991, forced many households to migrate, as the activities of a major rebel force, the Revolutionary United Front of Sierra Leone, led many rural households to move to cities, especially to the capital, Freetown. The war ended in 1999, after which some households moved back to their place of origin or migrated to new places in search of better jobs. In table 9.5, individuals are classified according to whether they belong to a household that migrated between 1991 and 1999, migrated after 1999, or never migrated (this group also includes households for which data on migration are missing). Given that the migration decision is rarely taken by children, and that most children were not alive yet before 1991 (and many were not born between 1991 and 1999), the estimates are presented only for adult men and women.

It turns out that in both rural and urban areas, and among both adult men and women, those who belong to households who moved after 1999 have the highest number of hours allocated to domestic work, while those who moved between 1991 and 1999 tend to have the lowest number of hours for domestic work. For example, in rural areas, among men, the average number of hours allocated to domestic work per week is 28 for those who migrated after 1999, and 17 for those who migrated between 1991 and 1999; among women, the average number of hours for domestic work is 52 for those who migrated after 1999, and 37 for those who migrated between 1991 and 1999. We provide these statistics because the decision to migrate is a major event for households, and the regression analysis in the next section shows that this decision correlates with domestic time worked. However, this correlation is difficult to interpret, because the links between this decision and time use may be complex; thus, in the next section, we will simply treat this variable as a control.

Finally, table 9.6 provides the time use statistics according to the structure of the household, namely, whether household members are of mixed genders or not. This is a way to look at how personal preferences affect domestic work. We compare the number of hours per week spent on domestic work for all-male households, all-female households, and mixed households. The results, presented in table 9.6, show that men in all-male households spend less time on domestic work than men in mixed households. This difference is especially large among rural men. In rural areas, men in all-male households allocate 14 hours per week to domestic work, while men in mixed households allocate 23 hours to such work. In all-male households, the time allocated to cooking increases significantly as compared to mixed households, but time for most other activities decreases. In all-female households, women spend much more time on domestic work than men in all-male households, but less time than women in mixed households. In urban areas, women in all-female households spend 26 hours per week on domestic work, while women in mixed households spend 35 hours; in rural areas, women in all-female households allocate 43 hours per week to domestic work while women in mixed households allocate 46 hours. The presence of children must always be considered as part of the demographic variables affecting time use, suggesting the need for regression analysis.

It should be noted that the Sierra Leone questionnaire has a fairly extensive list of domestic activities, including time spent supervising children. This detailed time use module, together with very low levels of access to basic infrastructure, tends to result in a high number of hours spent on domestic work. How do the domestic time use data presented for Sierra Leone compare to those in other low-income countries? In Sierra Leone, the average time spent on domestic work by women aged 15 years and older is 15 hours per week in urban areas and 46 hours in rural areas. This compares to about 23 hours nationally in Guinea (Bardasi and Wodon 2006a, 2006b) and 24 hours in Malawi (Wodon and Beegle 2006). In a review of UN surveys on time use, Charmes (2006) estimates that the domestic time work for women reached 24.4 hours per week in Benin, 46.2 hours in Madagascar, 45.9 hours in Mauritius, and 40.0 hours in South Africa. Thus, Sierra Leone's estimates of domestic time use are on the high side, but they are not outside the interval observed for other countries, since it is not that uncommon to find in other countries that women spend between 40 and 50 hours per week on domestic work alone.

Regression Analysis

The profile of time use according to individual and household characteristics presented in the previous section is useful, but it does not provide a precise idea of the correlates or determinants of domestic work. For example, as mentioned in the discussion of the relationship between domestic work and consumption level, the fact that there is a negative correlation in urban areas between consumption and domestic work time may not be directly related to the economic status of the household, but, instead, to the fact that richer households have access to better infrastructure services. For assessment of the links between individual and household characteristics and domestic work while controlling for the potential effect of other characteristics, regression analysis is needed.

In table 9.7, regressions for the determinants or correlates of domestic work are presented separately for urban men, urban women, rural men, and rural women. The dependent variable is the individual's total domestic work time per week. The independent variables include household per capita consumption, access to water and electricity, employment status in the labor market, migration status, and the gender type of the household. In addition, we also control for age, gender, education level, marital status, and religion, as well as for geographic location, household size, and household composition.

In most cases, the level of per capita consumption of the household does not have a statistically significant impact on domestic work time, except for rural men, where higher consumption is associated with lower workload. By contrast, access to water and electricity decreases domestic work time for both men and women in both rural and urban areas. The reduction in work time varies between 4 and 7 hours each for access to water and electricity, with time savings of a similar order of magnitude for men and women, as well as in urban and rural areas (yet, time savings for urban men in fetching water are larger than for rural men).

In terms of household structure, the impact of being in an all-male or all-female household is not statistically significant. Except for the case of rural men, individuals in households with a larger number of infants (aged 0 to 5) allocate more time to domestic work, probably in part because they need to take care of those infants. By contrast, the number of children aged 6 to 14 does not affect domestic work time for adults in a significant way in urban areas; and in rural areas, a higher number of children actually reduces the amount of domestic work performed by adults, presumably because the children play a larger part in the domestic work there. The same phenomenon is observed for the number of adults, which does not have a statistically significant impact on domestic work in urban areas, but does reduce the time allocated to domestic tasks in rural areas. The impact of the number of seniors is not stable across the four samples according to location and gender.

Finally, individual level characteristics also play a role in determining the amount of domestic work performed by the individual. First, the time spent on domestic work increases with age. Second, in most cases, education is not correlated in a statistically significant way with domestic work. Third, this is not the case for employment. In urban areas, there are no statistically significant differences in domestic work between those who have worked during the past 12 months in the labor market and those who are inactive (the reference category); but those who have not worked during the past 12 months also spend significantly less time (13 to 14 hours) on domestic work than either the inactive or those who have worked in the labor market. In rural areas, those who have worked over the past 12 months in the labor market have the highest burden of domestic work, followed by the inactive and those who have not worked during the past 12 months.

The migration variables (defined at the household level) show a similar pattern, with those who migrated after 1999 allocating the most time to domestic work, followed by those who never migrated, while those who migrated between 1991 and 1999 allocate the least time to domestic tasks (as mentioned earlier, this relationship is not necessarily easy to interpret, and additional work would be needed to better understand the transmission channel that could be at work here).

For women, being in a domestic union (as opposed to being single) leads to an increase in domestic work, which is especially large when the women are in an informal union. In rural areas, women of Christian or Muslim faith work more on domestic tasks than the excluded category (animists, agnostics, and so on).

It is important to note that the results presented in table 9.7 are indicative only. One issue is that of causality, which cannot be claimed with the limited analysis used in this study and in the absence of panel data, for example, to better measure the impact of access to basic infrastructure. Another issue is the possibility of the presence of non-linear relationships between the explanatory variables and the time use outcomes. This is not likely to be too serious a problem here, given that most of the explanatory variables are dichotomic and that we have allowed for non-linearity in the effect of demographic variables;

however, further tests could be performed. Still another potential issue is related to the type of econometric methods of investigation used. We have not compared the results of log linear regressions with those that could be obtained with matching methods, for example. In work by Bardasi and Wodon (2009) using data on Guinea, the results obtained with both matching methods and linear regressions were broadly similar.

Conclusions

Who bears the burden of domestic work in Sierra Leone? To a large extent, the results provided in this chapter confirm conventional wisdom: Women are found to work much more than men on domestic tasks, especially in rural areas. The workload of a rural adult female individual reaches more than 46 hours per week, a level that would be considered as a full-time occupation in many countries. A second finding is that, for many children, the burden of domestic work is high as well, reaching more than 20 hours per week on average in some cases. A third finding that was expected is the fact that access to basic infrastructure services (water and electricity) makes a large difference in the amount of time spent on domestic work. According to regression results, an adult individual living in a household with access to both water and electricity may expect his or her domestic work time to be reduced by 10 hours per week in both urban and rural areas.

The analysis in this study is descriptive, but it does have bearings for policy, although care must be taken before putting forth policy recommendations. For example, children in Sierra Leone today work a substantial number of hours, and incentives for parents to reduce this workload could lead to better education outcomes. Among incentives that have proven successful in increasing school attendance and reducing domestic work in many countries, for example, are conditional cash transfers. Yet, as suggested by Ravallion and Wodon (2000), while such transfers can indeed lead to more schooling, they may have only a limited effect on child labor if what gives is the child's leisure time.

Yet, some findings were perhaps less expected. Conventional wisdom on the division of labor within the household suggests that those who work in the labor market spend less time on domestic work than those who do not work in the labor market. The results presented in this study suggest a more nuanced outcome: some of those who work in the labor market may actually spend more time on domestic work than those who do not work in the labor market. In a country such as Sierra Leone, where jobs are mostly in the informal sector, which gives flexibility in terms of working hours outside of the home, this result perhaps could be explained by the dynamism of individuals who work in the labor market, that is, individuals who may also be ready to pitch in more at home. Other individuals might be less willing to put in a lot of effort, whether at home or outside it. This is, of course, speculative; it could also be argued that reducing the domestic work burden of women might potentially enable women to get better jobs in the labor market, instead of simply working longer hours in their current occupation. This could then have a much larger beneficial impact on household income and consumption. Still, while a much more detailed analysis would be required to understand the implications of this finding for the relationship between time poverty and income or consumption poverty, the results do suggest that care must be taken in discussing the potential reduction in monetary poverty that could be achieved by freeing time previously allocated to domestic chores through access to infrastructure services.

Note
1. Although causality cannot be claimed with the limited analysis used in this study, and other econometric methods of investigation could be used, the correlation is strong and access is likely to be exogenous.

References

Bardasi, E., and Q. Wodon. 2006a. "Measuring Time Poverty and Analyzing Its Deter-minants: Concepts and Applications to Guinea." In *Gender, Time Use, and Poverty in Sub-Saharan Africa,* ed. C. M. Blackden and Q. Wodon. World Bank Working Paper 73. Washington, DC: World Bank.

———. 2006b. "Poverty Reduction from Full Employment: A Time Use Approach." In *Gender, Time Use, and Poverty in Sub-Saharan Africa,* ed. C. M. Blackden and Q. Wodon. World Bank Working Paper 73. Washington, DC: World Bank.

———. 2009. "Access to Basic Infrastructure and Time Use in Guinea." Unpublished paper, Development Dialogue on Values and Ethics, World Bank, Washington, DC.

———. 2010. "Working Long Hours With No Choice: Time Poverty in Guinea," *Feminist Economics*, forthcoming.

Barwell, I. 1996. "Transport and the Village: Findings from African Village-Level Travel and Transport Surveys and Related Studies." Discussion Paper 344, Africa Region Series, World Bank, Washington, D.C.

Berio, A. J. 1983. "Time Allocation Surveys." Paper presented at the 11th International Congress of Anthropology Sciences, Vancouver, Canada.

Blackden, C. M., and C. Bhanu. 1999. *Gender, Growth, and Poverty Reduction: Special Program of Assistance for Africa 1998 Status Report on Poverty*. World Bank Technical Paper 428. Washington DC: World Bank.

Blackden, C. M., and Q. Wodon, ed. 2006. *Gender, Time Use, and Poverty in Sub-Saharan Africa*, World Bank Working Paper 73. Washington, DC: World Bank.

Charmes, J. 2006. "A Review of Empirical Evidence on Time Use in Africa from UN-sponsored Surveys." In *Gender, Time Use, and Poverty in Sub-Saharan Africa,* ed. C. M. Blackden and Q. Wodon. World Bank Working Paper 73. Washington, DC: World Bank.

Harvey, A. S., and M. E. Taylor. 2002. "Time Use." In *Designing Household Survey Questionnaires for Developing Countries, Lessons from 15 Years of the Living Standards Measurement Survey,* ed. M. Grosh and P. Glewwe. Washington, DC: World Bank.

Ilahi, N. 2000. "The Intra-household Allocation of Time and Tasks: What Have We Learnt from the Empirical Literature?" Policy Research Report on Gender and Development, Working Paper Series 13, World Bank, Washington, DC.

Ilahi, N., and F. Grimard. 2000. "Public Infrastructure and Private Costs: Water Supply and Time Allocation of Women in Rural Pakistan." *Economic Development and Cultural Change* 49 (1): 45–75.

Malmberg-Calvo, C. 1994. "Case Study on the Role of Women in Rural Transport: Access of Women to Domestic Facilities," SSATP Working Paper 11, Technical Department, Africa Region, World Bank, Washington, DC.

Ravallion, M., and Q. Wodon. 2000. "Does Child Labor Displace Schooling? Evidence on Behavioral Responses to an Enrollment Subsidy." *Economic Journal* 110 (462): C158–75.

Wodon, Q., and K. Beegle. 2006. "Labor Shortages Despite Underemployment? Seasonality in Time Use in Malawi." In *Gender, Time Use, and Poverty in Sub-Saharan Africa,* ed. C. M. Blackden and Q. Wodon. World Bank Working Paper 73. Washington, DC: World Bank.

World Bank. 2001. *Engendering Development: Through Gender Equality in Rights, Resources, and Voice,* World Bank Policy Research Report. Washington, DC: World Bank.

Part 5

Disparities in Bargaining Power

Chapter **10**

Gender Labor Income Shares and Human Capital Investment in the Republic of Congo

Prospere Backiny-Yetna and Quentin Wodon

Introduction

Despite general consensus on the existence of gender disparities in African labor markets, assessing their nature, extent, and implications remains a challenge. Databases provide incomplete and limited information on the relative situations of men and women. And empirical studies use diverse methodologies and definitions of employment and earnings, which makes comparability difficult, and focus mostly on urban areas (see, for instance, Appleton, Hoddinott, and Krishnan 1999; Brilleau, Roubaud, and Torelli 2004). Drawing on a meta-analysis of studies on the gender pay gap, Weichselbaumer, Winter-Ebmer, and Zwei-müller (2007) find that only a small minority of empirical studies conducted on the topic since the 1960s draw on African data.

In West and Central Africa, most of the household surveys available do not record labor incomes, or do so very imperfectly, in large part because most workers are involved in informal sector activities that often are not compensated through wages. However, the Republic of Congo is an exception: it is a fairly rich economy by African standards, in large part resulting from oil resources. Some 80 percent of the population lives in urban areas, especially in two major cities—the capital Brazzaville and Pointe Noire, where most of the oil-related activity is concentrated.

The conceptual framework and empirical methodology used in the section, "Impact of Gender Labor Income Shares on Consumption," of this chapter follow closely a similar paper on Senegal by Bussolo, De Hoyos, and Wodon (2009). The authors gratefully acknowledge comments from Jorge Arbache and Mayra Buvinic. The views expressed in the chapter are those of the authors and need not reflect those of the World Bank, its executive directors, or the countries they represent.

As a result of a high level of urbanization and a substantial share of the workforce involved in wage labor, it is feasible not only to compare the earnings of men and women, but also to assess how they affect consumption choices. Thus, the focus on the effect of labor incomes on consumption choices in this paper stems from recognition in the literature that higher labor incomes for women can have significant beneficial impacts for poverty reduction and human development.

As noted, among others, in Bussolo, De Hoyos, and Wodon (2009), whose analysis and framework this study follows closely, at least three different aspects of poverty can be related to the decisions made by various household members in terms of their allocation of time and their prospects for labor income. First, traditional consumption-based poverty is directly related to the earnings of household members, as well as to household size. Both factors depend in part on who is working in the household and how much various household members earn.

Second, the issue of relative power within the household (whether the household head or the spouse makes key decisions, either separately or jointly) also depends on the earnings of various household members. The unitary model of the household—which assumes that the household acts as if it were a single utility-maximizing individual with defined preferences and a budget constraint—has long been challenged by economists. Instead, what has emerged from the literature of the past 20 years is a bargaining model that assumes that household members differ in their preferences and engage in a negotiation process to maximize their personal utility (see, among others, Bourguignon and Chiappori 1992; Hoddinott and Haddad 1995; Browning and Chiappori 1998; Bussolo, De Hoyos, and Wodon 2009). This bargaining model implies that the income share controlled by women may have important long-term effects on investments in the human capital of children. The empirical evidence to date does indeed suggest that, when women are less engaged in income-generating activities, they have less influence on household decision making and on how the household invests in the human capital of children, which may reduce the likelihood that their children will avoid poverty in the future.

Third, time poverty—that is, working more hours than is desirable without much choice not to because of financial poverty—is an important welfare measure in its own right. It is the direct result of the decisions made within the household regarding the allocation of both domestic and productive work. For example, women tend to work much less in the labor market, but this is more than compensated for by long hours spent on domestic work, so that they tend to be more time-poor than men (that is, a larger share of women than men work long hours) (Blackden and Wodon 2006).

This study focuses on the second of the above three aspects related to the importance of the role of women in labor markets. It uses a recent, nationally representative household survey for the Republic of Congo—the 2005 ECOM

(Enquête Congolaise auprès des Ménages 2005) survey—to test the unitary model of household consumption. Congo is a good country for such an analysis because the correlation in the survey data between consumption and income is especially good in Congo. That is, income sources are not substantially underestimated in Congo as is often the case in other African countries.[1] This accuracy enables a proper analysis of the links between income data and consumption patterns. As in much of the rest of the literature, this study finds that a higher labor income share obtained by women does indeed lead to a higher share of household consumption allocated to investments in human capital (as proxied through spending for food, education, health, and children's clothing). The impact is not negligible and it is statistically significant, suggesting long-term benefits through children from efforts to increase female labor income.

This chapter is structured as follows. First, basic data is provided on income sources in Congo, as well as a brief analysis of the characteristics and correlates of wage income. This is followed by a description of the study's conceptual framework and empirical methodology to test the unitary model of the household. Next, empirical results are presented, followed by conclusions.

Income Sources in the Republic of Congo

Basic data on income sources in Congo, as well as an assessment of the characteristics and correlates of wage income as measured at the individual level are provided in this section. Since other income sources are measured at the household level, they cannot be disaggregated by gender. Given that wages represent a large share of total income in Congo, the problem of not being able to identify other income sources by gender is likely not to be too serious for the analysis that follows.

Data
Providing a context for the rest of the chapter, this section gives simple summary statistics on the various income sources obtained by households in Congo using the 2005 nationally representative ECOM survey. Aggregate income is calculated using two sources of data: the section of the survey questionnaire about income and revenue and the section about (cash) transfers received from other households. Income includes wages, profits from agricultural activities (including auto-consumption), profits from non-agricultural activities, public transfers (work pension, grants), private transfers, property revenue, exceptional revenue, and fictitious income (rent attributed to home-owning households and value of use of durable goods). The rent attributed to home-owning households and the use value for durable goods are considered as both consumption and revenue items. Where appropriate (in particular for wages), the aggregate

household income was calculated at the individual level before consolidating individual data at the household level.

The analysis is conducted on 4,774 households that declared a monetary income (excluding fictitious income). The 228 households (4.6 percent of the sample) with zero income were excluded from the analysis (these excluded households appear to be distributed relatively evenly across quintiles of living standards, thereby reducing the risk of selection bias due to non-response). We observe a rather good correlation between total household income and house-hold consumption, as suggested in table 10.1. Household income per capita increases with the standard of living quintiles, and the average annual house-hold income amounts to CFAF 1.753 million (Congolese francs), while consumption totals 1.516 million CFAF, that is, a ratio of 1.16.

Share of Households Receiving Various Income Sources

Table 10.2 provides data on sources of income in Congo. The analysis first considers how common income sources are in terms of the share of households receiving income from each source (beneficiary incidence). With the exception of fictitious income, the most common type of household income comes from non-agricultural enterprises, while the least common is income from property and public transfers. For almost 6 households in 10, a non-agricultural enterprise can be observed, more so in rural areas (7 in 10) than in urban areas (almost half). These enterprises are, for the most part, to be found in the informal sector and have few or no barriers to entry (low capital, absence of legislation, and so on), thus explaining the extent of the phenomenon. All types of households are concerned, both poor and non-poor, although in cities, this type of activity is relatively less common among households in the richest quintile of per capita consumption. After income from non-agricultural enterprises, private

Table 10.1 Household Income and Consumption by Quintile of Consumption in the Republic of Congo, 2005

	Urban		Rural		National	
	Income (CFAF 1,000)	Consumption (CFAF 1,000)	Income (CFAF 1,000)	Consumption (CFAF 1,000)	Income (CFAF 1,000)	Consumption (CFAF 1,000)
Poorest quintile	1,022.6	657.4	617.0	452.3	774.2	531.7
Second quintile	1,269.8	933.5	823.8	686.3	1,027.7	799.3
Third quintile	1,775.4	1,300.8	1,012.4	1,005.5	1,442.2	1,171.9
Fourth quintile	2,114.8	1,739.8	1,088.3	1,330.1	1,795.3	1,612.3
Richest quintile	4,282.0	3,800.1	1,763.5	2,246.6	3,708.2	3,446.2
Total	2,352.9	1,937.7	944.1	948.0	1,753.0	1,516.3

Source: Authors' calculations based on 2005 ECOM household survey. For more information on the ECOM survey, see Centre national de la statistique et des études économiques 2004.

Table 10.2 Household Income in the Republic of Congo According to Sources, 2005

		% households with this income			% household income			Share of households in income		
		Urban	Rural	Congo, Rep. of	Urban	Rural	Congo, Rep. of	Urban	Rural	Congo, Rep. of
Wages	Poorest	24.3	9.0	17.3	22.7	3.7	16.2	3.2	2.2	3.1
	Q2	35.2	6.2	22.3	33.3	8.3	27.2	8.3	5.4	8.0
	Q3	41.1	12.6	28.8	39.0	32.8	37.1	11.2	32.8	13.6
	Q4	47.8	11.8	31.9	53.0	12.2	42.9	24.0	14.5	22.9
	Richest	56.0	18.7	39.6	51.0	21.2	45.0	53.3	45.1	52.4
	Total	43.0	12.4	29.5	45.9	18.0	39.2	100.0	100.0	100.0
Income from agricultural enterprise	Poorest	24.1	95.2	56.6	8.7	51.3	23.3	23.9	18.9	19.9
	Q2	18.6	92.1	51.2	4.4	36.0	12.1	21.6	14.3	15.8
	Q3	14.6	86.2	45.5	3.0	29.1	10.9	16.5	17.9	17.6
	Q4	13.1	86.5	45.5	1.8	34.3	9.8	16.1	25.1	23.3
	Richest	6.9	71.5	35.4	1.1	18.2	4.5	21.9	23.8	23.4
	Total	14.3	84.8	45.5	2.4	29.3	8.8	100.0	100.0	100.0
Income from non-agricultural enterprise	Poorest	56.3	65.7	60.6	26.2	21.5	24.6	9.0	8.6	8.9
	Q2	54.3	71.7	62.0	27.2	27.0	27.1	16.5	11.7	15.0
	Q3	51.0	70.4	59.3	20.9	20.1	20.7	14.6	13.4	14.2
	Q4	45.5	75.2	58.6	15.3	25.4	17.8	16.8	20.2	17.9
	Richest	39.7	67.1	51.8	17.0	32.4	20.1	43.1	46.1	44.0
	Total	48.1	70.0	57.8	18.9	26.9	20.8	100.0	100.0	100.0
Public transfers	Poorest	11.5	1.4	6.9	9.8	1.8	7.0	9.0	10.2	9.1
	Q2	10.8	4.1	7.8	8.3	2.8	7.0	13.4	17.6	13.8
	Q3	11.8	2.6	7.8	5.3	0.8	3.9	9.9	7.8	9.7

continued

Table 10.2 Household Income in the Republic of Congo According to Sources, 2005 *continued*

		% households with this income			% household income			Share of households in income		
		Urban	Rural	Congo, Rep. of	Urban	Rural	Congo, Rep. of	Urban	Rural	Congo, Rep. of
	Q4	10.8	3.4	7.6	5.5	1.3	4.5	16.1	14.8	16.0
	Richest	8.2	5.6	7.0	7.6	2.4	6.6	51.6	49.7	51.5
	Total	10.4	3.6	7.4	7.1	1.9	5.8	100.0	100.0	100.0
Private transfers	Poorest	42.4	36.3	39.6	8.6	4.6	7.2	7.6	8.2	7.7
	Q2	46.3	39.9	43.5	6.8	6.5	6.7	10.6	12.5	11.0
	Q3	50.8	49.2	50.1	9.8	3.6	7.9	17.5	10.7	16.1
	Q4	54.0	52.9	53.5	8.0	9.8	8.4	22.5	34.5	25.0
	Richest	53.2	51.3	52.3	6.4	5.4	6.2	41.7	34.2	40.2
	Total	50.1	46.8	48.7	7.3	6.1	7.0	100.0	100.0	100.0
Revenue from property	Poorest	3.6	0.5	2.2	1.0	0.1	0.7	3.2	3.3	3.2
	Q2	7.8	0.4	4.5	1.8	0.1	1.4	9.8	4.3	9.6
	Q3	7.5	0.4	4.4	2.8	0.2	2.0	17.6	16.4	17.6
	Q4	5.8	0.4	3.4	1.4	0.4	1.2	14.0	52.3	15.0
	Richest	7.3	0.6	4.4	2.4	0.1	2.0	55.4	23.8	54.6
	Total	6.5	0.5	3.9	2.1	0.2	1.6	100.0	100.0	100.0

Other monetary revenue	Poorest	12.4	6.4	9.7	4.2	1.6	3.3	8.4	19.7	9.3
	Q2	12.7	5.6	9.5	4.2	1.1	3.4	14.6	14.6	14.6
	Q3	11.3	6.7	9.3	4.1	0.5	3.0	16.4	10.3	15.9
	Q4	8.6	3.2	6.2	3.0	0.5	2.4	18.8	11.7	18.2
	Richest	11.1	4.1	8.0	2.8	1.0	2.5	41.8	43.6	41.9
	Total	11.1	5.0	8.4	3.3	0.9	2.7	100.0	100.0	100.0
Fictitious income	Poorest	99.3	99.1	99.2	18.8	15.6	17.7	6.5	10.8	7.5
	Q2	99.4	99.7	99.5	14.1	18.3	15.1	11.5	11.6	11.5
	Q3	99.2	99.7	99.4	15.2	12.8	14.5	13.2	18.0	14.3
	Q4	99.7	99.9	99.8	12.1	16.1	13.1	20.8	21.4	20.9
	Richest	99.4	99.9	99.6	11.7	19.2	13.2	48.0	38.2	45.7
	Total	99.4	99.7	99.5	13.0	16.9	13.9	100.0	100.0	100.0

Source: Authors' calculations based on 2005 ECOM household survey.

transfers (for example, from other households) are the second most common source of income. Like income from non-agricultural enterprises, transfers are enjoyed by all categories of households.

The level of private transfers, at least in terms of the extent of the phenomenon, suggests a relatively high degree of solidarity in Congolese society. Almost half of all households benefit from a transfer from another household (in Congo or abroad), although this is not necessarily the case for poor households. By contrast, public transfers benefit only 7 percent of households. The beneficiary incidence is slightly pro-poor in urban areas (almost 11.5 percent of households in the first quintile are beneficiaries compared to 8.2 percent in the richest quintile), but poorly targeted in the rest of the country. In terms of benefit incidence, however, which takes into account the amounts received apart from who receives transfers, public transfers are clearly benefiting better-off households most.

Income from property and exceptional gains is the least common form of income. Income from property (received by less than 4 percent of households) can be observed in urban areas, mostly among more affluent households. This income may require an investment (real estate income, for example), and this investment is more often accessible by more affluent households. Finally, agricultural income is the third most common source of household income; yet, a large proportion of agricultural households do not receive monetary income from this activity and practice subsistence agriculture. Monetary agricultural income is observed for only one-third of households, while less than one-third earn wages from this activity. Monetary agricultural income is less common in the richest quintile than in the other quintiles. By contrast, wages are more likely to be received among better-off households.

Share of Various Income Sources in Total Household Income

What matters more for this analysis is the share of various income sources in total income. Wages represent the main source of household income, followed by non-agricultural enterprises; these two sources alone account for more than 60 percent of total income; however, the proportion of cash income represented by both sources is higher, since total income also includes fictitious income, such as the rental value of owner occupied dwellings, the use value of durable consumption goods, as well as auto-consumption.

Wages account for 39.2 percent of all income—the share of wages is higher in urban areas, where they account for 45.9 percent of income—and this is also the income source most positively correlated with standard of living. To illustrate this, wages account for almost 16.2 percent of income in the poorest quintile, 27 percent in the next quintile, and 45 percent of the richest quintile. Non-agricultural enterprises are the main source of income for households in the first quintile (representing a quarter of all income), slightly ahead of agricultural income, and well ahead of wages. If, however, auto-consumption is omitted from agricultural income, this source would fall behind wages for this category of households (the poorest quintile). Although more than two households in five practice an agricultural activity, agricultural income is relatively low, thereby explaining poverty among the rural population. Generally speaking, the small size of the areas farmed, low capital (implying low rates of mechanisation in agriculture), and insufficient use of inputs result in low output in the agricultural sector, which is more characteristic of subsistence agriculture, as illustrated by the high proportion of auto-consumption in agricultural income (almost half of agricultural income is in fact auto-consumption).

Public and private transfers represent close to 13 percent of household income, which is a relatively large proportion. This figure is higher in towns, where transfers account for almost 14 percent of total household income, compared to only 8 percent in rural areas. Examining the relative share of the different income sources in total household income highlights the importance of income from activity and shows that the labor force, the soil, and solidarity are the main factors of production of the population. Indeed, income from property, which is primarily income from capital, accounts for less than 2 percent of household income (although it must be noted that capital income may not be measured accurately).

The two most common types of household income are among those for which inequalities are most pronounced. With regard to wages, the poorest 40 percent of households account for only 11 percent of income from wages, whereas the richest quintile alone accounts for more than half of this source of income. Earning a wage is, to some extent, a privilege. It can be shown that a proportional increase in wages would benefit mostly the non-poor and would increase inequality (this can be demonstrated using a source decomposition of the Gini index of inequality), even if a proportion of the wages is redistributed among the households in the form of private transfers. Income from non-agricultural enterprises is also highly unequal. If it is hypothesized that in order to obtain a large income from this type of activity, a certain amount of capital is required—which, because of imperfections in the credit market, is more accessible to people who are already non-poor by means of auto-financing—one element therefore explains the other.

At the other extreme, agricultural income (including auto-consumption) is less unequal. The poorest 20 percent of the population account for 19.9 percent of agricultural income, and the richest 20 percent for 23.4 percent. Although a large number of poor people earn their living from agriculture, the non-poor nevertheless account for relatively more of this type of income. The explanation is the same as before: the non-poor have better quality means of production and they demonstrate higher productivity and higher income. Unsurprisingly, income from property is firmly in the hands of the richest households; the households in the highest quintile account for almost 60 percent of this category of income and the poorest quintile, only 3.3 percent.

Characteristics and Correlates of Wage Income

Wage-paying jobs are less likely among women, who also have a lower average level of education than men. Less well-educated people often have no choice but to resort to agriculture or self-employed non-agricultural activities, and the low returns from these jobs often force them into poverty. The public sector accounts for 46 percent of wage employment, while private firms account for 34 percent; large companies provide only 12 percent of wage-paying jobs. The importance of the public sector for wage work is also reflected in the employment structure of each economic sector. The services (administration, education/healthcare, and other services) account for more than 60 percent of wage-paying jobs. By contrast, trade and agriculture provide few wage-paying jobs (9 percent and 4 percent, respectively), and jobs in industry are rare (less than 9 percent).

As mentioned, analyzing the distribution of wages highlights substantial inequalities. The average wage is CFAF 149,000 per month (about US$300), but half of all wage-earners earn less than CFAF 80,000 per month. As expected, wages are affected by age (which is a proxy for professional experience) and education level. Taking the average wage of individuals under age 30 as a reference, the wages of people aged 30–39 are more than one-third higher and those of individuals 40-49 are almost twice as high. Similarly, wages increase significantly with level of education.

To confirm these results, we performed a standard regression analysis. The dependent variable is the logarithm of the hourly wage. The independent variables are education, professional experience (measured by the estimated number of years of professional experience), and other variables (gender, nationality, residence, institutional sector, and branch of activity).

The results (table 10.3) suggest good returns on education and professional experience, as well as a higher level of wages in the public sector than in other sectors. Individuals with lower secondary, higher secondary, and tertiary education earn wages approximately 40 percent, 74 percent, and 157 percent higher, respectively, than individuals with no formal education. However, there is no statistically significant difference in wages between a person who abandoned studies at the primary level and someone who never went to school.

With regard to professional experience, an extra year of work increases wages by about 2 percent, which results in relatively high wages for individuals over age 50. Compared to those working in private micro-enterprises, an individual with the same characteristics working in the public sector earns on average 83 percent more, whereas a person working in a large private company earns 66 percent more. Finally, with regard to the sector of activity, it is more advantageous to work outside the agricultural sector, in particular in mining (133 percent

Table 10.3 Determinants and Basic Statistics Concerning Individuals' Wages in the Republic of Congo, 2005

Variable	Details	Regression		Monthly wage and structure		
		Estimated parameter	Student T	Average wage	Median wage	Employee structure
Education	None	ref	ref	62,819	40,000	4.5
	Primary	0.0221	0.13	63,794	40,000	9.3
	Secondary 1	0.3342**	2.22	105,277	61,000	28.4
	Secondary 2	0.5560***	3.65	129,285	80,000	31.3
	Higher	0.9473***	6.02	263,879	113,000	26.5
Experience	Experience	0.0231***	2.69	—	—	—
	Experience squared	−0.0001	−0.62	—	—	—
Age	Under 30	—	—	91,719	46,000	17.6
	30 to 39	—	—	122,574	70,000	30.4
	40 to 49	—	—	166,962	98,446	32.2
	50 to 59	—	—	228,958	108,000	16.9
	60 and over	—	—	110,751	60,000	3.0
Gender	Male	ref	ref	158,207	83,000	74.8
	Female	−0.2296***	−3.38	121,867	60,000	25.3
Nationality	Non-Congolese	ref	ref	142,688	80,000	5.2
	Congolese	−0.1413	−0.88	149,376	79,000	94.8
Residence	Rural	ref	ref	91,222	60,000	18.2
	Urban	0.3196***	4.48	161,870	80,000	81.8
Institution	Public	0.6074***	6.38	190,581	100,000	46.3
	Large private firm	0.5085***	4.83	189,682	90,000	12.2
	Private micro-enterprise	ref	ref	125,104	65,000	22.0
	Associative firm	0.2435	1.40	72,382	60,000	3.8
	Home help	−0.3685***	−3.45	56,923	31,000	15.7
Branch	Agriculture	ref	ref	103,120	10,000	3.9
	Mining	0.8476***	2.78	235,115	122,000	1.3
	Industry	0.4300***	2.71	179,696	70,000	8.8
	Public works	0.3945**	2.00	145,085	75,000	5.0
	Transport	0.6958***	4.14	168,937	80,000	8.7
	Trade	0.6028***	3.81	79,573	60,000	9.3
	Services	0.4776***	3.14	119,758	65,000	18.3
	Education/healthcare	0.4458***	2.73	150,084	88,000	16.6
	Administration	0.3437**	2.14	186,468	90,000	26.5
	Other	0.3130	1.24	132,549	50,000	1.6
Constant	Constant	4.4477***	18.23	149,031.4	80,000	100
Statistics	Observations	1,610				
	R²	0.2881				
	Dependent variable	Logarithm of hourly wage				

Source: Authors' calculations based on 2005 ECOM household survey.
Note: **Significant at the 5% level. ***Significant at the 1% level.

gain versus agriculture), transport (101 percent), and trade (83 percent). The results also show a gap between men and women, with men receiving wages 21 percent higher than women, even after controlling for all the other potential determinants of wages discussed here.

Impact of Gender Labor Income Shares on Consumption

A detailed framework for the empirical work conducted in this study is provided in Bussolo, De Hoyos, and Wodon (2009). Here, we outline only the main points. Following Hoddinott and Haddad (1995), we use a simple model and estimation procedure to test whether a higher labor income share for women within a household influences the spending decisions of the household. The empirics rely on an expanded version of the Working-Leser expenditure system. In this econometric model, the budget share allocated to expenditure category j is a function of the log of household size, the log of per capita expenditure, the share of total income controlled by women (Y_F/Y), demographic variables, regional variables, and other controls:

$$S_j = \alpha + \beta_{j,1}\ln(H) + \beta_{j,2}\ln(E) + \beta_{j,3}\left(\frac{Y_F}{Y}\right) + \sum_{l=1}^{L}\gamma_{j,l}\left(\frac{K_l}{H}\right) + \delta_j X + \varepsilon \qquad (10.1)$$

where H is household size; E is per capita household expenditure; K_l is the number of household members within demographic category l; X is a vector with regional location variables and other controls; α, β, γ and δ are parameters to be estimated; and ε is a random component assumed to be normally distributed. Note that this specification implies that the sum of all parameters estimates for any regressor is equal to 1. This feature of the model is known as the "adding up restriction" (see Deaton and Muellbauer, 1980). The key variable is Y_F/Y, which captures the bargaining power of women within the household. We would expect that if women have a stronger preference for expenditure categories that directly benefit their children (such as education or health), an increase in that variable would cause an increase in the expenditure shares allocated to these categories. We expect that $\beta_{j,3}$ will be positive, which would reject the income-pooling hypothesis in favor of a more complex, intra-household bargaining process. Bussolo, De Hoyos, and Wodon (2009) provide a more thorough discussion of the implications of different values obtained in the estimation for assessing the impact of an increase in female labor income, not only on the share of spending allocated to various goods, but also the level of spending.

Following Bussolo, De Hoyos, and Wodon (2009), we consider several different types of expenditure categories, four of which are expected to have an especially positive effect on human capital formation and, more generally, the well-being of children: food, health, education, and children's clothing. The other seven expenditure categories are adults' clothing, alcohol, tobacco, housing, transportation, entertainment, and other expenditures. The shares of household members in different age and gender categories as a proportion of total household size are used as demographic controls. In particular, we use gender and age to form eight demographic categories: boys and girls below

6 years of age, boys and girls between 6 and 14, women and men between 15 and 59, and women and men 60 years old or more. Other controls include a dummy variable for each of the two main cities in Congo, as well as for other urban and rural areas (Brazzaville, the capital, is the reference category, with Pointe Noire being the other large city), and a dummy variable for female-headed households. The ratio Y_F/Y is formed by dividing female wage income for the spouse (or the household head when the household head is female) by the sum of the spouse's wage and that of the household head.

The average household in Congo has fewer than five members, each consuming slightly less than CFAF 300,000 a year (about US$600). In 2005, 13 percent of households were headed by women, and 14 percent were located in rural areas. The women's bargaining proxy Y_F/Y shows that female spouses contributed only 17 percent of total household wage income brought by either the household head or the spouse.

Before presenting the results of the regressions, it is useful to provide some basic statistics on the shares of total consumption allocated to various goods. According to the 2005 ECOM, the average household spends 39 percent of its total budget on food and more than a fifth (22 percent) on housing (this includes the imputed rental value of the dwelling when the household owns the dwelling). Health accounts for 4.5 percent of the total household budget; only 1.7 percent is allocated to education. Clothing for children receives on average 1 percent of the total household budget, well below clothing for adults, at 4.5 percent. Tobacco accounts for only a very small share of total consumption (0.2 percent), while alcohol is more significant, at 1.7 percent. Transportation represents 5.7 percent of the total budget, and entertainment 1.5 percent. All other expenditures account for 18.7 percent of total expenditure. The data in table 10.4 suggest that the share of total consumption allocated to food, human capital, and housing tends to be higher when the household head is female, and when more than 50 percent of the wage income is provided by the spouse. By contrast, when the household head is male or when more than half of the wage income is provided by men, spending for tobacco, alcohol, adult clothing, and entertainment is higher. The question is whether those patterns remain in a regression framework, controlling for a range of factors that may affect consumption choices.

The results of the estimations of equation (10.1) are presented in table 10.5. First note the high degree of variation in the R-squared across expenditure categories. For some goods, our specification captures a large share of total variation in expenditure shares across households, but for other goods, the fit is less good. The results suggest that location and family composition often have an impact on consumption choices. For example, households located in the two main cities spend less on food and more on housing, as expected. Richer households tend to spend less on housing and health and more on education, adult clothing, entertainment, and tobacco (although the impact of tobacco is small, with the

Table 10.4 Basic Statistics on Expenditure Shares (%) in the Republic of Congo, 2005

| | Sex of head | | | Female labor income share | |
	All	Male	Female	Below 50%	Above 50%
Food	38.8	38.4	40.2	38.2	40.0
Health	4.5	4.4	5.0	4.3	5.1
Education	1.7	1.6	1.9	1.6	1.8
Children's clothing	1.0	1.0	0.9	1.0	0.9
Adult clothing	4.5	4.7	4.0	4.8	3.9
Tobacco	0.2	0.2	0.0	0.2	0.1
Alcohol	1.7	2.0	0.5	1.9	1.1
Housing	21.7	20.8	25.0	20.4	24.3
Transportation	5.7	5.6	5.9	5.8	5.5
Entertainment	1.5	1.7	0.9	1.7	1.1
Other expenses	18.7	19.6	15.6	19.9	16.2

Source: Authors' calculations based on 2005 ECOM household survey.

share allocated to tobacco itself being small), indicating that these goods can be classified as "luxuries" in Congo.

Female-headed households tend to spend a smaller proportion of the house-hold budget on food (the coefficient is almost statistically significant at the 10 percent level) and alcohol. The result for the impact of female headship on food spending may appear surprising at first, but it may be a result of the fact that overall food caloric requirements, as opposed to other requirements for education, health, and other spending, may very well be lower for a household when the head is male.

Several (but not all) results of the coefficient estimates for the Y_F/Y variable reject the income-pooling hypothesis. First, women and men differ in preference in terms of their allocation of the budget to food, suggesting that a bargaining process is undertaken to determine how much of their resources should be allocated to this important expenditure category for human capital development. Controlling for differences in household size, total expenditure, demographic composition, gender of household head, and regional variations, an increase in women's income increases the level of resources allocated to food, with a 1 percent redistribution of wage income from the male head to his spouse increasing the food expenditure share by 0.04 percent. This is small, but nevertheless statistically significant at the usual levels.

The impact for education is even smaller (less than 0.1 percentage point), but, nevertheless, positive and also statistically significant. By contrast, a higher share of total wage income obtained by women decreases spending for adult clothing (by 0.1 percentage point for each percent of additional income share

Table 10.5 Correlates of Household Consumption Shares for Various Items in the Republic of Congo, 2005

Variables	Food			Health			Education			Children's clothing		
	Coefficient	t	P>t	Coefficient	T	P>t	Coefficient	t	P>t	Coefficient	t	P>t
Log household size	-0.001	-0.11	0.911	0.001	0.42	0.674	0.018***	9.12	0	0	0.09	0.924
Log p.c. consumption	-0.004	-0.72	0.471	-0.006***	-2.85	0.004	0.003**	2.4	0.017	-0.001	-1.42	0.154
Female income share	0.036**	2.49	0.013	0.002	0.36	0.718	0.006*	1.92	0.055	0	-0.22	0.826
Female head	-0.026	-1.64	0.101	0	0.03	0.98	0.002	0.62	0.534	0.003	1.39	0.165
Boys below age 5	-0.068	-0.89	0.373	-0.013	-0.48	0.632	0.012	0.68	0.496	0.041***	4.35	0
Girls below age 5	0.004	0.05	0.962	-0.009	-0.34	0.731	-0.006	-0.32	0.745	0.037***	3.99	0
Boys aged 6–14	-0.098	-1.32	0.188	-0.037	-1.47	0.142	0.036**	2.11	0.035	0.016*	1.71	0.087
Girls aged 6–14	-0.104	-1.41	0.159	-0.014	-0.53	0.595	0.041**	2.45	0.014	0.02**	2.24	0.025
Men aged 15–69	-0.149**	-2.12	0.034	-0.028	-1.17	0.243	0.02	1.25	0.211	0.01	1.19	0.234
Women aged 15–69	-0.120*	-1.73	0.084	-0.021	-0.88	0.379	0.022	1.36	0.173	0.009	1.11	0.267
Men aged above 60	-0.219*	-1.71	0.088	0.062	1.41	0.157	0.012	0.41	0.682	0.007	0.42	0.675
Pointe Noire	-0.051***	-4.85	0	0.006*	1.75	0.08	-0.001	-0.24	0.811	0.001	1.1	0.272
Other urban areas	-0.025**	-2.21	0.027	0.007*	1.92	0.055	-0.009***	-3.67	0	0.003*	1.87	0.062
Semi-urban areas	0.011	0.78	0.437	-0.001	-0.18	0.86	-0.017***	-5.54	0	0.002	1.18	0.237
Rural areas	0.042**	2.43	0.015	-0.005	-0.89	0.376	-0.022***	-5.53	0	0.001	0.4	0.693
Constant	0.536***	5.13	0	0.126***	3.51	0	-0.061**	-2.55	0.011	0.005	0.37	0.712
Number of observations	1384			1384			1384			1384		
R²	0.058			0.024			0.150			0.062		

continued

Table 10.5 Correlates of Household Consumption Shares for Various Items in the Republic of Congo, 2005 *continued*

Variables	Food Coefficient	t	P>t	Health Coefficient	T	P>t	Education Coefficient	t	P>t	Children's clothing Coefficient	t	P>t
Log household size	−0.001	−0.42	0.674	−0.001***	−2.73	0.006	0.002	0.68	0.496	−0.023***	−4.21	0
Log p.c. consumption	0.014****	6.25	0	0**	−2.2	0.028	0.005***	2.98	0.003	−0.062***	−17.15	0
Female income share	−0.011**	−2.06	0.04	0	0.32	0.751	0.004	0.97	0.333	−0.003	−0.27	0.784
Female head	0.004	0.66	0.509	−0.001	−0.96	0.337	−0.012***	−2.67	0.008	0.013	1.26	0.207
Boys below age 5	−0.003	−0.12	0.908	0.001	0.18	0.856	−0.002	−0.1	0.918	−0.127***	−2.63	0.009
Girls below age 5	0.017	0.59	0.552	0.005*	1.7	0.09	−0.003	−0.12	0.906	−0.15***	−3.14	0.002
Boys aged 6–14	0.002	0.07	0.942	−0.001	−0.3	0.767	−0.001	−0.07	0.948	−0.065	−1.38	0.167
Girls aged 6–14	−0.005	−0.18	0.86	−0.001	−0.21	0.834	−0.02	−0.91	0.361	−0.113**	−2.41	0.016
Men aged 15–69	0.002	0.07	0.942	0.001	0.3	0.762	−0.007	−0.35	0.728	−0.062	−1.4	0.161
Women aged 15–69	−0.01	−0.38	0.703	0.001	0.45	0.653	−0.002	−0.1	0.921	−0.009	−0.21	0.837
Men aged above 60	−0.041	−0.84	0.399	−0.001	−0.31	0.759	−0.045	−1.23	0.218	0.071	0.88	0.379
Pointe Noire	−0.005	−1.21	0.227	0	−0.14	0.893	0.002	0.65	0.518	−0.002	−0.23	0.819
Other urban areas	0.02***	4.62	0	0	0.7	0.481	0	−0.07	0.946	−0.021***	−2.98	0.003
Semi-urban areas	0.022***	4.09	0	0	0.1	0.92	0.013***	3.38	0.001	−0.046***	−5.22	0
Rural areas	0.013**	2.06	0.04	0.002**	2.48	0.013	0.014***	2.9	0.004	−0.044***	−4.05	0
Constant	−0.121***	−3.04	0.002	0.007*	1.85	0.065	−0.049	−1.64	0.101	1.089***	16.5	0
Number of observations	1384			1384			13 84			1384		
R²	0.060			0.027			0.026			0.201		

374

Variables	Transport			Entertainment			Other expenditures		
	Coefficient	t	P>t	Coefficient	T	P>t	Coefficient	t	P>t
Log household size	0.004	1.2	0.229	0.006***	3.14	0.002	−0.005	−0.86	0.389
Log p.c. consumption	0.003	1.2	0.231	0.007***	5.32	0	0.042***	9.96	0
Female income share	0.001	0.1	0.919	−0.006*	−1.74	0.082	−0.029***	−2.72	0.007
Female head	0.009	1.36	0.174	−0.001	−0.29	0.772	0.01	0.82	0.414
Boys below age 5	0.027	0.88	0.379	0.014	0.76	0.45	0.119**	2.14	0.032
Girls below age 5	−0.006	−0.21	0.831	0.003	0.19	0.847	0.107*	1.95	0.051
Boys aged 6–14	0.013	0.43	0.67	0.015	0.86	0.39	0.121**	2.23	0.026
Girls aged 6–14	0.019	0.65	0.518	0.022	1.26	0.208	0.152***	2.82	0.005
Men aged 15–69	0.024	0.86	0.391	0.029*	1.73	0.085	0.161***	3.13	0.002
Women aged 15–69	0.011	0.41	0.683	0.013	0.82	0.414	0.105**	2.08	0.038
Men aged above 60	0.048	0.93	0.355	0.037	1.22	0.221	0.07	0.75	0.453
Pointe Noire	0.007	1.62	0.105	0.004	1.7	0.089	0.037***	4.86	0
Other urban areas	−0.036***	−7.94	0	0.013***	4.98	0	0.048***	5.91	0
Semi-urban areas	−0.032***	−5.78	0	0.007**	2.14	0.032	0.041***	4.11	0
Rural areas	−0.026***	−3.75	0	0.007*	1.86	0.063	0.017	1.37	0.17
Constant	0.013	0.32	0.751	−0.103***	−4.19	0	−0.442***	−5.8	0
Number of observations	1384			1384			1384		
R²	0.097			0.049			0.133		

Source: Authors' calculations based on 2005 ECOM household survey.
Note: (*) denotes statistical significance at the 10% level, (**) at the 5% level, and (***) at the 1% level.

for women), entertainment (by less than 0.1 percentage point), and other expenditures (by close to 0.3 percentage point). The results obtained for the two gender variables in the regressions (the gender of the household head and the female labor income share) are illustrated in figure 10.1 (note that all effects are not statistically significant).

Given the parametric constraint imposed by equation 10.1 (the sum of the slopes for any regressor must equal 1), it may seem odd that only a few of the 11 parameters estimated on Y_F/Y are statistically significant (that is, statistically different from zero), but this has been observed in other instances (see, for example, Bussolo, De Hoyos, and Wodon 2009, on Senegal, where fewer parameters are statistically significant than those here). In order to come up with a summary assessment of the impact of the female labor income share on what can be considered broadly as investments in human capital, we re-estimate equation 10.1 by combining expenditures in two aggregate categories. The human capital category comprises spending for food, education, health, and children's clothing. All the rest is lumped together as the "alternative" category. The results in table 10.6 suggest that a 1 percent increase in the share of female

Figure 10.1 Impact of Gender Variables on Consumption Patterns in the Republic of Congo, 2005

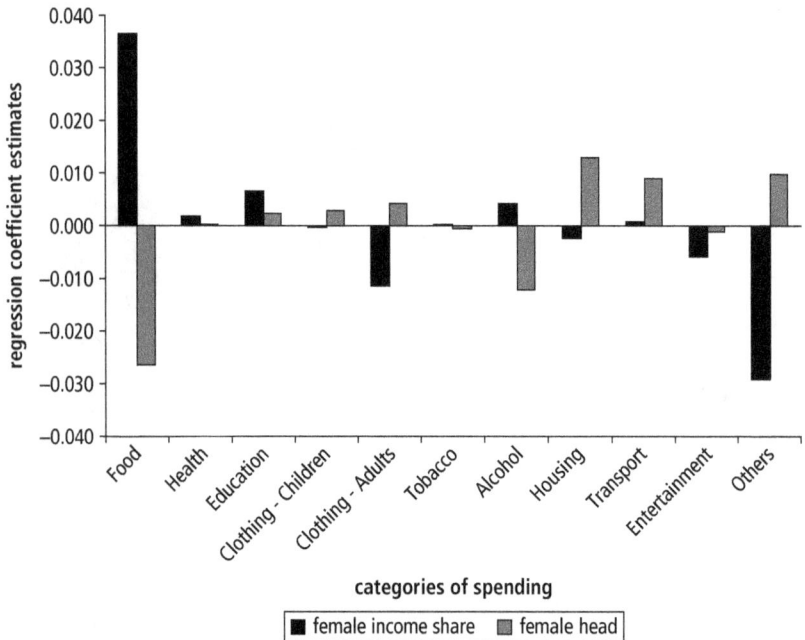

categories of spending

■ female income share ■ female head

Source: Authors' calculations based on 2005 ECOM household survey.

Table 10.6 Correlates of Household Consumption Shares for Two Aggregated Categories, Republic of Congo, 2005

	Food and human capital			All other expenditures		
	Coefficient	t	P>t	Coefficient	T	P>t
Variables						
Log household size	−0.005	−0.56	0.573	0.005	0.56	0.573
Log p.c. consumption	−0.069***	−12.42	0	0.069***	12.42	0
Female income share	0.042***	2.98	0.003	−0.042***	−2.98	0.003
Female head	−0.011	−0.72	0.471	0.011	0.72	0.471
Boys below age 5	−0.195***	−2.65	0.008	0.195***	2.65	0.008
Girls below age 5	−0.161**	−2.21	0.028	0.161**	2.21	0.028
Boys aged 6–14	−0.164**	−2.29	0.022	0.164**	2.29	0.022
Girls aged 6–14	−0.189***	−2.65	0.008	0.189***	2.65	0.008
Men aged 15–69	−0.220***	−3.24	0.001	0.220***	3.24	0.001
Women aged 15–69	−0.128*	−1.92	0.055	0.128*	1.92	0.055
Men aged above 60	−0.073	−0.59	0.553	0.073	0.59	0.553
Pointe Noire	−0.047***	−4.61	0	0.047***	4.61	0
Other urban areas	−0.048***	−4.43	0	0.048***	4.43	0
Semi-urban areas	−0.053***	−3.99	0	0.053***	3.99	0
Rural areas	−0.029*	−1.75	0.08	0.029*	1.75	0.08
Constant	1.690***	16.77	0	−0.690***	−6.85	0
Number of observations	1384			1384		
R^2	0.16			0.151		

Source: Authors' calculations based on 2005 ECOM household survey.
Note: (*) denotes statistical significance at the 10% level, (**) at the 5% level, and (***) at the 1% level.

labor income would increase total spending for human capital by 0.4 percent. A doubling of the female labor income share from 17 percent to 34 percent could thus increase the share of human capital–related expenditures in households by about 7 percentage points, which is relatively large.

Conclusions

As in many other developing regions, in Africa, labor income tends to be controlled by men. The results presented here show that, when women control a higher share of total labor income within the household, the household tends to allocate larger shares of its resources to investments that benefit their children. For each category of spending taken individually, the magnitude of the links between the female labor income share and the share of total expenditure allocated to a category may not be very large, but for human capital as a whole, the effect is not negligible. A doubling of the female labor income share from 17 to 34 percent could increase the share of human capital-related expenditures in households by about 7 percentage points, which is relatively large, but at the same time, many of the results obtained for good categories at a lower level of aggregation tend not to be statistically significant.

The evidence here suggests that in the Republic of Congo, as in other countries, the unitary household hypothesis does not hold well. Thus, this study, which has followed closely a similar analysis for Senegal by Bussolo, De Hoyos, and Wodon (2009), brings additional evidence to a growing body of micro-literature that has shown that the income-pooling hypothesis—namely, that what matters to household expenditure patterns is not who brings in the income, but the total available resources—is not supported by the data. This result signals that gender inequalities encompass not just inequalities of opportunities outside the households—such as inequalities in education, employment, labor remuneration, access to credit, and other dimensions—but also inequalities within the household, manifested mainly by inequality of power.

Can policy implications be derived from our results? Not in any specific way, but at a more general level, the results from the study do suggest that policies to boost women's bargaining power within the household could be beneficial for long-term investments in human capital. This could be achieved through educational and media campaigns targeted toward equality within the family, for example. Directing some public transfers directly or indirectly to women or creating access to credit programs with a focus on women could also be considered, although a detailed analysis would be required before making specific recommendations.

Note

1. In developing countries, and especially in Sub-Saharan Africa, income is often difficult to estimate through household surveys because most (or at least a large proportion) of the active population engages in independent and informal activities without keeping good account of the income received from such activities. Much of this income is also received in-kind, and when it is received in cash, it is often irregular, which makes it difficult for households to recall how much they actually earned. Consequently, any analysis of household income must involve a plausibility check, for example, by comparing income to consumption, a variable that is less subject to measurement errors. In the case of Congo's ECOM survey, total income for households is slightly higher than total consumption, and very well correlated to consumption. In most other West and Central African countries, total income as measured through the surveys is only at about half the value of the consumption of households, and thus substantially underestimated.

References

Appleton, S., J. Hoddinott, and P. Krishnan. 1999. "The Gender Wage Gap in Three African Countries." *Economic Development and Cultural Change* 47 (2): 289–312.

Bourguignon, F., and P. A. Chiappori. 1992. "Collective Models of Household Behavior: An Introduction." *European Economic Review* 36 (2–3): 355–64.

Blackden, C. M., and Q. Wodon, ed. 2006. *Gender, Time Use, and Poverty in Sub-Saharan Africa.* World Bank Working Paper 73. Washington, DC: World Bank.

Brilleau, A., F. Roubaud, and C. Torelli. 2004. "*L'emploi, le chômage et les conditions d'activité dans les principales agglomérations de sept Etats membres de l'UEMOA Principaux résultats de la phase 1 de l'enquête 1-2-3 de 2001–2002.*" DIAL Working Paper 6. Paris: DIAL.

Browning, M., and P. A. Chiappori. 1998. "Efficient Intra-Household Allocations: A General Characterization and Empirical Tests." *Econometrica* 66 (6): 1241–78.

Bussolo, M., R. E. De Hoyos, and Q. Wodon, 2009, "Higher Prices of Export Crops, Intra-Household Inequality and Human Capital Accumulation in Senegal." In *Gender Aspects of the Trade and Poverty Nexus: A Macro–Micro Approach*, ed. M. Bussolo and R. E. De Hoyos. Washington, DC: World Bank and Palgrave Macmillan.

Centre national de la statistique et des études économiques. 2004. ECOM 2004. Méthodologie de collecte. Ministère du plan, de l'aménagement du territoire et de l'intégration économique, Comité national de lutte contre la pauvreté, Bangui.

Deaton, A., and J. Muellbauer. 1980. *Economics and Consumer Behavior.* New York: Cambridge University Press.

Hoddinott, J., and L. Haddad. 1995. "Does Female Income Share Influence Household Expenditures? Evidence from Côte d'Ivoire." *Oxford Bulletin of Economics and Statistics* 57 (1): 77–96.

Weichselbaumer, D., R. Winter-Ebmer, and M. Zweimüller, 2007. "Market Orientation and Gender Wage Gaps: An International Study." Economics Working Papers 2007-12, Department of Economics, Johannes Kepler University, Linz, Austria.

Chapter **11**

Income Generation and Intra-Household Decision Making: A Gender Analysis for Nigeria

Diego Angel-Urdinola and Quentin Wodon

Introduction

Household decision making and resource allocation are critical for economic and human development. Many decisions made at the household level influence the welfare of the individuals living in the household as well as their communities. Decisions such as where to live, how to generate income, how much to invest and consume, and how many children to have constitute common dilemmas faced by households. The outcomes of such decisions are often linked to economic performance at the household level as well as in the aggregate for the country as a whole. In households with precarious opportunities (defined as living in a low-wealth environment with limited access to credit and limited labor opportunities), the intra-household dynamics of decision making and resource allocation may have an even greater impact on the welfare outcomes of family members.

Within households, many factors—age, marital status, culture, income level, and education—influence the dynamics of intra-household decision making. If various household members (including male, as opposed to female, members) have different preferences, it is expected that households will behave differently according to who controls household resources. For example, it is often argued that when women have better command over income sources, decisions on how these resources are spent tend to favor children more in terms of human capital investment (for example, Hoddinott and Haddad 1995; Bourguignon and

The authors gratefully acknowledge comments from Jorge Arbache and Mayra Buvinic. The views expressed in this chapter are those of the authors and need not reflect those of the World Bank, its executive directors, or the countries they represent.

Chiappori 1992; Browning and Chiappori 1998; Bussolo, De Hoyos, and Wodon 2009).

Lloyd and Blanc (1996; see also Blackden and Bhanu 1999) argue that children in female-headed households in Sub-Saharan Africa have better enrollment rates than those in male-headed households. Higher involvement of women in decision making within the household has also been shown to lead to better outcomes in terms of nutrition (see Piesse and Simister 2002, among others). Cooperative bargaining theory suggests that expenditure decisions are proportional to resource contribution (for example, Manser and Brown 1980; McElroy and Homey 1981). In this respect, as a woman's income increases as a share of total household income, so does her bargaining and decision-making power. Hoddinott and Haddad (1995) suggest that a doubling of the share of cash income held by women within a household may increase the share of the budget allocated to food by the household by about 2 percent, and may reduce much more significantly the shares allocated to cigarettes and alcohol (by 26 percent and 14 percent, respectively).

In the Uganda gender assessment prepared by the World Bank (2005), the analysis suggested similar differences between male- and female-headed households, with a higher share of consumption spent on alcohol and cigarettes in male-headed households, and a higher share spent on school fees in female-headed households, especially in the case of divorced and widowed heads. Evidence of the effects of female labor income share on household consumption patterns was also found by Backiny-Yetna and Wodon (2010) for the Republic of Congo, but the effects were not large and not always statistically significant.

While there is substantial evidence worldwide about the impact of women's income on intra-household decision making, including consumption allocations, the evidence for Sub-Saharan Africa remains limited, in part as a result of lack of comprehensive household surveys to conduct such analysis in many countries. However, good household surveys are becoming much more common, enabling research on gender-based decision making, as illustrated for Senegal, for example, by Bussolo, De Hoyos, and Wodon (2009), and for the Republic of Congo by Backiny-Yetna and Wodon in Chapter 10 of this volume.

Yet, even without a comprehensive household survey with detailed consumption and income data, it is still often feasible to conduct useful empirical work on these issues. The objective of this study is to document the extent to which income generation affects decision making within households in Nigeria, using the 2003 Core Welfare Questionnaire Indicator (CWIQ) surveys implemented in eight Nigerian states. While these surveys do not have income and consumption data, they do provide information on labor force participation and whether household members generate income for the household, as well as data on who makes the decisions within the household for a wide range of expenditure categories. This type of data can be used to assess, using simple statistical and econometric methods, the impact of income generation by women on their decision power within the household.

This chapter is structured as follows. The next section provides basic descriptive statistics on the differences in decision making within the household, as well as on differences in access to resources between the household head and spouse. Thereafter, bivariate probit techniques are used to quantify the extent to which income contribution influences a spouse's decision-making power on household expenditures in health, education, food, and on the use of productive assets. A brief conclusion follows.

Data and Basic Statistics

Using data from the CWIQ surveys implemented in eight Nigerian states in 2003, this section provides basic statistics on the roles of men and women in household decision making. The analysis relies on a one-page, special module on gender that was added to the standard CWIQ questionnaire by the National Statistical Office. Among other questions, the gender module asks respondents to answer the following: (1) whether each of the household members engage in a number of income-generating activities (fish smoking, food processing, soap making, crop farming, fishing, and others); (2) whether household members do household chores (fetching water, fetching wood, cleaning toilets, cooking, providing child care, caring for the elderly and the sick, and others); (3) whether household members take decisions in a range of areas (health, education, food, clothing, use of farmland, and sale of farm produce); and (4) whether household members spend most of their time on an economic activity, unpaid household work, child care, recreational activities, or other activities. The survey also provides information on who contributes the most to household income.

This study focuses on an analysis of the correlates or determinants of who is the main contributor to household income, and whether this affects the ability of the household member to participate in decision making in a range of areas. Before focusing on the interaction between income contributions and decision making, a few basic statistics are useful to provide context. The survey provides basic statistics showing whether men and women live in poor or non-poor households. For such statistics, in the absence of consumption data in the survey, poverty is defined using a household-level index of wealth obtained through standard factorial analysis conducted on the assets owned by the households, with a poverty line defined in such a way as to roughly reproduce poverty measures similar to the official figures (according to which, about two-thirds of the population lives in poverty). In conducting the factorial analysis, the first factor (which is defined statistically as a weighted sum of the various assets used to assess household wealth, in order for that factor to explain as much as possible of the variance observed in asset ownership between households) is used to represent the wealth index.

The 2003 CWIQ data suggest that, as is the case in many other African countries, Nigeria is still a male-dominated society. There are significant differences in roles played by men and women in Nigeria that influence their capacity to earn monetary income, and thus their intra-household decision-making power (see table 11.1). While one of every two men in Nigeria spends most of his time in an income-generating activity, a similar proportion of women spend their time in unpaid household work. The differences in economic roles are most

Table 11.1 Basic Statistics on Employment and Education by Gender in Nigeria

	Women %	Men %	Non-poor women %	Non-poor men %	Poor women %	Poor men %
Employment and access to capital						
Owns land	13.02	46.85	11.19	36.21	15.02	58.96
Employed (6–70 years old)	47.38	54.51	45.79	51.39	49.07	57.94
Main activity (6–70 years old)						
Economic activity	29.41	47.51	37.35	49.75	20.92	45.03
Unpaid household work	40.64	25.61	30.30	19.02	51.69	32.91
Takes care of the children	6.00	0.81	4.68	0.78	7.40	0.85
Recreation	9.15	9.95	9.72	10.10	8.53	9.78
Other activity	14.81	16.12	17.95	20.35	11.45	11.44
Education						
Literacy rate (all individuals)	39.78	62.41	59.20	81.24	17.80	39.30
School enrollment (6–15 years old)	62.40	64.81	83.06	85.94	40.30	43.19
Reasons to be not enrolled						
Too old	1.67	2.03	1.66	2.43	1.69	1.75
Completed school	28.06	34.32	17.37	30.41	39.53	37.03
School is too far	2.43	3.19	2.12	0.00	2.77	5.40
School is too expensive	26.82	29.03	26.24	34.86	27.45	25.01
Work (job / home)	7.89	7.55	9.16	8.32	6.52	7.01
Useless	10.18	12.69	10.64	8.55	9.69	15.55
Illness or pregnancy	5.39	1.31	5.40	1.52	5.38	1.17
Failed exam	2.59	11.13	3.40	6.42	1.73	14.38
Got married	5.27	1.17	4.53	0.00	6.07	1.98
Awaits admission	17.71	13.34	22.72	17.81	12.34	10.24
Other reasons	7.53	5.21	10.97	9.62	3.83	2.17

Source: Authors' estimate using Nigeria's CWIQ 2003.

striking in poor households. While only 30 percent of non-poor women engage in unpaid family work, the proportion is 52 percent among poor women.

The literature on Nigeria suggests that women do the most work in the subsistence agricultural sector, while men are given opportunities in the commercial sector. Households often encourage their male members to migrate in order to generate higher incomes through remittances and also in order to deal with a lack of sufficient farmland and capital in rural areas to make farming profitable (Chukwuezi 1999). In turn, male out-migration from rural areas is leading to the feminization of agriculture. By contrast, in the commercial sector, men are hired more easily than women, including to do weeding and other traditional woman's work. The monetization of a sector often shifts hiring practices in favor of men, with owners of commercial farms justifying the exclusion of women on the grounds that they are not able to work at the same pace as men, which is, however, doubtful. This may explain in part why when women are hired, they are often paid lower wages.

Despite doing a large share of the work in the agriculture sector, rural women often lack control over key farm inputs and decisions. A woman's right to own land is dependent on her relationship with her husband or male relatives. The risk of losing land rights has become a disincentive for women to invest in land. For example, land rehabilitation programs that require years to make land productive are not attractive to women who may have the land taken away once it becomes fertile. Women also lack control over the allocation of the labor of their children and at times even their own labor. In studying tobacco production in the north, Babalola and Dennis (1988) found that husbands controlled the allocation of their wives' labor. That is, women were assigned tasks in producing a labor-intensive crop owned and controlled by their husbands.

Improved farming methods, while increasing productivity, also increase the demand for women's labor. For example, applying fertilizer makes extra weeding necessary, and women do most of the weeding. In contrast, traditional male tasks, such as land clearing and preparation, are being mechanized. Access to credit is much more widespread for men than for women, who despite having better repayment rates, have less access than men. Even when women own resources, they may not have the power to make their own decisions about using these resources, and this may in turn result in the transfer of more woman-specific farm tasks (such as the processing and marketing of palm) to men.

The 2003 CWIQ survey data confirm the existence of differences by gender in decision-making power; these differences are especially pronounced in poor households. The empowerment of women in decision making within the household seems limited in Nigeria, especially regarding decisions for the use of capital goods in the household, such as land use, sale of agricultural produce, and decisions related to shelter. As shown in table 11.1, female land ownership is rare and the share of women who are the main contributors of income in a household with both head and spouse is very low (at 4 and 3 percent, respectively) for both poor and non-poor households. What is striking is the fact that women in non-poor households have much more decision-making power than women in poor households for virtually all areas of spending. For example, 40 percent of women in non-poor households have a say in decisions made about education spending, versus only 12 percent of women in poor households having this say. The same is true for decisions on land use and crop sales, with poor women again at a disadvantage.

The CWIQ data also show that literacy rates are significantly higher for men (62 percent for men versus 40 percent for women), and boys benefit from higher school enrollment rates than girls. Although net primary school enrollment is high and roughly similar for boys and girls in Nigeria, boys are more likely than girls to be enrolled by approximately 3 percentage points, and differences are larger at higher levels. Family responsibilities affect girls more than boys, even at a young age, and tend to magnify differences in schooling. In particular, while about 11 percent of girls are not enrolled in school because of marriage or pregnancy, this proportion is lower than 3 percent for boys.

Dealing with gender differentials in Nigeria is a complex matter. For example, gender roles are likely to affect human development at the society's level beyond the direct impact of decision making within households. One illustration is the apparent relationship between the sex of teachers and the school enrollment rates of girls as teachers, compared to boys, which is documented in a risk and vulnerability assessment prepared by the World Bank (2004). According to that report, about half the teachers in primary school are female. In secondary school, in contrast, the proportion of female teachers is lower. But in both primary and secondary schools, there is a clear positive relationship between the share of female teachers in a state and the share of female students. This relationship does not imply causality, since, apart from the female share of teachers, other factors may explain the fact that some states have a higher ratio of female-to-male enrollment than others. Still, the relationship suggests that gender patterns in Nigeria are correlated and multi-faceted, as well as deep-rooted in the functioning of society. Therefore, it is important to aim to develop integrated strategies to deal with such inequalities.

Monetary Contributions and Decision Power

In this section, the analysis focuses on the relationship between monetary contributions to household income and decision-making power on expenditure patterns. To do this, we restrict the sample only to male heads and female spouses who belong to a household where there is both head and spouse, excluding households where there is no spouse, as well as female-headed households. The reason for this selection is that in order to compare decision power between men and women, it is necessary to have both men and women in the household—which, in practice, means that both a household head and a household spouse need to show up in the data. When there is no spouse, decisions are made only by the lone parent, and when there is a female head, in the African context, this essentially means that the father or male household head has died or has migrated. Note that this exclusion does not lead to bias. It is simply that the analysis is carried over a subset of the population, but this subset is very large because most households have both a spouse and a head. For language simplicity, "men" will refer to male household heads, and "women" will refer to the spouses of household heads.

As a consequence of various inequalities between men and women, household decision-making power in Nigeria remains concentrated among men, especially in poor households. Most decisions on the use of productive assets (land use, crop sales, and shelter) are taken by men (see table 11.2). Although women participate more in decision making on food expenditures, heath, and education, men are still the main decision makers in these areas as well. Non-poor women participate more actively in the household decision-making process than poor women, especially in aspects involving health and education. Not surprisingly, non-poor women are also more likely to contribute through income to household expenses (for shelter, education, food, health, and clothing, among other things) than are poor women. The rate of contribution for non-poor women is 37 percent, versus 27 percent for poor women.

Decision patterns among men are roughly similar to those of women, whether or not the household is poor, although non-poor men are less likely than poor men to be involved in decisions involving education and crop sales.

Table 11.2 Contribution to Household Expenses and Decision Making by Gender and Poverty Status in Nigeria

	Women		Men	
	Non-poor	Poor	Non-poor	Poor
Main contributor of household income	0.04	0.03	0.93	0.93
Decides for expenditures on education	0.40	0.12	0.79	0.42
Decides for expenditures on health	0.54	0.33	0.94	0.90
Decides for expenditures on food	0.71	0.53	0.92	0.93
Decides for expenditures on clothing	0.57	0.34	0.90	0.87
Decides for expenditures on shelter	0.22	0.09	0.88	0.85
Decides for expenditures on land use	0.24	0.14	0.72	0.85
Decides for expenditures on crop sales	0.31	0.17	0.58	0.73

Source: Authors using Nigeria's CWIQ 2003.
Note: Sample = Heads and spouses belonging to non–single households.

Note that in some cases, the sum of the shares of the decisions made by men and women (that is, under our terminology by household heads and spouses) is below 100 percent. This is because other members of the households may make the decisions in some cases. For simplicity, our analysis here is bivariate, comparing household heads and spouses (who tend to make most decisions), but further analysis could be made regarding areas where other household members play a role.

Figures 11.1 through 11.8 illustrate how decision making evolves for men and women as they age. The graphs show the proportion of men and women involved in various decisions by age. There is a difference between decisions related to education and other decisions. In the case of education, as shown in figure 11.1, as both men and women get older, they are more likely to make decisions regarding education; the likelihood increases up to about age 60 and decreases thereafter (probably because younger individuals inherit the authority of the elder as they become the main providers of household income). Although the concave pattern of the decision curve for education is similar for men and women, the share of men who are decision makers is always larger than the equivalent share of women (the difference between both groups increases up to age 60 and then stabilizes). The probable reason for men's decision-making power on education increasing with age, and why at a younger age, neither men nor women make education decisions, may simply be because younger couples either don't have children yet or their children are not yet school age, so there are no education decisions to make.

The pattern for other goods looks more similar between different goods. As shown in figures 11.2 through 11.5, comparatively few women from early ages are likely to participate in decision making on spending for health, food, clothing, and shelter. In contrast, men's decision curves for these items are higher, flatter, and decrease only slightly with age. Women are likely to get more involved in decision making for these expenditure categories as they grow older, although they often reach a plateau relatively quickly. As for decisions regarding the use of the household's productive capital (land use and sales of productive farm output), women's involvement remains low throughout their life cycle, with only a slight increase with age (see figures 11.6 and 11.7).

To summarize, this study's findings suggest that women gain in terms of empowerment with age for all types of intra-household decision making that pertains to non-productive household expenditures. This may in part be a result of gains by women in terms of income generating activities as they age. Indeed the share of women who are the main source of income in their households increases from less than 1 percent among women of age 17 to between 5 percent and 10 percent for women above 30 years of age (see figure 11.8). The share

Figure 11.1 Decision Making on Education by Age and Gender in Nigeria (%)

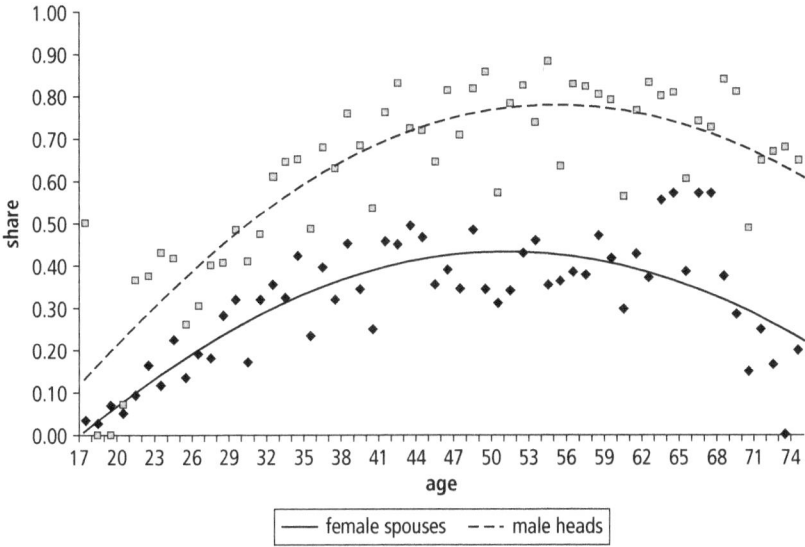

Source: Authors' estimate using Nigeria 2003 CWIQ surveys.

Figure 11.2 Decision Making on Health by Age and Gender in Nigeria (%)

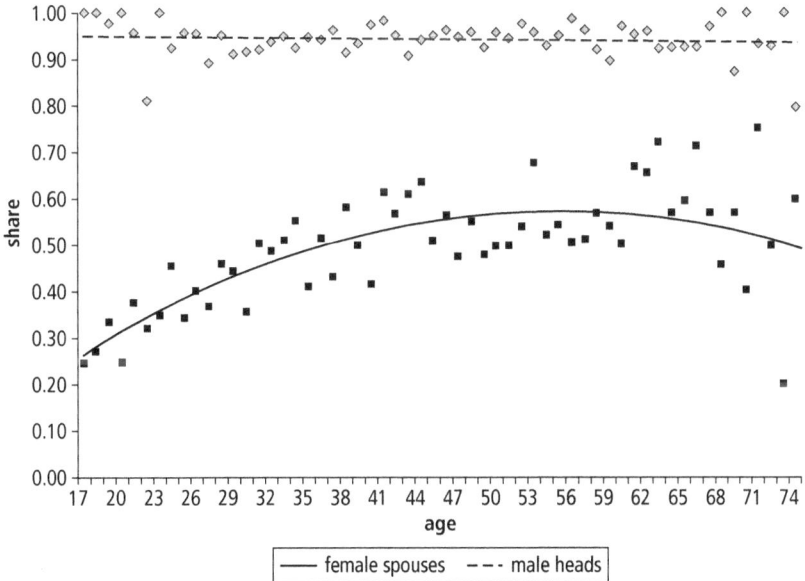

Source: Authors' estimate using Nigeria 2003 CWIQ surveys.

Figure 11.3 Decision Making on Food by Age and Gender in Nigeria (%)

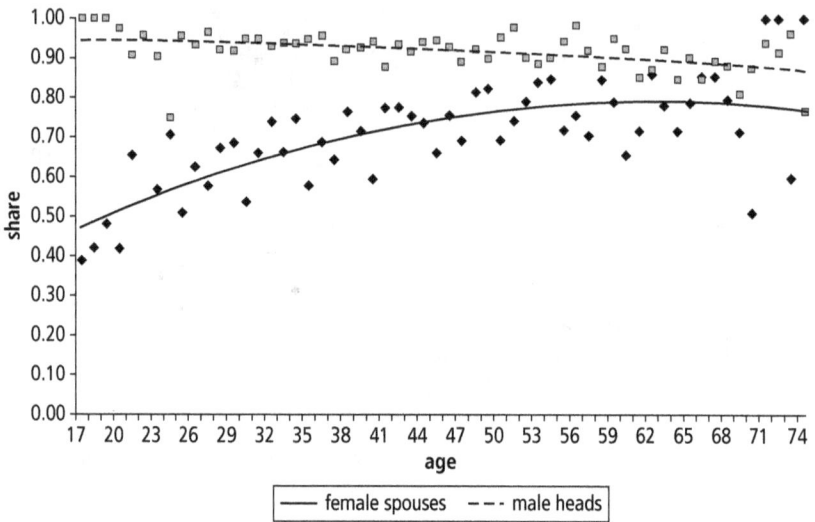

Source: Authors' estimate using Nigeria 2003 CWIQ surveys.

Figure 11.4 Decision Making on Clothing by Age and Gender in Nigeria (%)

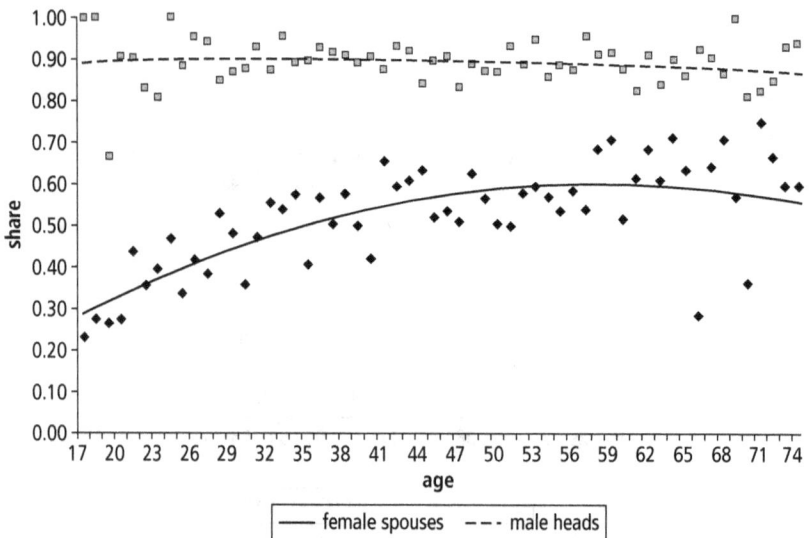

Source: Authors' estimate using Nigeria 2003 CWIQ surveys.

Figure 11.5 Decision Making on Shelter by Age and Gender in Nigeria (%)

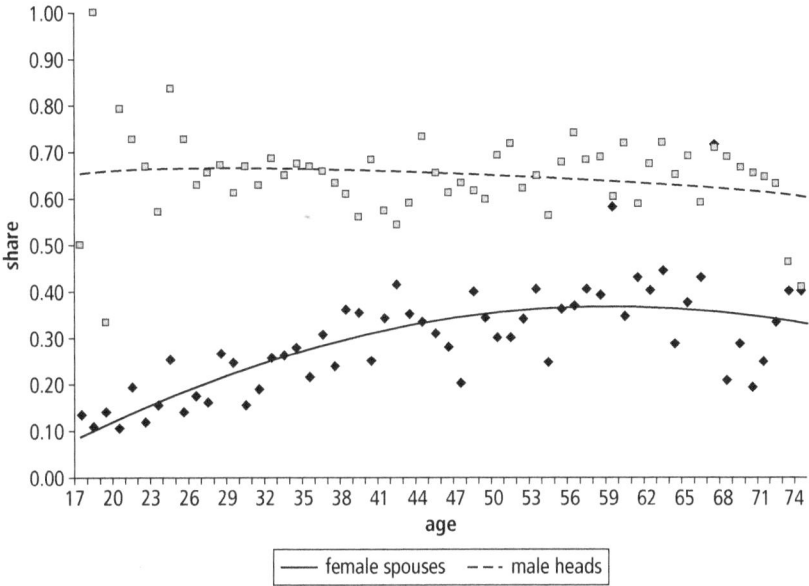

Source: Authors' estimate using Nigeria 2003 CWIQ surveys.

Figure 11.6 Decision Making on Sale of Farm Crop by Age and Gender in Nigeria (%)

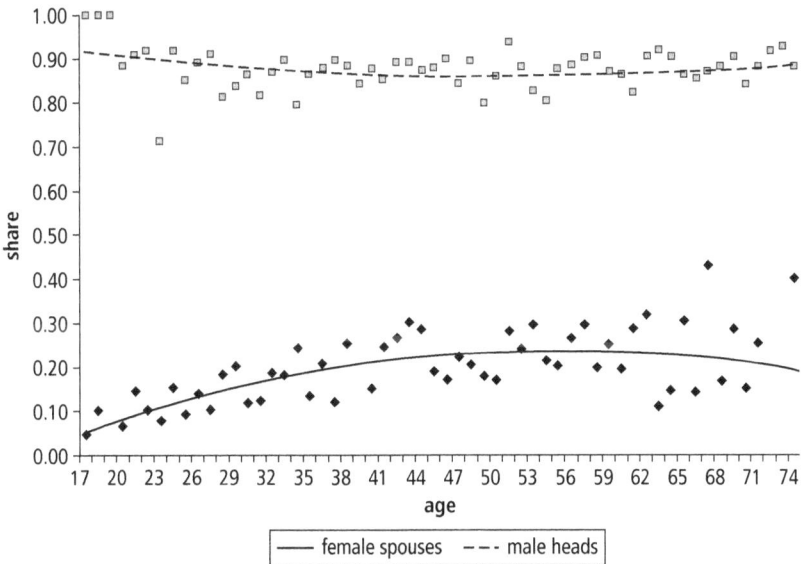

Source: Authors' estimate using Nigeria 2003 CWIQ surveys.

Figure 11.7 Decision Making on Land Use by Age and Gender in Nigeria (%)

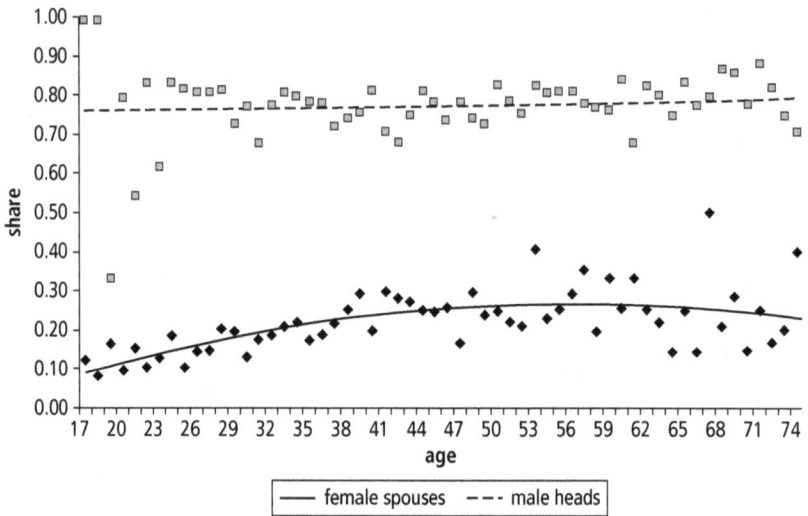

Source: Authors' estimate using Nigeria 2003 CWIQ surveys.

Figure 11.8 Main Contributor of Income in the Household by Age and Gender in Nigeria (%)

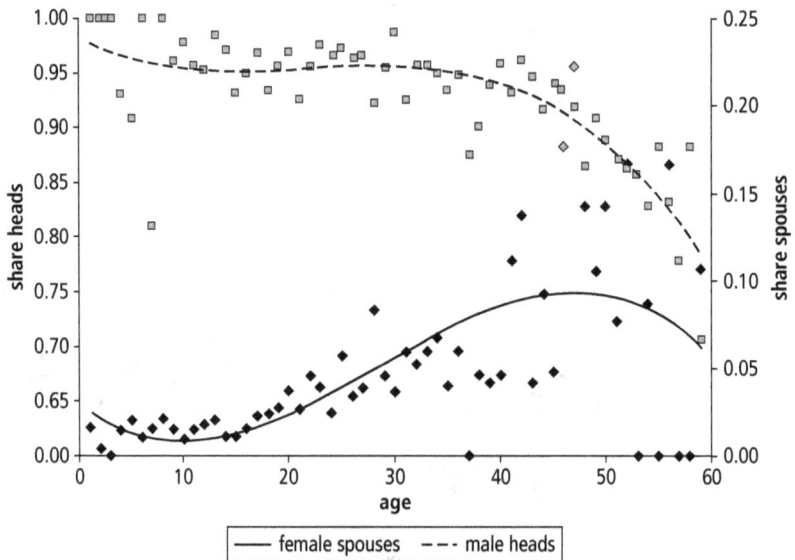

Source: Authors' estimate using Nigeria 2003 CWIQ surveys

of men as the main provider of household income, on the contrary, decreases significantly after they have reached age 65. The econometric analysis in the next section provides a better assessment of the correlates of decision making and income generation.

Econometric Analysis

In this section, a simple empirical model is developed to quantify how much income contribution by women affects their participation in household decision making. The analysis assumes that decision making and income contribution are jointly distributed outcomes, which means that both outcomes are decided jointly by household members, rather than sequentially. That is, the decision to contribute may be influenced by the decision-making power acquired in doing so, and similarly, the decision-making power depends on the ability to contribute (both outcomes depend on each other). We estimate for men and women separately the likelihood of decision making conditional on their contribution to the household expenditures, controlling for other observable individual and household characteristics that also may influence decision making and the probability that individuals contribute income to the household.

The determinants of income contribution and decision making are analyzed using a bivariate probit model. The need to rely on probits comes from the fact that dichotomic variables are observed as outcomes (that is, we observe only whether the household head or spouse contributes or not, and decides or not). Rather than estimating two probit regressions, we estimate the correlates of both outcomes together, because this enables us to assess the impact of one outcome on the other. In addition, bivariate probits generate efficiency gains in the estimation precisely because they take into account the correlation between the error terms of the two regressions for contribution and decision making, respectively. The estimation procedure enables us to compute the probability of participating in the household decision making conditional on whether the individual contributes to household income or not.

Denoting by D^* and C^* the latent and unobserved continuous decision and contribution variables, by D and C their categorical observed counterparts, and by X the vector of independent exogenous variables, the bivariate probit model is expressed as:

$$D^* = \beta'_D X + \varepsilon_D \qquad D = 1 \ if \ D^* > 0, \ D = 0 \ otherwise$$
$$C^* = \beta'_C X + \varepsilon_C \qquad C = 1 \ if \ C^* > 0, \ C = 0 \ otherwise \qquad (11.1)$$
$$E[\varepsilon_D] = E[\varepsilon_C] = 0 \qquad Var[\varepsilon_D] = Var[\varepsilon_C] = 1 \qquad Cov[\varepsilon_{D,}\varepsilon_c] = \rho$$

The impact of contributing income on the probability of making a decision on a particular issue is computed as the difference in the two conditional probabilities of making a decision:

$$\Delta P = P(D = 1 \mid C = 1, X) - P(D = 1 \mid C = 0, X). \qquad (11.2)$$

The set of exogenous variables, X, are age of the individual; household size; religion of the household (proxied by the type of household marriage, that is, whether Customary, Islamic, Christian, or another type of marriage); education of the individual (no education at all, incomplete/complete primary, incomplete/complete secondary, or tertiary education); a number of employment-related variables for the individual (employment status: whether employed, unemployed, or out of the labor force; type of employment: whether wage earner, self-employed, unpaid family worker, or firm owner; sector of employment: whether agriculture, manufacturing-construction-transport, wholesale-retail, public administration, or services); and several other variables such as whether the household owns a house; has access to electricity, water, and sanitation; whether the household head is a temporary migrant; and regional dummies to control for geographic effects.

The detailed results from the estimations are provided in the annex. We focus here on the estimates of the impact of income contributions to decision making using the method outline in equation 11.2. The results are provided in table 11.3. When they are the main contributor of income, women win substantial decision-making power and thus play a more active role of leadership in the household. The differences in decision power brought about by contributing income are largest for food, shelter, and health, where income contributions increase the probability of decision making by approximately 20 percentage points.

For example, in the case of expenditures for health, the predicted probability that women participate in the decision making is 43 percent when they do not contribute income, and this increases to 64 percent when they contribute income. For men, the corresponding reduction in the probability of making decisions for expenditures on health decreases by 18 percent when they do not contribute to the household's income. However, even when they contribute to cover most of a household's income, the probability that women will make decisions regarding the use of productive assets, such as land and the commercial use of agricultural output, remains low. To some extent, this same result is also observed with education.

An additional finding is that income contribution increases the level of decision making among poor women more than among non-poor women for health, food, and clothing. These results are provided in table 11.4. Yet for

Table 11.3 Impact of Income Contribution on Decision Making by Gender in Nigeria

	Men		Women	
	Probability	Standard deviation	Probability	Standard deviation
Education				
Decides if contributes	0.53	0.30	0.39	0.29
Decides if does not contribute	0.36	0.29	0.23	0.25
Difference	−0.17	0.08	−0.16	0.09
Health				
Decides if contributes	0.94	0.07	0.64	0.20
Decides if does not contribute	0.76	0.15	0.43	0.24
Difference	−0.18	0.09	−0.21	0.08
Food				
Decides if contributes	0.94	0.06	0.83	0.14
Decides if does not contribute	0.82	0.12	0.60	0.25
Difference	−0.12	0.07	−0.22	0.13
Clothing				
Decides if contributes	0.89	0.07	0.58	0.24
Decides if does not contribute	0.69	0.12	0.43	0.27
Difference	−0.20	0.06	−0.15	0.05
Shelter				
Decides if contributes	0.88	0.08	0.34	0.20
Decides if does not contribute	0.77	0.12	0.16	0.15
Difference	−0.11	0.04	−0.19	0.08
Land use				
Decides if contributes	0.77	0.23	0.27	0.25
Decides if does not contribute	0.66	0.26	0.16	0.20
Difference	−0.11	0.05	−0.11	0.07
Sell agricultural output				
Decides if contributes	0.65	0.25	0.26	0.30
Decides if does not contribute	0.51	0.25	0.21	0.27
Difference	−0.15	0.04	−0.05	0.04

Source: Authors estimates using Nigeria's CWIQ 2003.
Notes: Estimates based on sample of 10,702 men (household heads) and 13,260 women (spouses); differences in size of both samples are due to missing variables.

decisions involving household productive assets, such as land use, crop sales, and shelter, contributing income increases the level of decision making among non-poor women more than among poor women.

Table 11.4 Impact of Income Contribution on Decision Making by Gender and Poverty Status in Nigeria

	Men				Women			
	Non–Poor		Poor		Non–poor		Poor	
	Probability	Standard deviation	Probability	Standard deviation	Probability	Standard deviation	Probability	Standard deviation
Education								
Decides if contributes	0.72	0.24	0.37	0.25	0.59	0.26	0.23	0.20
Decides if does not contribute	0.54	0.28	0.20	0.21	0.38	0.26	0.10	0.15
Difference	−0.18	0.08	−0.17	0.08	−0.21	0.08	−0.13	0.08
Health								
Decides if contributes	0.96	0.05	0.92	0.08	0.75	0.18	0.55	0.18
Decides if does not contribute	0.81	0.13	0.73	0.16	0.55	0.24	0.33	0.19
Difference	−0.15	0.08	−0.20	0.09	−0.20	0.08	−0.23	0.07
Food								
Decides if contributes	0.93	0.06	0.95	0.06	0.89	0.12	0.77	0.14
Decides if does not contribute	0.80	0.11	0.84	0.11	0.72	0.24	0.51	0.22
Difference	−0.13	0.07	−0.11	0.06	−0.17	0.13	−0.26	0.12
Clothing								
Decides if contributes	0.91	0.06	0.87	0.07	0.72	0.21	0.47	0.19
Decides if does not contribute	0.73	0.11	0.66	0.11	0.58	0.25	0.31	0.21
Difference	−0.18	0.06	−0.21	0.05	−0.14	0.06	−0.16	0.05
Shelter								
Decides if contributes	0.89	0.07	0.87	0.08	0.45	0.20	0.25	0.14
Decides if does not contribute	0.78	0.11	0.75	0.12	0.23	0.17	0.09	0.09
Difference	−0.11	0.04	−0.12	0.04	−0.21	0.07	−0.16	0.07
Land use								
Decides if contributes	0.66	0.27	0.86	0.14	0.34	0.24	0.21	0.24
Decides if does not contribute	0.54	0.29	0.77	0.17	0.21	0.20	0.13	0.19
Difference	−0.12	0.05	−0.09	0.04	−0.13	0.06	−0.09	0.06
Sell agricultural output								
Decides if contributes	0.54	0.27	0.76	0.18	0.35	0.29	0.19	0.28
Decides if does not contribute	0.39	0.26	0.61	0.19	0.28	0.27	0.15	0.25
Difference	−0.15	0.05	−0.15	0.04	−0.07	0.04	−0.04	0.04

Source: Authors estimates using Nigeria's CWIQ 2003.
Notes: Estimates based on sample of 10,702 men (household heads) and 13,260 women (spouses); differences in size of both samples are due to missing variables.

Conclusions

In Nigeria, as in other Sub-Saharan countries, most of household decisions are made by men, who are the de facto household heads. Statistical analysis of CWIQ survey data suggests that men tend to have most of the decision-making power regarding the use of productive assets such as land use, crop sales, and shelter. Women participate more often in decisions on expenditures for food, heath, and education, but even in these areas, men more often than not remain the main decision makers. The decision-making power of women is especially low among poor households, in part, because in such households, the likelihood that women will be the main contributor of household income is much lower as well.

Simple econometric modeling suggests that, as expected, when they are the main contributor of income, women win substantial decision-making power. The differences in decision power brought about by contributing income are as large as 20 percentage points for food, shelter, and health spending. However, the impact is much smaller in relation to the use of productive assets. Finally, contribution income raises decision making more among poor than non-poor women.

Care must be taken not to draw strong policy recommendations from the limited and descriptive analysis in this chapter. Yet, some broad comments or suggestions can be made. This study found that increasing the contribution ability of women to household income leads to higher decision-making power for them within the household. This has also been shown by several other authors to lead to higher investments in the human capital of children, thereby leading to poverty reduction and higher income growth in the future. This result can be used to advocate for policies to increase women's ability to contribute to household expenditures, including policies raising the human capital of women, for example, through training and education programs specifically targeting women. Facilitating access to land (for example, through heritage law reforms or titling mechanisms) or access to credit (for example, through micro-credit interventions targeted to women) are all interventions that have proven successful in other countries to promote female entrepreneurship and, thereby, to increase women's income and bargaining power. However, a detailed analysis for Nigeria should be conducted before making any specific policy recommendation in favor of one type of intervention or another to improve the position of women in the household.

Annex Detailed Regression Results

Table 11A.1 Bivariate Probit Regressions for Women in Nigeria

	Decide education	Contrib. income	Decide health	Contrib. income	Decide food	Contrib. income	Decide cloth	Contrib. income	Decide land	Contrib. income	Decide crop sales	Contrib. income
Number of infants under–5	0.212 [4.82]***	−0.033 [0.42]	0.054 [1.59]	−0.033 [0.43]	0.042 [1.35]	−0.029 [0.36]	0.050 [1.40]	−0.043 [0.54]	0.042 [0.98]	−0.038 [0.48]	0.087 [1.93]*	−0.043 [0.55]
Square of number of infants	−0.044 [3.84]***	−0.014 [0.58]	−0.013 [1.69]*	−0.011 [0.51]	−0.008 [1.24]	−0.013 [0.55]	−0.014 [1.65]*	−0.010 [0.44]	−0.004 [0.39]	−0.010 [0.44]	−0.019 [1.62]	−0.009 [0.40]
Number of children (age 5–14)	0.295 [7.93]***	0.010 [0.18]	−0.012 [0.58]	0.029 [0.48]	−0.003 [0.15]	0.025 [0.42]	0.005 [0.24]	0.026 [0.43]	0.033 [1.12]	0.030 [0.49]	−0.019 [0.64]	0.027 [0.45]
Square of number of children	−0.039 [5.34]***	−0.007 [0.55]	0.003 [0.97]	−0.011 [0.81]	0.002 [0.56]	−0.010 [0.77]	0.001 [0.32]	−0.011 [0.80]	−0.001 [0.22]	−0.011 [0.85]	0.006 [1.33]	−0.011 [0.84]
Number of adults	0.189 [5.44]***	−0.015 [0.20]	−0.085 [3.53]***	0.005 [0.07]	−0.101 [3.93]***	0.010 [0.14]	−0.056 [1.96]**	−0.001 [0.02]	0.049 [1.26]	0.007 [0.10]	0.009 [0.24]	0.012 [0.15]
Square of number of adults	−0.013 [3.96]***	−0.005 [0.57]	0.006 [3.03]***	−0.007 [0.81]	0.006 [2.84]***	−0.007 [0.85]	0.003 [1.09]	−0.006 [0.75]	−0.005 [1.36]	−0.007 [0.81]	−0.001 [0.39]	−0.007 [0.87]
Number of elderly (age 65+)	0.096 [0.98]	−0.023 [0.13]	0.055 [0.66]	0.003 [0.02]	0.145 [1.68]*	−0.013 [0.08]	−0.088 [1.04]	−0.028 [0.16]	−0.044 [0.42]	−0.016 [0.09]	−0.012 [0.10]	−0.022 [0.13]
Square of number of elderly	−0.007 [0.16]	−0.059 [0.74]	−0.058 [1.59]	−0.061 [0.80]	−0.082 [2.20]**	−0.058 [0.77]	−0.009 [0.25]	−0.052 [0.69]	0.022 [0.49]	−0.053 [0.72]	−0.008 [0.18]	−0.053 [0.71]
Female–headed household	−6.325 [19.05]***	2.096 [2.59]***	0.684 [0.98]	2.089 [2.48]**	6.045 [31.09]***	2.120 [2.63]***	1.592 [2.72]***	2.133 [2.65]***	0.094 [0.15]	2.132 [2.57]**	0.259 [0.43]	2.089 [2.53]**
Age of household head	0.001 [0.10]	0.025 [1.23]	−0.011 [0.99]	0.025 [1.20]	0.005 [0.45]	0.023 [1.15]	−0.004 [0.33]	0.023 [1.12]	−0.010 [0.70]	0.022 [1.10]	−0.038 [2.75]***	0.025 [1.22]
Square of age of household head	0.000 [0.33]	0.000 [1.05]	0.000 [1.02]	0.000 [1.03]	0.000 [0.88]	0.000 [0.94]	0.000 [0.46]	0.000 [0.95]	0.000 [1.02]	0.000 [0.88]	0.000 [2.78]***	0.000 [1.04]
Age of spouse	0.042 [2.78]***	−0.003 [0.12]	0.028 [2.26]**	−0.001 [0.07]	0.024 [1.98]**	0.000 [0.01]	0.015 [1.19]	−0.001 [0.03]	0.013 [0.81]	−0.001 [0.07]	0.032 [2.14]**	−0.004 [0.19]

Square of age of spouse	0.000 [2.23]**	0.000 [0.69]	0.000 [1.73]*	0.000 [0.63]	0.000 [1.39]	0.000 [0.57]	0.000 [0.98]	0.000 [0.61]	0.000 [1.02]	0.000 [0.63]	0.000 [1.75]*	0.000 [0.78]
Head has customary marriage	0.073 [0.88]	0.177 [1.29]	0.166 [1.96]*	0.187 [1.37]	0.228 [2.33]**	0.155 [1.17]	0.110 [1.21]	0.185 [1.37]	0.018 [0.18]	0.188 [1.38]	0.088 [0.98]	0.189 [1.38]
Head has Islamic marriage	0.141 [1.29]	0.192 [1.02]	0.068 [0.68]	0.194 [1.03]	0.155 [1.41]	0.143 [0.79]	0.051 [0.49]	0.175 [0.94]	-0.275 [2.31]**	0.197 [1.06]	-0.208 [1.76]*	0.202 [1.08]
Head has Christian marriage	0.335 [3.40]***	0.259 [1.68]*	0.405 [4.10]***	0.280 [1.81]*	0.663 [5.54]***	0.246 [1.63]	0.386 [3.78]***	0.266 [1.74]*	0.172 [1.62]	0.281 [1.83]*	0.240 [2.35]**	0.270 [1.76]*
Head incomplete primary education	0.113 [1.20]	0.008 [0.05]	-0.086 [1.03]	0.006 [0.05]	-0.120 [1.25]	0.003 [0.02]	-0.059 [0.70]	0.011 [0.08]	-0.005 [0.06]	-0.004 [0.03]	-0.035 [0.38]	0.006 [0.05]
Head completed primary education	0.043 [0.64]	-0.256 [2.26]**	-0.046 [0.81]	-0.239 [2.15]**	-0.003 [0.06]	-0.247 [2.19]**	0.059 [1.05]	-0.246 [2.17]**	-0.081 [1.18]	-0.251 [2.21]**	0.049 [0.66]	-0.245 [2.15]**
Head incomplete secondary education	-0.050 [0.38]	-0.155 [0.87]	-0.139 [0.98]	-0.129 [0.71]	0.207 [1.47]	-0.107 [0.57]	0.002 [0.01]	-0.096 [0.53]	-0.232 [1.46]	-0.113 [0.63]	-0.181 [1.29]	-0.118 [0.65]
Head completed secondary education	0.157 [1.54]	-0.320 [1.94]*	0.055 [0.63]	-0.291 [1.76]*	-0.086 [0.92]	-0.267 [1.60]	0.029 [0.34]	-0.295 [1.77]*	-0.128 [1.31]	-0.290 [1.75]*	0.043 [0.36]	-0.295 [1.77]*
Head tertiary education	0.080 [0.79]	-0.171 [1.02]	0.013 [0.14]	-0.147 [0.89]	0.036 [0.37]	-0.132 [0.79]	0.088 [0.99]	-0.142 [0.84]	-0.163 [1.58]	-0.135 [0.81]	0.126 [1.20]	-0.139 [0.84]
Spouse incomplete primary education	0.108 [1.23]	0.336 [2.53]**	-0.001 [0.02]	0.329 [2.49]**	0.178 [1.81]*	0.324 [2.44]**	0.041 [0.48]	0.321 [2.42]**	0.076 [0.81]	0.347 [2.61]***	-0.048 [0.50]	0.335 [2.53]**
Spouse completed primary education	0.089 [1.20]	0.211 [1.81]*	0.041 [0.63]	0.180 [1.56]	0.004 [0.06]	0.193 [1.64]	-0.055 [0.90]	0.175 [1.50]	0.172 [2.24]**	0.210 [1.79]*	0.086 [1.06]	0.201 [1.72]*
Spouse incomplete secondary educ.	0.201 [1.69]*	-0.108 [0.47]	0.007 [0.06]	-0.135 [0.56]	0.045 [0.33]	-0.147 [0.61]	-0.021 [0.16]	-0.164 [0.68]	0.252 [2.03]**	-0.128 [0.55]	0.073 [0.59]	-0.143 [0.60]
Spouse completed secondary educ.	0.067 [0.64]	0.182 [1.08]	-0.174 [1.82]*	0.152 [0.89]	0.014 [0.13]	0.144 [0.83]	0.073 [0.76]	0.154 [0.88]	-0.070 [0.65]	0.154 [0.88]	-0.122 [1.03]	0.162 [0.93]
Spouse tertiary education	0.168 [1.12]	0.073 [0.32]	-0.149 [0.99]	0.053 [0.24]	0.075 [0.46]	0.051 [0.23]	-0.007 [0.05]	0.051 [0.23]	0.029 [0.19]	0.079 [0.36]	-0.222 [1.46]	0.081 [0.37]
Head unemployed	0.041 [0.19]	2.147 [4.75]***	-0.208 [0.98]	2.105 [4.66]***	-0.016 [0.07]	2.194 [4.86]***	-0.340 [1.83]*	2.198 [4.81]***	-0.067 [0.29]	2.193 [4.83]***	-0.245 [0.93]	2.193 [4.86]***

continued

Table 11A.1 Bivariate Probit Regressions for Women in Nigeria *continued*

	Decide education	Contrib. income	Decide health	Contrib. income	Decide food	Contrib. income	Decide cloth	Contrib. income	Decide land	Contrib. income	Decide crop sales	Contrib. income
Head not in labor force	-0.147 [0.85]	2.123 [4.84]***	-0.224 [1.21]	2.090 [4.80]***	-0.182 [0.99]	2.166 [4.95]***	-0.214 [1.47]	2.202 [4.96]***	0.099 [0.49]	2.191 [5.00]***	-0.200 [1.03]	2.210 [5.05]***
Head in public or parastatal sector	0.027 [0.16]	0.099 [0.40]	0.232 [1.72]*	0.114 [0.49]	0.137 [1.03]	0.120 [0.50]	0.028 [0.23]	0.153 [0.61]	0.143 [0.99]	0.146 [0.60]	0.133 [0.89]	0.140 [0.57]
Head wage earner	-0.341 [1.71]*	0.252 [0.56]	-0.280 [1.41]	0.216 [0.48]	-0.190 [0.94]	0.254 [0.57]	-0.253 [1.62]	0.245 [0.54]	-0.180 [0.90]	0.246 [0.55]	-0.222 [1.16]	0.250 [0.55]
Head self employed	-0.321 [2.25]**	0.180 [0.44]	-0.071 [0.44]	0.199 [0.48]	-0.087 [0.53]	0.225 [0.55]	-0.169 [1.36]	0.225 [0.55]	-0.088 [0.58]	0.243 [0.59]	-0.269 [1.78]*	0.237 [0.58]
Head unpaid family worker	-0.349 [2.11]**	0.822 [1.94]*	-0.481 [2.76]***	0.832 [1.94]*	-0.515 [2.94]***	0.844 [1.98]**	-0.424 [3.10]***	0.862 [2.02]**	-0.164 [0.92]	0.908 [2.12]**	-0.483 [2.77]***	0.899 [2.12]**
Spouse unemployed	-0.432 [1.77]*	-0.532 [0.98]	-0.518 [2.47]**	-0.510 [0.94]	-0.048 [0.25]	-0.427 [0.74]	-0.133 [0.68]	-0.451 [0.80]	-0.082 [0.32]	-0.447 [0.78]	-0.298 [1.14]	-0.468 [0.81]
Spouse not in labor force	-0.107 [0.50]	-0.460 [0.94]	-0.402 [2.13]**	-0.457 [0.93]	0.000 [0.00]	-0.327 [0.61]	0.184 [1.09]	-0.411 [0.79]	0.177 [0.76]	-0.370 [0.71]	-0.147 [0.62]	-0.426 [0.80]
Spouse in public or parastatal sector	0.093 [0.39]	-0.224 [0.91]	-0.203 [1.03]	-0.231 [0.92]	-0.126 [0.60]	-0.226 [0.88]	0.057 [0.29]	-0.213 [0.85]	0.082 [0.42]	-0.236 [0.95]	0.004 [0.02]	-0.238 [0.94]
Spouse wage earner	0.160 [0.56]	1.738 [3.36]***	0.363 [1.45]	1.742 [3.36]***	0.363 [1.48]	1.884 [3.34]***	0.355 [1.50]	1.817 [3.34]***	0.383 [1.48]	1.856 [3.40]***	0.088 [0.33]	1.832 [3.28]***
Spouse self employed	0.143 [0.72]	0.987 [2.06]**	0.240 [1.33]	0.964 [2.01]**	0.411 [2.54]**	1.105 [2.10]**	0.271 [1.67]*	1.034 [2.04]**	0.252 [1.22]	1.056 [2.08]**	0.209 [0.97]	1.034 [1.98]**
Spouse unpaid family worker	-0.142 [0.70]	0.804 [1.65]*	0.271 [1.49]	0.797 [1.64]	0.216 [1.31]	0.917 [1.72]*	0.143 [0.88]	0.850 [1.65]*	0.189 [0.88]	0.858 [1.66]*	-0.103 [0.47]	0.847 [1.60]
Head in manuf./constr./transport	0.041 [0.46]	-0.037 [0.23]	-0.023 [0.24]	-0.037 [0.23]	0.057 [0.61]	-0.036 [0.23]	0.045 [0.50]	-0.025 [0.16]	0.115 [1.18]	-0.032 [0.21]	-0.137 [1.42]	-0.030 [0.19]
Head in wholesale/retail	-0.035 [0.42]	-0.309 [1.90]*	-0.114 [1.66]*	-0.314 [1.93]*	-0.055 [0.82]	-0.303 [1.84]*	0.020 [0.28]	-0.305 [1.86]*	-0.348 [3.77]***	-0.301 [1.83]*	-0.479 [4.77]***	-0.294 [1.80]*

	(1)	(2)	(3)	(4)	(5)	(6)	(7)	(8)	(9)	(10)	(11)	(12)
Head in service/education/adm./other	-0.043 [0.51]	-0.385 [1.95]*	-0.093 [1.28]	-0.370 [1.94]*	-0.085 [1.22]	-0.391 [1.98]**	0.027 [0.36]	-0.403 [2.01]**	-0.015 [0.17]	-0.385 [1.99]**	-0.228 [2.48]**	-0.384 [1.99]**
Spouse in manuf./constr./transport	0.185 [1.18]	0.438 [2.26]**	0.075 [0.73]	0.408 [2.05]**	-0.114 [1.13]	0.397 [2.06]**	0.183 [1.78]*	0.409 [2.09]**	-0.571 [2.58]***	0.435 [2.28]**	-0.739 [3.15]***	0.424 [2.19]**
Spouse in wholesale/retail	0.002 [0.03]	0.121 [1.34]	-0.069 [1.23]	0.124 [1.37]	-0.205 [3.57]***	0.114 [1.26]	0.027 [0.49]	0.125 [1.38]	-0.543 [8.91]***	0.133 [1.47]	-0.525 [8.48]***	0.127 [1.40]
Spouse in service/educ./adm./other	0.059 [0.70]	0.324 [2.25]**	0.433 [6.64]***	0.317 [2.21]**	-0.028 [0.45]	0.311 [2.14]**	-0.037 [0.59]	0.304 [2.10]**	-0.645 [6.37]***	0.287 [2.00]**	-0.676 [7.78]***	0.292 [2.02]**
Individual owns house	0.365 [4.54]***	0.395 [3.57]***	0.319 [4.84]***	0.375 [3.36]***	0.851 [10.35]***	0.389 [3.50]***	0.462 [6.88]***	0.367 [3.35]***	1.204 [16.51]***	0.401 [3.64]***	1.078 [12.95]***	0.396 [3.64]***
Head temporary migrant	0.226 [0.80]	1.203 [5.33]***	0.220 [1.19]	1.167 [5.17]***	-0.151 [0.86]	1.163 [5.12]***	-0.120 [0.70]	1.175 [5.20]***	-0.451 [1.87]*	1.194 [5.28]***	-0.328 [1.49]	1.202 [5.39]***
Household has access to electricity	0.046 [2.05]**	0.120 [3.24]***	0.067 [3.19]***	0.121 [3.30]***	0.004 [0.16]	0.123 [3.30]***	0.068 [3.33]***	0.121 [3.26]***	-0.014 [0.52]	0.121 [3.33]***	0.032 [1.31]	0.122 [3.30]***
Household has access to piped water	0.077 [1.03]	-0.174 [1.24]	-0.129 [1.86]*	-0.166 [1.19]	-0.121 [1.73]*	-0.179 [1.27]	-0.011 [0.16]	-0.167 [1.19]	-0.078 [0.81]	-0.164 [1.17]	0.017 [0.17]	-0.164 [1.17]
Household has toilet facility	-0.005	0.122	0.092	0.126	-0.021	0.155	0.047	0.129	-0.479	0.127	-0.336	0.113
Wealth index	0.129 [3.82]***	-0.043 [0.74]	0.022 [0.74]	-0.041 [0.70]	-0.067 [2.05]**	-0.033 [0.55]	-0.028 [0.91]	-0.045 [0.77]	-0.019 [0.52]	-0.041 [0.70]	-0.033 [0.86]	-0.038 [0.65]
Wealth index squared	-0.008 [2.75]***	-0.003 [0.50]	-0.001 [0.41]	-0.003 [0.58]	0.005 [1.65]*	-0.004 [0.74]	0.001 [0.48]	-0.003 [0.53]	0.000 [0.14]	-0.003 [0.63]	-0.001 [0.42]	-0.003 [0.64]
Constant	-2.636 [6.80]***	-4.279 [5.72]***	-0.810 [2.56]**	-4.328 [5.77]***	0.289 [0.92]	-4.470 [5.71]***	-0.446 [1.47]	-4.365 [5.63]***	-1.109 [3.08]***	-4.415 [5.73]***	-0.430 [1.16]	-4.428 [5.69]***
Observations	13225	13225	13225	13225	13225	13225	13209	13209	13209	13209	13209	13209

Source: Authors' estimates using Nigeria's CWIQ 2003.
Notes: State dummy variables included in the regressions but not shown in the tables. (*) denotes coefficient statistically significant at 10% level, (**) at 5% level and (***) significant at 1% level.

Table 11A.2 Bivariate Probit Regressions for Men in Nigeria

	Decide education	Contrib. income	Decide health	Contrib. income	Decide food	Contrib. income	Decide cloth	Contrib. income	Decide land use	Contrib. income	Decide crop sales	Contrib. income
Number of infants under–5	0.232 [5.45]***	0.033 [0.76]	0.016 [0.40]	0.033 [0.74]	-0.079 [2.02]**	0.033 [0.74]	0.029 [0.77]	0.038 [0.85]	0.089 [2.55]**	0.036 [0.81]	0.037 [1.22]	0.038 [0.86]
Square of number of infants	-0.029 [2.79]***	-0.003 [0.53]	-0.009 [1.30]	-0.004 [0.57]	0.001 [0.13]	-0.004 [0.61]	-0.008 [1.05]	-0.005 [0.67]	-0.014 [1.79]*	-0.005 [0.69]	-0.005 [0.84]	-0.005 [0.69]
Number of children (age 5–14)	0.564 [17.04]***	0.035 [0.86]	0.079 [2.02]**	0.033 [0.87]	0.041 [1.05]	0.033 [0.88]	0.052 [1.68]*	0.034 [0.90]	0.055 [1.71]*	0.031 [0.83]	0.015 [0.55]	0.031 [0.82]
Square of number of children	-0.070 [10.44]***	-0.004 [0.45]	-0.008 [1.18]	-0.004 [0.61]	0.000 [0.01]	-0.004 [0.59]	-0.004 [0.79]	-0.004 [0.60]	-0.002 [0.28]	-0.004 [0.56]	0.000 [0.02]	-0.004 [0.56]
Number of adults	0.222 [6.68]***	-0.116 [2.25]**	-0.052 [1.00]	-0.106 [2.15]**	-0.106 [2.00]**	-0.113 [2.22]**	-0.037 [1.07]	-0.110 [2.20]**	0.095 [2.61]***	-0.116 [2.26]**	0.045 [1.36]	-0.116 [2.26]**
Square of number of adults	-0.012 [3.64]***	0.010 [1.86]*	0.007 [1.32]	0.009 [1.79]*	0.010 [1.79]*	0.010 [1.90]*	0.001 [0.30]	0.010 [1.86]*	-0.005 [1.54]	0.011 [1.92]*	-0.001 [0.26]	0.011 [1.93]*
Number of elderly (age 65+)	0.116 [1.08]	-0.135 [1.06]	0.217 [1.46]	-0.147 [1.15]	-0.048 [0.36]	-0.145 [1.11]	0.180 [1.56]	-0.119 [0.92]	0.035 [0.29]	-0.143 [1.09]	-0.130 [1.24]	-0.135 [1.04]
Square of number of elderly	-0.030 [0.57]	0.019 [0.36]	-0.071 [1.13]	0.030 [0.56]	-0.008 [0.14]	0.034 [0.61]	-0.057 [1.10]	0.022 [0.40]	0.015 [0.28]	0.026 [0.47]	0.058 [1.19]	0.024 [0.44]
Female–headed household	-7.759 [26.90]***	-1.265 [1.74]*	-0.711 [1.06]	-1.213 [1.63]	-1.452 [2.18]**	-1.195 [1.63]	-1.369 [1.80]*	-1.224 [1.58]	-0.625 [0.84]	-1.277 [1.68]*	-0.289 [0.38]	-1.250 [1.64]
Age of household head	0.014 [1.11]	0.015 [0.84]	0.047 [3.07]***	0.018 [1.00]	0.012 [0.81]	0.016 [0.93]	0.026 [1.91]*	0.016 [0.90]	0.004 [0.31]	0.019 [1.08]	0.012 [0.92]	0.018 [1.06]
Square of age of household head	0.000 [1.31]	0.000 [1.49]	-0.001 [3.76]***	0.000 [1.65]*	0.000 [1.42]	0.000 [1.56]	0.000 [2.72]***	0.000 [1.56]	0.000 [0.61]	0.000 [1.72]*	0.000 [1.21]	0.000 [1.69]*
Age of spouse	0.022 [1.56]	0.029 [1.52]	-0.031 [1.86]*	0.025 [1.33]	0.000 [0.01]	0.028 [1.47]	0.008 [0.51]	0.027 [1.44]	0.014 [0.98]	0.025 [1.29]	0.006 [0.44]	0.025 [1.32]
Square of age of spouse	0.000 [1.24]	0.000 [2.11]**	0.000 [1.68]*	0.000 [1.96]**	0.000 [0.25]	0.000 [2.14]**	0.000 [0.38]	0.000 [2.08]**	0.000 [1.15]	0.000 [1.92]*	0.000 [0.68]	0.000 [1.96]*

Head has customary marriage	0.316 [3.07]***	-0.343 [2.66]***	-0.152 [1.00]	-0.378 [2.88]***	0.100 [0.86]	-0.376 [2.83]***	0.024 [0.22]	-0.373 [2.89]***	0.089 [0.90]	-0.356 [2.77]***	-0.031 [0.34]	-0.358 [2.76]***
Head has Islamic marriage	0.403 [3.19]***	-0.154 [0.94]	-0.178 [1.16]	-0.182 [1.08]	-0.254 [1.92]*	-0.185 [1.11]	-0.080 [0.66]	-0.178 [1.07]	-0.150 [1.31]	-0.168 [1.02]	-0.210 [2.01]**	-0.160 [0.95]
Head has Christian marriage	0.436 [3.61]***	-0.481 [3.31]***	-0.112 [0.66]	-0.509 [3.50]***	0.150 [1.14]	-0.503 [3.40]***	-0.048 [0.38]	-0.517 [3.58]***	0.062 [0.57]	-0.498 [3.46]***	0.089 [0.89]	-0.490 [3.39]***
Head incomplete primary education	0.254 [2.42]**	-0.006 [0.05]	0.249 [1.44]	-0.012 [0.10]	0.163 [1.40]	-0.013 [0.10]	-0.010 [0.10]	-0.015 [0.12]	0.211 [1.78]*	-0.006 [0.05]	0.114 [1.19]	-0.006 [0.05]
Head completed primary education	0.320 [4.75]***	0.310 [3.21]***	0.093 [1.10]	0.300 [3.10]***	0.193 [2.28]**	0.311 [3.19]***	0.127 [1.59]	0.286 [3.01]***	0.176 [2.46]**	0.309 [3.16]***	0.124 [1.94]*	0.314 [3.20]***
Head incomplete secondary education	0.226 [1.49]	0.077 [0.28]	0.015 [0.09]	0.053 [0.20]	0.115 [0.69]	0.074 [0.27]	0.108 [0.74]	0.043 [0.16]	0.147 [1.09]	0.075 [0.27]	0.093 [0.79]	0.078 [0.28]
Head completed secondary education	0.355 [3.63]***	0.063 [0.45]	0.136 [1.05]	0.102 [0.73]	0.183 [1.49]	0.081 [0.57]	-0.029 [0.24]	0.076 [0.54]	0.061 [0.65]	0.076 [0.54]	0.197 [2.25]**	0.088 [0.62]
Head tertiary education	0.430 [3.69]***	0.085 [0.63]	0.172 [1.13]	0.109 [0.81]	0.220 [1.67]*	0.118 [0.88]	0.128 [1.02]	0.081 [0.60]	0.083 [0.82]	0.113 [0.84]	0.228 [2.37]**	0.119 [0.88]
Spouse incomplete primary education	0.163 [1.54]	-0.208 [1.72]*	-0.051 [0.30]	-0.202 [1.66]*	-0.326 [2.85]***	-0.240 [1.97]**	0.123 [1.01]	-0.212 [1.76]*	-0.048 [0.41]	-0.234 [1.92]*	-0.232 [2.38]**	-0.239 [1.95]*
Spouse completed primary education	0.148 [1.88]*	-0.072 [0.62]	-0.004 [0.04]	-0.102 [0.89]	-0.153 [1.64]	-0.106 [0.92]	0.060 [0.66]	-0.089 [0.79]	0.097 [1.20]	-0.094 [0.81]	0.045 [0.64]	-0.099 [0.85]
Spouse incomplete secondary educ.	0.345 [2.24]**	-0.146 [0.70]	-0.281 [1.55]	-0.111 [0.56]	-0.284 [1.90]*	-0.127 [0.61]	-0.056 [0.38]	-0.105 [0.53]	-0.004 [0.03]	-0.132 [0.65]	-0.081 [0.70]	-0.132 [0.65]
Spouse completed secondary educ.	0.082 [0.72]	0.071 [0.48]	-0.067 [0.45]	0.071 [0.48]	-0.216 [1.56]	0.046 [0.31]	-0.036 [0.26]	0.068 [0.47]	-0.210 [1.97]**	0.050 [0.34]	-0.298 [3.02]***	0.049 [0.34]
Spouse tertiary education	0.095 [0.52]	0.220 [1.15]	0.212 [0.84]	0.188 [0.99]	-0.088 [0.47]	0.164 [0.85]	0.073 [0.42]	0.215 [1.11]	-0.001 [0.01]	0.182 [0.94]	-0.220 [1.56]	0.171 [0.89]
Head unemployed	-0.499 [2.30]**	-1.492 [4.79]***	-0.541 [2.00]**	-1.455 [4.72]***	-0.312 [1.21]	-1.507 [4.88]***	-0.051 [0.18]	-1.455 [4.63]***	-0.160 [0.71]	-1.502 [4.81]***	-0.141 [0.69]	-1.507 [4.80]***

continued

Table 11A.2 Bivariate Probit Regressions for Men in Nigeria *continued*

	Decide education	Contrib. income	Decide health	Contrib. income	Decide food	Contrib. income	Decide cloth	Contrib. income	Decide land use	Contrib. income	Decide crop sales	Contrib. income
Head not in labor force	-0.618 [3.34]***	-1.525 [5.33]***	-0.858 [3.66]***	-1.479 [5.25]***	-0.428 [1.91]*	-1.522 [5.40]***	-0.443 [1.81]*	-1.481 [5.17]***	-0.358 [1.87]*	-1.520 [5.31]***	-0.200 [1.19]	-1.509 [5.26]***
Head in public or parastatal sector	-0.063 [0.35]	-0.186 [0.97]	0.136 [0.57]	-0.173 [0.90]	-0.201 [1.01]	-0.157 [0.81]	-0.401 [2.39]**	-0.169 [0.89]	-0.099 [0.81]	-0.175 [0.92]	-0.270 [2.06]**	-0.162 [0.85]
Head wage earner	-0.075 [0.35]	-0.043 [0.14]	-0.452 [1.44]	-0.062 [0.21]	0.061 [0.23]	-0.102 [0.35]	0.297 [1.11]	-0.062 [0.21]	0.041 [0.21]	-0.083 [0.28]	0.188 [1.01]	-0.094 [0.31]
Head self employed	-0.423 [2.62]***	-0.138 [0.55]	-0.277 [1.37]	-0.129 [0.52]	0.177 [0.89]	-0.154 [0.62]	-0.025 [0.11]	-0.143 [0.56]	-0.100 [0.58]	-0.151 [0.59]	-0.069 [0.47]	-0.161 [0.62]
Head unpaid family worker	-0.518 [2.95]***	-0.486 [1.81]*	-0.602 [2.83]***	-0.484 [1.83]*	0.241 [1.07]	-0.503 [1.90]*	-0.139 [0.56]	-0.493 [1.84]*	-0.177 [0.92]	-0.494 [1.82]*	-0.089 [0.54]	-0.503 [1.84]*
Spouse unemployed	-0.160 [0.52]	0.589 [2.04]**	-0.007 [0.02]	0.598 [2.10]**	0.270 [0.79]	0.619 [2.18]**	-0.150 [0.51]	0.564 [1.98]**	0.067 [0.26]	0.627 [2.20]**	-0.140 [0.60]	0.575 [2.01]**
Spouse not in labor force	-0.112 [0.39]	0.431 [1.63]	0.200 [0.63]	0.415 [1.61]	0.568 [1.77]*	0.456 [1.75]*	0.293 [1.11]	0.399 [1.52]	0.271 [1.13]	0.440 [1.68]*	-0.014 [0.06]	0.395 [1.50]
Spouse in public or parastatal sector	-0.217 [0.86]	0.069 [0.30]	-0.501 [1.66]*	0.036 [0.16]	0.273 [1.08]	0.072 [0.31]	-0.397 [1.72]*	0.041 [0.18]	-0.142 [0.63]	0.053 [0.23]	0.161 [0.83]	0.062 [0.27]
Spouse wage earner	-0.322 [0.95]	-0.802 [2.56]**	0.059 [0.15]	-0.754 [2.42]**	0.093 [0.26]	-0.746 [2.39]**	0.256 [0.83]	-0.775 [2.45]**	0.166 [0.55]	-0.757 [2.45]**	-0.245 [0.89]	-0.808 [2.61]***
Spouse self employed	-0.160 [0.57]	-0.251 [1.03]	0.517 [1.68]*	-0.255 [1.07]	0.468 [1.48]	-0.238 [0.99]	0.363 [1.44]	-0.268 [1.11]	0.273 [1.18]	-0.251 [1.04]	0.248 [1.17]	-0.287 [1.18]
Spouse unpaid family worker	-0.236 [0.84]	-0.084 [0.34]	0.056 [0.18]	-0.088 [0.36]	0.538 [1.67]*	-0.064 [0.27]	0.013 [0.05]	-0.100 [0.41]	0.290 [1.24]	-0.073 [0.30]	0.037 [0.17]	-0.101 [0.41]
Head in manuf./constr./transport	-0.115 [1.10]	0.156 [1.16]	0.029 [0.20]	0.155 [1.16]	0.085 [0.71]	0.156 [1.17]	0.002 [0.02]	0.152 [1.14]	-0.527 [5.57]***	0.149 [1.12]	-0.570 [6.57]***	0.134 [1.00]
Head in wholesale/retail	-0.011 [0.13]	-0.060 [0.48]	-0.183 [1.67]*	-0.089 [0.70]	0.088 [0.75]	-0.076 [0.60]	-0.114 [1.21]	-0.093 [0.74]	-0.426 [5.31]***	-0.073 [0.56]	-0.420 [5.72]***	-0.083 [0.64]

Head in service/education/adm./other	-0.066 [0.78]	0.132 [0.76]	-0.088 [0.72]	0.098 [0.56]	0.044 [0.46]	0.113 [0.65]	-0.114 [1.23]	0.092 [0.53]	-0.397 [4.79]***	0.115 [0.66]	-0.374 [4.70]***
0.103 [0.59]											
Spouse in manuf./constr./transport	0.160 [1.13]	-0.394 [2.29]**	-0.130 [0.90]	-0.411 [2.44]**	0.146 [0.85]	-0.419 [2.48]**	0.109 [0.75]	-0.426 [2.53]**	-0.573 [4.27]***	-0.412 [2.39]**	-0.574 [4.51]***
-0.415 [2.41]**											
Spouse in wholesale/retail	0.002 [0.03]	0.098 [1.16]	0.092 [1.16]	0.109 [1.28]	0.140 [1.65]*	0.114 [1.36]	-0.011 [0.17]	0.110 [1.29]	-0.465 [6.88]***	0.118 [1.38]	-0.467 [7.80]***
0.123 [1.44]											
Spouse in service/educ./adm./other	0.103 [1.41]	-0.191 [1.69]*	0.628 [6.44]***	-0.186 [1.63]	0.309 [2.79]***	-0.196 [1.73]*	0.312 [3.49]***	-0.185 [1.62]	-0.256 [3.02]***	-0.199 [1.74]*	-0.110 [1.53]
-0.187 [1.64]											
Individual owns house	0.099 [1.84]*	0.034 [0.47]	0.204 [2.95]***	0.041 [0.57]	0.109 [1.76]*	0.033 [0.45]	0.094 [1.57]	0.038 [0.53]	0.800 [16.09]***	0.031 [0.42]	0.736 [15.53]***
0.033 [0.46]											
Head temporary migrant	-0.307 [1.55]	-0.778 [3.58]***	-0.149 [0.62]	-0.754 [3.49]***	-0.252 [1.21]	-0.738 [3.39]***	0.247 [1.24]	-0.744 [3.43]***	-0.148 [0.68]	-0.759 [3.54]***	-0.047 [0.24]
-0.761 [3.57]***											
Household has access to electricity	-0.029 [1.19]	-0.087 [2.51]**	0.038 [1.07]	-0.093 [2.68]***	0.036 [1.20]	-0.094 [2.72]***	0.017 [0.56]	-0.092 [2.73]***	0.003 [0.12]	-0.092 [2.70]***	0.002 [0.09]
-0.090 [2.61]***											
Household has access to piped water	0.183 [2.33]**	-0.221 [1.93]*	-0.244 [2.39]**	-0.237 [2.07]**	-0.072 [0.66]	-0.211 [1.82]*	-0.076 [0.84]	-0.216 [1.89]*	0.043 [0.58]	-0.216 [1.87]*	-0.060 [0.86]
-0.210 [1.82]*											
Household has toilet facility	-0.122 [0.76]	0.157 [1.00]	-0.236 [1.17]	0.134 [0.83]	-0.300 [2.03]**	0.137 [0.84]	-0.317 [1.98]**	0.139 [0.86]	-0.178 [1.51]	0.157 [0.96]	-0.134 [1.14]
0.140 [0.86]											
Wealth index	0.131 [3.61]***	-0.014 [0.29]	0.112 [2.40]**	-0.004 [0.09]	0.148 [3.36]***	-0.011 [0.22]	0.152 [3.61]***	-0.003 [0.07]	-0.099 [2.61]***	-0.014 [0.28]	-0.035 [0.95]
-0.015 [0.30]											
Wealth index squared	-0.005 [1.45]	0.004 [1.00]	-0.005 [1.16]	0.004 [0.85]	-0.011 [2.81]***	0.004 [0.91]	-0.008 [2.12]**	0.004 [0.84]	-0.001 [0.25]	0.004 [0.96]	-0.006 [1.70]*
0.004 [0.97]											
Constant	-1.696 [4.10]***	2.159 [4.34]***	0.202 [0.44]	2.158 [4.33]***	0.117 [0.26]	2.194 [4.39]***	-0.575 [1.39]	2.207 [4.41]***	0.199 [0.52]	2.205 [4.41]***	0.085 [0.24]
2.249 [4.48]***											
Observations	10671	10671	10671	10671	10671	10671	10671	10671	10671	10671	10671
10671											

Source: Authors' estimates using Nigeria's CWIQ 2003.

Notes: State dummy variables included in the regressions but not shown in the tables. (*) denotes coefficient statistically significant at 10% level, (**) at 5% level and (***) significant at 1% level.

References

Babalola, A., and C. Dennis. 1988. "Returns to Women's Labour in Cash Crop productions: Tobacco in Igboho, Oyo State, Nigeria." In *Agriculture, Women and Land: The African Experience*, ed. J. Davidson. Boulder, CO: West View Press.

Backiny-Yetna, P., and Q. Wodon. 2010. "Gender Labor Income Shares and Human Capital Investment in the Republic of Congo." In *Gender Disparities in Africa's Labor Market*, ed. J. S. Arbache, A. Kolev, and E. Filipiak. Washington, DC. World Bank.

Blackden, C. M., and C. Bhanu. 1999. *Gender, Growth, and Poverty Reduction*. Special Program of Assistance for Africa 1998 Status Report on Poverty, World Bank Technical Paper 428. Washington, DC: World Bank.

Bourguignon, F., and P. A. Chiappori. 1992. "Collective Models of Household Behavior: An Introduction." *European Economic Review* 36 (2–3): 355–64.

Browning, M., and P. A. Chiappori. 1998. "Efficient Intra-Household Allocations: A General Characterization and Empirical Tests." *Econometrica* 66 (6): 1241–78.

Bussolo, M., R. E. De Hoyos, and Q. Wodon. 2009. "Higher Prices of Export Crops, Intra-Household Inequality and Human Capital Accumulation in Senegal." In *Gender Aspects of the Trade and Poverty Nexus: A Macro–Micro Approach*, ed. M. Bussolo and R. E. De Hoyos. Washington, DC: World Bank and Palgrave Macmillan.

Chukwuezi, B. 1999. "De-agrarianization and Rural Employment in South Eastern Nigeria." Working Paper 37 African Studies Centre, University of Leiden, the Netherlands.

Hoddinott, J., and L. Haddad. 1995. "Does Female Income Share Influence Household Expenditures? Evidence from Côte d'Ivoire." *Oxford Bulletin of Economics and Statistics* 57 (1): 77–96.

Lloyd, C. B., and A. K. Blanc. 1996. "Children's Schooling in Sub-Saharan Africa: The Role of Fathers, Mothers, and Others." *Population and Development Review* 22 (2): 265–98.

Manser, M., and M. Brown. 1980. "Marriage and Household Decision Making: A Bargaining Analysis." *International Economic Review* 21 (1): 31–34.

McElroy, M. B., and M. J. Homey. 1981. "Nash-bargained Household Decisions: Toward a Generalization of the Theory of Demand." *International Economic Review* 22 (2): 333–49.

Piesse, J., and J. Simister. 2003. "Bargaining and Household Dynamics: The Impact of Education and Financial Control on Nutrition Outcomes in South Africa." *South African Journal of Economics* 71 (1): 163–72.

World Bank. 2004. "Nigeria: Poverty and Vulnerability—A Preliminary Diagnostic." Unpublished manuscript, Human Development Department, Africa Region, World Bank, Washington, DC.

———. 2005. "Uganda: From Periphery to Center: A Strategic Country Gender Assessment." Poverty Reduction and Economic Management, Africa Region, World Bank, Washington, DC.

Index

Figures, notes, and tables are indicated by f, n, or t following the page number.

ECO-AUDIT
Environmental Benefits Statement

The World Bank is committed to preserving endangered forests and natural resources. The Office of the Publisher has chosen to print *Gender Disparities in Africa's Labor Market* on recycled paper with 30 percent postconsumer fiber in accordance with the recommended standards for paper usage set by the Green Press Initiative, a nonprofit program supporting publishers in using fiber that is not sourced from endangered forests. For more information, visit www.greenpressinitiative.org.

Saved:
- 10 trees
- 3 million BTUs of total energy
- 952 lbs CO_2 equivalent of greenhouse gases
- 4,585 gallons of waste water
- 278 pounds of solid waste

green press
INITIATIVE

www.ingramcontent.com/pod-product-compliance
Lightning Source LLC
Chambersburg PA
CBHW050448270326
41927CB00009B/1657